THUNDER SHAMAN

THUNDER SHAMAN

MAKING HISTORY *with* MAPUCHE SPIRITS *in* CHILE *and* PATAGONIA

ANA MARIELLA BACIGALUPO

UNIVERSITY OF TEXAS PRESS

Austin

Requests for permission to reproduce material from this work should be sent to:
Permissions
University of Texas Press
P.O. Box 7819
Austin, TX 78713-7819
http://utpress.utexas.edu/index.php/rp-form

All images and maps are courtesy of the author.

♾ The paper used in this book meets the minimum requirements of
ANSI/NISO Z39.48-1992 (R1997) (Permanence of Paper).

LIBRARY OF CONGRESS CATALOGING-IN-PUBLICATION DATA
Bacigalupo, Ana Mariella, author.
Thunder shaman : making history with Mapuche spirits in Chile and Patagonia /
Ana Mariella Bacigalupo. — First edition.
pages cm
Includes bibliographical references and index.
ISBN 978-1-4773-0880-6 (cloth : alk. paper)
ISBN 978-1-4773-0898-1 (pbk. : alk. paper)
ISBN 978-1-4773-0881-3 (library e-book)
ISBN 978-1-4773-0882-0 (non-library e-book)
1. Mapuche Indians—Patagonia (Argentina and Chile)—Rites and ceremonies—
History. 2. Shamans—Patagonia (Argentina and Chile) 3. Patagonia
(Argentina and Chile) I. Title.
F3126.B33 2016
305.898′720827—dc23
2015021068

doi:10.7560/308806

For Francisca Kolipi Kurin,
who upon seeing this would say, I hope,
"I have arrived, dear old ones. I have returned."

CONTENTS

CONTENTS

ACKNOWLEDGMENTS

Thunder Shaman is the result of many years of friendship and ethnographic research with Mapuche in the Quepe area of Araucanía in southern Chile. I am grateful to machi Francisca Kolipi Kurin, who demanded that I become her ritual helper and write her shamanic "bible," and to all who collaborated in its creation and in determining a propitious time to write it after her death. Many thanks to people in the communities of Millali, Chihuimpilli, Imilco, Nahuelhual, and Huenchual who taught me to understand the world through shamanic notions of history and time and talked to me about the lives and practices of Mapuche shamans Rosa Kurin and her successor Francisca Kolipi.

Particular thanks go to Francisca's children and grandchildren and to the Ancao, Añiwal, Calfuñir, Huenchuñir, Katrikura, Lefian, Millañir, Morales, and Sandoval families, who shared their lives with me and welcomed me into their homes. I am also indebted to the many Mapuche scholars who generously shared their perceptions of history and temporality with me: Sergio Caniuqueo, Luis Cárcamo Huechante, Andrés Cuyul, Rosendo Huisca, Leonel Lienlaf, Elisa Loncon, José Mariman, Doris Millalen, Rosamel Millaman, Yolanda Nahuelcheo, Juan Ñanculef, and Eduardo Rapimán. I trust that my gratitude for their openness and my deep admiration for their ways of understanding time and history are evident in the pages that follow. I am also grateful to German settlers Elizabeth Schleyer and Carlos Lüer for sharing their perspectives on their history with me.

A number of foundations funded different stages of the long-term research (1991–2015) required to write this book. I gratefully acknowledge the International Federation of University Women, Fundación Andes, Fundación Conycit, Dirección de Investigación (Universidad Católica de Chile), the Gender Institute Faculty Research Award (University at Buffalo), the UB 2020 Scholars Grant for Excellence in Cultural, Historical, and Literary/Textual Studies (University at Buffalo), and the Outstanding Young

Investigator Award (University at Buffalo). For funds that provided time for writing this book, I acknowledge the John Simon Guggenheim Foundation, the Rockefeller Foundation, the Rockefeller Bellagio Foundation, the National Endowment for the Humanities, the Radcliffe Institute for Advanced Study Fellowship (Harvard University), the National Humanities Center Fellowship (Rockefeller Foundation and National Endowment for the Humanities), an Ethel-Jane Westfeldt Bunting Fellowship (School for Advanced Research in Santa Fe), and a Humanities Institute Faculty Research Fellowship (University at Buffalo). For providing space for writing I acknowledge the Department of Anthropology and the Center for World Religions at Harvard University, the Lozano Long Institute of Latin American Studies (University of Texas at Austin), and the Latin American Studies Center at the University of Toronto. I am grateful to the Max Planck Institute for the Study of Religious and Ethnic Diversity for funding the indexing of the book.

I presented versions of various chapters of *Thunder Shaman* at seminars and colloquia, and the participants inspired me to extend my thinking. I thank the organizers of those events for their gracious invitations, commentary, and support. Many thanks to the participants in "Magic and Mysticism in Indigenous Traditions: Contested Terms, Material Objects, and Charismatic Figures" at the Center for the Study of Religion at Ohio State University, organized by Lindsay Jones; "Autobiographical and Biographical Narratives of Lowland Indigenous People," organized by Suzanne Oakdale and Magnus Course at the University of Edinburgh; the Society of Fellows in the Humanities at Columbia University, organized by Brian Goldstone and Eileen Gillooly; the Hemispheric Institute and Department of Anthropology at NYU, organized by Marcial Godoy, Diana Taylor, and Fred Myers; the Department of Religion at the University of Florida, organized by Robin Wright; the Committee on the Study of Religion at Harvard University, organized by Michael Puett; the Andean Studies Colloquium at Harvard University, organized by Gary Urton; the Radcliffe Institute for Advanced Study at Harvard University, organized by Judith Vichniac; the National Humanities Center, organized by Geoffrey Harpham; the Interdisciplinary Colloquium in Indigenous Studies at the University of North Carolina, Chapel Hill, organized by Emilio del Valle Escalante; the Department of Anthropology at the University of Wisconsin, Madison, organized by Neil Whitehead; the Coloniality/Modernity and Geopolitics of Knowledge Working Group at Duke University and the University of North Carolina, Chapel Hill, organized by James Peacock; the Department of Anthropology at the University of Pennsylvania, organized by Marshall Knudson; and the Department of Anthropology's Feminist Research Alliance and TransAmericas workshop at SUNY, Buffalo, organized by Phillips Stevens, Kari Winter, and Camilo Trumper.

Special thanks to Michael Frisch, Florencia Mallon, Paul Stoller, and Robin Wright for their comments on the entire manuscript. I am grateful to a number of colleagues who commented on drafts of chapters: Marjorie Balzer, Debbora Battaglia, James Brooks, Michael Brown, Manduhai Buyandelger, Luis Cárcamo Huechante, Jorge Canizares Esguerra, Jennifer Cole, Andrés Cuyul, Jeffrey Ehrenreich, Matthew Engelke, Carlos Fausto, Jennifer Gaynor, Laura Graham, Gastón Gordillo, Fernando Santos Granero, Jonathan Hill, Jean Jackson, Michael Jackson, Laurel Kendall, Bruce Mannheim, José Mariman, Antonia Mills, June Nash, Suzanne Oakdale, Daniela Peluso, Joanne Rappaport, Douglas Rogers, Steven Rubenstein, Rosalind Shaw, Helmut Schindler, Andrew Strathern, Charles Stewart, Pamela Stewart, Gary Urton, and Michael Winkelman.

For ongoing conversations that helped me write a manuscript true to both Francisca's project and my own, I thank Jim Bono, David Carrasco, Jean and John Comaroff, Giovanni Da Col, Jean Dennison, Tom Dillehay, Pat Donovan, Sarah Elder, Emilio del Valle Escalante, Michael Herzfeld, Jaime Ibacache, Bruce Jackson, Webb Keane, Michael Lambek, Catalina Laserna, Tanya Luhrmann, Jacob Olupona, Stephan Palmie, David Schoenbrun, Andrew Shryock, Cecilia Vicuña, Jenny White, Neil Whitehead, Ken Wissoker, and Vera Zolberg. I am also grateful to Margaret Humphrey for helping me interpret Francisca Kolipi's medical records.

I am grateful to Clara Antinao, Rosendo Huisca, Doraliza Millalen, and Juan Nanculef for their careful translations of recordings from Mapudungun to Spanish. I thank Leila Juzam, Marcelo Mendoza, Yolanda Andrea Lopez Sanchez, and Marcelo Gonzalez Galvez for transcribing the interviews. Many thanks to Sergio Caniuqueo, Rodrigo Levil, Pamela Maturana Arias, Carolina Schiolla, Myriam Duchens, and Cecilia Sepúlveda for obtaining data I needed from various archives in Chile, to Jessica Bright and Maria McQuade for organizing the references, and to James Stamos for creating the maps. My deepest thanks to Sarah Soliz and Merryl Sloane for their careful editing and to all the staff at the University of Texas Press, especially Casey Kittrell for his support and wise council.

PERMISSIONS

Preliminary versions of chapters 2, 5, and 7 have appeared previously as journal articles: "Mapuche Struggles to Obliterate Dominant History: Mythohistory, Spiritual Agency, and Shamanic Historical Consciousness in Southern Chile" appeared in *Identities: Global Studies in Culture and Power* 20(1):77–95, 2013; "The Potency of Indigenous Bibles and Biography: Mapuche Shamanic Literacy and Historical Consciousness" appeared in *American Ethnologist* 41(4):648–663, 2014; and "The Paradox of Disremembering the Dead: Ritual, Memory, and Embodied Historicity in Mapuche Shamanic Personhood" is forthcoming in *Anthropology and Humanism*.

I am grateful to George Munro for allowing me to use three of the photographs he took of Francisca Kolipi, and to Helen Hughes for allowing me to use one of her photographs.

I obtained permission to publish this book from Francisca Kolipi, her living children, her sons-in-laws, and the *longko* of the communities of Millali, Imilco, Nahuelhual, and Huenchual. I also obtained permission from all the interviewees whose quotes are included in this book.

THUNDER SHAMAN

CHAPTER ONE

MAKING HISTORY *in* FRANCISCA KOLIPI'S BIBLE

On May 22, 1960, southern Chile was hit by the most powerful earthquake ever recorded in human history—a 9.6 on the Richter scale. People in the Mapuche community of Millali, in the Araucanía region of southern Chile (fig. 1.1), believe that the colossal earthquake resulted from cosmic chaos provoked by the deplorable behavior of European settlers and by the state control, infighting, and sorcery that followed in the colonists' wake. The earth serpent Trengtreng punished the transgressors with the earthquake and a volcanic eruption (both associated with the powers of the earth), which were meant to destroy the world. Alejo Huenchuñir, a great-grandson of machi Rosa who lived in Millali, said, "When the hill, the earth, is angry at us, it makes noises; it says *huechii*. It makes thunder, earthquakes, and breaks the world."

Kinship, the ownership and inheritance of land, and social and political roles link the past with the present. In moments of great crisis this historical continuity is severed. The historicity of the present and the cosmic balance both collapse. At moments of crisis, the forces of the world boost the power of chosen Mapuche to another realm, initiating them as shamans (machi). The cosmic and temporal order is accessible only through the machi's altered states of consciousness. In dreams, visions, and trances, machi simultaneously experience different temporalities—past, present, and future.[1]

In 1992, seventy-year-old Francisca Kolipi, a Catholic machi, described how the force of Mapuche thunder machi was unleashed by the devastating earthquake of 1960, when at the age of thirty-nine she was struck by lightning and possessed by the spirit of Rosa Kurin:

My stomach fell as if they had cut it off. I ripped off my sweater and my shoes. I only wanted clothes from old times: *chamall* [woolen wrap], *ükülla* [shawl], people without makeup. I was trembling. I didn't

FIGURE I.I

Map of southern Chile and Argentina detailing the research area
(map commissioned by author).

FIGURE 1.1
(continued)

eat anything. I was skinny and yellow. I was like crazy. My head was drunk. . . . The sky opened and I was hit by lightning. [The spirits] brought me down my *kultrung* [drum] and my *kaskawilla* [sleigh bells], my *wada* [calabash rattle]. Then I looked upward, and there was a big stone—my *likankura* [spiritual stone]—a bull, [and] my horse. It was my power. They told me to get it. I held my apron out, and they brought down all the herbal remedies I should use. They got my eyes and my right arm and gave them power. People came here and slept outside and said that God was going to finish off the people. "No, the people shall live," I told them. . . . My stomach swelled up. I could only eat boiled apples. I told them to cook sheep liver and stomach for the hill. . . . The hill burst, the thunder burst on the hills. The hills, they have power. . . . Every day it trembled, every day there was lightning and thunder, every day I played my *kultrung*. . . . The earthquake calmed down, and I saved the world. I was a powerful machi. Now Ngünechen [the Mapuche deity] bosses me. I cannot decide things on my own. (March 24, 1992)

Soon after, Francisca had a dream with Catholic significance:

I went up a big thick pole to the Wenu Mapu. Just like on the day of Saint Peter, the sky opened up. . . . And they gave me clover, beans,

---

MAKING HISTORY *in* FRANCISCA KOLIPI'S BIBLE

maize, potatoes, wheat, lentils. . . . And as I was coming down, old man God with a long mustache said, "I am going to give you luck." (March 24, 1992)

Mobile, mounted thunder machi like Rosa and Francisca transcend the divisions of time; they travel to different worlds and times as masters of multiple realities. They use their multitemporal knowledges to reorder time and weave hope back into the world. In her initiation narrative, Francisca located herself and her source of knowledge in the past—"I only wanted clothes from old times." She then described how she experienced herself in multiple temporalities at once. In the present she was a Catholic thunder machi saving the world from destruction and predicting that people would survive. But she also saw the future in which she would become this machi and simultaneously saw herself as a machi who had already saved the world. Francisca was given a drum, sleigh bells, a spiritual stone, and herbal remedies, but she also recognized them as already hers, and she had already used them in a future time. God gave her *vista* (psychic sight) and gave power to her right arm,[2] which proved that she was a good Catholic machi espousing a morality in which good predominates over evil. But Francisca also experienced her right arm as already having power and as telling her about people's thoughts and emotions. Francisca described Saint Peter opening the heavens for her and God promising to give her luck in the future; she also saw them as already giving her luck and abundance in the form of produce.

This multitemporality is expressed through machi's unique ability to share multiple relational and individual personhoods with beings from different worlds and times and through machi's inherent ambiguity, which allows them to cross boundaries. Like many indigenous people (Oakdale and Course 2014; Strathern 1992), Mapuche persons are multiple. They expand their personhood by incorporating aspects of others in a variety of contexts. At the same time they condense those aspects into a concrete, singular person with a fixed destiny. Machi complicate this process because they are never singular persons. Minimally, those who are machi are double persons: humans permanently inhabited by a machi spirit who preordains them as shamans and shapes their everyday lives and actions. By virtue of their shamanic destiny, machi are simultaneously collective ancestral persons and historical individuals whose personhood is embodied in material objects and living entities (Bacigalupo 2010, 2013, 2014). Machi also share this personhood with spirits, animals, and deities in diverse ways during both ordinary and altered states of consciousness. In trance, machi can become multiple beings at once—simultaneously shaman and spirit, human and divine (Bacigalupo 2004a, 2007:45–47, 68–69, 100–110).

Francisca's acquisition of shamanic power—as well as others' perceptions of her use of that power—was the mediating event of her life. Her thunder-based kinship with machi Rosa, her narrative about saving the world from destruction, and her dream of Catholic support legitimated her community-focused rituals, in which she gained knowledge about the world, killed evil spirits, challenged power inequalities, resisted state agents, and healed suffering. As a good machi who had the power of God in her right arm, Francisca would sit on the right side of God and be blessed on the Day of Judgment. But Francisca was also suspected of sorcery because the wild power of thunder is not subject to human morality and can be used by sorcerers to destroy and cannibalize their own spiritual and blood kin.

Francisca spoke and acted within her own social and political context. She sometimes sought personal gain, took sides in the conflicts among factions within Millali, and was said to hex her enemies, including the *longko* (community head). Some viewed Francisca as an *awingkada* (meaning "like a *wingka*," or non-Mapuche). They questioned her legitimacy because she was a thunder machi initiated late in life and had no formal training. Others envied Francisca's wealth and power and called her a sorcerer because she violated Mapuche and Chilean patriarchal gender norms: she made her money independently outside the home and did not distribute sufficient favors to the community; she refused to remarry when she was widowed; and she was considered by some to be manly, aggressive, and amoral (Bacigalupo 2010, 2014). Aware of these criticisms, Francisca feared that her spirit would not be reborn in a new shaman's body after she died. To make sure that her spirit would not be lost, she demanded during our first face-to-face meeting that I write her biography as a "bible."[3]

SHAMANIC HISTORICAL CONSCIOUSNESS IN FRANCISCA'S BIBLE

Although Francisca and I had been aware of each other for years, it was not until November 1991 that we met—at her home in the community of Millali, a *reducción* (reservation) near the town of Quepe. Although Mapuche reservations have a defined land base and communal identity, they are not outside the purview of the state government. On the walls of Francisca's home, posters of a bikini-clad calendar girl and Rambo with his machine gun, along with an award for third place from the local soccer club, competed with three Catholic images: one of the pope, another of the Virgin Mary that read "This is the house of God," and the third of Saint Francis, Francisca's patron saint and master of animals, ecology, and agriculture (fig. 1.2). There also were two framed photographs. One showed her in the

FIGURE I.2
Author with Francisca Kolipi in her home (photo by Francisca's grandson Cesar Mellado).

full regalia of a Mapuche shaman, standing beside Francisco, her only son; the other was a wedding picture of her and her husband, José (Pancho) Calfuñir. Hanging from a nail was a *kultrung*, a drum made from a bowl of laurel wood covered by a goatskin. Francisca divined the causes of illnesses and invoked Jesus, the Virgin, and Mapuche spirits as she used herbal remedies, massage, and drumming to heal patients of a variety of ailments. She prayed for the well-being of her entire community, divined the future, and voiced local perceptions of the past and history in Mapudungun, the Mapuche "language of the earth," and in Spanish, the official language of Chile.

Francisca stared at me quizzically, her gray hair braided neatly under a blue headscarf, her weathered brown face wrinkling as she spoke. "You are *champuria* [mixed race] like me, but you think like Mapuche. Your mother's family is from Argentina, like mine. You will dream a lot. I will teach you about machi practice, and then you will help me heal. You will be my granddaughter. And then you will write a bible about me and I will never die" (November 3, 1991). Dumbfounded, I scanned Francisca's blue-painted living room for clues about what a bible meant to her and why she wanted me to write one about her, since she could not read.[4]

Crammed on a rickety shelf were a small black-and-white television, some gardening tools, and a large, dusty black Bible that some Catholic nuns had given her. Francisca also had on her shelf a copy of *Enseñan-zas de la primavera ancestral* (Teachings of the Ancestral Spring), a book published a year earlier by the Chilean philosopher Ziley Mora. Although Francisca was not featured in Mora's book, she believed that the picture of the two of them that appeared on the cover would legitimate her in the eyes of her non-Mapuche patients. "This way people know I am a good machi," she boasted. "But now I need a bible about *me*."

I first thought that Francisca was using the word *bible* because she saw her story as an authoritative divine truth that, through my ethnography, would mediate between God's word and ordinary language. Perhaps, I thought, Francisca wanted me to create a shamanic bible to compete with the one revered by evangelical Christian Mapuche, a sacred text containing her divine words rather than those of God, Jesus, the apostles, or the devil. This assumption was not completely wrong, but as we worked together I came to learn that she saw a different purpose for the bible she wanted me to write. Francisca's mutable and multiple identities, as well as my own, led her to think that if I learned about her shamanic practice through dream-ing and rituals, I could write a text that would stand in for her—it would be a potent shamanic object with a performative function. The book would store and textualize her power, circulate it through time and space, heal, and enable communication between the living and the dead and between Mapuche and non-Mapuche. It would be a shamanic history, and it would challenge the dominant culture's understandings about Mapuche and their society.

I gradually came to understand that Francisca sought to legitimate her-self and her shamanic forms of history-making in local eyes and in the eyes of the Chilean majority. Francisca practiced a bold kind of history-making, not replicating the enclosed otherness with which indigenous practices are often described, whether for repression or romanticized celebration. Since the nineteenth century, Chilean settlers, priests, soldiers, politicians, his-torians, and other intellectuals have fossilized female and male shamans dressed in women's clothing as symbols of the folkloric past.[5] These percep-tions have permeated the Chilean national imagination: machi are viewed as lacking historical consciousness. In this limited perspective, historical consciousness is conceived as a modernist assumption of the Global North about a linear temporal relationship in which events are organized into past, present, and future. Although most people do not experience the past through historicism, there is a great deal of tension among three distinct notions of the past: as events documented by professional historiographers through the discourse of fact and objectivity; as beliefs about a shared past experienced through collective memory (Seixas 2004:9–10); and as the machi's achronological narratives about the past and their experiences of the past through altered states of consciousness.

Some historians of Latin America have used social historical approaches to refine national histories by bringing in local memory and popular struggles (see Mallon 1995, 2005; Stern 2001). But people in the Quepe area experience Chilean national history more straightforwardly as positivistic *wingka* history, which has often been used as a weapon of repression and control. This is the kind of national history learned at the local school, on the radio, and through the discourse of right-wing settlers. And this is the history people seek to obliterate with their shamanic narratives. Throughout this book I hold to a more general contrast between shamanic histories and the descriptions of Chilean history constructed by *wingka* through the chronological narration of archival "facts." The machi's experience of shamanic rebirth; the combination of cyclical and linear histories, temporal dislocation, and multitemporality; and the indissoluble links between spirituality, politics, and ecology challenge positivist, linear notions of history.

The Chilean national imagination has rejected machi narratives as premodern, nonobjective, irrational, and ahistorical in contrast to national linear narratives. That machi could be historical agents has been unthinkable for a Chilean state that has leveraged positivist historiography, secularism, and Judeo-Christian thought to eradicate machi practice—erasing it from the archives and from the making of Chilean history.[6] As is so often the case, what is unthinkable is that which is too threatening to be comfortably acknowledged. As healers of both individuals and the body politic and as agents of history, shamans are marginalized because they challenge the colonialist institutions of authority and the secular ethnic histories that have been constructed for Mapuche. Machi can be males who often wear women's scarves, jewelry, and shawls during rituals. Their machi activities often preclude them from performing the ordinary roles of women and men, and spirits expect them to be celibate, although some machi are married and have children. Machi embody cogendered identities and use this multiplicity in rituals to mediate between other times, worlds, and beings.[7] Machi are morally ambiguous persons whose spirits are usually inherited through the female line and often by granddaughter from grandmother. Their powers are not controlled by chiefs, by the Mapuche patrilineage, by Chilean authorities, by Mapuche resistance movements, or by priests (Bacigalupo 2001, 2004d, 2007:140–163; fig. 1.3).

Because machi are marginalized by the state and are not tied to a specific place, group, or ideology—or even to a specific human body or life—they can offer what Steven Feierman (1995) has called a "partially autonomous

FIGURE I.3

Male and female machi praying at the step-notched rewe, *which is flanked by branches of the* foye *and* triwe *trees (photo bought at the market in Temuco).*

critique" of local and colonialist authorities and structures of power. Machi use their matrilineal spiritual genealogies to weave what Michel Foucault (1979:31) called an alternative "history of the present" and to revive local histories that have been marginalized by positivist historiography in the context of current Mapuche circumstances and utopian ideas of the future.

Francisca defied academic categories about native histories and defined her own political struggles for decolonization.[8] She endorsed the Mapuche notion that truth is tied to a world of values, not to the dichotomy of fact and fiction. Francisca argued that her narratives were *verdadera historia* (true history) that could not be reduced to "stories," which for her were synonymous with lies, recalling Global Northern notions about myth (Lévi-Strauss 1987), "creative productions" (Lambek 1998:111), "historical imagination" (Comaroff and Comaroff 1992), and "discursive engagements with the past" (Course 2010). Francisca drew on indigenous knowledge as the point from which she created connections with researchers and their understandings of history.

Although Mapudungun has no term for "history" or "myth" and Mapuche do not always subscribe to the kind of history written by scholars in the Global North, Mapuche do understand shamans' narratives and experiences historically and use the Spanish term *historia* (history) rather than *memoria* (memory) when speaking about them. Scholars have characterized memory as lived experience, as a particular perspective on the past (Nora 1989), as remembrance of past events and experiences, and as a past that is stored and transmitted (Battaglia 1992:14). Memory is seen as distinct from history, which is defined as a representation of the past that attempts to synthesize different perspectives. But machi reject this distinction between memory and history and focus instead on how different individuals and groups encode, understand, and reconstruct the past using multiple strategies and forms. The machi's perceptions resonate with some anthropological perceptions of historical consciousness as the basic assumptions that a society makes about the shape of time and the relationship of events in the past, present, and future. Determining how people in a particular society assume the past to be and how they produce stories requires an ethnographic history of that particular society (Stewart 2012:2; Lambek 2003).

For machi and other people in Millali, historical consciousness is itself shamanic. They remember, experience, enliven, and sometimes deliberately disremember their past—that is, they produce history—through texts, ritual objects, spirits, embodied ritual experiences, and oral biographies of their machi. Francisca wanted all of this included in her bible. She and her community engaged different notions of time and history to produce multiple modes of shamanic historical consciousness. Mapuche narratives and embodied experiences of the past are often achronological and episodic and can be used in different forms in a variety of situations. They are constantly assembled and reassembled in relation to specific sociopolitical and historical circumstances and activities that are not explicit in the narratives themselves.

This book is Francisca's bible; it is both a study of shamanic historical consciousness in Millali and an agent in the transformation of that history. It explores machi and community members' assumptions about the nature of time and the relationship between past, present, and future. This book is also about the role of shamans and spirits as effective historical agents who transform and make history through healing and remaking the world—as seen through the life and ritual practices of Francisca Kolipi. Francisca's shamanic history and practices propelled her patients from what they were to what they believed they were or would become. I have written neither a Global Northern–style history of the Mapuche and their shamans nor an ethnic history of the kind authored by Mapuche intellectuals to support their sense of identity in relation to the Chilean state.[9] Rather, I seek to understand rural Mapuche notions of time, history, continuity, change, and agency through a shamanic lens.

Machi use the temporal simultaneity of altered states of consciousness to reshape history. Through ritual, they draw on and remake the powers of the past to heal in the present and to forge a better future. Machi fuse historical events with individual lives in order to contextualize local histories within larger Mapuche origin stories and cyclical processes; they then rehistoricize and resignify these origin stories in new, changing contexts. Mapuche use temporal dislocation to conflate their current realities, identities, and experiences with colonial and postcolonial events and figures from other moments in their histories. In doing so, they construct nonlinear histories of intra- and interethnic relations and create a moral order where Mapuche become history's spiritual victors. By exposing and reflecting on all of these, I aim to show how machi are constituted by historical-political events yet also actively and imaginatively constitute those events through shamanic imaginaries and narrative forms.

All of this helps clarify what Francisca Kolipi meant, and what she was seeking, when she asked me to write her biography as a bible. In the Global North, biography is often seen as separate from history, not as a form of historiography. In contrast, Mapuche—like many Latin American indigenous peoples (Basso 1995, 2003; Kopenawa and Albert 2013; Taylor 2007; Oakdale and Course 2014; Wright 2013)—see the biographies of prominent individuals as central to engagements with temporality and history-making in a variety of everyday, ritual, and political contexts. Francisca occupied a pivotal role in her community, and her biography is a testimony about historical processes: change and continuity, conflict and harmony, sorcery and healing, disremembering and remembering, death and rebirth. She was an active agent within a complex constellation of cultural logics, social fields, and modalities for constructing history. Focusing on Francisca's story—on her position as a mestiza who was both within and outside the community and on her many transgressions—also reveals norms, practices, and notions of Mapuche personhood that might not otherwise become evident, including its relationship to spirits and to history.[10]

Notions of personhood and individuality in the Global North differ from Mapuche notions, in which biographies are conceived as an oscillation between singular lives that condense the experiences of others and collective lives that incorporate the experiences of others and represent the collective.[11] Shamans' personal narratives make connections among different times, worlds, and beings by placing dreams and altered states of consciousness in the context of colonization, missionization, and urbanization.[12]

Francisca embodied and resignified Rosa Kurin's shamanic spirit, and through stories, songs, and spirit possession she told of the community's past in order to interpret its present and grant it agency in relation to the dominant Chilean society. Francisca's narratives about her life were therefore never just her individual memories but included those of Rosa and the other spirits she embodied. Shamanic histories aggregate the personal experiences of shamans, recognize the periodic embodiment of the spirits of past shamans in new machi, and identify shamanic spirits alternately as collective and individual identities. The names and identities of prominent shamans and chiefs are collapsed into those of deceased ancestors or primordial characters in the creation of regional histories (Bacigalupo 2010).[13] In her bible, Francisca wanted me to include stories about how she and others in Millali obliterated political and economic ideologies in order to remake Chilean history in an achronological shamanic form. Like other spiritual practitioners around the world, machi mimic, parody, and oppose colonialism, and the themes of their stories relate to socialism, neoliberalism, and dictatorship.[14] Machi subject the characters, events, and powers in these structures to their own spiritual ideologies, including a shamanic logic of temporal dislocation and a Mapuche moral history of engagement with nature and its spirits.

As a wild, drumming, thunder shaman–warrior mounted on her horse, Francisca narrated her mastery over time and space while her spirit traveled to other times and places to gain power and knowledge and to conduct spiritual warfare against enemies, including forestry companies and settlers. As a tame machi bride who was possessed by spirits and subservient to their sociospiritual order and demands, Francisca narrated her people's attachment to the sacred landscapes of Millali, which are imbued with Rosa's power and populated by the spirit masters of particular ecosystems, and to her shamanic tree of life, or *rewe* (*axis mundi*), a carved pole flanked by branches, which allowed her to travel to other spiritual worlds from that particular location in the landscape. As a daughter, wife, and mother, Francisca narrated her conflicted kinship history through blood and marriage and told larger stories about the Mapuche's engagement with ethnic others and about the moral and social norms that shaped and constrained her shamanic practice. Francisca also became what she called a *machi civilizada* (civilized shaman) with a broad vision of the universe because she selectively incorporated *wingka* knowledges and technologies into her ritual practices and took their power to further Mapuche goals. But she also noted the ambivalent identities and conflicted histories that offer moral teaching for Mapuche themselves: Mapuche who act like *wingka* become selfish sorcerers.

THE HISTORIC POWER OF FRANCISCA'S BIBLE

My reading of Francisca's political and intellectual motives for asking me to write a bible about her deepened considerably over time. But it was only after her death in 1996 that I came to understand the larger ritual implications of her request and its consequences for shamanic healing and rebirth. This involved my moving from appreciating the historicism and transformation of personhood embedded in her request to focusing on her choice of the Catholic Bible as the particular basis for imagining historical power.

Of all books, the Bible has had the greatest influence on native religions and governance in the Americas. A nonindigenous textual object, it has come to play a central role in indigenous Mapuche shamanic identity and power. Through her use of the Catholic Bible, Francisca recast the world of orality, shamanic power, and spirits, and in doing so, she reconstructed history.[15] She displayed a copy of the Bible in her living room as an object of power that she could shamanically appropriate for the benefit of her patients.[16] She prayed and smoked over her Bible to "awaken" God's words. She placed leaves of the sacred *foye* and *triwe* trees in it to "activate" their medicinal properties before making herbal treatments. She rubbed the Catholic Bible on her patients' bodies during healing and then slammed it shut when she managed to trap an evil *wekufü* spirit within its pages.

It was Francisca's identity as a *champuria* Mapuche shaman, an expert in the control of the economy of alterity, that allowed her to effectively transform a non-Mapuche sacred text into an object infused with shamanic power that could alter the temporalities of death and rebirth. Mapuche have decolonized their relationship to Bibles, resignifying them to express complex local notions and practices, and they use a variety of Bibles as differentiated vehicles for memory, blending different streams of sacred knowledge. The Lutheran Bible stores the powers of devils and the landowners who destroyed Mapuche morality and sociality; the Capuchin Catholic and Anglican Protestant Bibles store the power of God and the magic of literacy; and bibles written by Mapuche prophets celebrate Mapuche rituals and an alternative ethnic and historical consciousness. Machi dream of celestial bibles that will narrate their biographies in the sky.

Francisca conceived the bible she wanted me to write about her as an intertextual object that would link biography, ritual performance, and personhood with graphic and alphabetic literacy. Through that linkage Francisca's bible would have the ability to transform the world and the future, and her words would spread to a distant audience and continue to exert her shamanic power and agency—"the capacity for meaningful action" (Harris 1989)—even in her physical absence.[17] She insisted that her bible have indented quotations of her shamanic prayers, "powerful little words like in the Bible" (July 15, 1996). When future shamans smoked and chanted over her quotations, the powers they held could be extracted, transformed, and used for a variety of ends.

This shamanic bible I have co-created with Francisca is somewhat like the shamanic antibible that emerged from the collaboration of Yanomami shaman Davi Kopenawa and anthropologist Bruce Albert (Kopenawa and Albert 2013). Francisca and Davi both appropriated the Bible to produce authoritative books about indigenous shamanic knowledge with the idea that white people would respect their texts as they respect the Bible. Both shamans have shown how spirituality, human life, politics, and ecology are inextricably linked, and they have integrated different political and academic categories, using multiple voices, in order to engage with and transform the reader and the world. But where Kopenawa experienced the fixing of his oral shamanic knowledge into a written form as an intellectual compromise justifiable only to convince a wide non-Yanomami public to support his political struggle on his people's behalf, Francisca saw her bible as a dynamic, subjective object. The words in her bible would store her power and be activated by future shamans, who would smoke and chant over them to effect her most important shamanic transformation: the rebirth of her spirit in another shaman's body, reincorporating her story into her community's history.

For Francisca the creation of this bible would immortalize her powers in another way too. "When I die, my words will stay in the book," she said (February 25, 1992).[18] Although the speech, rituals, and lives of individuals are ephemeral, words printed on a page are more permanent. Thus, Francisca's bible would both perpetuate Mapuche notions of historical continuity through spiritual rebirth and expand Mapuche notions of history and literacy.

It is this potential for rebirth that makes machi crucial to the transformation of Mapuche personhood and the production of Mapuche history. Machi are unique in the ways that death transforms their personhood. The historical process of disremembering them soon after death, and their eventual re-remembering, transforms machi spirits from individual figures into generic, ancestral ones, and then back. When machi die, their communities may depersonalize them as generic ancestor machi. This means stripping them of their individual thoughts, emotions, and personal relationships to others; merging their actions with those of earlier deceased machi; and remembering them for their positive social actions—such as having saved the community from an earthquake or a flood. Later, as their spirits are cleansed of their negative qualities, they can be reborn in the bodies of new machi. In this way machi are reindividualized and rehistoricized. The new machi will carry the temperament, skills, and ritual performance style of the machi whose spirit she inherits. Shamanic spirits are thus transformed and recycled at different historical and political moments in linear time, which gives them both relational-collective and individual identities. Narratives about Rosa and Francisca trace the history of their shared shamanic spirit as it has been transformed over time through remembering and disremembering.

It is in this particular sense that Francisca believed that the words and photographs printed in the book I would write could capture her essence, and in this way she would never die. But it is also why Francisca's family asked me not to write her bible after her physical death in 1996. At the time, they felt that my writing her bible would call her spirit back. They were focused on deliberately disremembering Francisca's controversial mestiza individuality so that her spirit would leave and merge with the collective ancestral spirit of all machi, the *filew*, to create historical continuity. They also sought to erase her memory because her life story reflected uncomfortable factional conflicts between hierarchical and egalitarian ideologies and included accusations of witchcraft in the community.

But in 2009, new circumstances caused Francisca's family to change their minds: the factionalism had eased and the community had begun to flourish. Displaying the messiness of time, memory, and human agency, people now remembered Francisca in an altered form, recasting her as the benevolent shaman who had brought prosperity to Millali. They merged Francisca's identity with that of her shamanic predecessor, machi Rosa. The family could now individualize her again within the new historical and political context. And so they asked me to write her bible after all. As part of the ancestral spirit of all machi, she would take a new textualized form. She would be reborn. This bible would constitute Francisca's new indigenized identity, grounding her positive shamanic powers in her role as a mediator for the collective, and recording Millali's history as traced through her.

This book is my response to Francisca's and her family's requests. Part "ethno-ethnohistory" (Turner 1988), part bible, and part a collection of my own interpretations, *Thunder Shaman* shows that for Mapuche, memory is a complex, heterogeneous process conditioned by local political circumstances, cosmic events, and shamanic transformations of personhood through death and rebirth. Unlike their Euro-American counterparts, the autobiographies and biographies of machi are generally not renderings of shamans' historical lives, but rather episodic tales of their origins, dramatic transformations, shamanic power, suffering, and shifting personhood. Machi engage in complex relationships with others from different times and places, including Christian saints, Spanish conquistadores, German settlers, and anthropologists, as well as with animals, spirits, and spirit masters of the forest.[19] I will maintain the fragmented, achronological nature of these narrations as I tell Francisca's story and, in less detail, Rosa's in Mapuche terms: as illustrations of particular modes of shamanic history-making rather than as linear biographies.

MILLALI: THE "PLACE THAT SHINES"

Francisca Kolipi (1921–1996) and her shaman predecessor, Rosa Kurin (1873–1955), both lived in a rural Mapuche community thirteen kilometers from the city of Temuco and five kilometers from Quepe, the nearest town. The *longko* who headed the community at the time was Pascual Calfuñir. Locals call the community Millali (originally Millaleu), meaning "Precious Place" or "Place that Shines," because they believe that the hill that rises above it "has power and shines at night. It has a gold mine and a huge amount of water in it. When it bursts, it is like a water pump. At night it thunders, and you can hear the people who live in it talking and laughing." Millali was first settled by hunters, gatherers, and horticulturalists around AD 1000 (Dillehay 1990:37). The different kinds of arrowheads, ceramics, tilling instruments, stone beads, ritual artifacts, musical instruments, and weapons found on the Millali hill indicate that this place was used continuously by Mapuche until the land was expropriated by the Chilean government and sold to settlers in 1885. Today, fifty-eight families live scattered over some 253 hectares of land, outside the bounded municipality.[20]

Millali is an important site because of its sacred landscapes, which are populated by a variety of spirits. People in Millali and the neighboring Mapuche communities of Imilco, Chihuimpilli, Nahuelhual, and Huenchual—the last two partly subsumed within the town of Quepe—know Millali as a place of *newen* (power). Alberto Huenchuñir from Millali told me, "All the trees around here have power. If you cut one down, you die. The stones you see [on the mountaintop] are bulls that came down from the sky with a big copper bell and went to the top of Millali" (June 20, 2007). On the Millali hill are three places of enormous significance: the *boldo* tree where Rosa Kurin obtained her shamanic powers and where her spirit lives; RukaÑamku, Millali's ancestral place of origin and the resting place of ancestral souls; and, adjacent to RukaÑamku, an old cemetery called Rüga Platawe, where Mapuche buried jewelry, ceramic vessels, and gold coins among the roots of a hollow laurel tree for the dead to watch over. The waterfall of Millali, the rock that machi Rosa once envisioned as a bull, and the streams where people in Millali panned for gold are also sites of spiritual power. In addition, each of the ecosystems in the forest on the Millali hill is guarded by a *ngen* (owner) of that particular ecosystem.

People in the neighboring communities also know Millali as a place of sorcery. "Dancing lights come down from the hill to curse people's houses," one person told me. "At midnight there is a standing horse and a dog [associated with the underworld] that stay there till dawn, and a fox [a trickster or sorcerer] roams and howls when someone is going to die. The machi from Millali are powerful, but they can also be bad witches," and "last year eight people died from witchcraft" (June 5, 2007). Alberto Huenchuñir added, "Many things come out in the evening in Millali. The kids get evil eye and sickness every time they go there. My granddaughter arrived vomiting. My grandson had a cold with fever and diarrhea. We heard loud thumping and laments at night. So I grabbed my kids and got a knife and told the *wekufü* not to bother them. People in Millali are strange [and] distrustful. They are afraid of their own relatives" (June 20, 2007).

The inhabitants of Quepe draw on a language of urbanity, civilization, and rationality—as well as the influence of three evangelical churches, two Catholic ones, a biomedical health clinic, and three schools—to distance themselves from the spirits and shamanism that are prevalent in Millali, even though most people in Millali have been baptized and combine Catholicism and Chilean biomedicine with shamanic practices in their everyday lives (Bacigalupo 1996a, 2001). Chihuimpilli boasts two schools, a

Catholic chapel, and a paved road, in contrast to the narrow, muddy dirt track leading to Millali, which has deterred both Catholics and evangelicals from building churches or schools there. People in Chihuimpilli claim that they are more secular and civilized than the people in Millali and that the spirits from Millali "don't go" to Chihuimpilli. For people in Millali and Imilco, however, being "civilized" does not mean being *awingkado*—like a wingka, or outsider—which implies a loss of Mapuche culture. Rather, to them being civilized means having a broad knowledge of Mapuche and non-Mapuche ways of thinking that can be deployed strategically for the well-being of the community. People in Millali alternately construe themselves as civilized because they have a broad knowledge of the world and as wild because they possess ancient shamanic knowledge of native plants and of the spirit owners of the forests.

In terms of the chronology of the Global North, the community members of Millali share with all other Mapuche a post-Columbian history of loss of life and land. Before colonization, the lush Mapuche region in Chile stretched from the Andean foothills to the Pacific coast, between the Mapocho River and the southern island of Chiloé. These varied environments allowed Mapuche to develop economic activities that included hunting, fishing, gathering, and incipient agriculture. The men also were accomplished guerrilla warriors who resisted first the Inca in the fifteenth and sixteenth centuries and then the Spaniards from the sixteenth to eighteenth centuries; the Mapuche also expanded into the Argentine Pampas and Patagonia. They were one of the largest indigenous populations and remained sovereign until the imposition of the reservation system between the Bío-Bío and Calle-Calle Rivers in 1884. After the Argentine and Chilean armies defeated and massacred Mapuche groups in 1879 and 1883, respectively, the Mapuche lost 9.5 million hectares of land (Bengoa 1999:61).

The state originally sold the Mapuche's fertile land to European settlers known as *colonos*, who established *fundos* (large farms), and more recently land has been sold to transnational forestry companies.[21] Araucanía became a two-tiered rural colonial economy with large race, class, and cultural distinctions between the wealthy landowners of European descent and the poor Mapuche living on reservations (Richards 2013:2). More than a million Mapuche live in Chile today, 6.25 percent of the population.[22] Sixty-two percent of Mapuche are *wariache*, or city dwellers, and 38 percent live in rural communities.[23] Thirty percent of Mapuche live in the Chilean capital, Santiago. Nevertheless, territory and the landscape remain central to Mapuche history, ontology, and identity.

The relegation of Mapuche to reservations combined the state's modernizing project—to expand its economy and territories and to incorporate

Mapuche as citizens—with a postcolonial project to control and "civilize" Mapuche by transforming their sociopolitical system, usurping their lands, exploiting their resources, and abusing the people (Mallon 2009). The Ley de Radicación de Indígenas (Law of Indigenous Settlement) was promulgated in 1866 to legally map the indigenous territories that were being incorporated into the Chilean state. Technically the law provided protection from usurpation by preventing the formal subdivision and sale of Mapuche lands. In practice it ushered in the largest expropriations of Mapuche land, which occurred during the granting of *títulos de merced* (land titles) between 1900 and 1930 (Bengoa 1991:372).

Between 1884 and 1929 the Chilean state issued to Mapuche lineage heads 3,078 titles for 475,422 hectares of land on the reservations (Bengoa 1991:355; Marimán 1990:1–13). But in 1927, the Chilean government produced a new document abolishing the legal inalienability of the reservations, and 784 of them, amounting to 131,000 hectares, were split into private landholdings and sold to non-Mapuche. A further 168 reservations disappeared from the written record (Bengoa 1999:59). In 1979 the dictator Augusto Pinochet wrote a law abolishing the communal character of the reservations, and many Mapuche who had rented their land to non-Mapuche people never recovered it.

The policy of the Chilean state toward Mapuche and their lands has been consistently two-faced. On the one hand, Chilean legislation protects indigenous lands from usurpation and charges the state with mediating between the Mapuche and broader society. On the other hand, Chilean private property laws and the state both support entrepreneurial activity (Mallon 2005:234), and local governmental institutions favor non-Mapuche landowners. The land titles for Millali and Imilco, for example, recognize only a fraction of the Mapuche's original holdings and include the worst lands. A man from Millali told me that the Mapuche received just a "pure stone quarry" because the government had already sold the best lands to the colonizers.

The democratic regimes that followed the Pinochet era, from 1989 to the present, have defined Chile as a multiethnic country and recognized Mapuche as an ethnicity in ideological and political terms, but they have failed to meet the Mapuche people's needs. The indigenous law passed by President Patricio Aylwin in 1993 protected some land and water rights and created the National Corporation of Indigenous Development (CONADI) to implement the state's policies relating to indigenous people. However, Mapuche quickly became disenchanted with this law because it does not grant them self-determination, autonomy, or significant political or participatory rights within the state; nor does it acknowledge their communal practices and traditional positions of leadership (Mallon 2005:225). Contemporary Mapuche have the right to vote, but they are marginalized from national politics, and their own political systems go unrecognized.

Although the democratic governments increased the number of development projects, they prioritized national and transnational economic interests, used Mapuche land for modernization projects, and sought to incorporate Mapuche into the global economy.[24] In 2008 the Chilean government ratified a key law on indigenous peoples, the International Labor Organization convention, but it has made little progress toward implementing the law's provisions. The Mapuche's political demonstrations, demands for self-determination and autonomy, and attempts to retake their previously seized territories from non-Mapuche landowners, timber companies, private energy firms, and state highway authorities have all resulted in escalating violence between the national police and the demonstrators. All democratic presidents starting with Ricardo Lagos (2000–2006) have used Pinochet's anti-terrorist law to indict Mapuche activists, *longko* (community heads), and shamans as indigenous terrorists and threats to national sovereignty and security. The government of Sebastián Piñera (2010–2014) has built an international airport in the Quepe area despite the protests of local Mapuche. Mapuche in Millali view this project as a confirmation of their perception that all Chilean governments, regardless of their political leanings, are anti-Mapuche.

Today, the community members of Millali, like other Mapuche living on reservations, experience extreme poverty. They eke out a living by farming wheat, barley, rapeseed, beets, and potatoes on small plots of eroded land; by raising sheep, pigs, and occasionally a few cattle; and by selling textiles at the bus stop in the city of Temuco. Land disputes among neighbors and with settlers and timber companies are common. Although in 2009 Millali recovered the acreage granted under a land title from 1909, these are the worst land parcels and only a fraction of the community's original holdings; moreover, the population has increased exponentially since the early twentieth century and can no longer survive on the yields of the reservation lands. Consequently, at least some members of every family in Millali work as wage laborers for farmers or forestry companies or in the city as maids, bakers, night guards, or construction workers.

Mapuche from the Quepe area have a long history of ethnic intermixing, factionalism, and shifting alliances. Beginning with the arrival of Spaniards in the sixteenth century and continuing until the ultimate defeat of Mapuche in the late nineteenth century, the indigenous people fought a prolonged guerrilla war, and descendants of some of the guerrillas settled in Millali. In the eighteenth and nineteenth centuries, Mapuche men from the Quepe area married Spanish and German women captured from farming settlements in Chile or Argentina in order to enhance their political and spiritual powers. Mapuche marriages to Chilean *wingka* increased during and after Colonel Gregorio Urrutia's pacification campaign (1861–1883), the goal of which was to incorporate Mapuche into the Chilean state. Rosa Kurin, the most powerful and prestigious shaman in the area, was half Patagonian Mapuche and half German, and she incorporated both Mapuche and German powers into her practice. Colonel Urrutia embraced machi practice, had a son with Rosa, and in 1882 built a fort with no strategic value on top of the sacred mountain of Millali in order to protect Rosa's shamanic powers and local history. And people in Millali engaged with me both as an anthropologist and as Francisca's *champuria* ritual helper.

MY COMPLEX RELATIONSHIP WITH FRANCISCA AND MILLALI

I first met Mapuche people when I was five years old, at my maternal grandparents' farm in Rio Negro, Argentine Patagonia, where I spent my summers until I graduated with a degree in history from the Catholic University in Chile in 1988 and left for the United States to begin doctoral studies in anthropology at UCLA. Many of these Mapuche were seasonal workers from the Quepe area in southern Chile and knew Francisca well. My grandparents' farm was next to Rosa Kurin's birthplace, so Francisca had heard about my family long before we met.

Virginio Ancao worked as the foreman on the farm between 1952 and 1992, when it was sold. When I returned to southern Chile in 1991, I met Virginio's brother Euladio Ancao, the *longko* of the neighboring community of Nahuelhual, on the road that connects Quepe to Chihuimpilli, where many people stop to buy beer and to purchase meat from the animals that he butchered on the back patio. Euladio adopted me as his niece, and his family began inviting me to community events and rituals and introduced me to a number of machi and other Mapuche, including Francisca. I shared an apartment with friends in Temuco, where I typed up notes on my laptop and bought supplies, but I often stayed with Francisca in Millali, which at that time had neither electricity nor running water.

Francisca described me as *champuria*—both the same as and different from her—because my father is part indigenous Peruvian Quechua and because I spent a lot of time with Mapuche. She refused to acknowledge that I was Peruvian because Mapuche had fought the Inca expansion from Peru to Chile (1483–1485), and instead she saw me as *champuria* from Puelmapu "where the earth ends" (Manquepi in De Augusta 1996) in Argentine Patagonia to the east, an area associated with Mapuche kin, allies, health, abundance, power, and good fortune. In the nineteenth and twentieth centuries Mapuche men gained wealth, power, and prestige by traveling to Puelmapu to exchange and ally with other indigenous groups, to obtain powers from sacred stones that made them invincible, and to raid other indigenous groups and colonizers to obtain cattle, horses, and white women captives (León 1991; Bello 2011).

However, Francisca and I were different kinds of *champuria* women: I stood apart because of my education and economic status, and she stood apart because of her shamanic knowledge and power. Because of our different backgrounds, we held different worldviews, but these expanded naturally and mutually as we worked together. I sought to understand Francisca's shamanic historical consciousness on her terms and to analyze her contributions to larger anthropological understandings of temporality, agency, and power. Once I gained her trust, Francisca sought to understand my role as an anthropologist, to incorporate me into her world, and to teach me about shamanic lore because she believed I had the ability to serve her needs as a mediator between worlds. Francisca shared her life stories and ideas with me, and I reciprocated with my own stories and my long-term commitment to producing her bible. An implicit pact of solidarity developed, and the data I collected became both the product and the stake of the ethnographic relationship.[25]

My friendship with Francisca combined disinterested generosity on both our parts with what we each hoped to gain from one another in this collaborative project. She was generous in providing information and knowledge and in asking me to become her ritual assistant, and she also sought small benefits from working with me: I drove Francisca to the hospital, to the local pension office, to the crowded farmers market, and to visit patients, friends, and family. I gave her and other people clothing, household items, medicine, farm implements, and food, which made their lives somewhat more comfortable. I did not give my Mapuche friends money because that would have implied that they were selling knowledge, something that could be associated with sorcery. But I often paid for repairs to the Mapuche homes in which I stayed, donated musical instruments, funded the performance of collective rituals, and, like her Mapuche patients, paid Francisca for her healing services. People in the Quepe area often used Mapuche kinship terms to create fictive kin relations with me, but they also referred to me as a friend who was outside of the kinship system. Francisca called me *chuchu* (granddaughter) and *wenüy* (friend), and other Mapuche referred to me as *lamngen* (sister, cousin), *ñaña* (an affectionate term for consanguineal sisters), or *wenüy*.

Francisca was sympathetic to my interest in learning about shamanic practices and historical consciousness, and she prayed for my success: "She is taking me everywhere in a truck and has come to help me heal. I ask you [God] to give her a lot of luck. She is a professor and wants to learn. Give her a lot of strength and knowledge about our culture. . . . She speaks well of me in other places. She defends me. She respects me. She is a good woman. I ask that you help her in all her work" (February 2, 1995).

As a woman I had easy access to the world of shamanism, which is dominated by women and celibate men and deals with domestic crises, with conflicts within families and between neighbors, and with ungrateful children, unfaithful spouses, and issues of fertility and childbirth. After my divorce in 1997 I enjoyed some of the relative freedom accorded in Mapuche society to separated women and widows. Yet as a single woman I could attend a machi's public ritual performances and talk to people there only if a Mapuche man accompanied me. Often this was Euladio Ancao, one of his sons, or Domingo Katrikura, a *longko* from the community of Chihuimpilli. At the same time, my friendship with Francisca meant that I was unwillingly incorporated into the local web of machi alliances and accusations of sorcery, which barred me from developing close relationships with her enemies.

I also gained experiential knowledge as a patient of several machi. Francisca treated me holistically for melanoma, depression, bad luck, the stress of academic life, the emotional upheaval of marriage and divorce, and the uncertainty created by multiple moves in and between Chile, the United States, and Canada.

In some contexts, Francisca construed me as being "like a Mapuche" because of my knowledge of shamanic lore. Once she tied red wool around my arms and ankles and her own to protect us both from evil *wekufü* spirits. But I was a non-Mapuche when she asked me to go outside and shoot *wekufü* with her revolver while everyone else remained inside. Since I did not have any Mapuche ancestors, she reasoned that I was under no serious risk of evil-spirit possession. In still other contexts, Francisca saw me as Mapuche because I was able to re-create my identity strategically for my own benefit and that of Mapuche.

These different constructions of my identity were often entwined, shifting rapidly and strategically depending on the situation. One day we were coming home from an all-night healing ritual. I was driving my truck along a dirt road with Francisca beside me. She was wearing her ritual machi attire, but I had changed into my jeans. In the bed of the truck were other people in full ritual attire, two drums, two *trutruka* (horns), *kaskawilla*, and the payment for the healing ritual: a sheep, three decanters of wine, and a sack of flour. We came to an intersection, where a police officer stopped us. Because it is illegal in Chile to have passengers in the bed of a truck, we assumed he was going to fine us and make the people in the back get out. This would be a problem because on Sundays there were no other means of transport in the area. As we stopped, I adopted a heavy American accent, flashed my UCLA identification card, and said, "These people in the truck are working for me." The policeman nodded and let us go on. Those in the truck cheered. Francisca said that now I was a "true Mapuche." The problem was solved because I had assumed the voice of the privileged gringa in charge (whereas in the United States, ironically, I was considered a nonimmigrant alien, an outsider, the other). Although I had worked under Francisca's orders all night at the ritual, I was quickly able to reconstruct myself and manipulate the situation in order to protect the group (Bacigalupo 2003:42).

Despite my honorary Mapuche status, Francisca and other people in Millali sometimes stressed that I could pass as a gringa because I am an urban woman with curly hair. I am also the granddaughter of a Hungarian farmer in Argentina for whom Euladio Ancao and other Mapuche men from neighboring communities had worked. I was particularly useful in the city because I possessed the car-driving, place-finding Spanish literacy that could help my Mapuche friends access banks and administrative offices.

When Francisca and I ran errands in Temuco, she played the role of a poor, ignorant Mapuche farmer and denied being a machi (which is looked down on by some non-Mapuche urbanites). Once, in the office where Francisca collected her monthly pension, she asked the secretary about a medicinal plant on the desk, an herb that Francisca knew well and used often in her own curing. Francisca listened and thanked the woman for "teaching" her, but later she told me that the secretary had no idea what she was talking about. Francisca thought this pretense of ignorance was necessary in order to avoid conflict in the city. However, the roles Francisca and I played were reversed in the community, where Francisca had the power and knowledge. When I learned and incorporated Mapuche knowledge and practice into my behavior, Francisca called me Mapuche. When I made mistakes or asked too many questions, she either got angry or excused me, saying that I could not learn everything since I was *champuria*.

I learned much about machi notions of history through my experiences as Francisca's ritual assistant, but I did not seek to become initiated as a machi, nor did I try to develop shamanic power through drum-induced trances and visions. I felt it would be unethical for me to assume a spiritual role but then be unable to fulfill the commitments that machi make to their patients, community, and ritual congregation.

Francisca believed that with my connection to Rosa's birthplace and my roles as her literate *champuria* ritual assistant and ethnographer-scribe, I could write a bible that would circulate her power after she died and would be read by literate Mapuche and non-Mapuche alike. Though nonliterate, Francisca understood the power of writing. "I need you to write my stories, to copy my force," she told me (February 25, 1992).

Sometimes Francisca claimed control over the recording technologies and content of the bible: "Bring your recorder," she would say. "I have something important to say." Or, more directly, "Put it in the book" (November 21, 1991). She also believed that photographs and tape recordings capture a machi's essence and could be used by a sorcerer to harm the machi. So she consulted with her spirit about which part of the rituals I should photograph or otherwise record. Assessing my intentionality when taping or taking photographs was crucial. "I wait and see if the spirit says you are working with the heart with good intention," she explained. "Then it is okay to record so that you remember what is said, as long as it is written later in the bible about me" (November 21, 1991). Francisca asked that my photographs only be shown in my own articles and books. That way, presumably, my intentionality would protect her. Francisca's spirit was apparently amenable to my presence, to my learning from her, and to my writing a book about her. But it had limited patience. When my photographs were blank or when my tape recorder jammed, Francisca would claim that "the spirit got tired and ate them" (fig. 1.4).

Francisca was pleased when I validated her shamanic histories and practices and when I participated in them. She nodded in approval when I understood her explanations for these histories and practices. Francisca agreed that I could add my own ethnographic and ethnohistorical analysis to explain Mapuche relations to the written word, to the Bible, and to her shamanic bible "for the gringos to understand the thunder machi" because she wanted her bible to have international reach. At other times she grumbled about my "stupid questions," which seemed unnecessary to her but whose answers I needed so I could put her words into a non-Mapuche context. Francisca and I decided that this would be an intertextual bible with her voice, actions, and analyses in dialogue with mine throughout, just like our everyday interactions and ritual collaborations.

I believed that a collaborative approach with the explicit presence of the ethnographer in the text would be the most useful for illustrating how I came to know what I know, and it would make clear the kind of mediation occurring between the shaman and the reader. I have selected the quotes

FIGURE I.4

*Francisca, her granddaughter Bernardita, and her great-grandchildren drawing
Francisca's machi initiation by thunder and earthquake (photo by author).*

and observations by Mapuche that best illustrate Francisca's and other Mapuche's shamanic conceptualizations of history, and I intersperse them with my interpretations. My long-term connection with Mapuche and my close friendship with Francisca has allowed me the unique experience of cross-identifying with her. She trusted me to put her life and practice in writing in ways that would be meaningful to both of us, and I hope I have succeeded in bringing out the richness of her thoughts.

Francisca and I coproduced the knowledge included in this bible by building alternative shamanic conceptual frameworks and by showing how these relate to academic debates on historical consciousness and temporality as well as to Mapuche ethnopolitical struggles and efforts by activists and scholars to decolonize the production of knowledge.[26] Francisca's discourses and practices challenge academic authority, the conceptual framework of historical consciousness, and the exclusion of indigenous shamans from the symbolic economy of power. She offered a moral critique of the indiscriminate, extractive forestry industry and the global economy, and she created new forms of exchange wherein spirituality is linked to broader sociopolitical and ecological changes and the production of knowledge.

Although Francisca and I collaborated in the making of her bible, her voice in this book is mediated by my own identity, the dynamics of field-work, and the requirements of academic writing. Well aware of the power dynamics of language, Francisca asked me to write both English and Spanish versions of her bible. The English version would circulate widely to legitimate her life and practices in the global textual community, whose perceptions hold more weight than those of the Chilean state in the worldwide economy of power, and the Spanish version would tell her story more locally, in the community, and serve shamanic temporalities by circulating her force to bring about her rebirth. This book about Francisca's shamanic discourses and practices is therefore not just an academic narrative with shamanic content, but an example of shamanism in action, where Francisca can speak about spirits to Mapuche and *wingka*, and about Mapuche and *wingka* to spirits, all through a *champuria* intermediary who is at once anthropologist and ritual assistant.

Francisca's bible—like other (auto)biographical accounts coauthored by scholars and indigenous people (for example, Kopenawa and Albert 2013; Raoni and Dutilleux 2010; Reuque 2002)—seeks to decolonize the unequal exchange that has marked ethnographic relations in the field and to serve as a local political instrument. But Francisca did not want to appear as the coauthor of this book. She wanted me to write about her as a spiritual authority in order to transmit her knowledge to the world after she died and to bring about her rebirth.

Because this book is the result of my relationship and collaboration with Francisca, it is what Deborah Reed-Danahay (1997:9) calls an autoethnography—a narrative that places the author within a social context and that is both method and text. It includes Francisca's contextualized self-narrative as well as my own. Francisca's tale of her life is in some ways what Lawrence C. Watson and María-Barbara Watson-Franke (1985:2) describe as a "self-initiated retrospective account." Francisca did not prepare a long narrative about her life before speaking to an anthropologist, as did Prepori, a Kayabi shaman (Oakdale 2007:65). But she told many stories about her initiation into power as a machi, her suffering, her struggles with various sorcerers, her notions of who was Mapuche and who an outsider, her success at healing, and her relationships with Chilean presidents.

Francisca's bible also contains a life history drawn from a series of unstructured interviews and informal conversations that I recorded between 1991 and 1996. Francisca told me about her childhood and her family genealogy; her relationships with family, friends, and the community; her analysis of community factionalism and sorcery; her social critiques of *wingka* and Mapuche; her shamanic historical narratives; and her predictions for the future. I have retained the texture of Francisca's narrations: she used different discursive registers in direct and quoted speech and shifted from personal memories to accounts of historical events to visions and dreams to tales of spirits and characters from primordial times.

In addition to the archival research I conducted in Santiago and Temuco (2007–2009), I have drawn on my observations of everyday interactions, meetings, and rituals in Millali (1991–2013); the community's collective memory after Francisca's death (1997–2013); community members' reactions to archival documents about them (2007–2013); and their perceptions of shamanic biographies and the use of my research over time. Throughout the book, I quote from my conversations with a variety of rural and urban Mapuche (farmers, artisans, community chiefs, professionals, intellectuals, and people who work in nongovernmental organizations), and I have integrated these conversations with archival documents about Millali and machi, academic work by anthropologists, reports from the Chilean media, and my own experiences in what Lila Abu-Lughod (1991) calls an "anthropology of the particular." Finally, I have drawn on the methodologies of narrative and dialogical anthropology to reflect on my participation in Francisca's life as her friend, ethnographer, and *champuria* ritual assistant.[27]

In writing their histories, I have followed community members' requests that I use the real names of people and places rather than pseudonyms. They criticized my previous works on machi hybrid healing practices (1996a, 2001) and on shifting gender identities and performances (2007) for my use of pseudonyms to protect the identities of subjects talking about sensitive topics. Community members saw this as withholding credit from the speaker; this "took away the person's power" and "made the conversation unreal." They explained that in order to revive the machi spirit's power and allow it to come back, I should use Francisca's name and the real names of all the people appearing in this book. I have honored this request, although in a few cases I have obscured the identities of people who made controversial statements that might provoke retaliation; in such instances, I refer to "a Mapuche man" or "a Mapuche woman."

MAKING HISTORY IN FRANCISCA'S SHAMANIC BIBLE

This book includes my analysis of the various strategies Francisca and other Mapuche in the Quepe area used to create a shamanic historical consciousness. Each strategy is presented in its own chapter, each focuses on specific kinds of temporality or forms of reshaping history, and each is expressed through one or more modalities that cut across the various strategies: object, narrative, ritual, text, dream, factional conflict, landscape, and death and rebirth.

Chapter 2 shows how settlers' perception that they are bringing "civilization" to the "savage" Mapuche are countered and obliterated by Mapuche shamanic narratives that mythologize shamans and other historical characters, and also by the employment of rehistoricizing and politicizing narratives about primordial times in new contexts. I demonstrate how Mapuche in Millali resignify colonial and modern binaries about the "time of civilization" and the "time of wilderness and warfare" as meaningful coordinates for moral and political self-fashioning. Mapuche and settlers both practice forms of temporal dislocation and intergenerational memory that conflate specific moments of the past and present. But they take opposing positions, highlighting different historical moments to justify their contrasting temporalities. Machi Rosa and other Mapuche in Millali countered German settlers' notions of the "time of civilization" by collapsing the identities of men from the German Schleyer family into one savage, immoral devil. They have created Rosa as a multitemporal machi who restores the cosmic order. Machi Rosa's transnational shamanic and ancestral mobility has obliterated Chilean national history while legitimating a Mapuche ethnonational project that transforms outsiders into local personages and defines Mapuche as the spiritual victors of history.

Chapter 3 introduces Francisca's multitemporal dreams, which she used to narrate the origins of her powers and paraphernalia. She used these visions to synthesize and mediate between time periods, producing and reshaping the world and its history, as well as to justify my role as her ritual assistant. I show how this multitemporality is grounded in machi's multiple perceptions of personhood. Francisca exemplified the tensions between different relations of kinship—constructed socially, spiritually, or through blood—and the process of *awingkamiento*, which is associated with sorcery.

Chapter 4 explores the ritualized relationships between illness, healing, embodiment, and history. I show how Mapuche in Millali understand illness and healing as the history of interethnic conflict and how Francisca ritually embodied ancestral spirits of the past and ritually reshaped the present and future, battling colonialist spirits from different historical periods. Francisca's complex healing strategies used and were propelled by three ritual modes of historicization: divinations in which she embodied the past to see the future through dreams; sacrifices to effect healing in the present and construct a better future; and multitemporality to assert her position as a prestigious machi from the past and to then reinsert herself back into machi history.

Chapter 5 analyzes how Francisca and other Mapuche have engaged the

Bible and official documents as objects of power, using them in both political and spiritual ways to challenge the way the Global North perceives historiography and postcolonial relations, as well as to produce Mapuche history and new forms of shamanic literacy.

Chapter 6 shows how Francisca and other Mapuche have reinterpreted the achronological times of civilization and savagery through the lens of thunder shamanism in response to the shaking of Mapuche communities by military power, state violence, neoliberalism, transnational forestry companies, and the discourses of terrorism. I explore how Francisca and other Mapuche have linked unmediated thunder from the time of wilderness and warfare to the spirit masters of native forests, ancient warriors, and even the contemporary Chilean military, enlisting these to conduct spiritual warfare against their enemies. Francisca and other machi have created a Mapuche cosmopolitics that combines spiritual, ecological, social, and political factors with realpolitik in order to counter settlers' construction of Mapuche as "savage terrorists." This cosmopolitics is deeply intertwined with Mapuche experiences of state-sponsored violence and their struggle for self-determination. I show how the Mapuche dream and create revisionist historical narratives to end violence by drawing on an existential form of civilization focused on human capacity and on forms of being rather than geopolitical histories.

Chapter 7 explores the local processes of remembering and disremembering Francisca's shamanic spirit following her death, and the transformation of her personhood and objects through death and rebirth.

Chapter 8 ends the book with the community's reflection on reconciling the multiple modes of historicity coexisting in their lives with what I argue are their contributions to current studies on history and memory.

In many ways Francisca's biography is representative of Mapuche culture. But her *champuria* identity serves as a counterpoint to it, and her contested identity and practices and her varied relationships with people and spirits illuminate some of the internal divisions in native communities. Francisca's mutable and multiple identities—and my own—led her to think that I could write her bible, which offers a lens through which to see how Mapuche shamanic historical consciousness is produced and mobilized; how shamanic narratives of the past construct the present and rewrite local history; and how change and its agents are conceived in shamanic practice. Francisca's bible calls for a rethinking of pan-Mapuche notions of history and this people's complex relationship with non-Mapuche, with whom they have intermixed for generations and whose world Francisca understood they might transform through a shamanic historical consciousness.

CHAPTER TWO

MOBILE NARRATIVES *that* OBLITERATE *the* DEVIL'S "CIVILIZED HISTORY"

One cold winter day in June 2007, ninety-eight-year-old Feliciano Lefian and his younger Mapuche counterparts Alberto Huenchuñir and Domingo Katrikura told me the shamanic history of Rosa Kurin, Francisca Kolipi's shamanic predecessor. She was a powerful German-Mapuche thunder shaman from Patagonia who came to Millali in 1879 and saved it from chaos and destruction. Rosa was central to Millali's history: she used her powers and her mixed ethnic identity to incorporate the colonizers into Millali's history, challenge their notions of civilization, subject them to shamanic logic, and then obliterate the history of colonization.

Feliciano, Alberto, and Domingo created a *koyang* about Rosa—a condensation of different narratives into one. During an implicit process of negotiation, they interrupted and corrected one another, added details, and told jokes. The three men had credibility to tell the story: Feliciano's grandfather was a cousin of Rosa Kurin's father, and Feliciano was also Francisca's cross-cousin. Although he was forty years younger than Rosa, she had lived to the age of eighty-two, so Feliciano spoke with the authority of someone who had known her well and had witnessed some of her life events. Alberto spoke as Rosa's favorite grandson; he remembered her fondly and had listened to her stories as a child. Domingo was a *longko* from the neighboring community of Chihuimpilli. He was knowledgeable about local history, and his grandmother had known Rosa well.

Mapuche narratives are always open, unfinished, and subject to negotiation and reinterpretation. But this *koyang* was cited by many people in Millali as the official version of the story—one that I should write down:

The Argentine army began exterminating the indigenous people of the Pampas and Patagonia and incorporating their territories into the new Argentine nation-state [in 1878–1879]. Many families of the Kurin lineage, along with others, fled west over the Andes into Chile. Six-year-old Rosa and her German-born mother, both blue-eyed redheads, left Argentine Patagonia on horseback and headed west for Chilean Araucanía, carrying with them as protection a thunder stone [*tralkan kura*; fig. 2.1] that held the spirit of an ancient Patagonian warrior-shaman. The stone belonged to Rosa's father, a Mapuche *longko* named Kurin, or "Dark One" [after whom the Rio Negro and the province were named]. Kurin had been born in Araucanía but had spent most of his life in Patagonia, raiding rival indigenous groups and the farms of Spanish, German, and British settlers for cattle, horses, and captives. Rosa's mother had been among the settlers whom Kurin took captive during a raid on Buenos Aires [in 1872]. He stole her on the rump of his horse, and nine months later Rosa was born. Kurin's stone was a portal to other shamanic worlds and it carried the histories of shamans and warriors of his lineage: their alliances, battles, their travels on the paths between Patagonia and Araucanía, their rituals at oracles and sacred places to divine their destiny, to become invincible, to gain shamanic and political power and wealth, and their linkages with spirits and people from other worlds and times in the past and the future.[1]

Rosa and her mother ended up in Millali. There, Kurin's cousin Manuel Lefian adopted them. Rosa became a machi suddenly at the age of twelve, when she had a vision of a bull that wore a gigantic copper bell. It climbed to the top of the hill above Millali, the community's cosmic place of origin, where a battle between the primordial earth and water serpents was believed to have taken place. This bull became emblematic of the force of the community of Millali. [To Mapuche, visions of bulls are associated with the water and earth spirits of specific places, collective *ngillatun* rituals, and cosmic and political events; sometimes, they announce violence and conflict to come. Machi who have visions of bulls are often considered both strong and unruly.] In Rosa's vision, the bull turned to stone so that she could use its magical power to protect the community. The power Rosa acquired from visions of animals and her thunder stone allowed her to make rain, to beat enemies and sorcerers, and to become a persuasive orator like the ancient warrior-shamans.

After climbing the Millali hill with her father's thunder stone, Rosa went into a trance beside a gigantic boldo tree that was said to possess ancestral spiritual powers. Lightning and thunder circled her and struck around her head, initiating her immediately as a thunder machi who incorporated within herself both the dangerous power of foreigners and the Mapuche power of thunder.

FIGURE 2.1
Tralkan kura, *or thunder stone (photo by author).*

Domingo elaborated: "Rosa controlled lightning bolts on the top of the Millali hill. Nobody could beat her" (June 4, 2007).

All shamans gain the power to heal and to divine from spirit masters of the ecosystem (*ngen*), ancestral and astral spirits, and the Mapuche deity Ngünechen through dreams, visions, and altered states of consciousness. Thunder machi are exceptional in that they do not experience any initiatory shamanic afflictions, such as boils, fevers, fatigue, partial deafness, or blindness; nor do they go through a period of training with a master shaman who teaches them drumming and healing techniques, songs, and recipes for herbal remedies. Mapuche consider thunder machi to be especially powerful because the primordial force that initiates them is enormous and cannot be controlled by humans (see Mege 1997:13–18), and thunder machi are well known for resolving battles between conflicting forces in the world, a role for which Rosa is remembered in Millali.

By July 2010, fifty-five years after Rosa's death, people in Millali recalled the late nineteenth and early twentieth centuries as a period of enormous political, economic, and cultural change—a time of cosmic chaos. They saw Rosa as the machi who had saved Millali from destruction. Along with non-Mapuche historical figures of the time, Rosa had become a character in Millali's shamanic history—a spiritual leader who transformed the chaos provoked by the settlers into a new world order.

Generally Mapuche perceive the reliability of stories as contingent on the closeness of the narrator to the people and events being recounted, as well as on the storyteller's prestige. They consider stories based on witnessing and spirit possession to be the most reliable, followed by stories that can be traced to a prestigious narrator. The reliability of a Mapuche narrator is encoded linguistically. Stories that are preceded by the disclaimer *urke* in Mapudungun or *se dice que* ("it is said") in Spanish cannot be attributed to a specific person or place and are thought to be less convincing. However, narratives about primordial times do not need validation because people tell them in a historical time that did not exist when the earliest events took place (see Gow 2001). Through the shamanic history surrounding Rosa Kurin, the Mapuche in her community have mythologized and obliterated the Chilean history of geopolitical conquest and civilization and used their spiritual agency to rehistoricize and repoliticize their own shamanic narratives and to construct a new world.

HISTORICAL CONSCIOUSNESS, MYTH, AND HISTORY

Some anthropologists accept the Euro-American conception of time as natural and given, projecting this notion onto others' schemas: history is construed as chronological, objective, and coherent. Myth, by contrast, is seen only as a model for understanding the world and how to act in it; by definition, it is nonlinear, atemporal, fictional, and nonsystematic (Finley 1965). Some scholars argue further that the potential for historical thought exists only in literate societies where analytical and chronological thinking is fostered through the critical reading and interpretation of conflicting reports about a single event (Goody 1977).

Claude Lévi-Strauss distinguished between "hot" societies, which perceive a linear history changing over time and construct a future in response, and "cold" societies, which view time as a model for understanding the world, limited to the cyclical repetition of myth and necessarily denying the future.[2] Likewise, Marshall Sahlins (1995), characterizing history as a chronological set of events bringing about change, claimed that indigenous societies were devoid of history and instead created static mythic structures until they encountered history and change as introduced by societies in the Global North. Structuralists view shamans as representatives and practitioners of a logic in which indigenous myths actually absorb the historical events and processes they seek to obliterate in order to reestablish a sense of social equilibrium (Lévi-Strauss 1981:607; Gow 2001:19, 291). The open-endedness of myth allows for the inclusion of different kinds of outsiders, who are then subjected to its logic.

All these perspectives ignore the ways in which the historical perspective is also constructed by and bound up with the European conquest of the globe (Cohn 1981:227–229). It precludes Europeans from seeing shamans and spirits as embedded and acting in history, and thus inevitably obscures their roles as hybrid mediators and historical figures inhabiting the same world as everyone else. In addition, as Hayden White (1973, 1978) points out, the essentialized nature of historical thought as distinct from myth ignores how both frameworks are imagined through the language historians use. History is not reality, distinct from myth, which is imagined as fiction. Rather, history is simply a particular expository style that is generally accepted. History and myth offer intersecting but distinctive kinds of truth; they are verbal representations of reality that outline some domain of human experience (White 1978:110).

There are no terms for *history* and *myth* in Mapudungun. For Mapuche there is no one expository style or specific temporality that represents their indigenous understanding of time.[3] Instead, Mapuche shamans, like the Amazonian Piaroa (Overing 1990), distinguish between a "before time" history and a "today time" history, but weave both together in shamanic narratives that make and reshape worlds. "Before time," also known as *rüf kuyfi* ("true time"), is the primordium, when the conflicting forces of creation, transformation, and destruction shaped the world (Huenchulaf, Cárdenas, and Ancalaf 2004:24; Curivil 2002:19–20). This preceded humans, morality, temporal sequentiality, and space; it is where the Mapuche locate narratives such as the story of the primordial serpents Trengtreng and Kaykay. "Today time," in contrast, is where the Mapuche locate the creation of morality, sociality, gardening and hunting, space, and sequential time. "Today time" is further divided into *füta kuyfi* (the remote past), *kuyfi* (the recent past), *fachantü* (the present), and *ka antü* (the future).

Lévi-Strauss's perception of time as a binary opposition ignores indigenous understandings of time as an ongoing process that includes the past, present, and future simultaneously. Anthropologists capture the past, present, and future in social processes as they arise, change, and decline—only to be reinvented (Nash 2015). Mapuche understand the temporal world not as single and unified, but as multiple. The primordium is never imagined as a time of beings who once existed but are no longer in this world. Spirits are constantly brought into the present from the primordial past, and shamans are multitemporal beings who necessarily experience themselves in primordial times, the recent past, the present, and the future in order to perform rituals to convert chaos to cosmos, illness to well-being. Mapuche shamanic power is produced and reproduced through local, embodied narratives about the primordium that reinterpret larger historical processes through a shamanic lens. In rituals and in shamanic histories, the distance between "today time" and "before time" collapses.

Like Amazonians (Hill 1988; Wright 2013), Mapuche see in the primordial world a conceptual framework through which shamans interpret changes in the social order in the present and the recent past. Narratives about the primordium are not simply reenactments of "before time," but history in a most fundamental sense: they are deployed to explain why a condition or transformative process exists. They also provide a foundation for reflection and action in the present. Beings from the Mapuche "before time," like the serpents Kaykay and Trengtreng, take on "today time" moral characteristics through historical transformations: the evil water serpent Kaykay becomes the settler Schleyer, who destroys the cosmos, and the good earth serpent Trengtreng becomes machi Rosa, who saves and reorders the world.

Rosa's shamanic history combines *nütram*, which are chronological narratives of the recent past recounted by a witness—such as family histories, local events (Huenchulaf, Cárdenas, and Ancalaf 2004:24; Curivil 2002:19–20), biographies, and Mapuche ethnic histories (Marimán et al. 2006)—with *piam*, which are collective stories about the primordium (Curivil 2002:19–20). Rosa and the Mapuche are constituted by historical-political events while they actively reconstitute the same events through shamanic imaginaries and narrative forms.

As the community of Millali has done with Rosa's story, historical outsiders are incorporated into the structure of the myths, and their inclusion also permits the historicizing and politicizing of these tales in a range of temporal contexts, including the very recent past (Hugh-Jones 1988:130; Santos-Granero 2007; Cepek 2009). *Wingka* can be added as the other in history because before the *wingka* existed, there were primordial others (the Inca, the dead, the spirits). Whatever form it takes, the other is necessary for the collective sense of the indigenous self. Thus in the telling of Rosa's shamanic history, non-Mapuche historical figures, such as the Chilean colonel Gregorio Urrutia and the German settler Schleyer, play central roles, as do specific events in the nineteenth-century Mapuche history of subjugation to the Chilean and Argentine states.

The Mapuche's reinterpretations of the history of colonization figure prominently in their shamanic narratives about the past in "today time." As Michael Taussig (1987) argues, shamanic power is produced and reproduced by complex historical processes—including the cultural and social mixing called *mestizaje*—brought about by colonialism, capitalism, and missionization. Mapuche in Millali incorporate, embody, and resignify settlers' oppositional relationship between *el tiempo de civilización* (the time of civilization) and *el tiempo de lo silvestre y la guerra* (the time of wilderness and warfare), which Mapuche translate as *el tiempo de ngen-mawida y weichan* (the time of the spirit owners of the forests and warfare). Both Mapuche and non-Mapuche understand the concept of civilization in moral, cultural, and political terms. But they disagree about who occupies the position of "the good civilized person" and "the evil savage," and they use different narratives about their relationship with the land to justify their belongingness—the most essential of all modes of connection and a kind of primordial, ahistorical *ur*-belonging (Comaroff 2001:658–659; Geschiere 2009:2). Settlers and Mapuche create histories as a form of intergenerational memory, conflating particular moments and exemplary people from the past and present. But they highlight different historical moments to justify their contrasting temporalities.

Lévi-Strauss's conception of myth leaves little room for historical agency because he made no allowance for an indigenous historical consciousness (Fausto and Heckenberger 2007). But Mapuche shamanic histories and historical consciousness are rich in agency. Narratives about a primordium that is constantly brought back into specific moments past and present allow for the historical agency of primordial beings, spirits, and humans (Fausto and Heckenberger 2007; Rappaport 1998:208; Salomon 1999:37; Wright 2013).[4] Shamanic histories convey this by embodying "the ability to act both within and upon larger social forces" (Sider 1998: xviii), in addition to expressing ideas about native ethnic identity, personhood, and ontology. They draw on a notion of spiritual agency that underlies the transformative nature of Mapuche personhood and identity.

The cyclical, synchronic *piam* narratives about the *rüf kuyfi* intersect with the linear, diachronic Mapuche shamanic histories (*kuyfi*) in Millali. The result is a sort of spiral along which people and events both repeat themselves and move through time. Shamanic histories both mythologize shamans and other historical characters, and rehistoricize and politicize myths in new contexts. Mapuche use these shamanic histories to challenge the conventional Chilean history—the history of their subordination to the state—to present themselves as the spiritual victors of history, to resist ethnocide, and to construct a new place for themselves in the world.

THE POROUS BOUNDARIES AND
MOBILE HISTORIES SURROUNDING ROSA'S STORY

Mapuche practice multiple belonging rather than identifying with one place. Since the sixteenth century, through practices surrounding marriage, kinship, shamanism, work, male initiation rites, and collective rituals, Mapuche have belonged to multiple places in what is now southern Chile and Argentina (Bacigalupo 2001, 2007; Bello 2011). Like Australian Aborigines (Jackson 1995:66, 122, 140), Mapuche hold that an intimate connection exists between persons and the landscapes they call home. "Home" is a relationship with the places to which a person's thoughts and dreams return, but it is also a web of relationships with people and other beings through kinship, ritual, and affinity, without whom life would cease to be meaningful. Relationships between people are therefore also articulated as relationships between places. For Mapuche, these relationships are further complicated by temporality: places evoke particular stories about times past. Shamans and chiefs expand these temporal and spatial dimensions to include spiritual realms and interethnic alliances.

Mapuche wish to remain an ungoverned people and have what James Scott (2009) would call a history of deliberate and reactive statelessness. They have consistently deployed a complex sociopolitical system of shifting alliances between mobile lineages to resist the Incas, the Spaniards, and the Chilean state. Mapuche also adapt their economic practices to current conditions; in the twenty-first century they combine subsistence agriculture and animal husbandry with salaried work. Such shifting economic profiles and a more general sociopolitical polymorphism do not allow the state an easy point of leverage and thus have proved well suited for evading incorporation into state structures.

The mobile histories that tie Mapuche to different places and times are expressed through dreams, visions, and transportable ritual objects like drums and thunder stones. For example, after the wars among rival Mapuche groups and with the Argentine and Chilean states subsided, the Wenteche-Patagonian shamanic military complex remained alive in Millali through the visions, dreams, and practices of machi like Rosa. As a thunder machi galloping on her spirit horse in ecstatic flight between Chile and Patagonia and other spiritual worlds to gain knowledge and to battle evil spirits, she carried the histories, powers, and sacred places of other thunder shamans and chiefs in her thunder stone, her drum, her body, and her prayers. Like that of Buryat shamans (Buyandelger 2013:63), Rosa's knowledge was also internally mobile: she used her agile mind to transform history through selection, remembering, and improvisation.

HORSEMANSHIP AND SPIRITUAL MOBILITY

Machi Angela: Old Man mounted on your horse, Old Woman mounted on your horse, Young Man mounted on your horse, Young Woman mounted on your horse . . . come together with your four saddled horses to see this sister [Francisca] and strengthen her spirit of service,

strengthen her heart. She must mount her horse with good faith to regain
her vitality and the activities of her machi being.
Machi Francisca: I need a horse to make me feel happier, stronger.
I will not get sick, because Chau Díos will be watching over me.
I will be invincible. (January 27, 1995)

Animals offer another spiritual dimension to machi mobile histories. Machi gain knowledge, power, and control over the spirit world and are healed through horsemanhip and mastery over spirit animals in the same way that Mapuche horsemen gained manhood, prestige, power, and wealth in the eighteenth and nineteenth centuries by raiding farms in the Pampas and Patagonia for cattle, women, and horses.[5] Mapuche warrior-shamans have incorporated the Patagonian horse, bull, sheep, and *ñandu* (ostrich) and powerful stones into Mapuche shamanic, historical, and military ideologies. Visions of bulls enable them to conquer enemies through violence, and visions of horses allow them to conquer enemies through negotiations and parliaments (Bengoa 1991:88; Marimán et al. 2006:73; Mallon 2008). The *longko* Mangin owned a white horse (white and blue are the colors of the sky) that he "brought from the moon." It told him the future and allegedly killed Kolipi, a rival Nangche *longko*, with sorcery.

Visions and dreams of animals and spirits are deeply intertwined with particular kinds of time and space. Machi gain wild, unmediated powers if they experience visions and dreams of wild animals (such as jaguars and snakes), forest spirits, thunder, or lightning in untamed landscapes associated with the past. Machi gain powers of sorcery if they have visions of dogs or pigs, which are believed to share spiritual essences with *kalku* and *wekufü* spirits. Machi gain controlled shamanic knowledge if they have dreams and visions of horses, sheep, chickens, shamanic paraphernalia, or ancestor spirits in sacred domestic landscapes associated with the present and future (Bacigalupo 1996b). Machi exchange spiritual essences, personhood, and bodily substances such as breath, blood, and saliva with sheep and horses. The spiritual relationships with these Mapuche shamanic animals reflect a complex understanding of personal consciousness in which machi are separate agents but at the same time share selves with their spirit animals (fig. 2.2). Francisca told me, "I dreamed they gave me a horse. My power is riding on a horse. Now I am strong and will jump like a horse" (February 5, 1995).

Machi are kin to their spirit animals and to the other machi who initiate them. When machi become spirit brides who seduce their spirit husbands into possessing them, they are seen as spirit sheep: obedient to the demands

FIGURE 2.2

Machi exchange spiritual essences, personhood, and bodily substances such as breath, blood, and saliva with "spiritual" sheep and horses during rituals (photo by author).

of spirits, expressing local histories, and linked to families by blood and by marriage. These relationships with Mapuche shamanic animals reflect the gendered dynamics of marriage and seduction, possession and ecstasy, and mastery and domination, as well as those of hierarchical kinship systems (Bacigalupo 2004a).

A machi's relationship with a spirit horse involves an explicit hierarchy—the machi's domination over spirits—associated with masculinity, warfare, mobile histories, and engagement with outsiders. Machi become mounted spiritual warriors who gallop to other worlds, gaining knowledge and killing evil spirits and foreignness. Mapuche expressions about lifting, elevating, and raising—especially those about mounted horsemen who travel to the sky—are metaphors of communication with the divine. Mounting and other mastery over animals are symbols of virility, fortitude, agility, and prestige for machi, as they were for colonial Spanish and Mapuche warriors who battled each other between the sixteenth century and the late nineteenth.

Machi conducted spiritual warfare against Spanish souls using lightning and thunderbolts as weapons (Bacigalupo 2007:118). Today, weapons and war imagery give machi knowledge and strength; they use guns, knives,

FIGURE 2.3

During a collective ngillatun *ritual, Mapuche circle the field on their horses in what is called the* awün. *Through this ritual they do battle against the wind and celebrate the power of equestrianship, the horse, and Mapuche identity (photo by Helen Hughes).*

and war cries to kill illness or drive it from the bodies of their patients or from their land, households, and communities. Machi's spiritual warfare aggressively emphasizes the opposition between, on the one hand, Mapuche traditions, life, and self, and, on the other hand, non-Mapuche cultures, death, and otherness (Bacigalupo 1998). Machi replay and transform history through ritual, performing the attributes of the Spanish colonial and Chilean national armies and using the power they gain for healing or destruction. All collective *ngillatun* rituals include the *awün*, in which Mapuche mounted warriors, shouting war cries and carrying flags and lances, gallop counterclockwise around the ritual field performing and creating mobile histories (fig. 2.3).

ARCHIVAL NARRATIVES: MAPUCHE INCORPORATION AND THE RESERVATION SYSTEM

Machi mobile histories in general, and Rosa's in particular, explicitly emerged in the context of the warfare and shifting alliances among Mapuche and between them and Spanish, Chilean, and Argentine authorities throughout the nineteenth and twentieth centuries. Controlling the western part of the provinces of Arauco and Araucanía, the Nangche faction of Mapuche led an insurrection against the Spaniards during the 1700s (Rodriguez 2001:84). When Chile became independent from Spain in 1810, these Mapuche sought to negotiate with the new government and integrate into Chilean society. In contrast, the Wenteche faction, which controlled the eastern Andean foothills in Araucanía (see Bengoa 1991; Guevara and Mañkelef 2002; Pavez 2003), continued to fight the Chileans, seeking to make them respect the treaties Mapuche had signed with the Spaniards in 1641 and 1726, which recognized Mapuche sovereign territories south of the Bío-Bío River. In the nineteenth and twentieth centuries, Mapuche social organization became increasingly patrilineal and patrilocal (Bechis 1994) and power and wealth became concentrated in the hands of the most powerful *longko* (Bello 2011:53).

Wenteche allied with natives from Argentine Patagonia under the leadership of *longko* Kalfukura, creating the Mapuche Confederation in Salinas Grandes in 1835. Contemporary Mapuche view this confederation as the basis for a Chilean-Argentinean transborder Mapuche nation known as Wallmapu, which is central to twenty-first-century Mapuche demands for sovereignty and self-determination. Wenteche signed new treaties with the Chilean state in 1860 and 1880 that recognized the autonomy of the Mapuche nation south of the Bío-Bío River (Bacigalupo 2004c, 2007). By 1861, however, the Chilean state had declared itself owner of the lands of Araucanía and sought to incorporate all Mapuche territories through the War of Pacification (1861–1883). The goal was to exclude Mapuche from the nation-state (Pinto Rodríguez 2003) and erase them from the sociopolitical landscape to allow space for the allegedly "culturally superior European settlers" (Villalobos 2000a, 2000b).

Historically, Mapuche from the Quepe area acted as intermediaries between rival lineages with whom they traded and intermarried. The descendants of the Wenteche and Nangche became chiefs of communities in Quepe. Mapuche from there were known as warriors, but they recognized the superiority of the Wenteche *longko* from Makewe (Guevara 1913:450; Guevara and Mañkelef 2002:129), with whom they allied in skirmishes. After the Mapuche people were defeated by the Chilean and Argentine armies in the late nineteenth century, members from the Wenteche Millañir, Añiwal, Epuñir, Kura, Wenteche-Patagonian Lefian, Kurin, Nangche Kolipi, and Coñuepan lineages moved to the Quepe area. Many of the descendants of these people became *longko* of the communities there. Between 1846 and 1884 Mapuche also took captives from the German farming settlements in Chile and Argentina (see Rausch 1999:42), including Rosa's mother.

By 1878, despite decades of tenuous alliance between the Mapuche Confederation and several Chilean and Argentine governors, Argentine national discourse constructed Wenteche as barbarian invaders preventing the local indigenous people from becoming civilized Argentine citizens (Lazzari and Lenton 2002; Walther 1973; Zeballos 1981). The alliance shattered that year as the Argentine general Julio Roca and the Chilean colonel Gregorio Urrutia coordinated efforts to exterminate the native people of the Pampas and Patagonia in Argentina and the Arauco and Araucanía provinces in Chile (Bengoa 1991:260–261; Delrío 2005).

Between 1877 and 1883 Urrutia founded many strategic forts and towns throughout Araucanía in order to put down rebellions, mark the sovereignty of the Chilean state over Mapuche land, and facilitate communication and transportation between the Chilean enclaves (Navarro 1909:221–230; Urrutia 1882). After the Mapuche people were defeated in Argentina in 1879, many fled to southern Chile. By that time, however, the Chilean pacification campaign was underway to incorporate Mapuche into the Chilean state. In November 1881, Urrutia defeated a pan-Mapuche insurrection in Temuco, where Wenteche, some Nangche, and other Mapuche groups allied for the first time. As Urrutia's army advanced south toward Millali, the *longko* from the Quepe area fought one last battle near the Quepe River on November 20, 1882. Euladio Ancao recounted, "We fought alongside the Manquilef and the Hueche against the Chileans to keep our land. . . . We were cornered by the *wingka* at the river. Urrutia came with Winchester repeating rifles and massacred [us]. The river flowed with blood. . . . Many Mapuche women married *wingka* men, and *longkos* also got *wingka* women captives" (December 18, 2001).

In 1884 the Chilean government completed its "pacification" of the Mapuche by forcing them onto *reducciones* (reservations), which put an end to Mapuche autonomy. Mapuche were required to live in one place and practice intensive farming and animal husbandry instead of continuing their environmentally sustainable uses of the land. These reservations became the communities of Millali and its neighbors. The Spanish term *reducción*, meaning "to order" or "to bring to reason" (Covarrubias Orozco 1995 [1611]:350, 854), was a metaphor referring to the process of "civilizing" the "irrational," "disordered" spaces of indigenous people (Rappaport and Cummins 2012:221). Members of several lineages of both the Wenteche and Nangche factions moved to the Quepe area, escaping from the colonists who had taken over their communities.[6] Ironically this nineteenth-century "civilized economy" did little for the development of Chile or Mapuche.[7] Mapuche who stayed on the *reducciones* were forced to live on small plots of reservation land, endured a subsistence economy, and became dependent on the settlers for jobs to supplement their income (Marimán 2000).[8] The eventual incorporation of Mapuche into the Chilean economy did not occur through agriculture but through the paid work of those who migrated to the cities or labored for the colonizers.

According to the Law of Indigenous Settlement (Ley de Radicación Indígena) of 1866, the reservation land granted to Mapuche was to be consolidated and the Mapuche's community rights formalized before any land was sold. But in practice parcels were auctioned off to private landowners and colonial companies before Mapuche settled their land claims (Mallon 2001:147, 160). The law distinguished vacant land, which was the property of the government, from indigenous land, which could be sold but only with the authorization of the "governor of Indians" (Donoso and Velasco 1928:35–37). But the government deemed much of the land used by the native people to be vacant, and the governor of Indians readily authorized the sale of indigenous land to European and Chilean colonizers. In cases of land disputes, the Tribunal of Indian Affairs prioritized settlers' land titles over indigenous titles (Bengoa 2004). Many settlers also usurped Mapuche lands by moving fences and by falsifying property titles.[9]

GERMAN SETTLER FANTASIES: SCHLEYER BRINGS "CIVILIZATION" AND HISTORY TO THE "SAVAGE" INDIANS

The Germans were bold entrepreneurial visionaries and pioneers in adverse conditions where everything had to be done because nothing existed. . . . They integrated their destinies with that of their second home through diverse institutions of public well-being. . . . It was only through the rationality, order, development, and progress brought by the German settler that the history of the region was created.

—HUNTER 1992:48–54

Fort Freire was created [on top of the Millali hill] with the purpose of clearing land for farming, dominating the Araucanians [Mapuche] to create populations that would know how to farm the land and breed cattle so that the Indians would learn and live better. But they [Mapuche] didn't turn themselves in because they didn't believe in the advances and progress of civilization and thought that they would lose their lands and would be dominated by the wingka.

—MUNICIPALITY OF FREIRE, UNTITLED DOCUMENT, 1983

The Chilean state sanctifies the settlers' historical narratives and rejects the Mapuche's perceptions as irrational, subjective, illegitimate, and a threat to national security. Although the times of civilization are expressions of kinship and intergenerational memory for both groups, they are unequal because the state and its violence are allied with the settlers' view of history and kinship. The Chilean government's fantasy that European settlers brought "civilization" to the "violent savages," "opportunistic and predatory thieves of cattle and white women," "immoral nomads," "lazy treacherous drunks," and "perverse sorcerers and spirits" that inhabited "wild lands" (*El Mercurio de Valparaiso*, January 30, 1856; León 1995:25–26; Pinto Rodríguez 2003:158–170; Bacigalupo 2007:111–138)[10] is closely tied to the development of ideas of history in the Global North and the modern national project. The encounter between self-governing and state-governed peoples is styled as a contest between the savage and the civilized, the backward and the modern, the nomadic and the sedentary, the people without history and the people with history (Scott 2009).[11]

Anthropologists have challenged the civilized/savage dichotomy because it perpetuates the domination of some people over others, denies indigenous peoples their specificity (Trouillot 2003:8, 12, 23, 28), and rejects their existence in the same time frame as the nation-state in the Global North (Fabian 1983). But these issues continue to shape the politics and theories around the conquest of natives as well as the memories of the colonizers and the colonized in Chile today. Settlers' perceptions of bringing "civilization" to savage Araucanía collapse nineteenth-century colonizing narratives into contemporary realities, while Mapuche shamanic narratives contradict and obliterate this history. Below, I engage Francisca's interpretations of the achronological times of civilization and savagery through her practice as a thunder shaman. In chapter 6, these reemerge in the context of state violence and military power, neoliberalism, the practices of transnational forestry companies, and the discourses of terrorism.

Because Mapuche had resisted state governments for three centuries, refusing "civilization" by "peaceful" means, the state justified settlers' use of force to destroy them.[12] European colonists massacred Mapuche people, torched their homes and fields, and took Mapuche women, land, and animals. "They imprisoned Mapuche, locked them into a *ruka* [house made from straw], and then set fire to it, exterminating the Indians in the flames" (Coña 1995 [1927]:287). These were the brutal techniques of the "civilizers," but their savagery was projected onto the natives so settlers could occupy the place of order, normality, and progress. Settlers then used "selective amnesia" (Mallon 2005:58) to conveniently forget the origins of their estates and power. Today's interethnic conflicts flow from these expropriations and the abuses perpetrated by the state and the colonizers (Comisión de Verdad Histórica y Nuevo Trato con los Pueblos Indígenas 2008:389–390).

Settlers' "productive" exploitation of lands and forests is deeply intertwined with the idea that literate, sedentary colonists create a history that is rational and linear. But the historical narratives deployed by settlers are neither. In order to sustain their fantasies, contemporary elite descendants of German colonizers use temporal dislocation to create historical continuity between different narratives—those of their late nineteenth-century settler ancestors and those of Germans during World War II. They have created a single, continuous, intergenerational memory of settlers' legitimacy and their cultural and racial superiority to justify their "civilization" of the region and the state's support for their version of history. It is from within this frame that the German settler Elizabeth Schleyer told me the story of her family, conflating the identity of Juan Schleyer, the first German colonizer in the region, with the identities of his son Carlos, his grandson-in-law Uwe Roth Schleyer, and other descendants, thereby maintaining and extending nineteenth-century colonizing narratives. By molding time in this way, Elizabeth Schleyer legitimated settlers' beliefs, their stories about the past, and their social status, wealth, and sense of belonging.

Between 1868 and 1885, well before the people of Millali had been constituted as a community and granted titles to their own land (which did not occur until 1909), the Chilean government auctioned off 90 percent of Millali's most fertile land to colonists—mostly Chileans but also Juan Schleyer (1840–1925). At that time, the government actively recruited German and other European colonizers to populate southern Chile, offering for a nominal price fertile lands south of the Bío-Bío River that belonged to Mapuche (Pinto Rodríguez 2003; Casanueva 1998:89).[13]

Schleyer was the first German colonizer in the vicinity of Temuco to own private property, and he is still celebrated in Chilean national discourse for bringing "civilization" and "progress" to the area. In 1868 he founded a farm called Santa Ana, where he and his family first lived. It was located on the flatlands by the river, seven kilometers from the original fort of RukaÑamku, which was built on the sacred hill in Millali—a place of primordial origins where collective *ngillatun* rituals were once held to replicate Mapuche cosmogony and ensure fertility and well-being. In 1885 Schleyer bought huge expanses of land around what is now Villarica, Freire, and Quepe, including the Millali hill, for cattle raising, milk production, and intensive agriculture. He built the town of Freire and its railroad station, ran a profitable lumber business, and became the local railroad superintendent and the first mayor of the town. In the 1960s the Schleyers

FIGURE 2.4

The stone marking the location of Fort Freire, founded by Colonel Gregorio Urrutia on what is today the Roth Schleyer farm (photo by author).

moved their farmhouse to the flatlands at the top of the sacred Millali hill and expanded their cattle-breeding and dairy industry.

Today, a well-traveled dirt road leads up one side of the sacred hill in Millali through the manicured fields of the Roth Schleyer family farm. The farm extends for thousands of acres between the towns of Freire and Villa-rica—farther than the eye can see. One cold day in June 2007 I visited the farm. Rolls of hay in neat lines waited to be collected while a group of well-fed cows stared as I drove by. A stretch of barbed-wire fence parceled off an equestrian field with clusters of trees, a sandpit, little hills, a lagoon, and a reconstruction of the wooden lookout tower of Fort Freire, which was built there by Urrutia. The Schleyers' watchtower and the remnants of the fort symbolize both the colonization of the Mapuche and the military repression faced by contemporary Mapuche activists, who demand sovereignty and the return of their ancestral lands. The road forks to the right and ends abruptly at a small office building where on the day of my visit dairy farmers discussed how to increase milk production. Opposite the office is a monument marking the place where Fort Freire once stood, and next to it stands a huge dairy shed with pine and eucalyptus plantings looming in the background (fig. 2.4).

A stocky, blonde, blue-eyed sixty-five-year-old woman emerged from one of two wooden family houses with pitched roofs built in the 1960s in the style often favored by German descendants in southern Chile. Like most German settlers, the Schleyer family spoke German, attended the German school and club, and married other German settlers. Elizabeth Schleyer, a member of the fourth generation of Germans in the area, had invited me to lunch to talk about her family's perspective on the history of the region and their relationship to the Mapuche and the land.

In our conversation, Elizabeth sought in several ways to justify the symbolic and physical violence done to Mapuche and their lands since the nineteenth century. First, she argued that the German settlers were native to the southern region of Chile because they were born of the soil and therefore had an irrefutable right to belong. "We are from here," Elizabeth told me. "Our ancestors came from Germany in the 1860s, and we maintain our German citizenship but have lived here all of our lives." Second, she embraced the German idea of cultural superiority that was prevalent during World War II, arguing that the privilege and dominance of German settlers was, in Pierre Bourdieu and Loïc Wacquant's (1992) terms, deserved rather than built upon a system of domination. Elizabeth claimed that the native lands were "impenetrable wild forests" that were an obstacle to production: "Nobody lived here. This is our land because we bought it from the state and because we work it. The Mapuche didn't even have agriculture, animals, or timber, and we taught them. We made the history of this region" (June 28, 2007). According to Elizabeth, the German work ethic and civilizing project had transformed the region's landscapes into civilized, productive territories populated by properly organized, subjugated mestizos and Mapuche. Like other settlers, she and her family asserted claims of belonging that required politically charged attempts to exclude Mapuche natives, who needed to be subjugated and civilized for the well-being of "society" and the nation (Congreso Nacional 1912; Klubock 2006:542, 545).

Elizabeth's narratives about Chilean history and colonization were not entirely consistent. She argued that the region was composed of empty lands that settlers needed to develop through intensive farming and the timber industry. The manicured fields, the dairy barns, and the eucalyptus plantations, to her, had etched "civilization" into the landscape. But Elizabeth also recognized that these "empty" lands were populated by indigenous people when the Europeans arrived. She resolved the tension between these notions by representing the Mapuche as lazy savages from Argentina who did not own the land because they were nomadic hunters with no notion of private property and had not developed the land through intensive agriculture. Elizabeth drew on what Arjun Appadurai (2006:5) has called "predatory identities": she excluded Mapuche from the Chilean state by arguing that they are not even legitimately indigenous. Chilean newspapers and historians supported this position throughout the nineteenth and twentieth centuries, arguing that Mapuche were obstructing progress in the region and should not be allowed to own land.[14] Because they deny that the land is a central part of Mapuche identity, settlers hold contemporary indigenous land claims to be unfounded (Richards 2013).

Elizabeth Schleyer saw her family as the rightful owners of the land because they had bought their properties from the state and because their commitment to live on and work the land surpassed that of Mapuche people, who often sell their land and move to cities: "These are our lands where we live and that have been worked by our family for generations. We learned in a seminar that half of Mapuche live in Santiago. If land [is] so important to them, they would stay and work the land like us" (June 28, 2007). Furthermore, the Chilean state upholds settlers' right to the inheritance of land through societies in which family members have shares that can only be traded and passed among themselves. Elizabeth explained: "The fourteen sons and daughters of Juan Schleyer created a society where members can only sell their shares to someone within the society. That way, the lands stay in the family."

CHANGING SYSTEMS OF MAPUCHE IDENTITY AND AUTHORITY ON THE RESERVATION

Mapuche used to have collective land tenure systems, but most of these were lost with the imposition of the reservation system. The reservations destroyed the mobile lifestyle enjoyed by allied patrilineages occupying limitless land because the reservations have precise boundaries, and Mapuche people cannot obtain new land (Bengoa 2000; Pinto Rodríguez 2000; Stuchlik 1976). The reservations also produced a radical reorganization of Mapuche systems of power and authority. During prereservation times, the most competent son of a *longko* inherited his father's position. A *longko* controlled the distribution of land within his community and led the *ngillatun*, the collective prayers offered and sacrifices made to request well-being, abundance, and protection. Machi inherited their powers through the mother's side of the family, often through a maternal grandmother. Families that produced machi and *longko* were more prestigious and held power over those that did not (Bacigalupo 2007).

The reservation system imposed a third type of authority in the south-central valleys, and this realignment persists today. A secular, elected president manages the community and negotiates with the government over issues such as land claims. In Millali, members of the Calfuñir and Huenchuñir families, descendants of the prereservation *longko*, usually take on the roles of president and administrative officials. The other *longko* still hold some local political authority and power, although the introduction of the secular administration has eroded some of their ability to negotiate with *longko* from other communities (Mallon 2009; Martínez 2009). These *longko* are chosen for their knowledge and oratorical ability, which they gain through dreams and visions, and they organize *ngillatun* rituals and perform priestly roles.[15] The machi's authority stems from their role as intermediaries between humans and spirit beings. They, too, are hired to perform *ngillatun*. In Millali there is a good deal of tension and competition between machi and *longko* over the performance of these rituals (Bacigalupo 1995, 2010).

A source of conflict during Rosa Kurin's lifetime was the Mapuche people's changing views of ethnic intermixing and of participation in Chilean society. Previously, Mapuche had viewed *mestizaje* as an effective strategy for expanding alliances and power and for subduing powerful foreigners who had entered into their cultural framework. Mapuche in the areas of Quepe, Boroa, and Makewe particularly intermarried with white women captives who were highly valued in local systems of prestige, wealth, and exchange (Bello 2011:198–207; León 1991; Núñez de Pineda y Bascuñán 1996:38–39). Like many other native peoples, Mapuche fit well with Lévi-Strauss's (1991) notion of "openness to the other": the idea that self-realization is possible only through the knowledge, incorporation, and embodiment of the viewpoints of both human and nonhuman others. While social otherness remains a central concern in indigenous representations of the past (Hill 1988:10), natives believe that by becoming like the others, even if only partially, they will be able to understand, pacify, and establish social relations with them and will have access to their possessions and powers (Gow 2007:300; Santos-Granero 2009a; Vilaça 2006:512). But since spiritual, political, and economic powers are all parts of the same historical field (Gordillo 2003:121), ethnic intermixing became suspect when Mapuche lost their lands and sovereignty to non-Mapuche settlers and were placed on reservations. Chilean non-Mapuche (wingka) people, American or European (gringo) people, and even mixed (champuria) people were distrusted in Millali. Mapuche began to limit their openness to the other in order to avoid "becoming like wingka."

By 1930 some Mapuche, inspired by the Mapuche leader Manuel Aburto Panguilef, had begun to draw on essentialist notions of ethnic identity based on blood in order to protect themselves from assimilation. Other Mapuche sought ways to participate in Chilean society on equal terms (see Crow 2010; Mallon 2010; Menard 2003:7–8; Menard and Pavez 2007:51). The nation of Chile today does not subscribe to the concept of *mestizaje*, and culture is racially constructed and used to justify social differences and systematic racism against Mapuche (Richards 2013:8, 17). Sergio Villalobos (2000a, 2000b), a Chilean historian, continues to draw on outdated notions of racial purity to argue that "pure" indigenous Mapuche people no longer exist because they have mixed with non-Mapuche. The people are therefore mestizos who cannot demand to be recognized as a native nation or claim their ancestral territories.

HYBRID IDENTITIES AND COMPLEX AFFILIATIONS IN ROSA'S TIME

The people I consulted in Millali believed that when Rosa arrived there, the spirit of a powerful deceased shaman was roaming the community, seeking someone to initiate as a new machi in whom this spirit would be reborn. One man told me that a member of the deceased's family dreamed that the spirit said, "'I am leaving very sad because I looked to the north, the south, the east, and the west, and I didn't find any good men or women [to choose as a machi].' . . . But that spirit continued wandering around and finally seized Rosa. She understood the spirits and she had relatives in Millali, so her shamanic power could emerge in that place" (June 15, 2007).

Rosa was a good candidate for the shamanic spirit for two reasons. First, she had spiritual power drawn from the Patagonian shamanic-military complex. Her father's Kurin lineage and all Wenteche warriors possessed spiritual powers derived from ancestors and special stones: they could make rain, were persuasive orators, and were invincible—superior to their Nangche rivals (Bengoa 1991:88; Marimán et al. 2006:73; Mallon 2008). When she arrived in Millali as a child, Rosa already possessed the power of her father's thunder stone. Second, she was of mixed ethnicity, which placed her in a condition of otherness. People of mixed gringo and Mapuche descent are thought to possess special powers because they see the world as both insiders and outsiders, and Rosa was one of only a few blonde or red-haired, blue-eyed German-Mapuche machi in Araucanía (Bengoa 1991:85; Vicuña Mackenna 1939).

People in Millali believed that because of her mixed ethnicity, Rosa could mimic and spiritually appropriate the power of Germans and make it part of her practice as a Mapuche shaman. Domingo Katrikura explained,

"The mix of Mapuche with German comes out way too intelligent and powerful . . . because the German is quick in his reactions and has the power of wealth, political connections, and the ability to work all the time, . . . and the Mapuche is spiritual and has the power of the ancestors and the land. That's why Rosa was so powerful. All of those powers were part of her machi practice" (June 26, 2007). Rosa was closer to the realm of the dead—"nonhuman social outsiders" (Viveiros de Castro 1998:482)—than other people were because she was an ethnic outsider and had no consanguineal relatives in the community. As a shaman, she could move among the perspectives and identities of humans, animals, spirits, insiders, and outsiders without losing her Mapuche humanness. Therefore, she could mediate with deceased spirits more effectively than others could.

Yet despite her mixed ethnic heritage, Rosa was considered Mapuche because she was raised and lived with Mapuche. Alberto Huenchuñir said, "Rosa's thought [rakiduam], [her] mentality, was Mapuche because she was raised Mapuche, even though her blood was mixed." Another man added, "She was brought up as a Mapuche so she could become a machi. [She] was just as Mapuche as anyone else in Millali" (June 27, 2007). Mapuche, like Amazonians, believe that consubstantiality—the sharing of a common nature, substances, affect, and memories—is generated by "proximity, intimate living, commensality, mutual care and the desire to become kin" (Vilaça 2002:352). People in Millali endorsed Rosa as a true machi because she used her difference in ways that healed, she promoted the collective well-being, and she behaved according to Mapuche social and moral norms.[16] She spent her life learning how to balance her identities as an ethnic outsider and as a shaman with her identity as a Mapuche who married into Millali.[17] Mapuche in Millali place Rosa in a sacred space and time and see her as creating a new interethnic order.

When Rosa was in her twenties, she married Ignacio Huenchuñir, a member of the local Wenteche family. The two had no children of their own, but Rosa had six children with other men, which gave her a circle of relatives in Millali. Present-day community members explained to me that all of Rosa's offspring were legitimized as the children of Ignacio Huenchuñir, and all but one of them used the Huenchuñir family name. People in Millali did not condemn Rosa. On the contrary, they accepted her sexual openness on the grounds of her alterity: she was a half-German shaman. Mapuche in Chile and Argentina during the nineteenth century intermarried freely with outsiders and had no notion of racial or ethnic purity (Bengoa 1991:111, 369). They stressed relational identities over those of blood kinship and drew on inclusive discourses of ethnicity. They assigned particular prestige to non-Mapuche wives, whose "purported sexual skills

FIGURE 2.5
Silver figure of a pregnant thunder hawk machi.
Francisca Kolipi identified this as the machi
Rosa Kurin from RukaÑamku (nest of hawks)
(photo by author).

brought social wealth and prestige to their husbands" (Brooks 2008:255; So-colow 1987:117). Some people in Millali celebrated Rosa's various liaisons as auspicious because her mixed ethnicity created kinship ties between Germans and Mapuche from Chile and Argentina, and her kinship with spirits brought well-being to the community.

Rosa formed one of her most important alliances with Urrutia, who led the final military campaign against Mapuche in Araucanía. Rosa, it is said, used strategies of intimidation, negotiation, and incorporation to protect the people of Millali and neighboring Imilco from being massacred. First she climbed the Millali hill and frightened the Chilean soldiers with a spectacular lightning storm (fig. 2.5). Then she healed the wounded Chilean soldiers and, in exchange, asked them to build a road for Millali. Finally, she seduced Colonel Urrutia, and they had a son together. Urrutia became kin to her family and therefore kin to the community. Urrutia also performed Mapucheness: he ate Mapuche food, believed in shamanic powers, and used Mapuche herbal remedies when he was sick. People in Millali credited Rosa with transforming the colonel into a supporter of their community.

Urrutia had an ambivalent relationship with the Chilean state and military. In 1882 he had Fort Freire built on RukaÑamku, atop the Millali hill. Although Urrutia justified the construction to the Ministry of War by saying that it allowed him to control the adjacent valley, the place had no economic or strategic military value (Urrutia 1882). Instead, it held tremendous symbolic importance for the community. It was on RukaÑamku that the first *ngillatun* rituals to ensure fertility and providence were performed in Millali, and it was there that Rosa received her shamanic powers. People in Millali today believe that Urrutia recognized the spiritual significance of RukaÑamku and built Fort Freire there to protect this sacred site.[18] But by the end of 1882 Urrutia signed a treaty with Mapuche, incorporating them into the Chilean state and ending the War of Pacification, and thus regained his credibility with the government.

Throughout her lifetime, Rosa was known for her powerful shamanic healings and collective fertility rituals and for her ability to control the weather. She was wealthy in local terms because she was well paid for her shamanic services and also bred cattle for sale. She displayed her wealth by wearing her full shamanic regalia and heavy silver jewelry every day. But she was also a generous machi who redistributed her wealth to the community by giving less fortunate Mapuche gifts of apple cider, potatoes, and meat and by contributing animals for collective rituals.

In 1950 the Wenteche families of Millali split into competing factions; one was led by the Huenchuñir and Calfuñir families and the other by the Millañir family. All three families belonged to the lineage of the fox (*ngürü*, abbreviated as *ñir* when used in names), an animal that Mapuche see as a trickster, as a mediator between the living and the dead, and sometimes as a witch. Some people in Millali attributed the factional division to the fox lineage's trickster nature. Others attributed it to conflicts between the Millañir and Huenchuñir families over the leadership of the community and its land, which the Chilean government had further reduced in 1947.

The rupture produced social disorder, conflict, and charges of sorcery. It manifested most visibly in the performance of the *ngillatun*, which normally includes an entire community. Until the split, Rosa had presided over Millali's periodic *ngillatun*, but at that time Pedro, the head of the Millañir family, claimed that the Virgin Mary was forcing him to break away from the rest of the community and perform a separate *ngillatun* in a different field. His nephew told me, "Pedro saw the Virgin dressed in white at a place on top of the Millali hill, Rüga Platawe [Shining Silver Hill of Abundance], and where they say there is gold. She [the Virgin] told him that if he wanted his brother to heal from thrombosis, he would need to organize and preside over separate *ngillatun* rituals. The Virgin told him to name the *ngillatuwe* San Pedro [Saint Peter] so that they would have access to the gates of heaven" (June 18, 2007). Because the Huenchuñir family and its allies, the Calfuñir family, drew on the prestige of the Wenteche-Patagonian military-shamanic power held by Rosa, a Huenchuñir by marriage, the Millañir family sought legitimacy in Catholicism.

Rosa, by that time seventy-seven years old, was devastated by the split, which would continue through 2004, and she refused to perform any more rituals. She predicted that the split would produce cosmic chaos and that in a few years there would be a major earthquake that would destroy the world unless a machi intervened. One day in 1955 she decided to die. Her granddaughter Norma recalled, "I was a baby [at the time], but my mother explained that Rosa didn't suffer at all. She asked that they bathe her and change her clothes. She began to play her drum softly because she didn't have strength. And she sat up and fell asleep" (June 20, 2007). In a very short time, her identity and life story became mythologized.

CIVILIZED COSMIC SHAMAN AND SAVAGE SETTLER DEVIL

Immediately after Rosa's death, her family and neighbors in Millali began to memorialize her as a larger-than-life figure, merging her life story with stories of cosmic events during primordial times. They also associated Rosa with the sacred boldo tree on the Millali hill. Alejandro Huenchuñir said, "Her power was there. We heard babies [which are associated with fertility] crying [there] and saw two beautiful *metawe* [ceramic vessels] that then disappeared" (June 28, 2007). The family had carved on her gravestone the words "Rosa Kurin died at the age of 110. Remembrance by her son and grandchildren." Rosa's descendants did not locate her on a linear timeline by including her birth and death dates on the gravestone, as is customary in Chilean cemeteries. Rather, the number 110 places her in the primordial "before time" because when people in Millali want to speak about events or people of a different time or cycle, they say "more than a hundred years ago."

Ultimately the mythologization of Rosa came to be bound up in much larger issues. Rosa took on charismatic qualities as someone who had saved

Millali from military repression at the hands of Colonel Urrutia and also from natural disasters. Mapuche in Millali viewed the sociopolitical and economic transformations resulting from the loss of their land, their territorial sovereignty, and their way of life in the late nineteenth and early twentieth centuries as nothing less than a cosmic catastrophe. By construing colonization as a moment of chaos in a larger cyclical process that would eventually end, giving rise to a new order, the rural Mapuche of Millali challenged linear Chilean historical narratives of progress and civilization brought by settlers (Navarro 1909:221–230) and the linear ethnic national histories written by urban Mapuche intellectuals.[19]

In the shamanic history told in Millali, cosmic disorder resulted from the appropriation of the Millali hill by the German colonist Juan Schleyer in 1885, and only Rosa's shamanic strength saved the community from destruction. Domingo Katrikura explained the background:

> RukaÑamku was a Mapuche community and the place of our origins where we had our first *ngillatun*. Little old ladies lived in their *ruka* [straw huts] before, but Schleyer tricked them. He gave them a dish full of silver peso coins and took their land away. The little old ladies didn't speak Spanish and didn't know how to defend themselves. . . . Schleyer had a pact with the devil and was friends with the military. He came to take all the good land and threw Mapuche out. The military built a cave in RukaÑamku; it was a *renü*, a place where witches go to get power.[20] And from there, they shot at the Mapuche all night. The Mapuche were afraid. The Ñamku, Curihual, and Nawelpi families that lived there loaded what they could on a bullock cart, abandoned their lands, and went to live with their relatives. These lands are now part of the farm owned by the Roth Schleyer family, and the families who had lived at RukaÑamku don't even have a place to raise two cows. (June 15, 2007)

In acquiring the hill, Schleyer expropriated two sites of enormous significance to the people of Millali: RukaÑamku and, adjacent to it, an old cemetery called Rüga Platawe, where Mapuche buried jewelry, ceramic vessels, and gold coins among the roots of a hollow laurel tree. By taking these places, Mapuche say, Schleyer stole the wealth, power, and resources of Millali. In the local shamanic history, he did so by imitating machi Rosa and tricking the local dwarves (*kofkeche*), who were brought into being from the primordial past and lived hidden from sight in the present, guarding Millali's treasures. Here is the *koyang* assembled in 2007 from the accounts of different narrators in Millali:

Before, people from Millali got gold from the hill and the river and accumulated gold coins. Not trusting the bank, they buried their gold at Rüga Platawe, and dwarves guarded it to increase the wealth of the Millali hill. Mapuche also buried their dead there with jewels and treasures. Machi Rosa asked the dwarves to give her some gold from the river to buy a horse for the *ngillatun* ritual for everyone's benefit. Schleyer saw this, and when he bought the Millali hill and made it his farm, he copied Rosa and tricked the dwarves. He told them to give him gold so that everyone in the community would benefit. The dwarves allowed gold to swim into his pans in the river. Schleyer bought Quilas Bajas and made a gold mine on the farm, and the dwarves worked underground and brought him the gold through a well in his house. But the gold was only for himself. Schleyer put a lock on the farm's gate so that no Mapuche could look for gold there anymore.

In a letter to the National Corporation of Indigenous Development (Corporación Nacional de Desarrollo Indígena, CONADI) dated August 31, 2007, the people of Millali wrote that the loss of Rüga Platawe "caused confusion and shortages in the community because we lost all our wealth and power." In their "political economy of life" (Santos-Granero 2009d), Mapuche believe that the vital force that animates the universe is finite, scarce, and unequally distributed. Mapuche have experienced the gringos' theft of this life force through territorial dispossession and the extraction of gold and timber from their former lands. According to this perception, gringos not only exploit, dispossess, enslave, and kill natives (Brown 1984; Varese 1973), but they also use their evil powers to harass them (Santos-Granero and Barclay 2011:155, 158). One man from Millali complained, "Now the Germans own the hill and have taken its power. That's why they are wealthy and invincible. All the *ngen* are dominated by Schleyer. That's why his land is so fertile and ours is so poor" (June 22, 2007). In Rosa's shamanic history, the individualistic, capitalist intentions of the gringo transformed the dwarves (normally, helpers of the *ngen*) and other spirits into evil beings who sucked the labor, blood, and life force from Mapuche.

The perceptions of people in Millali of *patronazgo* (patronage) and of Schleyer as the dominator of the *ngen* and the earth resonate with older Mapuche concepts. Mapuche tended to build strategic relations with persons who acknowledged them and from whom they could gain power, rather than with institutions or representatives of political ideologies. Mapuche desired the cattle, land, and other forms of wealth and connection that the patrons had, and they sought close relationships with them for those reasons. When Juan Schleyer arrived in 1860, people in Millali sought to ally with him to gain his protection and favor through the paternalistic institution of *patronazgo*. Schleyer served as a godfather to people in the community, took sick people to the hospital, and donated animals for *ngillatun* rituals. He also became the owner and patron of *ngen* spirits.

Most Mapuche believe that *ngen* need to be propitiated in order for Mapuche to gain access to an ecosystem and its resources; otherwise, the *ngen* will capture and possess a Mapuche's spirit or punish the individual with illness. But European and Chilean settlers have the ability to take over a *ngen*'s powers and are not affected by its punishments. The term *genche* (owner of the people) first appeared in 1606 and referred to the Spanish patron and landowner, who held social, economic, and political power over his Mapuche workers and the *ngen* (Valdivia 1887 [1606]). The term *ngenmapun* (owner or dominator of the earth) appeared in the eighteenth century and was associated with the devil and with the hierarchical political and religious structures imposed by non-Mapuche settlers like Schleyer (Febres 1882 [1765]). Mapuche counteracted the foreign powers of *genche* and *ngenmapun* in the spiritual realm by creating in the nineteenth century a pan-Mapuche deity called Ngünechen, who combined the power of all the Mapuche nature spirits and the ancestral spirits who live in the sky (*wenupüllüam*) and became the patron, dominator, and governor of the earth and its people (Bacigalupo 1997).

For Mapuche in Millali, the gringo Schleyer represented a new form of alterity that required new mediators (mischievous dwarves) and new forms of mediation (helping, guarding, and enslavement). In Mapuche narratives, the devil's serpents usually guard treasures for Mapuche or grant them power and wealth if they feed milk to the serpents. In Rosa's story, it is dwarves—nonhuman beings without ethnicity—who guard the treasures of Millali. Her story incorporates dwarves not only as guardians of treasure but also as mediators between the shaman Rosa and the *ngen* spirits, as well as between the sorcerer Schleyer and the same spirits. When Rosa ultimately recovered the spiritual powers of Millali through her rituals, the dwarves became her helpers. They are symbols of the shifting, contextual construction of ethnicity, identity, and alterity in Millali.

Another way to understand the story of the dwarves is through Michael Taussig's (1993:xviii) notion of mimesis, the magical replication of the beings, objects, rituals, or practices of powerful others for the purpose of obtaining their power. The memory of that appropriation is then erased, negating the power of the other (Santos Granero 2007:59). People in Millali believe that by mimicking Rosa—becoming partially and temporarily like her in order to trick the dwarves—Schleyer reversed the relationship in which the dominated mimic the dominators in order to appropriate their power (Taussig 1993). As a gringo and the legal owner of the Millali hill, Schleyer held economic and political power over the people of Millali. But it was only when he mimicked Rosa's shamanic rituals that her spiritual power became his, and he was able to obtain gold from the Millali hill. Rosa had asked the dwarves for gold to finance a ritual for the collective good, which subordinated capitalistic accumulation to circulation (Steven Rubenstein 2007). Schleyer inverted this economy of power, subordinating circulation to accumulation by keeping the gold for himself and locking out local Mapuche.

In sharp contrast to Chilean national narratives about Schleyer's role in bringing civilization, morality, and progress, the people of Millali place him in their shamanic histories as a savage sorcerer who made pacts with the foreign devil. Similar behavior is widely attributed to white patrons throughout Latin America (Edelman 1994:62; Gould 1990:30; Nash 1993:191–194). People in Millali claim that the immoral German settlers made these pacts with the devil in order to gain wealth, power, and an obsessive work ethic, which allows them to exploit the reproductive power of the land and animals through intensive farming and logging. They harvest greater yields without concern for soil degradation or the spirit masters of ecosystems. Machi Juan believed that settlers "write their contracts with the devil in blood on crinkly mauve paper in an office in [the city of] Temuco run by a Chilean to become rich.[21] The devil, who is Lutheran, makes the land give them good harvests, lots of animals, and cheap workers in exchange for years of their lives or those of their children. Settlers have no morals. They are selfish, wealthy, greedy. They suck the life out of the land and then just steal more land" (December 17, 2001). The Lutheran devil is bent on increasing production through capitalistic exploitation, but this production is ultimately destructive of life, growth (Taussig 1980), Mapuche society, and morality.

The devil brought by European imperialism to the new world symbolizes the contradictory ways in which natives and colonizers understand each other, which is an important aspect of the political and economic history of colonialism (Taussig 1980:169). The devil is united metonymically and symbiotically with the white *patrón* through a pact that grants the *patrón* power over his indigenous workers (Gordillo 2004:137; Turner 1986). The Germans believe that the "civilized" Protestant ethic gives "moral sanction to profit making through hard work, organization, and rational calculation" (Yankelovich 1981:247; Rose 1985), along with deferment of gratification, repayment of debt, and avoidance of luxuries. The settlers claim that they keep the salaries of Mapuche low so they will work more hours; otherwise, they will have too much time for leisure. The image of the rich, white *patrón* points to the cannibalistic aspect of labor exploitation: the consumption of the bodies of indigenous people by settlers' hunger for profit (Gordillo 2004:131); and Mapuche believe that German settlers in league with devils literally treat their workers like animals and eat them. One Mapuche man linked the German settlers to a story published by the Municipality of Freire about a "tall, fat woman cannibal" at Tres Esquinas who allegedly killed people and made them into mincemeat for empanadas: "One day the neighbors heard a lamentable scream . . . and the people say that the people who disappeared there were made into empanadas. In the end they did an investigation and the justice system found traces" (Municipalidad de Freire 1983:23).

Mapuche also view the Lutheran devil's capitalistic mentality of individual gain and indiscriminate production as savage and immoral because it clashes with Mapuche ideals of civilized morality and sociality, which include communal work, parliaments, egalitarianism, and the value of leisure and socializing. For Mapuche, creating and maintaining alliances for collective agricultural work, local politics, group rituals, and socializing are central to a civilized community life.[22] Mapuche sociality demands that people be polite, moral, engaged in reciprocal behaviors, and working toward collective well-being. Mapuche in Millali believe that Germans become individualistic, selfish, violent, and angry because they have been made *piru longko* (crazy, literally meaning "worms in the head") by the devil. A Mapuche man said, "The Germans' blood boils. They are rude, angry, and selfish because they have contracts with the devil. Nothing can stand in their way. . . . Schleyer is the man of a thousand devils. When something breaks or a worker doesn't do his job, . . . he becomes angry, crazy. The workers are scared" (July 2007).

People in Millali collapsed the identity of Juan Schleyer into those of his son Carlos, his grandson-in-law Uwe Roth Schleyer, and other descendants. Then they mythologized "the gringo" as one gigantic, powerful sorcerer, "Schleyer," who received fertile fields, wealth, and power in exchange for the lives of his family members—the price, Mapuche believe, that people who make pacts with the devil typically pay (Bacigalupo 2007; Schindler and Schindler-Yáñez 2006). The intermittent light from the lanterns on Schleyer's carriage as he visited his properties at night became the evil fireballs (*cherufe*) that accompany the devil and his sorcerers on their nightly voyages (Municipality of Freire 1983:10–11, 15).

People in Millali believe that members of the Schleyer family use fireballs and the *chonchon*, a flying sorcerer's head, to coerce their workers. One man said, "The lantern of the old gringo, we call it *chonchon* because it flies at night to scare us. Ever since the gringo traveled on his properties at night, the *cherufe* have been coming down the hill to harass us at night and make sure we obey him" (June 27, 2007). Another man in Millali elaborated, "Schleyer is a giant that has magical powers he gets from a brown square bread [pumpernickel] given to him by the devil, and that's why he is wealthy and strong. . . . He works day and night stealing riches from the soil, planting trees, tilling the land, and taking its gold. He never sleeps. Nobody can beat him. . . . He has the strength of a bull. . . . He is very intelligent; nobody can fool him. He knows what you are thinking. He sees everything" (January 5, 2008). Mapuche in Millali portrayed the devil as "a huge man who comes down from the farm and lurks at the community center to do sorcery in Millali." In this mythologized image, Schleyer is the epitome of the feudal, colonial settler who took Mapuche land and exploited Mapuche workers. As a stranger, Schleyer was considered closer to the realm of animals and spirits than to the human realm.

Because the mythologized Schleyer—as devil and giant—has a nonhuman body, some Mapuche say he experiences the world differently from the way humans do. Eduardo Viveiros de Castro (1998:479; 2003), writing about Amazonian peoples, called this belief perspectivism: the idea that nature is variable and culture is constant and homogenous, which places indigenous and nonindigenous humans, spirits, and animals in different, incommensurate worlds. According to this theory, although all beings share the same generic spirit, each kind of being sees the same world differently because of the body it inhabits.[23] One woman in Millali said, "The giant Schleyer is very blond and that's why he thinks like the devil. He wants all the riches, all the land, all the power. He doesn't have animals on half-share like us. He doesn't help the neighbor. He gives nothing. He takes it all" (June 17, 2007). In other contexts, however, people in Millali viewed the historical Juan Schleyer as a person with a body like theirs and the ability to communicate with them in the same language.

Mapuche do share a world and a language with Schleyer and the devil even though they do not share a lot of wine or conversation, and they usually see the differences between themselves and the devil at the level of culture, behavior, thought, and history, rather than nature and the body. What distinguishes the devil is his savage, immoral, capitalistic mentality of individual gain and indiscriminate production that works against Mapuche morality and sociality. According to people in Millali, Schleyer promoted his reputation of having a pact with the devil in order to keep cattle thieves off his land. The Mapuche image of the devil is at once a moral judgment and a historical comment, which replicates the way shamanic histories link the primordial and the historical.

Whatever they may have thought of the historical Schleyer, Mapuche in Millali made the mythologized version of him the agent of the cosmic chaos of colonization. Correspondingly, they re-created Rosa Kurin as the primordial Trengtreng serpent, who retook the spiritual power of Millali from Schleyer and restored the cosmic order and meaning to their world through her ritual intervention in history. They merged the events of the early twentieth century into cyclical time by incorporating them into the primordial conflict between the earth serpent Trengtreng (associated with the east, the Andes, and life) and the water serpent Kaykay (associated with the west, the Pacific Ocean, and death).

According to people in Millali, the loss of their sacred hill, the realm of Trengtreng, caused such cosmic disorder that in 1933 Kaykay tried to destroy the world with a flood. Only ritual action by Rosa restored the balance between the two serpents and saved the community. Alberto Huenchuñir related the story as it was handed down from his grandfather:

> The hill burst open like a motor pump, spewing water everywhere. Even the horses were knocked over. There was a huge wind, huge rain, for many days. It almost turned the world around. . . . There was thunder, and evil started. The stars fell onto the earth, and a gigantic bull with a bronze bell came down from above with clouds. This happened in front of Lefian's house. Everyone saw it. . . . Rosa climbed the hill and sacrificed two sheep and hung them on the sacred *boldo* tree to calm the waters. The thunder and lightning possessed her. . . . A lot of people got together to pray, all wet. . . . We were surrounded by water, and people from another community screamed, asking us if we were alive or dead. Rosa said, "We are going to do a *ngillatun*. Everyone must cover themselves with white cloth, white wool, and follow the white horses at the front. And this is how we are going to calm the fury of the water [Kaykay] and the hill [Trengtreng]." Rosa floated in the water while she prayed, and little by little the water subsided. All the *ngen*, the forces, obeyed her. My father said that's how my grandfather told it. (June 15, 2007)

In this shamanic history, community members identify Rosa with a shamanic spirit from the primordial "before time" (*rüf kuyfi*). But simultaneously they see her as embodying shamanic history through her engagements with Urrutia and Schleyer and with historical changes, contexts, and contingencies. People associate Rosa with the Mapuche narrative of the primordial deluge, the flood produced by the struggle between Trengtreng and Kaykay. In this creation story, most of humanity drowns or is transformed into sea creatures. Some humans are helped by Trengtreng and survive on the mountaintops, but they resort to cannibalism, producing further cosmic disorder. When only one couple is left, a shaman goes inside the mountain and reveals that the two must pray and sacrifice their only child by throwing him into the water to appease the divine anger. The couple perform the sacrifice, the water is frozen inside the mountain, and order is restored in the world (Bacigalupo 2007:46–47).

For the people of Millali, Rosa Kurin was a multitemporal machi because she drew on the powers of the good earth serpent to defeat the evil water serpent, control the flood, wrestle the power of the spirits back from Schleyer, and reestablish balance in the cosmos. After those events, the relationship between Schleyer, the devil, the dwarves, and other spirits changed radically. They say that Schleyer had initially tricked the devil by feeding him the lives of his Mapuche workers instead of those of his family members.[24] When the devil realized what had happened, he turned against Schleyer, killing his two adult sons in violent accidents in order to feed on their blood. One man explained, "Mapuche who work in the Schleyer house don't last very long. At around midnight [the savage time of the devil], the *patrón* would appear. Then the Mapuche would suffer bad luck and die. . . . When the devil realized [this], he possessed the nephew of Uwe Roth Schleyer from Germany and made him shoot his cousin, . . . and Uwe's other son was galloping on his horse when the devil put barbed wire between two trees and decapitated him" (June 15, 2007).

The dwarves and spirits in Millali who had been tricked by Schleyer during the cycle of chaos tricked him in turn. In January 2010 Hernan Huenchuñir (Alberto Huenchuñir's son) smiled smugly as he pointed to two pits dug by "the gringo" at the base of the hollow laurel tree in the old cemetery of Rüga Platawe: "The gringo saw the laurel tree shining at night, and he thought he would find the gold buried there. He brought a machine to detect gold and started digging but found nothing. The dwarves showed him the treasures and then made them disappear, mocking him. . . . The *metawe* with gold coins are buried deep among the roots of the laurel tree, and the dwarves make them move under the ground, so the gringo will never catch them."

By mythologizing the men in the Schleyer family as one long-lived sorcerer who produced chaos by usurping Millali's land and local spirits and by mimicking Rosa's shamanic powers, the people of Millali construe the Chilean state's subjugation of them as sorcery. By mythologizing Rosa as the restorer of cosmic order at a moment of radical socioeconomic and political reorganization and ethnic intermixing, they regain spiritual control over their land and the spirit beings and re-create their community's place in a new historical context. Through these processes, both Rosa and Schleyer become multitemporal beings with spiritual agency and transformational power who remain immanent presences in the community. They are also periodically rehistoricized in new contexts as Mapuche employ a cyclical narrative outside of linear, historical time in order to create historical continuity.

Many Mapuche believe that the chaos produced by the deluge is periodically repeated in a different form, although gringos are always to blame. Rosa created a new kind of interethnic order in Millali, but Schleyer kept the Millali hill and large plots of community land. This set the stage for the cosmic chaos and earthquake of 1960, when Francisca was initiated as a machi. By then factionalism and internal conflicts over the remaining land, the destruction of the ancestors' land, and loss of knowledge of the Mapuche past had led to the destruction of the community's lineages. The good earth serpent Trengtreng was furious: he would rather destroy the world and humanity by earthquake than allow a world without the past to exist. But according to some people in Millali, Rosa's spirit returned and possessed Francisca, initiating her as a machi who would appease the anger of Trentreng and save the world.

SHAMANIC HISTORY, IDENTITY, AND AGENCY

As the shamanic history of Rosa Kurin shows, Mapuche shamans have historical consciousness, and their phenomenological "true history," based on their embodiment of spirits and forces, allows them to mediate between different worlds, identities, and beings. Their historical consciousness is made intelligible to ordinary people through the narration of shamanic histories, which become a means for conveying native agency based on the transformative capacities of spiritual power. And because shamanic narratives construct the spiritual agency of natives as superior to the political agency of settlers, they can obliterate the dominant history, reverse the colonialist dynamics of subordination and mimicry, and create new worlds and histories.

Shamanic histories reconcile the tension in anthropology between what Frank Salomon (1999) referred to as the otherness of natives' history and a recognition of indigenous people's historical agency. Shamanic narratives are radically other not because they are isolated from hegemonic or indigenous ethnic histories, but because they subject these histories to a logic by which human and nonhuman beings act as historical agents, and natives become the victors of history. Furthermore, shamanic histories are able to reconcile many different rural and urban representations of the past—life histories, kinship histories, ethnic national histories, and narratives about *rüf kuyfi* and *kuyfi*—to contest the dominant national history. Shamanic narratives are deeply historical in that they incorporate outsiders and describe the radical changes the people have experienced. But at the same time, natives rework the dominant historical narratives, characters, and events to reflect their own stories, structures, and ontologies of becoming. Indigenous people may simultaneously obliterate a traumatic history and register it in a new ritual form (Fausto 2007; Severi 2000)—or, in the Mapuche case, as new shamanic histories.

In shamanic histories, agents—including charismatic characters, primordial beings, and spirits—mark the beginnings and ends of cyclical phases in a spiraling pattern. People in Millali saw the Mapuche's military defeat and Rosa's flight to Chile as marking the end of a cycle of warfare; the personal, spiritual, and military power of warrior-shamans; and their transnational political alliances. The invasion of Gregorio Urrutia and his relationship with Rosa marked the beginning of a cycle of subjugation of the Mapuche to the Chilean state and the creation of complex interethnic relationships. The appearance of Juan Schleyer marked the beginning of a cycle of cosmic and social chaos produced by colonization and the loss of land. German settlers claimed cultural and racial superiority and viewed as markers of civilization their practice of intensive agriculture, their capitalistic and individualistic ideologies, and their aggressive entrepreneurship. Mapuche, by contrast, see these traits—as well as the anger and violence they attribute to Germans—as markers of the colonists' savagery, linked with the Lutheran devil. The mythologization of Rosa Kolipi Kurin marked the beginning of a cycle of restoration of the cosmic order. And she sought to project this new order into the future after she died by possessing Francisca and making her a machi.

Shamanic histories also show that natives mediate the relationship between alterity, identity, and agency through multiple modes of incorporation and transformation of the other, including commensality, sex, childbearing, marriage, fictive kinship, and the internalizing of colonial hierarchies. Rosa's shamanic history is rife with the ambiguous appropriations that have helped people in Millali make sense of their *mestizaje*, their relationships to others, their lives, and their humanity. Viveiros de Castro (1998) argues that alterity, not identity, is the default state in Amazonia, but among Mapuche in Millali the two alternate.

Although Rosa is the hero of the story because of the way she used her Mapuche shamanic powers, she was part German, and she created a beneficial alliance by having a child with the Chilean Urrutia. During her lifetime she moved from a position of alterity (as a German and a shaman) to one of identity with kin (as a Mapuche wife, a mother, and a person who protected the community). After her death she moved back to a position of alterity (as a primordial Mapuche shaman), although her identity with kin remained through her immanent presence in the community. Schleyer occupied a position of alterity because he was a European of German descent and, in his mythologized persona, could take the form of a giant, devil, or evil spirit. At the same time, he was identified as human when he showed his benevolent side as an honest, hard-working *patrón*, a godfather, and a donor to the Mapuche community. Urrutia was simultaneously the conquering Chilean military commander (a position of alterity) and, under Rosa's influence, a man who protected the community. Rosa's shamanic history shows how subjects continuously move between celebrating alterity in order to gain power and domesticating difference in order to identify with kin and develop a sense of belonging.

Shamanic histories are also commentaries about the transformational nature of native personhood and native ethnic identities. Rosa's shamanic history negates the power or superiority of outsiders by attributing these characteristics to temporary dynamics and mimicry. Rosa appropriated the powers of the Germans and made them her own as soon as she was initiated as a shaman; they then became her permanent, intrinsic shamanic powers. Schleyer gained power only temporarily by mimicking Rosa's rituals and claiming her shamanic powers as his own. Because Rosa already possessed the power of Germanness, she did not mimic Schleyer, nor was she impressed when he copied her shamanic rituals. She drew on her intrinsic German-Mapuche shamanic powers to wrest spiritual control of the Millali hill away from him and restore order, even though the historical, human Schleyer kept the land. The story portrays Rosa as inherently powerful and morally superior to outsiders because she used her alterity for the well-being of the community rather than for individualistic, capitalist purposes.

In their transformational capacity, shamanic histories are central to the agency of natives and to the anthropological endeavor. Mapuche resistance movements have used shamans and their drums as their symbols and have fostered an increasing "shamanization of indigenous identities" (Conklin 2002:1058) and a politicization of the shaman role. Shamanic notions of power based on spirits, the life force, and traditional knowledge have become central to Mapuche ethnic politics and are used in both ritualistic and political ways (Bacigalupo 2004c). As ontologies, not epistemologies, have become anthropologists' true objects of study (Argyrou 1999), we have recognized that native discourses speak about the world, not just about the native society and mind (Viveiros de Castro 2003). And shamanic histories enable new ontologies: Mapuche create themselves as beings with inherently superior spiritual agency who can make a better world for themselves. In their new world, Mapuche have obliterated historical trauma, Chilean temporality, and Mapuche mortality. Shamanic histories are not static myths but contested narratives expressing contradictory histories and politics. By remembering Rosa and telling her story, the people of Millali attempt to gain control over their present and future. By challenging their traumatic history through Rosa's superior spiritual powers and morality and by making her presence immanent in the community, they hope to achieve equality and immortality.[25] This new world of hope allows people in Millali to move away from internal conflicts and factionalism to create a form of historical consciousness that promotes group solidarity and agency and that has the potential to support political mobilization.

Five years after Rosa's death, her spirit was believed to have reemerged and thus was rehistoricized during a series of natural disasters: a thunderstorm, a devastating earthquake, and a tsunami. Some Mapuche say that Rosa's powers as a thunder shaman, her temperament, and her ritual practices were reborn in Francisca's body, that Rosa's spirit seized Francisca and initiated her immediately as a machi to reestablish order in the world. Francisca's maternal grandfather, Manuel Lefian, was Rosa's father's cousin. When Francisca became initiated as a machi, she claimed Rosa as her maternal grandmother and replaced her maternal surname, Lefian, with Rosa's surname, Kurin. Francisca then became known as Francisca Kolipi Kurin. As I demonstrate in the next chapter, Rosa's and Francisca's powers, lives, and ethnically mixed genealogies became intertwined through blood and spiritual kinship. At the same time, Francisca's life and practice were interpreted differently within a fractious new historical context.

CHAPTER THREE

MULTITEMPORAL VISIONS
and BAD BLOOD

"Get up, lazy people!" Francisca screamed at 5:00 a.m. "Cesar, make a fire. I had a dream." I woke abruptly from my sleep. Cesar, Francisca's grandson, stumbled into the kitchen to light the wood stove. Francisca was lying next to me, breathing heavily. Her hands were clammy. The date was February 3, 1995, a few days after machi Angela's complex *datun* healing ritual for Francisca. She was still drinking herbal medicine for healing. I reached for the candle under the bed but instead felt Francisca's knife and a bottle of *aguardiente* (a distilled liquor made from sugar cane), meant to protect her against evil *wekufü* spirits during the night.

"Was it a good dream, *Papay* [old woman]?" I asked.

"I dreamed that I was lying on a bed of remedies, and several machi were here healing me. There were herbal remedies everywhere. That means that Ngünechen is hurrying me to have a *machi pürun* [renewal ritual]. I am going to have to do this in March. And I will need a tame horse. Now I have to pray at my *rewe*. Ngünechen is telling me so," she said anxiously. "My stomach and my right hand are swollen. Did you have a bad dream, Mariella? You were writhing like a snake."

"I don't have bad dreams. I have bad fleas," I joked, trying to relieve some of her anxiety. Francisca chuckled and got out of bed.

Francisca's daughter Aurora, Cesar's mother, also was living in Francisca's house. Aurora entered the room with a candle. She picked up Francisca's *kultrung* and went to heat it on the kitchen stove to make the tone of the drum deeper. I stuffed my tape recorder in the pocket of my sweatpants and picked up Francisca's sleigh bells. "No pants," Francisca said. I pulled a long black skirt over my pants and tied red string around Francisca's wrists to protect her from evil spirits. She tied a blue scarf around her head.

We walked outside to her *rewe* (*axis mundi*), where Francisca's spirit lived. The *rewe* faced the living room and consisted of three carved wooden statues from successive *machi pürun*. Each had painted blue arms and a

FIGURE 3.1

Francisca Kolipi prays as she strikes her rewe *with a knife to awaken its power.
The* rewe *consists of three carved wooden statues tied together and flanked by
branches of the* triwe *and* foye *trees (photo by author).*

painted blue heart, and the statues were tied together and flanked by sacred
foye and *triwe* branches (fig. 3.1). I placed the tape recorder on a stool; Aurora brought the drum; and Francisca performed a prayer in Mapudungun,
accompanied by drumming. I jingled the sleigh bells (fig 3.2). Periodically,
Francisca made me repeat phrases after her. She began by asking Chau
Díos (Old Man Ngünechen) and Ñuke Díos (Old Woman Ngünechen) to
give her knowledge through dreams: "Chau Díos, Ñuke Díos, ancient machi from the transparent earth above, sitting with your legs crossed. You
have all the knowledge of the worlds and know all places and times. Give
me your knowledge in dreams. Have compassion with your daughter." After the prayer, Francisca and I huddled by the wood stove and drank yerba
mate as she recounted her dreams about her shamanic powers and her ritual
objects. I had heard these narratives before, but Francisca repeated them to
impress upon me their monumental importance.

Dreaming and other altered states of consciousness provide individuals
with knowledge of a multitemporal spiritual reality (Kracke 1987) in which
communication and shared personhood with beings from other worlds are
possible. The *püllü* (spirit) travels outside the body and outside time to gain
knowledge and power from good spirits, or it may suffer harm from evil

MULTITEMPORAL VISIONS *and* BAD BLOOD

69

FIGURE 3.2
Francisca Kolipi plays her kultrung *(drum) while her granddaughter
plays the* kaskawilla *(sleigh bells) (photo by George Munro).*

spirits. Machi may invite spirits to come into their dreams or to possess
them and take over their bodies to grant them knowledge and power. Or
machi may travel to other worlds to plead with, bribe, and cajole spirits for
knowledge.[1] The acquisition of information about the past through these
altered states of consciousness is a challenge to the linear temporalities and
historicization of the Global North because "in dreams, a person encounters what he is, what he will be, what he has done and what he is going to
do, discovering the knot that ties his freedom to the necessity of the world"
(Foucault 1986 [1954]:47).

The multitemporality experienced in dreams, visions, and trance states
allows machi to synthesize and mediate between time periods to produce
and reshape history. Although Francisca lived in the present world mate-

rially, she was not of this world: her spirit was from the past, and she also lived in the future. Francisca's experiences of trance (*küymi*), vision (*perimotu*), and dream (*pewma*) connected her with Rosa and provided knowledge of the past. Like Baniwa prophets (Wright 2013), machi gain knowledge that surpasses all human knowledge, knowledge that effects change. Francisca learned ways to resolve cosmic chaos and to solidify relationships in the present, and she had visions of how to heal others and give them hope in the future. But altered states of consciousness are ambiguous modes of renewing the primordial in the present. *Kalku* (sorcerers) also use multitemporality to block Mapuche paths and futures, promote factionalism, and destroy knowledge and the family. People in Millali constantly scrutinized and reinterpreted Francisca's dreams, visions, and trance experiences in the communal context and in view of their relationships with her and her ethnicity.[2] Was she a shaman or a sorcerer?

In this chapter I analyze Francisca's altered states of consciousness and how people in Millali interpreted her ambiguous powers, healing practices, and ritual objects through discussions of blood and spiritual kinship, multitemporality, and sorcery. Some questioned Francisca's legitimacy because she had no patrilineal blood ties to the community, because she did not experience machi illnesses, and because she was initiated late in life without formal training. But others believed that Francisca created continuity with the past and promoted spiritual, social, and blood kinship in her life and practices.

MACHI FROM OLD TIMES AND SPIRITUAL KINSHIP

"Machi are not ordinary people. We don't live in this time," Francisca told me on May 12, 1995, as we sat on the bench outside her kitchen, watching pigs scramble for the cherries falling from her tree.

"What time do machi live in?" I asked.

"Old times. We only want things of the past. Ways of the past. The *filew* [ancestral spirit of all machi who possesses all wisdom] wants us to live in old times."

"But don't you also live in this time?" I asked. "You play cumbia on the radio. You like to ride in my truck. You don't wear your *chamall* every day. You ask me to rub your swollen feet with Calorub [an ointment from the pharmacy]. Aren't those things from this time?"

"Ay, Mamita," Francisca said. "I was also born on this earth, and I am a woman with a family, but people only want a machi who lives in old times. Ngünechen punishes me with *kastikukutran* [punishment illness] for wearing a dress and not a *chamall* and for listening to the radio instead of play-ing my *kultrung*.[3] Now, I can only eat *kako* [cooked wheat] and *mültrün* [Mapuche unleavened brown bread], no spaghetti or sweets. I can't listen to the radio anymore. My *likankura* [precious stone] and my *tralkan kura* [thunder stone] come from the volcano where old people live. They gave me the knowledge of old times."

Although all memory studies link the past, the present, and the future, the orientations of different spiritual practitioners within the temporality they experience—and their modes of engaging it—are strikingly differ-ent. Machi are not of this world (spiritually) because they are from the old times, but they live in this world in the present. Sakalava mediums in Mad-agascar experience the past as a burden that they carry on their backs; they speak about the weight of the past that they embody in rituals and carry in their lives in order to speak of the present (Lambek 2003). In contrast, Mapuche shamans *are* the past and are described as spiritually living in the past—in part because the past lives permanently in them, in the form of the spirit of the deceased machi they embody. With this basis in the past, machi rituals focus on divining and creating a better future for Mapuche.

Machi are judged on their ability to use their knowledge and power to fulfill social functions in the family, in their spiritual kinship with other machi, and in the community. Mapuche historian Sergio Caniuqueo de-scribed them as "reche machi che" (real machi people) because they obtain their knowledge and power from the past, both witnessed and primordial. Their social and spiritual roles are continuous with that past even though they live in the present. Caniuqueo explained to me, "People say machi and *longko* are living in the past [*kuyfi*] or the primordial past [*rüf kuyfi*] because [they are] anchored with old things and the past. And [their] *kü-palme*—lineage and social function—are determined by the past" (Janu-ary 7, 2012). Mapuche greet female machi as Papay (old woman) and male machi as Chachay (old man), regardless of their biological age, for the same reasons. Mapuche have anxiety about losing their connection with the past because they believe that losing that connection brings misfortune. Machi play a central role in keeping the past alive among Mapuche.

Mapuche construct machi *küpalme* through blood ties—procreation, filiation, and descent—as well as socially and spiritually through actions in the present. Both social and spiritual *küpalme* involve the transmission of the components of a person, including their embodied traits, physical characteristics, bodily substances, character, ability to fulfill social roles, and moral behavior. And both genealogical kinship and social kinship are constructed through a "mutuality of being" (Sahlins 2011:2). Nevertheless, as early as the beginning of the twentieth century, many Mapuche began to understand the kinship of blood ties as a natural, irrevocable fact that is in tension with the kinship acquired through the sharing of spirit essence, language, commensality, and spiritual relationships.[4] Mapuche intellectual Juan Ñanculef explained that "kinship and social memory [are] in *mollfün*, blood, the DNA. If the quality of the race is bad, we will have a conflictive society" (January 10, 2006).

People in Millali use blood and acquired kinship to define the categories of Mapuche, *wingka*, and *champuria*, as illustrated in Amelia Ancao's narrative about her grandmother Mercedes Rain Millañir: "My grandmother was a *wingka* captive. The Millañir and the Rain scraped her tongue and took the skin off the palms of her feet and hands and buried it so that she would not escape and so that she would learn to speak Mapudungun. They gave her a Mapuche name, she learned Mapudungun, wore a Mapuche *ükülla* [shawl], and she had six children with her husband. She became Mapuche." But on her deathbed, the importance of patrilineal blood ties reemerged: "Mercedes couldn't find her final rest among Mapuche because she was *wingka*. She agonized for many years. They had to go and get the priest on horseback to bless her before she could die" (June 14, 2007).

Mapuche understand living people on the basis of their social relationships with kin and non-kin, spirits, and animals. This is similar to beliefs found widely in Amazonia and Melanesia. Because Amazonian, Melanesian, and Mapuche people are "chronically unstable and forever partible" (Taylor 1993:318), they live in a dynamic state of "centrifugal sociality" (Course 2011:161). They find wholeness only in relationships with others (Vilaça 2005:460), by participating in larger social aggregates (Strathern 1992:86), and by incorporating the other into their individuality. Amazonian subjects view their experiences as replicating those of people of previous generations, and they express their continuity with their predecessors by using first-person narratives to recount the experiences of their ancestors (Viveiros de Castro 1992:2, 4; Oakdale 2002:172). Mapuche take this process to an extreme: they conflate the multiple identities of prominent people of different generations to create a singular individual figure who becomes central to the telling of biographical narratives (Bacigalupo 2013). This has happened with the Schleyer family as well as with Rosa and Francisca.

Mapuche social kinship includes both maternal and paternal features but has a patrilineal bias. Because Mapuche tend to be virilocal, men spend most of their lives with the people they share *küpalme* with, while married women are separated socially and spatially from their kin. Co-resident men, unmarried women, and children who share *küpalme* are said to be of one lineage, which leads to an ethic of mutual assistance and solidarity (Bengoa 1992:141; Course 2011). Matrilateral kin relations, in contrast, are characterized by perceived difference. Mapuche believe that sorcerers are most often women who have married local men but do not share blood ties with the patrilineage; therefore, they do not belong to the local system of descent (Faron 1964; Bacigalupo 1996c). Mapuche also view *wingka* outsiders and *champuria* as possible sorcerers. These authoritative views of social kinship persist, although in practice many Mapuche marry outside the traditional matrilateral cross-cousin system and live on the land of either the husband or the wife. *Longko* Euladio Ancao referred pejoratively to a Mapuche man who was unable to procure land in his own community and instead lived on his wife's land as *anükon*, literally, "one who obtains everything sitting down."

Mapuche spiritual kinship (*küpalme püllü*)—the transmission of a shamanic spirit, its qualities, and its knowledge of the past—is highly selective and usually matrilineal, although few matrilineal descendants are chosen to be machi. Those who are chosen often receive their shamanic spirit and knowledge from a deceased maternal grandmother or great-grandmother through dreams, visions, and possession. As Juan Ñanculef explained, "A machi has knowledge about a machi ancestor who died before she was born because the spirit, the blood, passes from the maternal great-grandmother to the great-granddaughter" (January 10, 2006). Machi are expected to become initiated early in life, "when there is no doubt that they were chosen by God," said Domingo Katrikura, "not like Francisca, who was initiated when she was old" (January 6, 2006).

Machi from the same cohort also share a mutuality of being and often refer to their master machi as "mother" and their machi colleagues as "sisters." They cluster in machi schools of practice, heal each other, and share similar powers, ritual paraphernalia, healing methods, and herbal recipes. Francisca claimed that good machi like her receive shamanic powers directly through visions or during catastrophic natural events, like thunder and earthquakes, "not like in school." But since thunder shamans do not undergo training in any particular machi school of practice, their powers are unknown and ambiguous. Some are said to practice ritual revenge and are accused of sorcery (Bacigalupo 2001). Machi Francisca was not invited to perform in the collective *ngillatun* rituals of the Millañir faction in Millali because she was a *champuria* thunder shaman of ambiguous lineage and because she incorporated non-Mapuche practices, such as love magic, which some people saw as a form of sorcery.

Nevertheless, Francisca was initiated by the prestigious old machi Avelina Sandoval (mother of Jorge Sandoval, who later became *longko* of Huenchual), who had also initiated Rosa Kurin, thereby incorporating Francisca into Rosa's spiritual matrilineage. Francisca belonged to the same machi cohort as Avelina's other initiates, Angela and Lucinda, who shared person-hood with each other and supported each other throughout their lives, and to the cohort of those who inherited their spirits after death. This sister-hood perpetuated the lineage's particular form of machi practice and par-ticipated in each other's rituals, including those to renew their machi pow-ers (*ngeikurewen*), collective rituals for well-being (*ngillatun*), and funerals (*eluwün*). Francisca initiated machi Juana and included her in the sister-hood. When Juana died, her machi spirit was reborn in the body of her granddaughter Maria Cristina, who became a machi and currently heals people in the Quepe area. Angela healed Francisca twice in 1995 and per-formed a ritual at her funeral in 1996.

Francisca personified the tensions between the relationships constructed through blood ties, social kinship, and spiritual kinship. Her life story ex-emplifies the anxiety that people in Millali have about ethnic intermixing and about losing their connections with the past and their identity through *awingkamiento*, which brings individualism, stinginess, and sorcery. Her story also reflects the conflicting feelings that people in Millali have about relationships with *wingka* and with other Mapuche subgroups. Francisca's straddling of Nangche and Wenteche regional identities and the *wingka* world serves as an allegory for her community's conflicted collective history and its relationship to the official national history.

BAD BLOOD AND CONTESTED GENEALOGIES

"I suffered a lot in this community, Mamita," Francisca cried as we col-lected leaves from her *palco* and laurel trees to prepare medicine for a pa-tient. "They abhorred me because my father was a *wingka*. And my grand-mother was a sorcerer. They said I had bad blood" (December 10, 1994).

Francisca was born in 1921 into a family of uncertain standing in Millali. She lived with her mother, Juana Lefian, and her maternal grandmother, Filomena Lefian, who was considered a sorcerer because of her vengeful character and questionable morality. "Filomena would play her *kultrung* se-cretly, and nobody knew who she was praying to," Francisca remembered. "The dogs would dig at the fence when she was around because the *añchimalleñ* [evil female dwarf spirit with red painted lips] wanted to come into the house" (December 15, 1991). Her mother baptized Francisca in the Catholic faith to protect her from evil spirits, to prevent nightmares, and to ensure that she did not inherit Filomena's sorcerer spirit.

Juana Lefian was afraid of local *kalku*, who are believed to have ob-tained their powers from the ancestors. *Kalku* can intentionally direct illness and misfortune toward a victim, and they may manipulate the victim's will and actions through the use of herbs, rituals, and amoral *wekufü* spirits, which are often conceived as evil in Millali.[5] *Kalku* are believed to use ritual manipulations and their inherited powers in order to separate a person's *püllü* (spirit) from his body and transform him into a *wekufü* spirit or do him harm. Filomena was believed to make contracts with evil *wekufü* spirits, who offer wealth and prestige in exchange for Mapuche bodily substances. People claimed that she sent these evil spirit helpers to seduce her victims, attack them, and suck their blood, breath, flesh, or semen.

Francisca protected herself from accusations of sorcery and illegitimacy through her association with her prestigious maternal grandfather, Manuel Lefian, Rosa's father's cousin, who connected the community to their Patagonian past. Francisca claimed that she inherited Wenteche Patagonian shamanic powers from her maternal line because the Lefian lineage had intermarried with the Kurin (machi Rosa's lineage) in Patagonia before migrating to the Wenteche territory of Millali in 1850, after Argentina proclaimed its independence. When Rosa migrated to Millali in 1879, the Lefians raised her as their own and supported her initiation as a machi. Francisca met Rosa and claimed that the machi was her grandmother.

Francisca's father, in contrast, was a non-Mapuche adopted into the Kolipi lineage from the enemy Nangche faction and had no connection with Millali's past. He was the biological child of a *wingka* man named Esteban Aravena and a *wingka* woman, who gave the baby to Numaihual Liña, the Mapuche widow of Juan Kolipi, who had settled in Millali in 1883 after the last battle between the Mapuche and the Chileans. After Juan died, Numaihual continued to live on his lands in Millali and raised Juancito as her son because she wanted a man to inherit the Kolipi name and lands. But even though Juancito Kolipi was adopted by the Kolipi family and raised in Millali, which made him Mapuche through social kinship ties, people in the community rejected him and his daughter because they were without Mapuche patrilineal blood ties and were *awingkados* from the suspect Nangche group. The Kolipi family sided with other Mapuche in the pan-Mapuche insurrection of 1881, and several Kolipi family members were executed by the Chilean army.[6] But many people in Millali viewed the Kolipi family as traitorous *awingkados* because they had a close relationship with the Chilean army, sought to integrate into Chilean society, and obtained the best lands from the government.[7] People in Millali also resented Juancito Kolipi for inheriting more land than anyone else under the Law of Indigenous Settlement. They described him as a selfish *wingka* who privileged his individual interests instead of redistributing his wealth to ensure equality among community members. Even the Chilean land surveyor questioned his ethnicity. Francisca described him as saying:

> "It seems that he's not your son, grandma, he is so white." And Numaihual responded, "Yes, he is my son. I birthed him." And then the land surveyor gave Juancito about eight hectares on the map. A lot. The community was angry. "Why did that *wingka* [Juancito] come here? Let's get him out," they said. And they made up lies about him. . . . He worked hard selling coal and wood. But they said he stole animals. . . . My father [Juancito] was sad. He told me, "Just as they abhor me, they will do the same to you." He left to Patagonia on horseback and never returned. I was twelve years old. (November 7, 1991)

Francisca grew up without a father and described her childhood with her sister, María, as one of suffering:

> We lived in a *ruka*, a house of straw. We were very poor; . . . we had lice. We only ate *pisku* [beans], eggs from the chicken run. We got a handful of flour for the day. . . . My mother made *lamas* [rugs] to sell and feed us. But we didn't even have a blanket. I left early in the morning and arrived late at night, watching the animals outside every day. . . . I had no shoes, no dress; . . . my heels were split. . . . When the animals shit, I would put my feet in it to get warm. I wore my mother's shawl when it rained. I got all wet. . . . If I lost an animal or a dog hurt it, she would beat me. . . . I went barefoot to the school on the Manzanar farm. The teacher punished me because I couldn't read, but she also took pity on me; she gave me clothes and shoes. (December 15, 1991)

When Francisca was seventeen years old, her mother and sister died, which she believed was the result of sorcery. According to Mapuche logic, neighbors or family members can hire a *kalku* to do a *trabajo* (sorcery job) to harm those with whom they have conflicts over money, land, belongings, or social obligations. Mapuche themselves can send sorcery, illness, or death to their enemies by linking anything that contains the essence, image, or bodily fragments of a person with an evil spirit, a dead person, or the underworld. Francisca believed that the Millañir had poisoned her mother and sister by tainting their food with a substance called *fuñapuwe*, which is composed of nails, hair, lizards, frogs, worms, earth from a cemetery, poisonous herbs, or parts of decomposing animals. She also believed that they had used *üñfitun*, whereby a victim's hair, nails, clothing, photograph, land, or belongings are contaminated by sorcery-laden substances. "They buried a big evil by our house, a dead dog. My mother dug it out and burned it. Then the neighbors put *fiñapuwe* in some bread they gave to my sister, María, [and] she died. My mother picked up some hexed coins and she died too. They were killed because the Millañir hated my father. They also hexed the scraping they took from my footprints [*pünon namun*]. That's why my feet swell and hurt" (January 24, 1992).

Francisca inherited her father's lands, which again provoked anger in the community because she had no blood ties to the Kolipi patrilineage. One woman said to me, "Francisca got all the best land because she is a *wingka* and a Kolipi with connections with the government. She benefited from both sides" (June 13, 2007). Shortly after receiving the land, Francisca severed her relationship with the Kolipi lineage and married José (Pancho) Calfuñir from the Wenteche faction. José Pancho paid Francisca's mother two horses, three sheep, and some money to marry her. Following Mapuche virilocal norms, she and her husband lived with the prestigious Calfuñir family. The Calfuñir were allies of the Huenchuñir, also from the Wenteche faction, and the family into which Rosa Kurin had married. Francisca hoped that this marriage would lead the community to accept her, granting her the same legitimacy that Rosa had and linking their life stories and subjectivities.

Francisca had three children with José Pancho—Francisco, Marta, and Aurora—and another daughter, Orfelina, with Froilan Huenchuñir, the grandson of machi Rosa and Colonel Urrutia. By then, however, the people of Millali had incorporated Christian values into their own system, and they judged Francisca's liaisons more harshly than Rosa's had been judged in her time. Neither the Calfuñir nor the Millañir attributed Francisca's conduct to foreignness. Instead, they labeled her a "dirty *champuria*" and a "*mujer de la calle*," a street woman; they considered her immoral, crazy, and lustful. Later, Alejo Huenchuñir, Froilan's son and the great-grandson of Urrutia and Rosa, married Bernardita, Francisca's granddaughter, creating further relations between the two families.

During the period of community hostility, Francisca experienced initiatory dreams about her machi animals, her ritual paraphernalia, and the future: "I would dream about a brown mare with a white star on its forehead and a plump sheep that would come to me. I dreamed about me playing the *kultrung* and the *kaskawilla*, wearing a *ükülla*. . . . I dreamed about people who were ill, about herbal remedies. I knew when my mother was going to die. I knew my in-laws were going to die" (March 20, 1992). Francisca ignored her shamanic calling, however, to raise her four children, who were born with the help of a midwife and a bottle of wine. She worked in the vegetable garden, cooked and cleaned, and wove textiles that she sold to provide for her family. Though she never went to Mass, Francisca had all her children baptized to protect them against evil and to give them godparents. She also made them all go to school to learn to read and write. Francisca put up with José Pancho's liaisons with other women because she needed him to plow the land with the help of his compadres and to earn additional money working on the Schleyer farm. But during the earthquake of 1960, Francisca could resist no longer. She was initiated as a machi suddenly at the age of thirty-nine. The community did not mythologize Francisca during her lifetime as they had machi Rosa; they could not come to a consensus about whether she had saved the world like Rosa or had caused the earthquake with her sorcery.

FACTIONAL NARRATIVES ABOUT
FRANCISCA'S CONTESTED INITIATION

The narratives about Francisca's initiatory experiences are disputed. They were created amid the internal conflicts in Millali about what it means to be Mapuche and interpreted in relation to the criteria used for choosing Mapuche political and spiritual leaders. Francisca and the prestigious Calfuñir, Lefian, and Huenchuñir families who supported her drew on the hierarchical model whereby *longko* inherited their positions. The Millañir who migrated to Millali from Maquehue, in contrast, embraced an egalitarian model whereby *longko* should be elected. But people in Millali recognized these conflicting beliefs neither as internal differences nor as aspects of struggles for power and leadership (Martínez 2009). Instead, they attributed them to sorcery. Anne-Christine Taylor (2007:146) has argued that factionalism sustained and revitalized indigenous identities and cultures, rather than making indigenous people more vulnerable to greedy colonists who wanted their land or labor, as is often assumed. But this revitalization was not without substantial internal complexity. Factional narratives about Francisca's initiation affected her experiences in the community, her power, her ability to tell stories, and the way others made meaning out of her experiences. The complex interactions between subject, experience, and the narratives central to a spiritual practitioner played out in a larger community context.[8]

According to members of the Calfuñir and Huenchuñir families, Rosa Kurin's powers as a wild Wenteche Patagonian thunder machi and her fiery temper reemerged in Francisca. Since Francisca's grandfather was Rosa's cousin, the families believed that Francisca had inherited Rosa's shamanic powers and that she had acquired them when she was possessed by Rosa's spirit during the earthquake of 1960. The Calfuñir-Huenchuñir faction associated Rosa and Francisca with the salvatory Trengtreng serpent. They believed that Francisca had saved the community from earthquake and flood, as Rosa had done thirty years earlier. Alejandro Huenchuñir explained, "At the beginning she didn't want to play her *kultrung* in the ritual field, but the chief begged her. She was possessed all the time and finished her ritual like thunder. Then the trembling [of the earth] stopped." The same bull (representing both conflict and wild powers) that had appeared to Rosa Kurin in a vision now appeared to the whole community in front of Francisca's house. "There was thunder and lightning, and then a bull came from the clouds above with a huge bell around its neck. It didn't step on the earth and filled the earth with stars" (June 16, 2007). To confirm Francisca's new status, Virginia Manquein, Rosa's daughter-in-law (married to Juan Benito Huenchuñir), gave Francisca traditional Mapuche women's attire: a *chamall* (black woolen wrap) and a *ükülla* (woolen shawl). Francisca's uncle made her a *kultrung*. He also carved her *rewe*. The Calfuñir and Huenchuñir families legitimated Francisca as a conservative Catholic woman who played a pivotal role in the community and asked her to perform in their collective *ngillatun* rituals to petition for fertility and the well-being of the community.

The Millañir faction did not recognize Rosa's spirit in Francisca. They argued that the separate field in which they prayed was the "true" ritual field because animals came to it of their own accord during the earthquake, kneeled at the collective *ngillatuwe* (cosmic tree of life), and bellowed. The Millañir held that Francisca's initiation was nothing more than a cautionary tale of factionalism, sorcery, and the perils of ethnic intermixing. Whereas Rosa was initiated when she was twelve and was therefore a legitimate machi, Francisca was thirty-nine, too old to become a machi. Members of the faction claimed that Francisca was selfish and did not defend the community against chaos and destruction like Rosa did, but in fact brought chaos and conflict to the community by embodying the spirit of her sorcerer grandmother (Filomena Lefian) and traitorous mestizo father (Juancito Kolipi). They associated Francisca with the punishing dimension of the Trengtreng serpent, claimed she had caused the earthquake of 1960, and viewed her uncontrolled trances as a sign of sorcery. In contrast, they associated machi Rosa with the salvationist dimension of Trengtreng.

The Millañir believed that Francisca had inherited the powers of sorcery matrilineally through her grandmother Filomena and that this blood tie superseded any shamanic power she claimed to have acquired as an adult from her spiritual relationship with machi Rosa. They also considered her to be a powerful *wingka* sorcerer. Some people in Millali claimed that Francisca killed her enemies with sorcery for personal gain. Unlike Rosa, Francisca did not have the socioeconomic status that comes with blue eyes, red hair, and noble Mapuche and German origins. Francisca's genealogy evoked painful memories of the time when Nangche, allied with the Chilean government, fought Wenteche and when Mapuche communities were torn apart by the conflicting values of their members. The Millañir faction used Francisca as a scapegoat for their anger and humiliation at having been dispossessed of their land and having to work as wage laborers for Germans and Chileans on land that had previously been theirs. Filomena Katrikura recalled the hostility: "'Go to your own cross,' they said. 'Do *küymi* [trance] at your own cross. You do not belong here. Leave!' they said, and chased her away with sticks" (June 15, 2007). Juan Millañir Lefian, who was from Rosa's Lefian lineage but from the Millañir faction, wanted to become a machi himself and displace Francisca, but his powers were weak, and he did not have enough of a following.

Despite all this, Francisca remained in the community and tried to restore her legitimacy by claiming that she had inherited the shamanic powers of the prestigious machi Rosa Kurin. Shamans who engage in the "traditionalization of shamanic subjectivity" (Oakdale 2005:79, 167) to gain regenerative powers often actively establish their authority by linking themselves to a prestigious past (Bauman 2004:150–152). By claiming that she was "like Rosa," Francisca appropriated the special powers of the mixed-race machi of earlier times. Francisca's efforts to align her mestiza identity with Rosa's were often futile, however. People in Millali had celebrated Rosa's mixed ethnicity, which placed her in a condition of alterity and increased power during the nineteenth-century process of colonization. But attitudes toward *mestizaje* had changed radically with the influx of European and Chilean settlers who took over Mapuche land and as Mapuche engaged in cultural and ethnic intermixing (Bacigalupo 2013). Many people in Millali viewed Francisca's engagements with difference as contrary to Mapuche social and moral norms because they believed she was more interested in her own well-being than that of the collective.

In contrast, the Calfuñir-Huenchuñir faction used relational and blood criteria to support Francisca as both a Mapuche and a *champuria* machi. Filomena Katrikura said, "*Champuria* machi like Francisca have just as much strength as Mapuche machi, because even those who have one drop of Mapuche blood can be machi all the same. Francisca sang everything in Mapudungun. She was raised in this community, so she was Mapuche" (December 13, 2005). Euladio Ancao said that Francisca thought like other Mapuche because she had Mapuche blood: "Francisca and we are of the same Mapuche blood. If we were *champuria*, we would be different in our thinking" (December 14, 2005). Alberto Huenchuñir argued, however, that Francisca's character was different because she was of mixed ethnicity: "Francisca was bad-tempered, nervous, because she was *champuria*" (June 16, 2007).

Despite the Millañir hostility, Francisca gained power as a healer of the body politic as she officiated in the Calfuñir-Huenchuñir *ngillatun* rituals between 1960 and 1982, until Julio Calfuñir became an evangelical Christian, refused to continue practicing Mapuche rituals, and uprooted the *ngillatuwe*.[9] Francisca was devastated: "I saved the community at that *ngillatuwe*. Now they hit that stick [uprooted the *ngillatuwe*]. I am ill" (May 9, 1995). The purpose of the *ngillatun* is to integrate the ritual community through sacrifice and to reinforce the reciprocal relationship with ancestral spirits and the deity Ngünechen.[10] *Ngillatun* also help Mapuche ward off diseases, natural disasters, sorcery, and conflicts with forestry companies and the government. Francisca believed that if the Calfuñir-Huenchuñir faction did not perform *ngillatun*, Ngünechen would punish them all with drought, scarcity, and poverty.

After Julio's conversion, Francisca dreamed that she should have her own *ngillatun* field: "I had a beautiful *milla lelfün* [shining flatlands] and a *ngillatuwe* in the middle, with the face and arms of Ngünechen painted in blue, where I prayed" (May 9, 1995). She created this *ngillatun* field next to her house, where she planted branches of *foye*, *triwe*, *boldo*, and *külon*. The *ngillatuwe* served as an *axis mundi* that connected the different worlds of the Mapuche cosmos to those who participated in the ritual and protected them from natural catastrophes, illnesses, infertility, and evil. Francisca's *ngillatuwe* faced east. "It looks at Patagonia," she told me.

Francisca began performing *ngillatun* rituals for the Calfuñir-Huenchuñir families in her own field in 1984. She combined them with *pürun* rituals to renew her machi powers because she did not have the resources to hold separate rituals. Francisca had few followers, however, because of her controversial reputation. Several families began to participate in the competing *ngillatun* rituals held by the Millañir group. Francisca performed her last *ngillatun* ritual for the Calfuñir-Huenchuñir families in 1990. Evil *cherufe* (fireballs) and a *witranalwe* (cowboy spirit) were reported in Millali; some people attributed them to Francisca's sorcery, while others blamed Segundo Millañir. Francisca dreamed that the community's *ngillatuwe* should be moved back to its old location and that all members should participate, but the community ignored her. In 2009, long after Francisca's death, Julio's nephew Osvaldo Calfuñir planted the old *ngillatuwe* next to his house, painted it, and put a helmet over its head. Some people in Millali believe that Ngünechen and Francisca's spirit are both angry with Osvaldo for this transgression and will make him crazy, poor, and sick.

HEALING OR CANNIBALIZING KIN?

Ancient machi, you know that sometimes they speak badly about us and call us sorcerers. It is true that we know the effects that plants produce and that we can manipulate them to do good. Although on some occasions we do the contrary. . . . Ngünechen made machi as well as kalku, *because there has to be good and bad powers in the world. Some make the family and heal. Others swallow the blood of their own family. Then there is no* kimün *[wisdom and morality derived from the old times]; people fight, they behave badly. They fail and there is no future.*

—FRANCISCA KOLIPI, PRAYER, MARCH 12, 1995

Although machi and sorcerers are not entirely different from each other, their relationships to kinship, temporality, and knowledge of the old times are antithetical. Machi and *kalku* both share in the life essences of animals, natural phenomena, and spirits, which they manipulate to direct the flow of energy between different worlds and to balance the conflicting forces of the universe. But machi divine the past, heal the present, and ensure a better future for the collective through the creation of historical continuity. *Kalku*, in contrast, cannibalize or consume the life force of their own kin and destroy Mapuche history, morality, and the social relations of the lineage for their own individual gain. *Kalku* introduce mental, spiritual, and physiological illnesses into bodies, both corporeal and political, instead of extirpating evil, as machi do. But since machi are multiple beings, they are always ambiguous. Like those of Amazonian shamans (Fausto 2002:121), machi's intentions are never theirs exclusively; nor can machi ever be certain of their own intentions. Shamanism and sorcery are part of a single epistemology, a theory of knowledge about the role of temporality in the making of the world and a set of analytical tools Mapuche use to make sense of their suffering and their complex relations with a multiplicity of others over time.

Mapuche sometimes imagine sorcerers, who are selfish and individualistic, as women and men who have turned against their kin or in-laws. Some people in Millali imagined Francisca to be a *kalku* who had obtained her powers of sorcery from her maternal grandmother, and whether she belonged to the local system of descent or had married into it, she was seen not as an outsider but as someone who could destroy communal solidarity from within. Accusations of sorcery flare up most often around people like Francisca who share both responsibilities and conflicts over communal obligations or property. That is, local sorcerers attack people and households for specific reasons that would not interest *wingka* or Mapuche from other ritual congregations (Bacigalupo 2007:37).

At other times Mapuche associate sorcery with the differences in prestige and wealth created by people's relationships with the *wingka* world. Since sorcery is a kind of negative kinship, many Mapuche today imagine *wingka* (outsiders by definition), as well as those who come from outside the lineage and act like *wingka*, to be the most powerful sorcerers. *Wingka* are imagined as sorcerers also because they effectively manipulate the powers of modernization, colonialism, and government—including the military and the law—for their own benefit. *Wingka* are wealthier than Mapuche and higher in socioeconomic status, and they are perceived as valuing individual gain over knowledge of the past and communal well-being—which is also proof of their sorcery. Mapuche who seem to ally with the forces of modernization may also be seen as having succumbed to *awingkamiento* and, by extension, as having become sorcerers. The social disruption caused by the loss of native land, impoverishment, and the necessity of wage labor has intensified the frequency of accusations of sorcery linked to *awingkamiento*, which is often cited as the root of illness, alienation, and evil.

Some people in Millali imagined Francisca to be an *awingkada* sorcerer. Because Francisca was a *champuria* woman with a Mapuche mother, a *wingka* father, and a maternal grandmother who was a sorcerer, yet also was a powerful thunder machi who had both blood and spiritual kinship with machi Rosa and Filomena, she and the legitimacy of her power were hotly debated in the community. She simultaneously embodied and was opposed to each of her identities. But Mapuche identify contextually and relationally,[11] and Mapuche identity categories that appear fixed are really in constant flux.[12] People in Millali expressed their ambivalence about Francisca's identities and power through factional conflicts over Mapuche egalitarian ideologies and hierarchical ideologies as they, along with Francisca herself, constructed various narratives about what it means to be Mapuche. Some focused on the collective good while others focused on the well-being of the families who had inherited positions of political and spiritual power. And Francisca's endorsement and transgression of social norms, her multiple alliances, and her shamanic practices at times reinforced and at times challenged both sets of narratives.

The pungent smell of boiling herbs rose from the pot in which Francisca was making medicine for a patient suffering from stomach pain, dizziness, and bad luck, a result of becoming *awingkado*. Francisca would invoke spirits and Ngünechen to heal her patients, sometimes at no cost, for the collective good. "Even if I am making my best soup, if a patient comes, I have to tend to them," Francisca said. "Even if they have no money, I must heal them. Ngünechen told me this in dreams" (January 15, 1992). Francisca, like other machi, held spiritual, moral, and judiciary authority in the community, and to the extent that shamans represent the forces of good and control the forces of evil on behalf of the ritual community, they play a political role (Dillehay 1985). Sometimes, however, Francisca transgressed social norms by seeking personal gain and promoting inequality: "I am a machi. I don't ask permission from anyone. Only Ngünechen bosses me. All I have earned has been from the sweat of my brow, Mamita. Before, I was very poor. I sold wood, coal, and textiles. Now, I heal patients, and that money is not for others to go spending" (May 7, 1992).

The fine line between shamanism and sorcery is always shifting. Francisca could not help other people and advance the collective interest unless she had power, and she only gained power if the spirits and their ritual congregation recognized her as a legitimate machi. As Steven Rubenstein (2002:243) points out, in this context it is impossible to distinguish between helping oneself and helping others, especially since shamans need recognition in order to acquire audiences and patients (Atkinson 1989; Tsing 1993; Steedly 1993). In order to heal, machi must promote themselves, which gains them individual prestige and wealth, but then they must give some of this wealth to the community and help those in need to gain further prestige. What distinguishes shamanism from sorcery is the way machi balance their call to help others with their desire for power and money. Those who are too selfless lose power, and those who are too selfish are accused of being sorcerers.

To defend their authority as powerful but selfless champions of health, life, and fertility, machi combat the forces of death and sorcery in *datun* healing rituals. Yet rituals themselves are ambiguous and can be defined as healing or hexing depending on the positionality of the observer. In order to heal someone who is sick, a machi needs to exorcise the evil spirit (presumably summoned by an evildoer) that attacked the sick person and send it back to the place it came from. But the evil spirit may go back and harm an innocent family member of the evildoer, in which case the machi who returned the evil to the place it came from has become a sorcerer.

Capitalist consumption and individual success, prestige, and wealth are simultaneously desired by machi and criticized as antithetical to spirituality, morality, and community values, such as egalitarianism and the common good (Bacigalupo 2005). Mapuche believe that shamans' powers decreased substantially after colonization as new positions of secular authority were introduced. Shamans became increasingly individualistic and less interested in the collective good, and accusations of sorcery aligned with the fractures that developed within the community as people took different positions on modernization, capitalism, and foreign influence. Francisca exemplified this belief: she did not have the same kind of power to heal and divine that Rosa Kurin did, and she did not perform *ngillatun* rituals for the entire community. Like shamans in Argentina (Gordillo 2003:119), Francisca increasingly used her skills for her own material advantage and used community conflicts to promote her power and dominate others.

The ideals of egalitarianism and social participation proposed by socialist president Salvador Allende (1970–1973) contributed to the increasing democratization of power in Millali and the loss of traditional Mapuche hierarchical sociopolitical and spiritual models. The Calfuñir, Lefian, and Huenchuñir families claimed that Allende was promoting sorcery via *awingkamiento*. The Millañir family, on the other hand, argued that egalitarianism and social participation were Mapuche ethnic values unrelated to Allende's socialism and agrarian reform. In their opinion, sorcery via *awingkamiento* was linked to the hierarchical models followed by the Calfuñir, Lefian, and Huenchuñir families, and to authoritarian leaders, capitalist settlers, and Francisca's own unruly behavior. In their view, these hierarchical models promoted the same kind of political and economic inequalities prevalent under colonialism and perpetuated by settlers. Both factions agreed that machi were chosen by spirits, not humans, but they disagreed on how to distinguish legitimate Mapuche machi from *awingkado* sorcerers, including integrationists, socialists, despots, and individualistic capitalists. Francisca's power and practices, as well as their meanings, were transformed through the conflicts over these different egalitarian and hierarchical ideologies.

Since Francisca had married into the prestigious Calfuñir family, she endorsed the Mapuche sociopolitical hierarchies that favored prestigious families over the Mapuche egalitarian principles that collective interests should predominate over individual interests and that those who have more must share their wealth. She became openly anti-egalitarian, sought individual gain, and tried to control others, including the Millañir family, which she opposed. Francisca's disdain for Segundo Millañir, the community head, political leader, and ritual orator, gained her the enmity of many people in the Millañir lineage. She challenged his authority by performing competing *ngillatun* fertility rituals with her allies from the Calfuñir-Huenchuñir-Lefian faction. According to Eduardo Añiwal, "Segundo and Francisca were armed with salt and flour and dead animals to throw sorcery in each other's land. 'Take your salt, take your devil,' they would say" (December 22, 2005).

The Millañir family challenged the hereditary leadership of the Calfuñir faction and the authority Francisca claimed as a machi. They read Francisca's support of Mapuche hierarchical models through the idioms of sorcery and capitalism, and they claimed that Francisca was an individualistic *awingkada* because she did not redistribute her wealth to the community. They believed that she made contracts with evil *añchimalleñ* and *witranalwe* spirits to become wealthy in exchange for her kin's blood, and some held Francisca responsible for the deaths of her husband, her son, and three of her grandchildren (Bacigalupo 2010). Francisca, in turn, argued that the members of the Millañir family envied her power and wealth. Moreover, she said that they endorsed the egalitarian principles because they had been influenced by secular, socialist, class-based *wingka* ideals, which would destroy Mapuche ethnic identity, shamanic power, and the land inhabited by the spirits.

Some community members endorsed "shamanic forms of social punishment" (Gordillo 2003:120) and used sorcery to neutralize the material resources of better-off Mapuche. According to Francisca, the Millañir family was jealous of the Calfuñir family's power and wealth and performed *üñfitun* sorcery:

> When someone has animals and things [like the Calfuñir], "Look, he is rich," they say. "He has everything. He has money." Then they are envious. "The *witranalwe* watches over his animals," they claimed. . . . They were jealous and did sorcery to him and his family. . . . They cut the ears and tail of the animals and took their hair to hex them, and the animals blew up, the bile swelled, and [they] died. . . . That year a cow and an ox died. My mother-in-law cried. . . . They buried a dead buzzard and a dead snake so that my in-laws and husband would die. . . . They buried a dog's leg so that I would be poor like a dog. My spirit protects me, though. (December 15, 1991)

In 1974 Francisca's husband, José Pancho, became very ill. Francisca gave him herbal remedies and performed *datun* healing rituals for him, but he did not recover. Francisca said she could not cure him because "God does not like the smell of husband and wife together." She took him from one machi to another to try to cure him, but he died later that year. Francisca had sold all her animals to pay for his healing, which left her destitute. Although General Augusto Pinochet had seized the presidency in a military coup in 1973, Francisca blamed the socialist government for not offering her aid: "When my husband died, I was so poor. I didn't have kerosene, I didn't have shoes, I had no animals. . . . The socialists said, 'Everyone is equal. We take care of the poor,' but when I was so poor and so hungry, they gave me nothing. They are liars, sorcerers" (February 2, 1992).

To people in the community, Francisca's poverty and the death of her husband showed that her powers of healing were reduced and that she, too, was vulnerable to sickness and death and no longer superior to others. The community concluded that machi in general were less powerful and more like *awingkados*: selfish and vulnerable to sorcery. By punishing Francisca (as she described it) for transgressing social norms and for not prioritizing collective interests, Mapuche redefined their identity and ideas about acceptable forms of power, rejecting both socialist, class-based ideologies (in which neither spirituality nor ethnicity are important) and authoritarian types of power.

Francisca then redefined her healing practices as being for the collective good and against authoritarian, capitalistic machi. She became skeptical and bitter about other machi, whom she now viewed as individualistic sorcerers interested only in their personal wealth: "Machi deceived me, they are swindlers. They just grabbed the money. That's why I don't like them. Even if I am dying, I'm not going to get a machi to do a *datun*. . . . 'Yes, he [José Pancho] will get better,' they say. Pure lies. . . . Then I had a dream where a tall man on a horse [the *witranalwe*] came and told me that he would die" (February 2, 1992). By viewing machi in this negative way, Francisca placed herself on an equal level within the community. She also critiqued her own behavior and reflected on her own inability to heal: "I must charge less [for healing rituals]. Ngünechen is punishing me. He breaks the force of my right arm. My bones, my blood, become weak and I cannot heal."

The mutually constitutive relationship between Francisca's physical body and Millali's social body is evident: Francisca's physical ailments represented her transgressions as well as Millali's factional conflicts, and her healing ability was contingent on her working for the collective good and following egalitarian social norms. In addition, Millali's social body was at war with itself, conflicted and disrupted by socialist and authoritarian ideologies. The distraught social body of Millali could only heal through transformation. Francisca and the Calfuñir family had to see the value of the collective good, and Millali had to redefine its Mapuche identity in egalitarian, ethnic, and spiritual terms against authoritarianism, individualism, and secular, capitalistic ideas.[13]

When people like Francisca are construed as sorcerers and are feared, they become sorcerers in a social and political sense, regardless of their practices. Sorcery has physical, emotional, and spiritual effects on people, and as Adam Ashforth (2000:247) has noted with reference to Sowetans in South Africa, "The sorcerer's power works on and through that fear of the sorcerer." In April 1995, machi Angela chuckled as she reported that she had healed machi Francisca and machi Genaro, who had been labeled dangerous sorcerers: "Now I have healed two *brujos* [sorcerers]."

"If they are *brujos*," I asked, "why did you heal them?"

She replied, "People say they are *brujos*. But they don't know their real self. Really, they are good people."

FRANCISCA'S MULTITEMPORAL DREAMS
OF MACHI RITUAL OBJECTS

For ordinary Mapuche, dreams relay messages about the future and knowledge about the spiritual world. People sometimes interpret dreams literally. At other times they believe the meaning is the inverse of the dream (Degarrod 1990:183, 1998:702). But machi dreams are almost always interpreted literally and are believed to reflect the individual morality of the machi. Francisca insisted that she had Catholic morality because through her dreams she incorporated the symbols of Catholicism into her spiritual practice, transforming and resignifying them in the process. She dreamed that the Virgin Mary, the moon, and Jesus were inextricably linked and gave her the ability to enhance abundance, fertility, and well-being for her patients:

> In a dream, a nun gave me the Virgin . . . so that the devil will not step on me. . . . I saw the moon has two people, man and woman. In the full moon I saw Jesus Christ, our savior. The new moon is the woman, the Virgin. It has sheep, pigs, horses, beans in it. The moon gave me power, voice. The moon is life. It makes people pregnant and defends people. The good people, when they die, they go to the moon. (February 1, 1992)

Like other multidimensional aspects of shamanic practice and community life, machi dreams are multitemporal experiences of the past, present, and future. They grant spiritual power and reveal the medicinal and spiritual qualities of herbs and the powers of ritual objects, which will allow the dreamers to become successful shamans or sorcerers. Ritual objects—a drum (*kultrung*), a step-notched *axis mundi* (*rewe*), sleigh bells (*kaskawilla*), herbal remedies—are "subjective objects" (Santos-Granero 2009c:9), and they become agents as they are inhabited alternately by the machi's personal spirit, by the generic *filew* spirits, and by Ngünechen. These machi objects also synthesize the Mapuche cosmos in their temporal and spatial dimensions.

Francisca dreamed she played the *kultrung* and *kaskawilla*; she heard advice from the old times and learned about the herbal remedies for different kinds of ailments, which "fell into her apron" from the sky. Francisca shouted four times into her unfinished drum to place her spirit in it. Inside it she also placed pairs and double pairs of corn kernels, seeds, charcoal, *llangkatu* (precious stones), and old coins before her husband covered the drum with the skin and tied it together with horsehair. From then on her drum was an object animated by her power and imbued with the history of her spirit. By playing her *kultrung*, Francisca entered into *küymi*, and her spirit was able to travel to other geographic locations and spiritual worlds. She said, "Ngünechen and two machi help[ed] me and gave me my loud *kultrung* that I love so much. . . . I play my *kultrung* so that we will do well on our path" (January 27, 1992). Francisca associated her rhythmic beating of the *kultrung* with the galloping of her spirit horse to other worlds and times. The drumming allowed Francisca's thunder machi spirit and Ngünechen to speak and give her knowledge and advice.

Machi Avelina, Angela, and Lucinda, from the same school of machi practice as Francisca, used blue and white paint (the colors of the moon, the Virgin Mary, and the sky, associated with good, purity, and creation, and inhabited by deities, by ancestral spirits, and by the sun, moon, and stars) to draw crosses on their drums, dividing the surface into quarters to represent the *meli witran mapu*, the fourfold division of the world to which a machi's spirit travels. In each quarter they painted stars and moons and associated them with fertility, healing, and the Virgin Mary. The quarters also represent the four corners of the Mapuche earth (*mapu*)—the everyday dimension where the Mapuche live and work, where the struggle between good and evil, life and death, health and illness takes place (Bacigalupo 2001; Dillehay 1990:89; Grebe, Pacheco, and Segura 1972; Marileo 1995). The *mapu* is populated by people, animals, and various *ngen* and associated with the colors of nature: blood red and green. The quarters of the *kultrung* also represent the four seasons, the four winds, the four celestial bodies (Grebe 1973), and the four principles of Ngünechen.

The center of the cross represents the middle of the earth, the place where the Mapuche locate themselves and their *ngillatuwe*, or collective altar (Marileo 1995:93–102). The center is also where the machi's *rewe* is located—representing both the center of the earth and the place where different worlds meet and communicate. The space above the *kultrung* represents the Wenu Mapu (upper skies); below is the Miñche Mapu (underworld), which is associated with the colors bright red and opaque black, and with cemeteries, whirlwinds, evil spirits, death, destruction, and pollution. A machi's spirit also travels there (Bacigalupo 2007:51–52). Francisca saw her *kultrung* as a model for the Mapuche cosmos and her spirit as traveling both horizontally and vertically through time and space, but she did not paint her drum because the powers she obtained directly from thunder and earthquakes were mobile and ubiquitous, and she believed that the lines constrained them.

Francisca dreamed that she befriended Rosa's *tralkan kura* (thunder stone), which had an autonomous soul that could not be controlled or tamed. This stone told Francisca that it would appear to her and that she should rub it on the faces of her patients who had become disfigured following a stroke. Shortly after that dream, a thunder stone appeared in her yard, and Francisca linked it to volcanoes, earthquakes, and the primordial time of cosmic destruction and reordering:

In my dream, they told me that people from old times live in the volcano. Mapuche go by the volcano to look for stones to be powerful and rich. If they are worthy, the stone reveals itself to them. If not, the volcano eats them. I have a *tralkan kura* that comes from the volcano. It is small and black, and it doesn't move. The ones that move, those are *kalku*. . . . My *tralkan kura* helps me control the lightning and the waters. . . . The stone can heal and protects from evil spirits. It cures people when their faces are twisted [because of a stroke]. . . . When people are bad, the volcano becomes angry and shoots out lava, and the mountains tremble. (May 24, 1995)

Like the *rewe* of most machi, Francisca's *rewe* was inhabited alternately by her personal spirit and by the generic *filew* spirit, who tied her to her husband's land and to her kin by blood and marriage. When a *rewe* becomes old and slanted, a machi usually changes it during a renewal ritual and leaves the old one to rot in a stream. Most machi have a step-notched *rewe* carved out of laurel, *pellín*, or oak, which faces east and which they climb while in an altered state of consciousness to connect the various human and spiritual worlds. Branches of the sacred plants *külon* (maqui or *Aristotelia chilensis*), *triwe* (*Laurelia sempervirens*), *foye* (*Drimys winteri*), and *rüngi* (bamboo) are tied to its side.

Francisca dreamed of a *rewe* consisting of carved wooden statues unlike any I had seen. She asked her uncle to make her *rewe* just as it appeared in her dream. None of the statues had steps, but they all had carved faces and arms "like people" painted blue, and they looked like *nguillatuwe* (*rewe* in a *ngillatun* field for collective rituals). Francisca explained the significance of her *rewe*:

> [The *rewe*] has a mouth, nose, eyes, ears, like people. . . . They tell me what to do through dreams. I dreamed that I should have a woman and two men—my *likanche* [precious people], my sergeants to defend me— that's why no machi can beat me. They live in the *rewe*. The smallest *rewe*, that is a woman. The others are men. If I only had a woman, they could trample me. . . . Ngünechen did not give me a dream of a ladder [to ascend the *rewe*] like other machi. I don't go up the *rewe* to pray. I pray from down below. I am a *pewütun* machi [omniscient machi who knows everything and can divine the future]. (February 10, 1995)

Francisca struck her *rewe* with a kitchen knife while she prayed, calling on the warring, exorcising aspects of her machi spirit. And she placed a volcanic rock—associated with masculinity and warfare—at the foot of her *rewe* to protect the *filew* against the attacks of evil spirits. She also occasionally placed flowers, food, grain, drink, and herbal remedies—associated with fertility and nurturance—at the foot of her *rewe* in order to feed the *filew* and to evoke healing. Patients sometimes tucked 5,000-peso notes into Francisca's *rewe* next to her other offerings while she prayed for them. She asked me to spit water over her head when she was entering into trance, to symbolize the rainbow (*relmu*) and her connection with the *ngen* spirits of the forest: "When the spirit comes, it gets very hot. The water refreshes the head and the spirit arrives well." To make it rain, Francisca placed a bowl of water from the stream beside her *rewe* and prayed to Ngünechen and the spirits of the sky: "I can control rain, thunder, and earthquakes," she said. "That's why I am a powerful thunder machi" (February 23, 1995).

Machi ritual objects also stood for Francisca's personal qualities and subjectivities and became extensions of her body. Francisca's objects demanded that she conform to their ritual needs. She told me, "When I am away for three or four days, my *rewe* calls me back in dreams. My *kultrung* screams that it must be played. Then my feet swell up; my head hurts. I'm dizzy. I have to come back and play my *kultrung* to feel well" (March 1, 1992). I observed this once, when Francisca and I were in Santiago performing an exorcism. She became restless and tired. Her legs swelled, her stomach hurt, and she hardly ate at all. Francisca's ritual objects—her headdress, thunder stone, ring, and this bible—link Francisca to the mobile histories of past shamans who embodied the spirit of thunder machi, to different places in Patagonia, and to the many layers of time in which this mobile spirit rode on a horse to different earthly and spiritual realms. By remembering these histories, Francisca invoked them and brought them to life in order to heal others. Francisca conceived of this bible I have written about her as another subjective ritual object that would store her power and that could be awakened by other machi, who would chant and smoke over it or dream about it.

DREAMING TO BECOME A RITUAL ASSISTANT

Francisca demanded that I learn about shamanic practice through dream experiences and illnesses and by performing as her ritual helper. She was happy to know that I dreamed about flying but disappointed that I had not dreamed about *rewe* and that I had been healed through biomedicine. Francisca concluded, "You have been healed from your illnesses, although you are still weak. You will continue to be ill. Your dreams will improve, and then you will dream about *rewe* and help me heal" (November 3, 1991).

On February 15, 1995, as Francisca prepared to visit a patient and his family in Longkofilu, she surprised me by saying, "I am going to heal them, and I need you to come as my ritual assistant." I was hesitant to accept, although I had grown close to Francisca since our first meeting in 1991. She referred to me as her granddaughter, and I often stayed at her house and traveled with her to healing rituals, where I prepared herbal remedies, shook tree branches, and played sleigh bells and rattles for her. But Francisca's granddaughter Bernardita had always been her main ritual assistant. I was afraid I might confuse the herbal remedies in the dark or fail to recognize when the skin of her drum needed to be heated over the fire to change its tonality. I wondered what the patient's family would think about having me as a ritual helper.

"What will they say if they see a *wingka* healing? What if I make mistakes?" I asked. Francisca was adamant: "I taught you many things, now you have to help me. If you do things badly, I will correct you." Referring to my mixed ethnic background and to her fictive kinship with me, she argued that I was not a *wingka*: "You are *champuria*, like me. You are my granddaughter."

Shortly afterward I had a dream in which I became Francisca's *metawe* (a ceramic vessel symbolizing the fertility of Young Woman Ngünechen, Üllcha Domo Ngünechen). I reported this dream to Francisca:

> The sound of the *kultrung* beats loudly. My heart dances to the beat of the drum. I look up and see a full moon and a *rewe* peering down at me, reaching for me with long blue arms. It rains hard, and I hear *kaskawilla* jingle as they fall from the sky. I have a body of clay. Yes, these are my thick legs. My skin is hard. It rains *muday* [a drink made from fermented maize and associated with milk or semen] from the sky. I open my big mouth and drink thirstily. Delicious *muday*, sweet and white. Shoots of many plants—*foye, triwe, quila,* and maqui—grow by the *rewe* and become trees. (February 19, 1995)

Francisca laughed and slapped her thigh. "You had a good dream," she said as she sucked her teeth. "It is good that you are a *metawe* and that they gave you *kaskawilla*. It is good that you saw the remedies growing. My spirit is happy. Now you shall come and heal with me." Francisca exhorted me not to believe in evil spirits: "You will not see *wekufü*. Then they cannot make you ill and weak. And I won't have to heal you. Your heart is strong. You will be invincible."

My role as Francisca's ritual assistant supported and complemented hers. Francisca had knowledge of the old times, whereas my vitality and fertility would enable me to put her knowledge into practice since Mapuche use *metawe* to give offerings to spirits and to Ngünechen at a machi's *rewe* or the collective *ngillatuwe*. Francisca considered my dream auspicious, a *metawe* offering to her *rewe*. Furthermore, I had bought *kaskawilla* from a Mapuche musician for Francisca, and these bells play a supporting role to the sound of the machi's *kultrung*. She handed the *kaskawilla* back to me, saying, "Now you will play this *kaskawilla* in all the places we go to heal. . . . You have learned to listen to the *kultrung*. Now, you will know when you need to heat it." For her, my dream signaled that her spirit had approved of our healing partnership. My role as Young Woman also fit Francisca's characterization of me as her granddaughter, her kin.

Together, Francisca and Bernardita had drawn a picture of Francisca's initiation for me. Now Francisca asked me to draw my dream of the *metawe* and *kaskawilla* for her, and she pinned it up in her living room as proof that I was a legitimate ritual assistant. She dreamed about *wa* (maize) and used some to make *muday*, which she poured at the base of her *rewe* before we left to go healing.

Francisca sought to legitimate her ambiguous shamanic powers and genealogies in the community and beyond by having me serve as her *cham-*

puria ritual assistant. By construing me as her Argentine granddaughter, Francisca augmented her legitimacy as a Mapuche-Patagonian shaman. By calling me a *champuria* woman who thought like a Mapuche, she defended herself against comments about her own *awingkamiento,* the implication being that she, too, thought and acted like a Mapuche. By transforming me, an anthropologist with *wingka* knowledge, into a granddaughter who gained machi knowledge as her ritual helper, she enhanced her role as a ritual expert and created spiritual kinship between us. She also stressed the advantages of being *champuria* or a "civilized Mapuche"—a person who possesses both Mapuche and *wingka* knowledges—because these allowed her to engage with many different kinds of beings in various places. As Francisca's ritual assistant, I tied the world of multitemporal dreams with real world historicity and with Francisca's biography, identity, and practice. Francisca and I would perform many healing rituals together, each of which highlighted a particular way of reshaping the past and the future.

CHAPTER FOUR

EMBODIED HISTORY: RITUALLY RESHAPING *the* PAST *and the* FUTURE

One summer night in January 1996, Francisca pulled her headscarf over her eyes and increased the tempo of her drumming as she invoked the Mapuche deity Ngünechen and the spirits of ancient shamans and chiefs. Her head rolled loosely as she entered into a trance (fig. 4.1). Serving as Francisca's assistant, I spat water over her head to enable Rosa Kurin's spirit to take hold of her body and share personhood with her.

In this state of possession, Francisca invoked past suffering and land expropriation and fused them with contemporary realities and concerns, conflating the periods of the wars between Mapuche and Spaniards (1546–1803), the battles between Mapuche and Chilean patriots (1814–1825), the appropriation of community lands by greedy *wingka* during the War of Pacification (1861–1883), the time of colonization (1884–1929), and the conflicts between Mapuche and the forestry companies, settlers, and the Chilean state (1929–present). Francisca's head bowed with the weight of the past as she spoke of the present and the future: "The ancient machi, the ancient *longko* from the earth above are speaking. . . . *Wingka* will bring more suffering for Mapuche. There will be tears, a lot of tears, a lot of sadness. There will be *malon* [raiding] and *weychan* [war]. Many spirit owners of the forests will die. There are people of another blood, of another thought—the *wingka*—who don't want our tranquility." Francisca embodied ancestral Mapuche spirits, narrated Mapuche's past suffering, and appealed to Mapuche chiefs, shamans, and warriors to defeat the evil spirits of landowners and forest loggers in the present—the sources of her patients' illnesses and of local conflicts over differences in wealth and prestige. She predicted that if Mapuche enacted their communal ideals of egalitarianism and solidarity, a new world order dominated by Mapuche would ensue.

The past is never dead (Sartre 2004 [1940]); rather, it is contained by, reshaped by, and ultimately fused with the present (Benjamin 1999:462;

FIGURE 4.1
Possessed machi with headscarves over their eyes, necklaces of
kopiwe *flowers, and shawls (photo by author).*

Lambek 2003:12; Shaw 2002:265). Those who have deep knowledge about the origins of things and of their futures have the power to mix past and future events and invent "today time" in their narratives (Overing 1990:611). Francisca drew from the "before time," the past, and the future in order to gain control of the present and create a new world. Spiritual practitioners around the world produce history by embodying and reviving beings from different historical periods in the present.[1] But machi are unique in that they both embody and collapse these temporalities—experiencing multiple times at once—in order to transform the future.

On October 27, 2007, Yolanda Nahuelcheo, the Mapuche coordinator of the National Ministry of Health in Araucanía, hired machi Ana and María to perform a blessing at an intercultural health meeting at the Rotonda de Curacautin. Historically, Curacautin (Gathering Stone) was a Mapuche road that crossed the Andes and was used by natives on both sides. In 1882 Chilean colonel Gregorio Urrutia fought and defeated Mapuche in this area, incorporated it into the Chilean state, and founded the fort and town of Curacautin. The spirits of *wingka*, Mapuche, and machi killed at this location in 1882 interrupted the blessing of 2007 and possessed the bodies of the two machi, linking their contemporary experiences with colonial memories and local forms of historical imagination.[2] Yolanda explained:

The machi began the blessing. Ana felt ill. She was attacked by evil *wingka* spirits. Her body felt cold, languid, and [she] had to lie down before leaving the site. The power of the place was too much for her. Her spirit was not compatible with the *wingka* spirits there. She confronted them and resisted that moment. María entered into trance and her *filew* [shamanic spirit] contacted the spirits of the Mapuche who died in a massacre there, including several machi. The spirits told her that this was the place where the last confrontation with the *wingka* took place, that many Mapuche had died there. When people die a violent death, their *püllü* remain as custodians of that place until someone performs a *tranatun* [ritual to send spirits to the Mapuche sky]. We were very moved; we cried. Not everyone knew how to confront it. We contacted the leaders of Lonquimay in Curacautin. They came to perform a ritual with the machi to balance out some of the damage that had been done and restore the energies of that place. . . . We sacrificed a lamb and prayed. We got branches of maqui and *triwe* trees and helped the machi. We sacrificed food and drink: *muday*, *kako*, and flour. . . . In trance María saw the image [spirit] of another machi in the sky. . . . The sound of the *kultrung* [and] the songs revived and released an entrapped machi spirit, who also went up to the sky to protect the community.

Francisca, Ana, and María embodied profoundly traumatic histories that moved the ritual participants and connected Mapuche to their past. The detailed stories they narrated were not just those of suffering spirits from Curacautin, but the collective history of loss and humiliation suffered by all Mapuche. Because machi have multiple personhoods shared with ancestor machi, spirits, animals, and forces of nature from different times and places, the stories they tell are always larger narratives about Mapuche experiences, perceptions, and morals, which resonate with the lives of the people who listen to them. Machi are masters at weaving dramatic personal histories into larger webs of meaning through deeply emotional performances that encourage people to retain a particular view of the world and that create an image of how the world ought to be.[3]

The lack of mourning rituals for the spirits in Curacautin—both the perpetrators and the victims of state violence—had kept them trapped in that place. Nobody had remembered them or ensured that they traveled to other realms through funerary rituals. The deaths of these individuals were both physical and social erasures, and their spirits emerged in the bodies of machi to tell their stories and be honored so they could be released from their suffering and merge with the ancestral spirits in another world. Like the uncontrolled Buryat spirits of the dead produced by Soviet-era purges

(Buyandelger 2013:88), the forgotten spirits of Curacautin are cultural metaphors for forced forgetting and violence. But they are also emblematic of the loss of Mapuche knowledge and ethnic identity. The merging of the spirits of the deceased with ancestral and *filew* spirits, in contrast, represents the collective ideal of Mapuche history and identity: historical continuity, cumulative knowledge, and participation in history through individual healing rituals as well as collective *ngillatun*.

The events in Millali and Curacautin point to four temporal modalities in which machi may embody, produce, and reshape interactive histories with spirits. First, the conflicted colonial past irrupted into the present via competing Mapuche and Chilean spirits. *Wingka* spirits attacked machi Ana and tried to assert their role as dominators of the Mapuche collectivity, while the spirits of deceased Mapuche voiced their suffering through machi María and demanded recognition and respect. Possessed by Rosa's spirit, Francisca narrated Mapuche suffering at the hands of colonizers throughout history.

Second, the machi in Curacautin confronted these spirits for the benefit of the contemporary Mapuche community. Machi Ana defied the *wingka* spirits: rather than let the other participants be harmed, she took on the illness until she was finally able to control the *wingka* spirits. But she did not attempt to appropriate their power to boost local autonomy from the state, because these spirits were too evil.[4] Machi María absorbed the suffering of the Mapuche spirits who narrated the tragic history of Curacautin. Francisca embodied generic Mapuche suffering in the past and mobilized Mapuche ancestral warriors' spirits to confront the present.

Third, Ana, María, and other participants restored the cosmic moral order through ritual sacrifice, appeasement, and honoring; they contained and reshaped the violence experienced by the Mapuche spirits. They erased the past of suffering, released the entrapped spirits, and restored the agency of the machi spirits. Francisca invoked the trauma of the past in order to transform it and heal patients' suffering in the present.

Fourth, the appeased machi spirits of Curacautin used their historical agency to protect the community of the living, encouraging Mapuche to salvage the best of the past, to make sense of the present, and to change the worst of the past to create a better future.

These incidents involving Francisca, Ana, and María challenge classic phenomenological approaches to shamanism in which shamans are seen as experiencing a state of being that is radically different from that of the modern Global North and its historiography. The conventional view highlights shamans' altered states of consciousness—dreams, visions, possessions, and ritual engagements with texts—as well as their ability to heal magical fright, the evil eye, soul loss, and other illnesses brought on by sorcery. Many scholars have reduced these experiences to discourses of social affliction that may then be analyzed as social texts. Yet the experiences of machi are better understood through scholarship on altered states of consciousness as sensory practices linked to alternative modes of historicization (Hirsch and Stewart 2005). In these, the past is mediated by the body of the possessed and comes into the present (Lambek 2003). Possession serves as a form of countermemory in which people embody, mimic, and mock the past (Stoller 1995), and dreams allow people to learn about new pasts and to divine the future (Stewart 2012).

The idioms of historicism of the Global North attempt to objectify the past as separate from the present.[5] Mapuche stories of past violence and the undead are expressed in a different idiom. They are not filtered through rational formulations of history as linear progress; nor are they subaltern discourses about history. Rather, they are sensory, embodied cultural memories (Stoller 1995; Connerton 1989) that "flash up in a moment of danger" (Benjamin 1969:255). They are translated through machi's bodies as gestures and movements that in turn convey and even produce history, power, and knowledge.

Dreams, visions, and ecstatic states such as possession are both perceptual and imaginative experiences. Perception—which is experienced as immediate and real—always has an imaginative dimension; it is shaped by our individual and cultural expectations. Altered states of consciousness express individual and collective imaginations that represent the habits of the past and that "offer solutions for the present, and suggestions for the future" (Stewart 2012:15). But they also do something more: they provide the sensory means by which machi and spirits transform temporality.

Since history (in the sense of the Global North) assumes that the world should be singular and unified, the metaphysics of multitemporality is often incomprehensible to scholars. Some have claimed that when the coherence of the present and the implicit links between past and present are threatened,[6] religion ensures the continued historicity of the present by momentarily dehistoricizing it through multitemporality. They argue that this stepping out of history—effected through dreaming, visions, and experiences of possession—enables a reacquisition of the present, which is then followed by a reinsertion into history (De Martinao 2012; Saunders 1995:333; Stewart 2012:214). But Mapuche do not experience multitemporality as dehistoricized. For them, multitemporality is a historical process linking the "before time" with "today time." Machi's effectiveness in ritual depends neither on their closeness to the events narrated (as in oral histories) nor on rational formulations based on archival documents and written representations (as in positivist historiography). Rather, it depends on their ability to embody and transform the suffering of the spirits from the "before time" and the historical past of "today time" in order to gain power in the present and create a better future for the collectivity.[7] By reordering the simultaneous temporalities of Mapuche cosmogony in rituals where multiple events happen at once, the machi is able to effect change in the current world—transform illness into healing—and produce a more promising future.

Anthropologists have argued that the memory of a biographical past should be kept separate from the invocation of a past of which one has no direct personal experience (Jackson 2007:81) and that histories constructed through altered states of consciousness offer historicizations rather than memories because they are elaborated from previously unknown pasts (Stewart 2012:215). The separation between the biographical past and the past of which people have no direct experience is irrelevant for machi, however. Since machi spirits are agents who travel to the "before time" and to various historical pasts in "today time," their experiences and memories of these various pasts become part of their machi biography and history. When the spirit of the thunder machi possessed Francisca, it gave her a genealogy that included thunder machi from the "before time" and the spirits of the various machi it had possessed during historical pasts, who were simultaneously part of Francisca and separate from her.

Machi's ability to embody and transform temporalities resides in history: they experience and convey the aggression and suffering of spirits from other times. But this ability also makes history: machi create collective Mapuche histories as well as their own, producing a complex layering of multiple forms of knowledge from different people and times. Spirits from different times may emerge in the bodies of humans in the present to perform history and to address current concerns. Memory can express the politics of the past as well as the ongoing struggles over ritual reformulations of history (Shaw 2002:84, 104). Francisca remembered the pasts of her thunder machi spirit, of patients, and of the Mapuche collectivity through her embodied practices. She "evoked the past, manipulated the present and provoked the future" (Stoller 1995:37). Francisca's—and, through her, Mapuche spirits'—reshaping of history during rituals provided her community with continuity and helped its members negotiate socioeconomic changes and new interethnic relations. Through possessions, visions, and dreams, Francisca connected with past shamans and locations in Patagonia and attempted to gain mastery over the indigenous and colonial past and to change the Mapuche's history—and ongoing experience—of power inequalities. The narratives about the past that emerged in rituals also became part of the community's oral history, told around the hearth in the cold of winter.

In the rest of this chapter I discuss Francisca's perception of illness and healing as the history of ethnic conflict and then analyze how her complex healing strategies were propelled by three ritual modes: divinations in which she embodied the past to see the future; sacrifices in rituals in order to effect healing in the present and construct a better future; and use of multitemporality to reshape her departure from the ideal cultural role of "machi from the past," which made her ill and required that she be healed by machi Angela.

ILLNESS AND HEALING AS THE HISTORY OF ETHNIC CONFLICT

Mapuche use the idea of illness as one major way to conceptualize the history of intra- and interethnic conflict because Mapuche factional conflicts and encounters with whites are experienced as painful, unwanted transformations causing changes in personhood that threaten ethnic identity.[8] As Anne-Christine Taylor has argued for the Ecuadorian Shuar, the suffering of bodies and the suffering of the world become interchangeable. To experience pain is to experience the world out of balance (2007:152–154). Mapuche believe that illness and chaos are created by acts of anger, greed, violence, deception, arrogance, or jealousy in primordial times, the remote past, or the recent past. But as I mentioned in chapter 2, intra- and interethnic conflicts in the present can also create illness, death, and chaos in the primordial world. A machi's diagnosis and healing are simultaneously historical explanations and unique creative acts that transform illness into health and chaos into order, and ritually remake the world, effecting changes in everyday life.[9] Since illness is carried by evil spirits whose presence is felt although they usually remain invisible, these spirits are often reshaped in the image of white outsiders and included in the Mapuche spiritual world.[10]

Mapuche also link illnesses with internal Mapuche conflicts produced by history, and they are often associated with losing the self and becoming like *wingka*. While illness can serve as a forum for articulating social conflict and lack of agency and for negotiating moral meaning, it can also provide a frame for understanding how misfortune is inherited individually and collectively. The actions of ancestors influence the lives of their descendants, and the actions of Mapuche as a collectivity affect future generations. Explaining misfortune through inter- and intraethnic conflict and inheritance can create anxiety and strain social relations. But this explanation also links it to illness, makes suffering meaningful, allows patients to cope (Kleinman 1988), and gives them a way to heal with the help of machi. Mapuche people hire machi such as Francisca to heal them from many forms of illness, both natural and spiritual in origin.

Mapuche ontological alterity is carefully articulated through historical and political processes (Bacigalupo 2001, 2004c, 2007; Briones 1998, 2007), and like other Latin American indigenous peoples, Mapuche reproduce, reconcile, unravel, and transform colonialist binaries.[11] The symbolism of *wekufü* is defined by the structure of Mapuche ontology and the way it has been transformed in a postsettler context. Mapuche construe *wekufü* both as older, ambiguous spirits who preceded colonization and represent internal conflicts, and as evil, non-Mapuche settler spirits. In Millali the following *wekufü* are conceived in both their Mapuche and settler forms: the *chonchon* (evil bird or flying *kalku*'s head), the *piwüchen* (winged serpent), the *cuero* (manta ray), *cherufe* (fireballs), *punkure* and *punfuta* (nocturnal spouses), and *kürüf* (whirlwinds that invade a person's homestead and land). *Wekufü* are amoral, numinous "non-person humans" (Course 2011) who lack the ability to engage in productive sociality, but they can be helpful and promote the collective well-being or they can be harmful and dangerous to humans (Foerster 1993:76; Kuramochi 1990:45; Schindler 1988).[12] Mapuche poet Leonel Lienlaf has described *wekufü* as balancers of forces (Sierra 1992:84–85), and Mapuche regularly make pilgrimages to the "saint stone *wekufü*" in Lumaco to ask for miracles (Schindler and Schindler-Yáñez 2006).

For Francisca—who was often the target of accusations of sorcery—illness, suffering, *awingkamiento*, and death were provoked by *wekufü* in the shape of *wingka* landowners, who suck dry Mapuche blood and identity. For her, the *witranalwe* took the form of a tall, thin, non-Mapuche cowboy mounted on a horse: an image of the typical feudal criollo settler who took Mapuche land and exploited Mapuche workers. The *witranalwe*'s wife, the *añchimallen*, is a white, luminescent dwarf with iridescent eyes who is often associated with urban models of femininity. These spirits will grant favors and wealth to their creators and will hex their enemies, but, like the devil, they require human lives in exchange. Eventually, their appetite for human lives and blood makes them turn against their owners and their families, causing the depletion of wealth, the increase of illness, and death.

In Millali, it was the actions of non-Mapuche—gringos and *wingka*—that Mapuche increasingly linked to their experiences of illness and sorcery. By equating non-Mapuche with evil, they reversed the political economy of spiritual power. In her construction of *wekufü* as evil *wingka* or gringos, Francisca actively combated settlers' power and values from within a Mapuche shamanic logic, and she was thus able to reduce internal Mapuche factionalism and accusations of sorcery. By perceiving *wekufü* spirits in the guise of wealthy non-Mapuche settlers, Mapuche effectively challenged *wingka* secularism and constructed hierarchy, wealth, and individualism as evil. But even though Francisca and other people in Millali attempted to break away from non-Mapuche values, they inevitably reproduced *wingka* systems of domination. Mapuche beliefs became twisted as *wingka wekufü* took over and became responsible for the ailments suffered by Mapuche individual bodies and social bodies. At the same time, by holding non-Mapuche *wekufü* responsible for these illnesses and for *awingkamiento*, people in Millali have been able to re-create their identity as a moral, spiritual culture. In Millali, where conflicts with outside ideologies are part of everyday life, Mapuche continue to use accusations of sorcery and *awingkamiento* as a tool to define what it means to be Mapuche and to police those who incorporate non-Mapuche ideologies.[13]

Francisca saw *awingkamiento* as decreasing her patients' faith in her healing practices, and thus increasing their risk of developing illness and alienation. She denounced *wingka* individualism, stinginess, and dishonesty as contaminating Mapuche and destroying collective well-being and local history. Francisca sometimes drew on a behaviorist definition of what it meant to be Mapuche—acting according to Mapuche norms, speaking Mapudungun, and performing rituals:

> Mapuche sons and daughters have changed a lot. They have become *awingkados*. This is not good for us. We no longer have a good heart, a good head. Everyone here thinks like *wingka* and not like Mapuche. They think they are making a prayer, and they are not doing it. They think they are sad, but they are not. It is pure lies. Everyone is faking. Everything has changed. Before, we had old people who gave good advice. Today, we no longer have those old people. Now, everyone wears pants. Men no longer use the *chiripa* [woolen breeches] as they did traditionally; women don't wear the *chamall*. Chau Díos Ngünechen gives us strength to recover what we were before. When we speak in Mapudungun, everything comes out so nicely, my heart is happy. Now, the young people don't speak Mapudungun anymore. (January 17, 1995)

Francisca advocated for the revival of older Mapuche practices, histories, rituals, spiritual systems, and ideals of collective well-being; she accused those who did not hold these values of being sorcerers and *awingkados*. Francisca was angry at the school in Chihuimpilli for punishing students who spoke Mapudungun and at parents for not teaching the language to their children. Her patients needed to know at least some Mapudungun in order to participate in her rituals. She used the terms *wingka* and *gringo* as insults to hurl at Mapuche participants who did not repeat her phrases in Mapudungun during healing rituals: "Speak, you idiots. I'm going to hit all of you. Why don't you speak? Are you gringos? What's wrong with you? You *wingka* shitasses are not helping. She [Mariella] is not Mapuche, and she is cooperating" (February 28, 1995).

In her healing rituals, Francisca used "hidden transcripts" (Scott 1990), which are less visible, more individual forms of resistance that are not necessarily part of collective indigenous struggles but have been adapted to the new historical conditions of class and ethnic confrontation.[14] Her rituals became a form of ethnic resistance to both *wingka* socialist ideas and the hierarchical right-wing ideologies of gringo settlers. During most of her career as a machi, she healed people from illnesses caused by non-Mapuche sorcery and *awingkamiento* by combating the *wingka wekufü* who had taken hold of their lives.

Francisca conducted all-night *datun* healing rituals to cure patients of a variety of sorcery-related and other kinds of illness. The healing rituals have ancient roots, but machi today heal in a holistic manner the illnesses related to the management and consequences of modernity: soul loss, evil spirit possession, spiritual punishment for transgression, stress, insomnia, alienation, depression, and bad luck. In the process, machi also legitimate Mapuche histories and political struggles for land recovery and sovereignty. Francisca prayed, gave her patients massages and enemas, performed smoke exorcisms, prescribed medicinal plants for patients to drink or use as poultices, prescribed pharmaceutical remedies, gave advice about social relationships, and showed patients how to regain control over their lives and their health by contributing to the collective good (fig. 4.2). Over the course of their healing, her patients were participating in shamanic productions of history in order to create a better future for themselves.

The most common types of *wedakutran* (negative spiritual illnesses) healed by Francisca were *wekufütun* (illness produced by an independent *wekufü* spirit) and *kalkutun* (illness provoked by a sorcerer who manipulates *wekufü* to penetrate the victim's homestead and land, jeopardize the normal functioning of the body and household, and afflict the victim's emotions and soul). *Wekufü* seduce, attack, trick, and trap the souls of living humans by lodging in their head, stomach, or chest, and they cause illness, suffering, loss of self, and death (Bacigalupo 2007:22–23). Francisca saw people with *wedakutran* as "animals whose mind has become disorganized and disoriented." Machi perceive the illness itself as frogs, insects,

FIGURE 4.2
*Francisca Kolipi prepares a poultice of herbal remedies
to rub on her patients (photo by author).*

snakes, worms, balls of coagulated blood, or feathers lodged in the victim's body. Like healers in northern Peru (Joralemon and Sharon 1993:249–250), machi speak about evil spirit possession by using metaphors of contamination and entrapment. Francisca exhorted her machi spirits to "expel the filth" and "untie the person from the *wekufü*."

Francisca also performed the *ülutun*, a diagnostic ritual without trance that includes prayers, massage, and the playing of rattles and sleigh bells. Francisca's *ülutun* allowed her to gain information about patients, their social relationships, their family's participation, and the incidents that preceded the illness in order to effect a cure. In the case of spiritual illnesses, machi must find out which *kalku*, *wekufü*, deity, or spirit is responsible; whether the illness is a positive or a negative one; and how to treat it. Positive spiritual illnesses pressure a person to become initiated as a machi or pressure machi to renew their powers. In the case of a negative spiritual illness, the machi must locate, cleanse, and then release the victim's soul; alleviate the victim's symptoms; reintegrate the victim back into everyday life; and provide a *contra*, or counterhex, as protection against future attacks.

Machi Francisca gained legitimacy and prestige for treating a large number of Mapuche and *wingka* patients, for combining empathetic and authoritarian healing techniques, and for speaking both Mapudungun and Spanish. Before seeing patients, Francisca usually dreamed about the required remedy and often about their family situation and the route to their house. In her practice Francisca drew on several older Mapuche healing therapies, which reinforce the connections between thought, emotion, and the body, in order to divine and heal her patients' suffering. According to her, patients had to have *küme piuke* (good heart), *küme rakiduam* (good thoughts and intentions), and faith in order for the cure to work. She made her patients take responsibility for their actions and participate actively in the healing process, adapting her rituals to their needs. She emphasized forgiveness, courage, faith, and hard work as requirements for healing. But she also practiced countersorcery against those who hexed her clients and friends. And she chastised her patients for transgressing Mapuche norms and for being greedy, stingy, and unfaithful.

Michael Taussig (1987:237) has argued that shamans in Colombia do not "become the Other" but seek to appropriate the other's power by becoming the "shock absorbers of history." The ways in which machi appropriate and resist this power are complex and often contradictory. In some instances Mapuche incorporate colonialist hierarchies and powers as qualities of the deity Ngünechen. They collapse their own sociospiritual hierarchies into colonialist ones to produce new and local forms. Ngünechen thus has incorporated Catholic, military, and Mapuche ancestral authorities: just as Ngünechen grants life, blessings, good crops, salvation, health, wealth, and remedies to Mapuche who perform rituals, so associations with landowners and political and military figures will bring Mapuche social and economic benefits (Bacigalupo 1997; Foerster 1993:78–80). In contrast, Francisca sometimes conceived Ngünechen as a punishing deity, the "eater of humans" who makes people blind when they look at the eclipse or when they are arrogant or bad.

In some instances, Francisca and other machi have brought foreign powers, objects, and images into their local epistemologies and ontologies while rejecting the underlying foreign systems of knowledge and beliefs. For Francisca, Catholic Bibles became ritual objects, the Virgin Mary was equated with the moon, Jesus was considered a machi and associated with the beat of the drum, and antibiotics were used for killing evil spirits. But some elements from these foreign systems of belief seep into machi practice more deeply and transform it. Catholic morality, alphabetic literacy, and the existence of "natural illnesses," for example, became part of Francisca's machi practice. Ngünechen's moral character challenged the unmediated power of thunder. Machi view *wingka* and gringos as devils who remain outside the system of shamanism and sorcery, but machi also incorporate *wingka* and gringos into their own healing epistemologies as evil spirits who bring illness, harm, and suffering to Mapuche.

Francisca rejected biomedicine, Catholicism, and modernity as systems of knowledge and belief. She resignified symbols, technologies, and characters from folk medicine, Catholicism, biomedicine, and literacy while remaining true to her notion of being Mapuche. Francisca believed, however, that some pharmaceutical remedies were effective, and she incorporated them into her healing. For example, she attributed the swelling of her feet to the actions of an evil *añchimalleñ* spirit and asked me to rub them with both laurel leaves and Calorub, an ointment for muscle pain that she bought at a pharmacy. She told her patients to take antibiotics "to help expel evil spirits." At the same time, Francisca held on to machi epistemologies of illness, and she explained to her patients that spiritual illnesses move around the body and can be healed only by machi: "My patient has passed through the hands of *wingka* and is tired of so many medicines and so many lies, so many words and so many promises. *Wingka* don't know about these illnesses; only machi know about them" (February 19, 1992). But some Mapuche criticized Francisca's hybrid healing practices.

Francisca became well known for treating problems related to fertility and birth: she dreamed about rituals "to make God bring babies down" and performed love and luck rituals. Some construed her love and luck rituals as sorcery because they involved "manipulating a person's will or destiny." Others criticized her for providing herbal contraceptives to women and therefore interfering with "God's plan."

Francisca identified with the Virgin Mary as the Lady of Sorrows who is morally superior to her Mapuche children, but who still grieves for them when they are ill. She painted her *rewe* and house blue and white (Marian and moon colors), and she hung a statue of the Virgin in her bedroom beside her *kultrung* because Mary gave her power and helped her exorcise evil spirits. In February 1992 she told me: "The Virgin takes care of you. The Virgin is good to heal people, to take out the filth." When Francisca died in 1996, her daughters painted her tombstone blue, hung a crucifix on it, and planted a *foye* tree at her feet. Francisca had told me, "In a dream I will die, and the Virgin will carry me to the Wenu Mapu." Nuns and the priest from the Church of the Sacred Cross in Quepe had visited her and given her an image of the Virgin Mary and a Bible in an attempt to convert her more fully to Catholicism. But she rejected the authority of the Catholic Church and much Christian dogma, particularly the notion of sin, the virginity of Mary (whom Francisca viewed as a fertility goddess), and the celebration of the crucifixion of Christ. Francisca associated dreams of crosses with death. She said, "I don't like the cross. Jesus Christ dies; there are crosses in the cemetery. To dream about the cross and flowers is bad. It means someone is going to die."

It was Francisca's multivalent approach to shamanism that allowed her to envision her power taking the shape of this bible I have written. As Taylor (2007:159) has argued, "Shamanism is the mirror image of alienation. It is the ability to control the polarity of the process of identification and to suck foreign beings into one's selfhood instead of the other way round." Francisca linked together distinct, unequal, but mutually transforming Mapuche and non-Mapuche relationships, practices, and discourses, and her complex healing strategies allowed her to embody three different modes of historicization. I turn first to Francisca's divination rituals, in which she embodied the past to foretell the future through dreams, psychic sight, her arm that contained shamanic power, and experiences of possession.

DIVINATION: EMBODYING THE PAST
TO SEE THE PRESENT AND FUTURE

"I dreamed that this place is charged with sorcery. The evil *wekufü* spirits are trapped between the mountains, which makes people envious. There are sorcerers everywhere," Francisca whispered, her voice barely audible above the clamor of stones from the dirt road hitting the bottom of my truck. It was February 22, 1995, and we had driven past the tourist town of Pucón, where the paved road ended, and through the lush, hilly countryside on our way to the community of Longkofilu to heal Segundo and his family. "The old *kalku* from the top of the hill hexed Segundo and his family because she wants them all to die so that she can get the land," Francisca concluded.

We snaked our way along the narrow muddy road riddled with holes and ruts. "I dreamed about this treacherous road," Francisca said. "There were many little *piwüchen* [evil *wekufü* in the form of small chickens] chirping, who became people near the cemetery, and then they got onto the bus. These bad *piwüchen* ruined the road so that we couldn't come to heal Segundo's house[hold]. But we are coming anyway."

I stopped suddenly as we reached a river flowing over the dirt road. "A *cuero*," Francisca said as she pointed to a small, dark, triangular shape floating downstream: a manta ray, an evil *wekufü*. The river looked too deep to cross. I wanted to turn back. "We will get stuck," I said. "What if the *wekufü* drown us?" Francisca glared at me. "You will not believe in *wekufü*," she argued with impeccable logic. "You go straight. I pray. Go." Francisca invoked the Mapuche deity Ngünechen and the warriors of the four skies and squeezed my hand. I pressed on the accelerator, and we made it across. The river was shallower than it had seemed. Francisca laughed as she slapped my knee: "It is good that you trusted me."

"How did you know it was shallow?" I blurted out.

"I am a *pewütun* machi [omniscient diviner shaman]," replied Francisca in a matter-of-fact manner. "Ngünechen gave me all the intelligence and power. He taught me everything from above. When something is going to happen, I dream, my right arm twitches, and the *filew* show me [in *küymi*, or trance]. And then I tell people."

I persisted: "You say you are a *kuyfi* machi [from the past]. So how does the machi from the past know the *ka antü* [the future]? Mapuche say this is a different time."

Francisca squinted at me and said, "The machi is from the past. The past takes hold of the machi and lights up the future behind her. So the machi advises what will happen."

Rosalind Shaw (2002:265) has written, "Memories are the prism through which the present is configured even as present experience reconfigures these memories. Memory works backwards and forwards." Francisca's account of her divinatory skills must be read according to Mapuche perceptions of the body in time. While most peoples imagine the past as behind them and the future in front, Mapuche reverse this imagined positioning of the body in time. According to Mapuche poet Leonel Lienlaf, the past is "always in front of us; it is what we see, hear, and know [through historical narratives, dreams, and experiences of possession]. [We view] the present as beside us, and the future as behind us because we don't see it and we haven't known or experienced it [except through machi]" (January 2, 2010). Walter Benjamin (1969), in contrast, envisioned "the angel of Western history" gazing at the ruins of the past but unable to awaken the dead and piece together what has been smashed because he is driven irresistibly toward the future. Mapuche also face the past, but the past is not in ruins; nor are the dead long gone.

Francisca had performed several divination rituals for Segundo and Anita (his younger daughter) at Francisca's home prior to our trip to Longkofilu. She had used gestures, movements, and sounds to divine the present and future of Segundo's family in what Paul Connerton (1989:72) would call the "primacy of ritual as a bodily habit" in the construction of memory. She used a holistic and practical approach to discover the natural and spiritual causes of the illness in Segundo's household, analyze its social context, and determine the cure.

Francisca had looked at the family's urine samples (*pe-wülleñün*), which were "dark yellow and thick with evil." She stared into their eyes with her *vista* (psychic sight) and saw that Segundo's children were hexed: Anita "runs to the woods like an animal and rubs her hands together.[15] No one will marry her. Carmen [the elder daughter] cannot think, because the evil has possessed her head. Joaquin [the youngest son] . . . wants to be like a *wingka*, and he is ill." Francisca diagnosed their misfortunes by drumming over Segundo's used undershirt; he and his house were hexed: "Segundo's house creaks and the dogs bark because of the sorcery. They have bad luck. Segundo's wife died. The witch made Segundo deaf. He cries all the time. . . . The *kalku* threw putrid dogs' legs on the wheat fields to make them barren. The *añchimalleñ* and *wekufü* spirits have been busy doing harm." Segundo told Francisca that his family had been attacked by evil spirits, which confirmed Francisca's divination. Anita described an attack by a cherufe spirit: it "pursued me and landed on my shoulder, and then the bone from my shoulder poked out." Segundo had seen a tall, thin *witranalwe* spirit cutting grass by the path.

The special powers in Francisca's right arm told her that the family was truthful and would complete the requirements for her healing ritual. Francisca said, "My arm pulls this way [to the right] and swells when people have faith; the healing will come out well. When it pulls that way [to the left], he has no faith, and I don't treat him. . . . Segundo waited too many days, and that's why the evil is so strong. I need to do a *datun* for them. They need my strong medicine to pray to the old people to change their luck."

In preparation for our trip, Francisca dreamed about the place where Segundo and his family lived and the medicinal plants each member needed to heal: "I dreamed that a *bruja* [sorcerer] buried dead dogs' legs in Segundo's field to make it infertile. She placed a small coffin full of feathers in the outhouse and contaminated earth from the cemetery on their threshold so that they would die. . . . I saw a plant growing next to the *palo trébol* tree that stands beside Rosa Kurin's sacred stone [on the Millali hill] that I should use to heal Segundo. They told me to leave coins and wool on the stone [as offerings]." Francisca then squatted and smoked cigarettes in the forest and used the smoke to locate the other medicinal plants that she had dreamed would heal the family.

Divination rituals are therapeutic because they reconnect a client's individual body and the social bodies to which he or she belongs with the physical world, the moral order (Kapferer 1997; Graw 2009; Holbraad 2012; de Boeck 1991; Werbner 2015), and the world of spirits in which his or her life may be reinterpreted and reinvigorated. Francisca had the ability to change people's bad luck and illnesses that were due to their own actions and those of others. But when her patients' problems recurred over time despite her healing practices, she explained this failure as the bad preordained destiny of her patients or as an evil spirit attacking the family. For Mapuche, evil is an external force that threatens to destroy the temporal and moral order established by the cyclical rebirth of spirits of the past and by endorsement of the ancestral ways. When people are hexed, they cease to act in socially appropriate ways and therefore lose their personhood and connection with the cosmic order. Anita ran to the woods like an animal. Joaquin wanted to become a *wingka*. Segundo cried and became deaf. Machi like Francisca heal disruptions in the temporal and moral order caused by sorcery, which often manifest as illnesses and social conflicts.

Evil spirits may appear in any form, and shamans alone are capable of judging their appearances and distinguishing between different forms of doubling. What appears to be a person may actually be a spirit that has taken on the person's form in order to harm people. Francisca had divined that she should trick the evil spirits who were mimicking people. She told Segundo's family, "If you see *añchimalleñ* [or] *witranalwe* that greet you like a person, greet them too so that they are not suspicious. Then I will defeat them."

Francisca and I reached the bottom of Longkofilu, where I parked my truck and we were met by Carmen and Anita. Francisca and Carmen made the steep ascent to Segundo's house in a cart pulled by oxen. Anita and I walked beside the cart. As we climbed, Francisca had a vision of the evil *witranalwe* spirit by the roadside. She confronted him and predicted his failure: "I will not give you medicinal plants. These are for my patients. They will be healed, and you will be defeated." Francisca was relieved that I did not see the *witranalwe* because then it could not attack me. Nevertheless, she tied red string around my ankles and wrists to ward him off.

Segundo's family welcomed us into their small wooden house and served us chicha made from fresh apples. After three gulps, Francisca slammed her glass down on the table and asked for the sacks of medicinal plants she had brought for the ritual. A neighbor who would serve as Francisca's *dungumachife* (ritual translator) arrived. We all sat in the shade of a large *boldo* tree, pulled the leaves from the different plants, and put them in various bowls as indicated by Francisca (fig. 4.3). She repeatedly demonstrated her knowledge by holding up a leaf, identifying it, and explaining how the spirits had told her to use it to heal Segundo's family. Many names of medicinal plants rolled off Francisca's tongue: *linco, triwe, boldo, rauli, quila, llankalawen, pulli-pulli, foye*. After she said each one, she exclaimed "Juy!" to stress the power of the plant's medicine. Finally, Francisca held up a leaf of *alwe lawen* and turned to Segundo: "This is to refresh the heart and the bone so that the sadness leaves. I dreamed I should give this to you to make

FIGURE 4.3

Francisca Kolipi, her daughter Aurora, and her patients Anita and Carmen strip off the
leaves of medicinal plants to make a poultice for a healing ritual (photo by author).

you feel encouraged and happy, and forget the finished one [Segundo's deceased wife]."

That night in Longkofilu, Francisca divined through spirit possession the larger social and moral causes of the suffering experienced by Segundo and his family, which complemented what she had learned through dreaming, psychic sight, visions, and the power of her right arm. Since the creation and manipulation of history in ritual is accomplished through the mimetic body of the shaman, the spirits and deities that also mimic Mapuche realities played a central role.[16]

Francisca sat on a low stool next to Segundo, who was lying on the floor of his living room with potted *foye* and *triwe* trees at his head and feet. Even on this dark night, she tied her headscarf over her eyes so that she would not be distracted from seeing the present and the future. Since spirits both duplicate human society and have the power to transform it (Lambek 1996), to bring them forth is to mimetically gain control over their mirror image of physical reality, which then transforms the power of the shaman. Francisca's power to diagnose and cure depended on "out-doubling the doubling of the spirit image" (Taussig 1993:127–128). She soon entered into trance, and Rosa's spirit took over her body and speech:

EMBODIED HISTORY

The old people from above feed me wisdom from all times. Today I can see everything. A sorcerer is trying to manipulate you and cause you harm. . . . She has sent her messengers [evil *wekufü* spirits]. . . . They have tried to transform your being. . . . I see people wandering in the forest without any destination, like animals without an owner. . . . There are people taking chalky stones from the cemetery to do you harm. . . . There will be suffering, bitterness, and crying in this family. . . . [Speaking to the family] The sorcery makes you fight among yourselves like dogs. You insult and hurt each other. You feel headaches and heartaches. You feel weak, dizzy, forgetful, and desperate. You don't know what to do. You are afraid. . . . [To Ngünechen] My patient's body itches. . . . Who can be happy with pain in the stomach, back, hip, knee, and cramps in the feet? . . . Sometimes he feels a lot of heat; he is weak. His heart is sad. He is confused with this illness. He believes that his heart and his head grow big. Sometimes he sees a dog [a symbol of sorcery]. . . . He doesn't remember his dreams. [To the family] You should be strong, united, to be healthy. Confront things as a family. . . . The sorcerer will not be successful because we have more strength and better spirits. . . . I am praying for you, my children, so that you will be well. . . . Now we shall clean these bodies and do good remedies so that the sorcery leaves.

The *dungumachife* (ritual translator) responded to Francisca:

You have clarified things with your wisdom and good machi powers. We are grateful for what you have told us. You see what we cannot see. You feel what we cannot feel. What you have told us is true [morally right]. You have consoled the hearts of those who are suffering.

Divination trances provide clues to the conditions underlying the pathologies of the social world. Francisca divined that the suffering and fighting experienced by Segundo's family were caused by a sorcerer and her evil *wekufü* spirit helpers, and she told the family to remain united and to have faith in her so they would be healed. She linked sorcery to the loss of Mapuche morality, spirituality, and history; to the hegemonic imposition of Chilean knowledge; and to the dispossession and conflict that had created an imbalance in the relationships among Mapuche families and communities and led to envy and jealousy among neighbors.

At other times, Francisca predicted natural disasters such as earthquakes, floods, and excessive snow, which she interpreted as divine punishment for Mapuche misbehavior. *Longko* Euladio explained, "I laughed when the machi said in trance that a huge snowfall would kill many animals. I said, this machi is crazy. And then there was a huge snowfall in the mountains, and many animals died. The machi was saying the truth. . . . The machi also said that the oldest *longko* [that is, Euladio himself] would die, and I almost died. If the machi hadn't intervened, I would have been dead. Machi are from the past, but they know the present and the future" (January 9, 2010).

In addition to the insights gained from divination, Francisca's ability to heal in the present and create a better future also depended on the efficacy of her sacrifices, her second mode of ritual historicization.

SACRIFICE AND HEALING: REORDERING THE COSMOS

They criticize us without reason, Father God. They say, "She has the heart of a machi to gain money." But don't we sacrifice ourselves? We didn't become machi just with one or two sheep. We spent a lot of money to pay for machi pürun *[initiation and renewal rituals] to be able to walk among many people. . . . "You will suffer and sacrifice yourself," Old Woman machi told me. We attend rich and poor people. That is our work. I go out to many different places in the cold winter. I spend entire nights without sleeping or napping on two hides on the floor. . . . I arrive home at 10 or 11 a.m., and in the evening I have to go out again. . . . It is a big sacrifice for my family because I am always gone healing other people. What can I do if Father God gave me that destiny?*

———

—MACHI ANGELA, JANUARY 28, 1995

Francisca laid on the floor covered with medicinal leaves . . . and then the helping machi entered into küymi, *trance, to heal her. . . . They [young male helpers] clashed the* rüngi *canes above her head [to help her enter into trance] and screamed above her head. I cried; . . . my tears fell. I felt such pity for the machi. . . . It was sad to see her thrown down there in trance on the floor, covered with medicinal plants, . . . to see how much a machi sacrifices herself and her spirit for the well-being of others. . . . But without sacrifice, there is no healing and no future.*

———

—AMELIA ANCAO, JANUARY 5, 2007, SPEAKING ABOUT
FRANCISCA'S *NGEIKUREWEN* RITUALS IN 1980

Machi sacrifice their lives, bodies, and spirits to reorder the moral cosmos, effect healing, and create a better future for others. Mapuche refer

———

to this huge sacrifice as *rume kutrankawün*—a great illness suffered to obtain something for the collective good (Juan Ñanculef, personal communication, July 22, 2014). The moral validity of sacrifice is tied to the perceived efficacy of ritual acts and the validity of the possible future worlds the acts of sacrifice seek to effect (Course n.d.). A machi's sacrifice is a form of remembering, but in order for the sacrifice to be efficacious, spirits must consider the machi worthy of the knowledge and power they give her, and she must be able to use the sacrifice to remember the past and create a better future for others. Like Maya *katun* cycles (Farriss 1987), Mapuche shamanic histories combine linear and cyclical time to provide guidelines for interpreting events in the present and in the past, help shape events as they unfold, and describe the human ritual agency required to keep time and the cosmos in orderly motion. While machi's sacrifice creates social order, sorcery disrupts it. Sorcerers sacrifice their victims' lives and well-being to gain wealth and power for themselves in the present. Machi combat the chaos provoked by sorcery, renew the power of the spirits, and reorder the cosmos through a very different type of sacrifice—the offering of their own labor, spirit, and personhood.

Machi will only be possessed and sacrifice their spirit for the well-being of others under specific conditions. Machi Juana's husband explained, "In the past, machi went into trance all the time to divine where the Spaniards were. But today, machi don't *küymin* [enter into trance] in [just] any place because it is ridiculed. The conditions have to be well established where she can enter in *küymi*. There has to be a *dungumachife*. This has to be decided beforehand. . . . We Mapuche have our rules. Just because a machi goes to a ritual does not mean that she is going to sacrifice her spirit. *No*" (December 27, 2001).

The performance of shamanic sacrifice and healing in order to create a better future is also a political act. Although the explicit goal of Francisca's ritual in Segundo's house was to produce healing, her ritual narratives pointed to a larger Mapuche history that was not an "incidental memory" (Cole 2001:133) secondary to the primary goal. Although instances of sorcery occur at different times and scales, they are intimately connected with each other: all forms of sorcery produce suffering and the destruction of cosmic time and moral order. Evil spirit possession, for example, makes a person depressed and unmotivated and causes their lands to become infertile. Francisca voiced the suffering experienced by Segundo and his family, but the family's suffering was also part of the collective reality of Mapuche people. Francisco Chureo (2001), the director of the Makewe-Pelales Mapuche hospital, has argued that the origin of Mapuche's depression is the lack of land and the breakdown of the family due to migration

(Menard 2003). Machi try to heal holistically the suffering, alienation, and chaos produced by colonialism and by growing social and economic inequalities by manipulating invisible forces that have an effect on physical bodies, communities, and land (Bacigalupo 2001, 2007).

I assisted Francisca in two all-night rituals during which she invoked the deity Ngünechen, the stars, and the spirit masters of the ecosystem to heal Segundo's family and change their future. The family had already taken several measures to protect themselves against evil spirits. For four consecutive days before our arrival they had drunk Francisca's emetic medicine to expel the sorcery. As counterhexes, they had tied red yarn around their wrists, painted white crosses on their doors, and drawn a circle of ashes around the temporary *rewe* they had fashioned so Francisca could connect with other spiritual realms.

During those rituals, the idiom of sacrifice also was applied more broadly to all participants in the healing process, and not just in relation to the work of the machi and the sacrifice of her spirit. Francisca highlighted the family's sacrifice of their labor and money to ensure that the healing would be effective. Segundo lay on a sheepskin on the floor, with a potted *foye* tree at his head and a laurel tree at his feet, which pointed toward the door on the east. Francisca placed the 40,000 pesos that Segundo had given her for the *datun* beside his head and prayed, "Segundo made a great sacrifice to get money for healing. He is paying for his recovery with money. So please help me heal him, strengthen his spirit and his heart. We will bring order back to this land." Patients' payments also help machi to recover the money they spent on initiation and assure them that their knowledge, powers, and services are valued.

Francisca also used the idiom of sacrifice to describe my participation: "Mariella sacrifices herself a lot for me. I told her, 'We are going far.' 'Yes, Mamita,' she said. She will play *wada* [gourd rattles] and *kaskawilla* [sleigh bells]. And she will rub medicinal plants on the sick person." Segundo nodded. The *dungumachife* turned to me: "My God sees that you are helping a machi. He is grateful for your sacrifice and is going to help you." Francisca pulled her headscarf over her eyes and prayed:

Old Man of the sky, Old Woman of the sky, of the rainbows, of the stars. Through my sacrifice and prayer, I give you these people who have come to ask for help. They have been humiliated. They are suffering. . . . I have come to cleanse and purify your children. We ask to be respected; we are praying with force and making sacrifices so that you listen to us and give us what we are asking for. . . . Help them be healed and united as a family. . . . I am sacrificing the best plants. My ancient ones have sent me here to sacrifice myself to return you to health and happiness. Then, you will have a future.

The *dungumachife* engaged in a highly stylized conversation with Francisca. I alternated between playing sleigh bells and massaging the patient's body with a mixture of crushed laurel leaves, other soothing herbs, and water. Segundo's children took their own turns at being the patient while the others shook short branches of laurel leaves (*iaf-iaf*) to induce healing. Then Francisca drummed loudly and signaled for me to rub all the patients' arms with another potion made of aguardiente and crushed bitter *foye* leaves, while she prayed to expel the evil spirits. The family shook *foye* branches to exorcise the evil *wekufü* spirits. Francisca then had a vision of an evil *añchimalleñ* spirit in the shape of a *wingka* woman, who behaved in ways that Mapuche associate with *wingka*: lying, practicing trickery, being stingy, and focusing on individual gain rather than the collective good. Francisca chided the spirit:

> Why have you done this? . . . You are *wingka* woman; you pretend to be people's friend, but you only do them harm. Other times you pretend to be a family member, but you are nobody's family. You have no friends, no family. You cannot continue seeding evil in the fields and hills. Leave my patients alone. Go back to where you came from. You wander around transforming yourself into anything, dog, cat, harming people and crops. . . . Go somewhere else where we won't see you again, you putrid dog. You shall not win. . . . We will humiliate and despise you. . . . Take your shiny stones, take your bones that you dug up. . . . We shall not admit you in this house. . . . We will make you lose all your strength. We shall shoot you. We shall burn you. We already beat you. We know who you are. We know you wish to harm people. That's why we are here, to make you lose all your power. . . . Because of our sacrifice, this illness will be healed.

Then Francisca circled inside and outside the house, drumming loudly to chase the evil spirits away. I followed, sprinkling a mixture of ammonia, aguardiente, and chili peppers in the corners of the house. The men followed me, thumping knives and axes on the floor and walls to cleanse them of evil spirits. Francisca threw a kitchen knife toward the door four times to test the *wekufü*'s power. Twice, the knives fell pointing toward the door, a sign that Francisca was defeating the spirits. Twice, they fell pointing toward the family, indicating that the sorcery was still affecting them.

FIGURE 4.4
A smoke exorcism made from wilkawe, foye, ruda, ajenjo, *chili peppers, salt,*
and sulfur expels evil spirits (photo by author).

Francisca took a break while Anita heated the *kultrung*. Sweat dripped
down Francisca's nose. Outside, Carmen and Anita prepared a *sahumerio*
(smoke exorcism) made from *wilkawe, foye, ruda, ajenjo,* chili peppers, salt,
aguardiente, vinegar, and sulfur, and Joaquin fired a gun from the roof
(fig. 4.4). The smoke snaked down the path, back to the alleged witch's
house, which Francisca interpreted as proof of the witch's culpability. During the night we heard the patter of footsteps and a dog barking outside the
house. Anita shot the revolver through the window, and the noise subsided.
Since dreaming is an important part of the ritual, at midnight all participants took a nap in order to dream. A few hours later I had a nightmare
about a huge dog that barked at the head of my bed. I screamed. Anita shot
through the window again. Segundo dreamed that the witch said, "I am
screwed now; they all know who I am," and left. Francisca saw this dream
as a sign that healing had begun.

Francisca completed the ritual with a prayer, reminding the spirits of the
sacrifices made and asking them to ensure the family a good future: "I have
sacrificed my words, my knowledge, my strength, and my remedies for this
family. . . . I have completed my work with your help, Old Father, Old

Mother Hawk, old people of the skies and mountains. . . . This family has sacrificed their money and work to ask for your help. Take care of this family and protect them from evil."[17]

Machi's confidence in the efficacy of sacrifice contrasts with notions held by philosophers and anthropologists. Philosophers in the Global North focus on the ethical dimensions of economic sacrifice—a disinterested gift that must be given without recognition or hope for a better future, a sacrifice with no reason or goal (Bataille 1992 [1973]; Keenan 2005:1, 178; Derrida 2007:113). Anthropologists often view sacrifice as an economic transaction from which some good will be received.[18] Some scholars see sacrifice as the irreversible destruction of a person, animal, or object in service of some future goal (Durkheim 2001 [1912]; Hubert and Mauss 1968 [1898]), such as creating something new (Mayblin and Course 2014; Lambek 2003). In contrast, a machi's sacrifice does not destroy her and is neither totally disinterested nor constrained by the logic of exchange. Like E. E. Evans-Pritchard (1956:21), Mapuche understand sacrifice both as communion with the divine and as a gift to others.

The power and wealth machi gain as a result of their sacrifice are ambiguous. They do gain knowledge, recognition, and prestige because of their spiritual powers and healing abilities. And patients make extraordinary financial sacrifices in order to pay efficacious machi well. But Mapuche believe that if a machi sacrifices her spirit for her own benefit rather than for the future of her patients, that machi will become ill and eventually die. Mapuche intellectual Juan Ñanculef explained that machi Eugenia died because she allowed the Chilean Museum of Pre-Columbian Art to make a video about her life and ritual practice for a fee. "One can't be sacrificing the spirit of the machi just for 70,000 pesos," he said. "Years later, the spirit punished her. She got cancer and ended up paraplegic in a wheelchair" (December 27, 2001).

The more power and wealth a machi gains, the more she is subject to accusations of sorcery—the other side of sacrifice. Those machi (like Francisca) who are sometimes labeled as sorcerers can become scapegoats for a community. The "sorcerer" then becomes the sacrifice, in "an efficacious act of casting out by destroying the person rather than an act of exchange with the divine" (Rio 2014), which allows community members to regain control over their lives and future. Francisca made others aware of her self-sacrifice to prove that she was not a sorcerer: "I sacrificed myself to heal my patients. But the money I got is to pay for my *pürun* to renew my powers, not for me" (September 3, 1996). Mapuche affirm both the ritual efficacy of machi sacrifice and the scapegoating of sorcerers.

The most important criterion of a machi as opposed to a sorcerer is to be recognized as a machi "from the past." But Francisca had not always performed the ideal cultural role of a machi from the past, and as a result she became ill and almost died. Machi Angela thus had to heal Francisca in a ritual that required Francisca to embody multitemporality—her third mode of ritual historicization. She then became a "true machi" of the past and was able to reinsert herself back into her present machi history.

EMBODYING MULTITEMPORALITY: RESHAPING THE PAST

When I am at home, I feel ill. When I don't leave to heal someone for over a week, I feel that I am dying. I lose my appetite. But when I leave to go and heal someone, my illness disappears; I don't even catch a cold. That's because machi must follow their destiny to heal people, the path of the machi from old times.

—MACHI ANGELA, JANUARY 25, 1995

Machi of the deep seas, machi of old times, you told me what medicine to use. You gave me a heart, Father God. You told me you shall help to heal humans. You have guided me to be present in any time or place. . . . May your daughter [machi Francisca] return to life. Your daughter has abandoned her machi [profession]. . . . Return the vitality to her heart, muscles, and head. . . . Defend and protect her. . . . You chose her heart, her tongue, to be machi from old times.

—MACHI ANGELA'S PRAYER FOR MACHI
FRANCISCA, JANUARY 28, 1995

The poetic ritual language of machi prayers and other forms of ordained speech depicts the real source of divine power as existing on a multitemporal plane. If a Mapuche shaman can access this plane, where distinct times become simultaneous, then she can be several different people at once.[19] The "machi from old times" must fulfill their destiny as machi by embodying the spirits from the past to see the past, present, and future simultaneously and partake in the cosmic reordering of the world.

Machi view possessions as multilayered ecstatic experiences in which the machi and the *filew* go into *küymi*, the *filew* acts as an intermediary between humans and Ngünechen, and the *filew* "speaks the words of Ngünechen through the machi's mouth" (Bacigalupo 2007:101–102).[20] Machi, like Panamanian Kuna chanters (Taussig 1993:109), are always retelling or reinterpreting something that was said before. Machi hear the message of Ngünechen through the words of the *filew* (generic machi spirit) and the *püllü* (individual machi spirit). The machi then repeats and interprets the words of the *filew* and the *püllü* in her ecstatic discourse. The machi's words are in turn repeated and interpreted by the *dungumachife*, who makes the machi's words intelligible to the ritual participants. Machi Francisca elaborated, "My head gets drunk, and the *filew* comes down and gets inside the stomach. It heats and compresses it. . . . Then the voice comes out and repeats what Ngünechen tells it" (April 19, 1995).

But Francisca did not always live up to her machi destiny or to her community's expectations of a machi from the old times. Some believed that her wisdom and her ability to see the past, present, and future were diminished because of *awingkamiento*, which made her vulnerable to sorcery and suspected of being a sorcerer herself. Furthermore, Juan, machi Juana's husband, observed that machi's powers are decreasing:

> Before, few people got the machi spirit. Now everyone wants to be a powerful machi. . . . It is the same ancient machi *püllu* that returns [in the body of new machi], but with less potency, with less *kimün* [wisdom] . . . because Mapuche are too *awingkados*. Mapuche now have another mind [they think like *wingka*], and machi have their tongues in a *wingka* context. We think of ourselves in Chilean history. People change, the Mapuche change, the wisdom changes, the destiny of the *wingka* changes. . . . These young machi are spoiled, arrogant, . . . and they don't know shit. . . . One of them was boasting that he was riding on seven horses. "If I want," he said, "I can make people fight and split." That's sorcery. The role of the machi is to heal and serve the community. . . . A traditional, good machi who has her position, her *kimün* beside Chau Díos, can say ten words, and she [the good machi] eats them [the arrogant machi], brings them down, and makes them fall. (December 20, 2008)

This juxtaposition of the old and the new, machi from the old times and Mapuche *awingkado*-sorcerers, made necessary a resurgence of the past. Machi Angela therefore performed a healing ritual to reshape Francisca's past and reconnect her with the spirits and deities by helping her to embody multitemporality.

At midnight on January 28, 1995, machi Francisca lay on the floor while machi Angela played her drum loudly over her, imploring Ngünechen to forgive Francisca for transgressing her role of machi of the past and to let her live. I had arrived at Francisca's house early that morning to find two of her daughters sobbing and Francisca lying on a mattress in the living room, dressed in her best black woolen wrap and wearing the heavy silver pin she used to protect herself from evil spirits. Her eyes were closed, her face was white and clammy, her hands were cold. I could feel no pulse. Her daughters said she had been dead for over two hours and that they had washed her and changed her clothes in preparation for the funeral. Francisca's daughters had sent me and her brother-in-law José to fetch Angela, who belonged to the same school of machi practice.

In addition to *nervios* caused by the breakdown of social and spiritual networks,[21] Francisca also experienced *wenukutran* (spiritual illness) and *kastikukutran* (punishment illness) because she had transgressed her role as machi of the past: she had neglected to make sacrifices for others, and she had not performed rituals to renew her powers. Furthermore, Francisca had sacrificed her spirit horse to feed the mourners at her son's funeral and to ensure that her son would travel to the Wenu Mapu (Mapuche sky). Francisca's premature slaughter of her own spirit horse, with whom she shared personhood, was a form of spiritual suicide that transgressed the shamanic temporal cycles of death and rebirth. The slaughter therefore lacked the moral validity and efficacy of a true sacrifice. When Francisca revived an hour later, Angela instructed her to drink manzanilla tea to calm down, to avoid getting angry, to start saving money to buy another spirit horse, to speak exclusively in Mapudungun, and not to watch television.

That night Angela treated Francisca in a *datun*, a complex healing ritual that involved bringing Francisca back in line with Mapuche expectations for a machi from old times by helping her to experience multitemporality and by renewing her powers and her relationships with ancient machi, deities, spirits, and her spirit animals. Francisca had framed me as "good, like a Mapuche person" and as "understanding Mapudungun" and "already knowing" so that I could help Angela heal her. Angela had nodded. Francisca had asked me to shake *foye* and *triwe* branches to scare off evil spirits and to play *kaskawilla*. She also had decided that I should record the first half of her *datun* (before midnight, when her illness would be diagnosed) but not the second part (when her future would be decided), lest it offend Ngünechen. Because the structure of this ritual was similar to the one Francisca performed for Segundo, I focus below exclusively on the healing of Francisca's temporal transgressions.

On the evening of January 28 I went with José to pick up machi Angela, her brother, who was also her *dungumachife*, and her niece, who served as her ritual helper (*ye-ülfe*). Angela prayed to her *rewe*, asking her spirit for permission to go and heal Francisca, and spat water on the *rewe* as an offering. When we arrived at Francisca's house, Angela inquired about her health. Francisca's grandson Cesar sacrificed a sheep for the machi. He slit its throat, and Francisca and Angela drank the warm blood mixed with chili to gain strength. The two of them bragged competitively about their shamanic powers and the patients they had healed. Meanwhile, José, Cesar, and I prepared the remedies for the ritual. José planted two bamboo canes as a temporary *rewe* outside the kitchen door on the east and tied *triwe* and *foye* branches to them. I placed soothing medicinal plants (*triwe, nulawen, limpia plata*) in one wooden bowl and the remedies meant to exorcise evil (*llanten, fulcon, foye*) in another. Francisca's daughter Aurora heated the skin of machi Angela's *kultrung* to make its sound deeper.

Francisca lay face up on a sheepskin on the floor, bare-breasted but wearing a petticoat, with her head toward the kitchen door. Cesar placed pots with *foye, triwe*, and *külon* branches at her feet and head. Angela sat on a low stool beside Francisca, smoking a cigarette in order to concentrate. She donned her silver breastplate and her headdress for protection against evil spirits and placed two crossed kitchen knives behind Francisca's head. She played the sleigh bells and *kultrung* softly as she invoked the spirits of the past and narrated in four phases the history of her calling, powers, and initiation, as well as Francisca's. Her *kultrung* was heated after each phase. She described Francisca as her "sister" and as a "daughter" of the deities who was destined to become a machi but ignored her destiny for many years:

> Old Woman who created machi, Old Man who created machi, you have destined us to exist and gave us wisdom and strength, this is why we are standing here before the *filew*. . . . We did not choose to become a machi. You told us we must be machi to help, to save the children [patients]. . . . When she was in her mother's womb, this daughter [Francisca] was destined to become an orator, a machi. . . . My sister [Francisca] is the descendant from a lineage of sacred singing women machi that does not end. . . . But she waited too long to become a machi.

Machi are not singular subjects but also embody the spirits and deities whom they mimic and about whom they chant.[22] They thus see the world through different "modalities of personhood" (Bem 1993), temporalities, genders, and points of view (Bacigalupo 2007:77).[23] Angela named a variety of nature spirits and ancestors, the deity Ngünechen, the Virgin Mary, and Jesus, all of whom duplicate the physical world of humans in terms of family relationships and social and spiritual hierarchies. By calling them forth into the ritual space and embodying them, Angela became simultaneously spirit and human to gain control of the world they represent.

During the healing ritual, Angela also embodied multiple other beings and therefore held different positions, each associated with a different time: Üllcha Domo Ngünechen, a young servant and daughter of Ngünechen from the present, who has the power of unbounded female fertility, childbirth, and the stars; Weche Wentru Ngünechen, a young servant and son of Ngünechen from the present, who has the power of Chilean military officers, masculinity, and lightning and kills evil spirits; Fücha Wentru Ngünechen, or Chau Díos, the old Father God from the past, who has the wisdom and power of the Christian God, Jesus, the apostles, the sun, and ancient *longko*; Kuse Domo Ngünechen, or Ñuke Díos, the old Mother God from the past, who has the power of fertility and the wisdom of the Virgin Mary, the moon, and ancient machi; the multigendered and multitemporal Ngünechen, who links worldly and spiritual realities; and a young sister, who is also equal to Francisca in the present, to embody and implement these different qualities and times.

Angela wiped the sweat from her brow, and her niece pulled Angela's headscarf over her face as she proceeded with the faster drumbeat—*trekan kawellu kultruntun* (the traveling horse)—on which machi gallop to other worlds and gain knowledge. Six young men from the community were also present, and they clashed *rüngi* above her head and screamed, "Ya ya ya ya!" Angela's head shook, and she entered *küymi*. Angela played a forceful beat often referred to as *tropümkultrunün* (Ñanculef and Gumucio 1991:5) as she began the *pewütun* (divination). The *dungumachife* spoke about good machi from the past and the damage wrought by *awingkamiento*. Angela spoke about Francisca's transgressions:

> *Dungumachife*: In the beginning, the Ancient Father created good machi, good *filew*, and that's why we lived on the breasts of the mountains. . . . But now that the land has become *awingkado*, it is different. . . . Mapuche thought has been tossed aside. People use *wingka* tricks. Some machi do too.
>
> Machi Angela: The daughter machi [Francisca] is ill, and the *filew* asked us to come. . . . *Filew* is kneeling and crying because her heart has declined. . . . This daughter left the language of the old machi leader, who is like a *choyke* [Patagonian ostrich]. . . . She doesn't have her machi animals; she hasn't performed her renewal ritual. . . . She has no strength. . . . She is wounded even in the place where she prays. . . . They sent her *witranalwe*. . . . It makes her ill and competes with her *filew*. . . . They [bad spirits] filled her heart with evil and left shadows in

her eyes. . . . Now she lost consciousness and has a fever. . . . She doesn't have muscles in her hands, she doesn't have blood of service [to the machi profession]. . . . She walks crooked; she has melancholy.

Bernardita (Francisca's granddaughter): On the day of the Ascension of the Virgin Mary [December 8], Francisca was going to renew her *rewe*. But none of her helpers showed up, . . . [and] her heart declined. Her own family harmed her.

Mapuche view challenges to the past and the amorality of sorcery as trapping and weakening people, tying them up, agitating them, contaminating them, knotting their life paths, and confusing them. Healing takes place as the machi exorcises the evil spirits lodged in the bodies, souls, hearts, and households of her patients by shooting or stabbing these manifestations and by purging and otherwise cleansing the patient. Angela rubbed Francisca's arms and legs with the blunt side of a knife to unravel the knots caused by Francisca's temporal transgressions and sorcery. She sought to purify and strengthen Francisca's spirit and lift it so she would be influenced by the healing powers of Ngünechen.[24] The healing process is the transformation from knotted to unraveled, contaminated to purified, weak to strong, and agitated to calm. The goal was for Francisca to regain her role of machi of the past (Bacigalupo 2007:75–76).

Angela sang and massaged Francisca with medicinal plants while her niece-helper played the *kultrung*. Then the helper and I rubbed Francisca's body with "soft" medicinal plants while Angela played her *kultrung* face down for maximum therapeutic effect. Francisca's daughters and I also shook *iaf-iaf* to induce healing. Machi Angela and the *dungumachife* asked Ngünechen to forgive Francisca for her transgressions and to help her so she would be integrated back into her machi practice, family, and community:

Dungumachife: Give her guidance and strength. . . . Your daughter machi [Francisca] is paying money to complete her designation. . . . Untie her tongue. Awaken her bones and spirit for service so that she can have her prayer, her discourse, her song [*tayül*].

Machi Angela: I am calming her illness. I am returning her elasticity. . . . Help me stretch and purify your children, . . . reorganize the middle of her body, blow on her, . . . revitalize her heart, blood, bones to become servants to the machi ancestor leaders. . . . Give her back her breath, infinity of ancestor machi, help the daughter machi. . . . If God allows, this machi shall recover. Defend her, encourage her. Don't let her be defeated. Bring her back to life, unravel her like a thread. . . . Give her a clear vision. Illuminate her on this dawn. Give her back her good machi dreams. May she do good prayers with a sincere heart, with a clean mind. Let her produce well-being. . . . Let her have her saddled spirit horse again. . . . You [Francisca] will go to many places singing your *tayül*, your sacred song. . . . Old Woman visionary, Old Man visionary told me this.

Then Francisca herself unexpectedly went into trance. She sat up and swayed, holding onto her breasts and playing sleigh bells as she faced east. Her body trembled. Cesar brought in her chosen shamanic spirit sheep and moved its front legs, making it dance to the music. By recovering her spirit sheep, Francisca strengthened her ties to her *rewe*, to the land in Millali, and to its forces. She also renewed her marriage to her spirit, her ties of affinity to the family of her deceased husband, and her position of subservience as a machi bride to her machi spirit and to Ngünechen, who granted her power and knowledge. Machi Angela had Francisca exchange saliva and *neyen* (breath and life) with her spirit sheep to reestablish her shared personhood with it. Francisca breathed on the sheep's nose and spat into her hand. The sheep licked the saliva, a sign that it had accepted her spirit. She prayed:

They gave me my sheep from above and I put it in my heart. Then I forgot my ways and my heart raced. I became ill. . . . My tongue was small and blocked. Now I have recovered my sheep, my heart, again and I can scream louder. Have compassion for me, Old Man from the sky, Old Woman from the sky. With my mentality and bones of service, heal me. We are doing the necessary things for my machi being. . . . Now you are supporting me again. . . . I have been revitalized. I have recovered my strength. . . . I am fulfilling my destiny. I will do my duty and perform the renewal ceremony. I believe in my heart again.

A machi's songs have a performative function: they bring about the healing and transformation that she requests. By singing about herself as a machi who must transform herself to become like a machi of the past, Francisca brought it about. At the same time, the prescribed formal speech of prayers limited her range of responses and stressed her public position (as a machi) along with a sense of social distance from and respect for the established spiritual, political, and social order (compare Bloch 1998; Irvine 1979). The deity Ngünechen would have machi from the old times channel the past to order the cosmos and heal the present and future, not intervene in the particular circumstances of Francisca's or Angela's life.

Anthropologists often distinguish between the shaman, who controls the alteration of her own consciousness, serves as a conduit for the spirit, and truly sees and interprets the healing images, and the patient, who gains awareness of her inner being and can talk but who does not truly see and whose trances and visions are controlled by the shaman (Laderman 1994:192; Taussig 1987:198). Machi Francisca was exceptional in being both patient and shaman. As a patient, she was ill because of her transgressions, but as a shaman, she controlled the alteration of her own consciousness and was able to access her own healing images and therapies. Along with Angela, Francisca became a conduit for the spirits, who demanded that she be a machi from the past.

After the ritual, Angela and Francisca regained normal consciousness. Francisca's daughters and I set the table for a feast, during which the *dungumachife* summarized the spirit's explanation of Francisca's illness (which I was allowed to record):

> The people [machi creators] who gave her life have not abandoned her, but she has made some mistakes. Her illness is caused by two different forces, and she has been informed about this in her dreams. . . . She hasn't performed the activities typical of her being. Before, she had a chosen sheep and saddled horse. Now she doesn't, say the celestial Mother, the celestial Father who chose her. . . . There is where she is failing. They almost took her machi language away. . . . Then a negative force came to visit her and her heart was left without strength. . . . But the hex has a limited time frame, which is now over. . . . She needs to ask for blessings. . . . She needs to renew the activities typical of her being [machi profession]. . . . She has to perform her prayers. . . . She will be given strength through her right hand, her hand of power.

Francisca concluded by erasing her previous transgressions and speaking from the embodied position of a machi from the past: "My *filew* moves my arm to play my *kultrung, kaskawilla*, my *wada* so I can heal. . . . My powerful lord is pressuring me to renew my powers. . . . My arm twitches."

The relations of the human and spirit worlds have an immediate effect on the machi's body, investing it with power and training it to perform rituals and emit signs. As Foucault (1979:25–26) argued, the body is always invested with relations of power and domination but "becomes a useful force only if it is both a productive body and a subjected body." Although most machi are punished by their spirits because they watch television or allow themselves to be photographed or filmed, few commit the major transgressions against machi being and temporality that Francisca did. Through her illness, Francisca learned that the spirits and deities would not tolerate her temporal misbehavior. If she wanted to live, she had to erase her previous transgressions, live as her ancestors did, locate her being and spirit in the ancestral past, and embrace multitemporality. Only then would she regain her agency, the gift of healing, and the knowledge to ensure a better future for others.

EMBODIED SHAMANIC HISTORIES

I have shown how different embodied forms of shamanic history-making emerge in Francisca's healing rituals and how they reshape the past, present, and future. Francisca embodied the past and divined the future through dreams and experiences of possession. She performed sacrifices in the present to effect healing and construct a better future. Francisca also embodied multitemporality to reshape her past and place herself in history.

Machi are custodians of the knowledge and power of the past, which they embody to pass on to future generations.[25] But machi like Francisca also fuse past, present, and future, and they ritually embody, reproduce, and reshape these times to forge a better future for Mapuche. Like the Colombian Nasa (Rappaport 1998:9–10), Mapuche conceive of their history as based on a moral link with their past, which is activated to achieve their political goals, including challenging their current relations with the Chilean state and constructing a better future for themselves as they follow "their own vision of existential transcendence" (Brown 1996:731). Through her divinations, healing rituals for others, and the ritual that restored her as a machi of the past, Francisca located her own body in a state of multitemporality to gain knowledge and power from the spirits. She also linked her body, her personal history, and those of her patients to Mapuche collective histories and sought to restore the cosmic and moral order and her own reputation as a good machi through self-sacrifice.

Healing rituals allow people to reshape the world by "regimenting present activity and by invoking futures and pasts that set the present in perspective" (Stewart 2012:212–213). Mapuche rituals transform the past into "images of the past," narratives about "what should have happened" (Morphy and Morphy 1985:462), "condensing the experience of the conquest and creating analogies with the hopes and tribulations of the present" (Taussig 1984:88). Thus, the present, replete with its own interests and preoccupations, appropriates and revises the past (Jackson 2007:80). Like Australian Aborigines (Goodall 2002:12; Attwood 2005:248, 249), Mapuche view different time frames as blurring into one another, each incorporating new experiences, notions, and forms. Buryat shamans in Mongolia distinguish between personalizing the distant knowledge of the past through memory and dispersing the knowledge of individuals to larger groups, making history (Buyandelger 2013). Mapuche call both of these processes history because living shamans are never just individuals, and therefore their narratives and performances are never just personalized knowledge of the past. Machi are always multiple persons, which allows them to experience different times at once.

Dreams, visions, and spirit possessions are modes of historicizing that express Mapuche understandings of temporality in their own terms. Machi experience multitemporality to reorder the world and then return to the present. They transition from "unconscious temporalization to everyday historical consciousness, from internal temporality to articulated history" (Stewart 2012:215). As Sartre (2004 [1940]) argued, imagination is what allows people to think of something beyond the current perceptible reality, which then allows them to think about changing the current reality. But Francisca experienced the spirits and people of the past and their histories as real, not imagined, which allowed her to transcend the present through ritual action. Dreams, visions, and spirit possessions are forms of agency for machi and their patients, enabling them to change their situation by looking into the future and into the past to find ways of acting in the present. In addition, the future often takes the form of the past as transformed by utopian dreams of the present.

Since machi ideally *are* the past, during possession they are expected to partly anticipate and know the future and be able to select moments from the past to create "what will happen." When Francisca failed to fulfill her destiny as a machi of the past, she also failed to create what would happen. But she recovered this ability once she located her personhood and identity as a machi of the past.

Francisca projected her ability to ritually reshape the past and the future onto her understanding of the Catholic Bible and other documents as shamanic objects of power. As I show in the next chapter, Francisca believed that through her ritual practices and sacrifices she could change history by reviving the collective past represented in contemporary documents to grant community members a better future. She also believed that my bible about her would speak to people of a distant future and store the powers animating her universe.

CHAPTER FIVE

SHAMANIZING DOCUMENTS *and* BIBLES

Official documents and Bibles have contrasting meanings and uses for the Mapuche and for the Chilean state, which are shaped by conflicting perceptions of the relationship between power, orality, and the written word. Chilean state narratives about history, social identity, and citizenship are tied to the documentation practices of the Global North, which marginalize and oppress nonliterate indigenous people, particularly machi. Birth certificates and identification cards determine Mapuche's legal existence, and land tenure documents define the legal owners of land. Mapuche, in contrast, associate the authoritative texts of church and state—the Bible, community land titles (*títulos de merced*), censuses, maps, identification cards, and Chilean laws—with state surveillance, the political and legal power of non-Mapuche people, and the illegal usurpation of Mapuche land. Mapuche often view the actions and documents produced by the state as instances of sorcery.

Indigenous South American peoples without their own systems of alphabetic writing often have conceptions of time, history, and agency that differ from those of people who create a writing-based, positivist historiography. They also engage with literacy in different ways.[1] Some scholars have argued that many nonliterate indigenous peoples had their own pre-Columbian systems of inscription, which were later linked to European alphabetic script, and thus the production of indigenous legal documents could grant native peoples legitimacy in the eyes of the Global North and could reconfigure native memories, identities, and political practices (Rappaport and Cummins 2012; Salomon and Niño-Murcia 2011). Others have argued that natives use secular texts as powerful ritual objects independent of European ways of reading and understanding the alphabet (Erikson 2004; Gow 1990; Guzman-Gallegos 2009; Platt 1992; Rappaport and Cummins 2012). But little attention has been given to how indigenous peoples produce sacred texts and use them to make political statements, narrate alternative histories, and circulate shamanic power.[2] In addition, the specific question of how spirits, agency, literacy practices, and history intersect remains largely unexplored.

Francisca was interested in the words of powerful texts (*chillka newen*) both sacred (Christian Bibles, Mapuche prophetic bibles, and ethnographies of machi) and official (land tenure and other legal documents). Machi and their followers consider the powers of church and state that emerge from Bibles and official documents as analogous to a machi's own power. Francisca read official documents and Bibles using graphic literacy practices. She also used them as ritual objects storing shamanic power. She viewed the words in these documents as animated shapes "dancing all over the page," from which she could extract power. Like Songhay healers in Niger (Stoller 1980:129), she conceptualized "powerful words" as energy or as living entities that have an existence separate from the domains of human, animal, and plant life. By using powerful texts as ritual objects, machi like Francisca evoke a shamanic graphic and performative literacy and a shamanic temporality, which take precedence over the rational, secular epistemological assumptions that underlie positivist historiography.[3] The bible Francisca wanted me to write as her personal legacy would be readable through both shamanic and ordinary literacies. It would carry her shamanic powers and extend them into the future. It could also be read by literate Mapuche and non-Mapuche, giving them a way to remember her after she died.

In this chapter I show how Francisca and other Mapuche engaged the colonialist power embedded in official documents and Bibles by avoiding, subverting, and exceeding the limits of the state archive in ritual and political ways. Mapuche sometimes have avoided census takers and mapmakers to prevent discrimination, conscription, and other perceived threats to their autonomy. At other times they have subverted the archive by using different names and by feeding officials false information to protect the community and for personal benefit. And Mapuche have exceeded the official archive by creating their own records and by appropriating the state's legal language in order to produce documents denouncing settlers and requesting land restitution. People in Millali consider these petitions analogous to acts of countersorcery. Mapuche also produce their own bibles to create shamanic literacies, store shamanic power, and promote shamanic rebirth, which challenges outsiders' perceptions of machi as nonliterate and ahistorical.

Mapuche shamanic literacies further our understandings of indigenous *grafismo*—the secular intersection of orality, performance, and alphabetic script. Mapuche transform the power imbued in official documents and Bibles and wield it in spiritual and political ways to challenge the dominance of the state and church. In this chapter, I analyze how spirits acquire historical agency as they animate sacred texts, transforming them into objects that permanently store shamanic power and that produce indigenous history. I show how the new medium of permanent shamanic text-objects challenges postmortem shamanic transformations—from historical figures to ancestral ones, and then back—and in the process creates new forms of shamanic indigenous history.

HISTORICAL TIME AND THE MARGINALIZATION OF MACHI

The idea that machi are historical agents is unthinkable in the dominant analytical modes of positivist historiography and Judeo-Christian thought.[4] Michel Foucault (2006:xxxii) showed that a discourse premised on the irrationality and nonliteracy of people from the Global South was a system of exclusion and repression developed by nineteenth- and early-twentieth-century Europeans to justify the concept of time as a unified, meaningful, and moral order, and history as linear and text-based (Khalfa 2006:ix–xx). To Europeans, positivist historiography is a factual, written representation of the past, which is separate from the present and the future, and is composed according to rational principles (Hirsch and Stewart 2005:263–264). A "critical rational discourse" will reveal "real facts" and will result in a coherent proposition, a final interpretation, or a self-evident, undeniable truth (Povinelli 2002:9, 11, 32). Karl Marx and Max Weber argued that "civilized" Judeo-Christian religions are compatible with rationality, modernity, and history, but native religions are not.

This historicism operated as a "normal science" (Kuhn 1962), and experiences of multitemporality—past, present, and future coexisting now (Stewart 2012:10)—went unrecognized or were considered deviant. Thus, historical time measured the distance between the "civilized" Global North, meaning the rational, scientific, secular modern state, and the "premodern" Global South, populated by irrational, nonliterate, shamanic indigenous people (Chakrabarty 2000:7). This colonialist, historicist paradigm served as a strategy for denying what Johannes Fabian (1983) called coevalness— the participation of both natives and colonizers as protagonists in the same time and space. This view denies that all human beings think and act both rationally and irrationally (Jackson 2007:235–236) and does not take indigenous systems of knowledge seriously.

Beginning in the eighteenth century, priests, intellectuals, and politicians in Chile adopted European historicism to argue that Mapuche lacked notions of time and religion and should therefore be excluded from history (Molina 1901 [1787]:86–87; Barros Arana 1888:104–105). The Jesuit priest Diego Rosales (1989 [1882]:29) discounted the Mapuche cyclical histories traced through the sun and moon, along with the Mapuche's generic notions of the past, as "lacking a structure of different times and a register of years." Historians construed Mapuche's nonliteracy and shamanic practices as expressions of unreason and barbarism that led them to believe in superstitions and to adopt "perverse practices," including sorcery.[5] The state deemed nonliterate Mapuche and shamans unfit to be Chilean citizens because they did not participate fully in history. Because shamanic histories that include oral narratives, spirit possession, and the ritual use of documents threatened the state's institutions of power and authority and its secular histories—as well as Mapuche patrilineal kinship narratives—shamans were absented from the archives as historical agents, and Chilean historians reduced them to the realm of folklore.

The legacies of colonialism include the separation of spirituality from politics and science, the construction of indigenous thought as predominantly religious, and the exclusion of indigenous people from the spheres of political power and history. Francisca sometimes internalized these colonialist perceptions, viewing her inability to read and write alphabetic text as a condition of her inferiority: "If I knew how to read, shit, who knows where I could be? Who knows what I could do? They wouldn't have tricked me. But I went to school for only one year, and didn't do the homework. I didn't know how to read my book. I used my book to hit other children and to kill bugs" (December 15, 1991).

Relegation to the realm of unreason and spirituality put Mapuche in an impossible bind. If they advanced their own worldview as an alternative to a secular Global North worldview, they risked reifying and reinforcing the split between unreason and reason that oppressed them. But by not invoking their own worldview, which combines politics and spirituality, they risked abandoning the symbolic system underpinning their distinct identity and history (Jackson 2007:241–247). In the face of this dilemma, the dominant Chilean definitions of history and morality gradually permeated Mapuche organizations without appearing to be imposed—a classic example of the workings of Gramscian ideological hegemony.

During the nineteenth and early twentieth centuries Mapuche organizations sought to legitimate themselves in national discourses as practitioners of secular politics. Unión Araucana rejected the ancestral culture and argued for assimilation and modernization, while the Sociedad Caupolicán promoted the gradual incorporation of Chilean national values into Mapuche culture (Foerster and Montecino 1988). Gender bias played a conspicuous role in this process of accommodation. Both organizations viewed female machi as ignorant, nonliterate, deceitful women who disobeyed their husbands, used poisons to weaken or kill men, tricked innocent people, and made others believe in sorcery.[6] The organizations petitioned the government to prohibit machi practices as "fraudulent" and "uncivilized" and to ban community-wide rituals as "immoral" and "irrational."[7] As a result of this convergence of state and Mapuche leadership, machi practices were considered illegal medicine in Chile until the advent of democracy in 1990. Shamans were rarely jailed, but out of fear many of them denied that they were machi.

Meanwhile, the Chilean state upheld written documents as more truthful and reliable than Mapuche oral histories and denied full citizenship to all nonliterate Mapuche (Menard and Pavez 2005:217),[8] although Chilean legal documents granted indigenous people some limited land rights. As part of Mapuche's incorporation into the state, literate Mapuche were forced to get identification cards (*cédula de identidad*) like other Chilean citizens. These documents gave Mapuche the power to vote, to do business with Chileans, and to shape their identities, political agency, and everyday lives. But nonliterate Mapuche were not considered full citizens, with the right to vote and possess identification cards, until 1972.

As represented by the ID cards, Mapuche have ambivalent connections with Chilean national identity. They value these documents as powerful objects symbolizing both their past alienation from citizenship rights and their current status as full citizens.[9] Some Mapuche have said that identification cards "made us people" (Briones 1993:81). But by the late twentieth century, Mapuche had begun co-opting official documents like ID cards as objects of power that they could transform for their own purposes. In March 2000 a group of machi asked Alejandra Krauss, the Chilean minister of development and planning, to create special ID cards that would legitimate them as "machi central to Mapuche traditions," who practice legal medicine and are neither sorcerers nor practitioners of illegal medicine. Although the government never produced such special machi identification cards, some machi claim that their national ID cards document their legitimacy as shamans rather than sorcerers.

Such counterhegemonic use of ID cards has been a significant but limited Mapuche response to state-sponsored objects and power. Individuals who believe that they are poor and marginalized because they do not have state-issued documents do not link that condition to the exploitation that has produced and shaped the ID card regime. Machi may argue that they are construed as sorcerers by the Chilean majority because they do not have legitimating shamanic identification cards. But that is not the same as confronting the deeper marginalization deriving from the Chilean biomedical system and the misogynistic Christian church, for example. There is, however, a more complex dimension to Mapuche resistance. Mapuche have devised some substantial mechanisms for avoiding, resisting, and subverting the colonialist archive and its historicist assumptions.

AVOIDING AND SUBVERTING THE ARCHIVE

Mapuche today see official documents both as instruments of colonization tied to the political and legal power of the Chilean nation-state and as powerful texts they can challenge, mimic, and manipulate in spiritual and political ways. In chapters 1 and 2, I showed how since 1866 the colonizers and the Chilean state have created laws codified in official documents, such as land titles, to facilitate the state's ongoing modernization project and to enhance its efforts to control and "civilize" the Mapuche people. Here I focus on the various paths Mapuche have taken in resisting the colonizing discourses embedded in official state documents.

Some avoided census takers and mapmakers, adopting invisibility in the written record as a defensive strategy against discrimination, conscription, and other threats to their autonomy.[10] But invisibility was sometimes a counterproductive strategy in terms of land rights. Domingo Katrikura explained that "the census officials wrote down the names of those present that day, but those who fled were left out. . . . Since there were no bridges to cross the Quepe River, the census officials just went along the banks. Those who lived in inaccessible places didn't appear in the census and didn't get land titles" (June 4, 2007).

Other Mapuche subverted the archive by giving false names to census officials, adding or deleting family members to gain benefits, or defining non-Mapuche writings as sorcery. The Mapuche's use of two different naming systems proved especially frustrating for officials creating censuses and genealogies. The term *küga* refers to a lineage that traces its descent from a totemic animal or plant or from a primordial ancestor.[11] The Chilean naming system, in contrast, focuses on nuclear families rather than lineages, decreasing the "lineage power transmitted by the lineage name" (Bengoa 1991:71). The adoption of the Chilean naming system had a major impact on Mapuche communities. The prefixes *Calfu-* (blue), *Huenchu-* (male), and *Milla-* (gold) once referred to particular individuals. Today, however, lineage names and prefixes are joined together and used as family names, which are preceded by first names that are often non-Mapuche. Feliciano

Lefian explained, "Before, we were all one lineage. Calfuñir, Huenchuñir, Epuñir, Nahuelñir, and Millañir—we were all foxes [ngürü, abbreviated as the suffix -ñir]. But when the reservation system came, each head of household had to have his own name. They changed their names, and the lineages came apart" (July 7, 2010).

Mapuche in Millali sometimes countered this impact by turning to the older Mapuche system, in which sons are named by the addition of a prefix to the lineage name. Two of Pascual Calfuñir's sons were named in this way: Linconñir (lance-fox lineage) and Nahuelñir (lion-fox lineage). Pascual's other children, however, were named according to the Chilean system, which is based on the father's name: José Calfuñir, Santiago Calfuñir, and Delfina Calfuñir. Since sons without their father's surname are not recognized as heirs, many change their names to adjust to the Chilean system. Linconñir became Linco Calfuñir and Nahuelñir became Nahuel Calfuñir (Feliciano Lefian, July 17, 2010). Additionally, some officials recorded people's nicknames rather than their formal names, or they misspelled their names, confounding the archive even further.

Mapuche in Millali stress the continuity of persons and lineages by naming boys after prestigious men in the patrilineage and thus fusing their identities, histories, and deeds (Bacigalupo 2010). In Millali when I was visiting regularly, there were three José Calfuñirs, two Manuel Lefians, two Juan Millañirs, and two Juan Kolipis. People rarely distinguished between the living men with the same name, in effect subordinating chronological time and individual histories to the ancestral memory of the lineage. Just as individual ancestors become part of generic spirits and deities, individual men can become generic ancestors of a lineage, and individual machi can become machi ancestors. This Mapuche practice challenges the Global North notion of a unified self, and more specifically challenges the dominance of an official census record that requires each person to be registered independently under a unique name.

Some Mapuche purposefully subvert the archive by giving false names to census officials, believing that to reveal their actual names would give outsiders spiritual power over them (Smith 1855:222). Mapuche in Millali also register adopted children as birth children and register migrants to the community as locals in order to obtain further resources or land from the government. In 1909 machi Rosa Kurin claimed Juan Huenchumilla and Luis Santos as her sons so they would get some land in the community because Mapuche who could not prove legal possession of their lands with a título de merced were considered settlers by the state. When a census was conducted in Millali after the 1960 earthquake, Mapuche men claimed as their own all the children they raised or who were born to their wives even if they did not father them. Ignacio Huenchuñir, for example, claimed Rosa's eight children as his own although he fathered none of them. And Francisca's father, Juancito Kolipi, was a child of *wingka* but was raised and documented as Juan Kolipi's legitimate son. If people in Millali were having a conflict with family members at the time a census was taken, they would often adopt the surname of a friend or of a prestigious Mapuche family.[12]

Francisca provided different versions of her name in different contexts. When she was interviewed for a popular non-Mapuche magazine, she called herself Francisca Kolipi Araneda to emphasize her relationship with *wingka* and her ability to perform folk medicine. At other times she labeled herself Francisca Kolipi Kurin to emphasize her relationship with the powerful machi Rosa Kurin. And to claim the lands she had inherited, she used the name Francisca Kolipi Lefian, asserting her ancestral connection with community land and the Wenteche regional identity.

Many people in Millali laughed when I showed them official documents about their community. They pointed out errors in people's names and in the constitution of families, and they dismissed disputes between community members as gossip. Carmen Añiwal told me, "All the fights between the ancient ones are here. . . . But Mapuche also told the officials many wrong names, and the officials wrote it down as correct. Some families are missing people, and others include people that belong to different families. They are all mixed up" (June 15, 2007). Community members understood census documents not as real genealogies but as snapshots of the political relationships between people and their government at particular moments in time, which are therefore open to subversion strategies that minimize the control exerted by state texts. However, Carmen found that the census officials did do something useful: "The officials wrote down the names of the ancient ones that died long ago and we forgot. And now the schoolteachers tell the children to find out the names of their ancestors, so then we look them up in the little books you gave us."

People in Millali were able to use state-issued documents to construct versions of their family history in the Global North idiom that a schoolteacher would understand. This highlights the methodological limitations of a purely textual approach to constructing history, which leaves out the people who speak their histories and do not write them. In contrast to these now-subverted documents, people in Millali stress their understanding of shamanic histories as "true history." They have now merged older Mapuche graphic systems with the European alphabet to create new kinds of shamanic literacy.

In "The Writing Lesson," Claude Lévi-Strauss (1955) used a narrow understanding of writing to argue that indigenous peoples have oral cultures that are oppressed and alienated by European systems of inscription. The nineteenth-century explorer Edmund Reul Smith (1855:221–222) saw the alphabet as the only measure of civilization and labeled the Mapuche as uncivilized for not having one. Such normative judgments, and even Lévi-Strauss's more nuanced estimation, share an inaccurate assumption: that there is a severe dichotomy between written and oral cultures that is closely related to the civilized/primitive divide.

But long before the arrival of the Spanish conquistadors in the sixteenth century, indigenous peoples used systems of inscription and visual communication in which signs stood for referents rather than sounds, as they do in alphabetic systems (Salomon and Niño-Murcia 2011; Santos-Granero 1998).[13] Mapuche created graphic designs in textiles and glyphic inscriptions on silver jewelry that can still be read by the older generations and by shamans like Francisca. These designs and inscriptions are "metadiscursive images of a seemingly durable, shareable and transmittable culture" (Silverstein and Urban 1996:2). They describe family and primordial histories, ritual events, and forms of social and political organization.

With this dimension of literacy and inscription in indigenous cultures, it is not surprising that during colonization Mapuche and many other indigenous peoples found it natural to link their own graphic systems and forms of representation to European alphabetic script (Gow 1990; Hugh-Jones 2010; Perrin 1986; Platt 1992; Bacigalupo 2014). Mapuche gradually incorporated legal document writing into an indigenous *grafismo* (Salomon and Niño-Murcia 2011), a social process of interactions between orality, ritual acts, bodily experiences, and alphabetic and pictorial forms. Francisca saw the paintings on her *rewe* as akin to written words, and she viewed alphabetic writing as designs with force that act but do not speak. She was interested in the graphic quality of writing—the size and distribution of words on a page—not in words as visual representations of speech (cf. Gow 1990:92).[14]

Clearly, Mapuche textual interpretation presupposes a multimedia base. The Mapuche term *chillka* (which derives from the Quechua term *quilca*) refers to the material in which an inscription is made (stone, wood, vegetable, paper). But the term can also allude to letters, inscriptions, and designs and to reading, decipherment, interpretation, and learning (Cárcamo-Huechante 2011:146; Gerbhart-Sayer 1985; Gow 1990). The term *writing* is more often translated as *wirin*, which refers to something that has been inscribed or drawn and also denotes lines, signs, designs, and sketches (Erize 1960:206).

Writing produces texts, but not all texts have the same value or power. Francisca distinguished between *chillka newen* (texts with power) and *la chillka* (dead texts), which are neither official documents nor bibles. She said that if she tried to read schoolbooks, newspapers, or personal letters, her spirit would "slap her down with *kastikukutran* because learning by reading 'dead texts' breaks the force of the machi" (January 10, 1992).[15] Francisca classified all Christian Bibles as *chillka newen*, but she differentiated between the Lutheran Bible, which holds the devil's words; the Catholic and Anglican Bibles, which hold God's words; and the bible I would write to store and circulate her shamanic power after her death.

When I gave Francisca a copy of my monograph "Adaptación de los métodos de curación tradicionales mapuche: La práctica de la machi contemporánea en Chile" (Adaptation of Mapuche Traditional Healing Methods: The Practice of Contemporary Shamans) in 1996, she smoked tobacco over my quotations of machi prayers—"powerful little words like the Bible," she called them—to awaken them. "That's the power of Ngünechen, Jesus, everyone. The little words are the machi, the word, the knowledge. I smoke it, and that makes my bones strong. I become invincible. . . . In my book, you will have little words. Powerful words" (July 15, 1996).

Francisca wanted me to channel her spiritual power through my writing, in much the same way that she channeled spirits. If machi read a text, they give it authority. If they experience the text and smoke over it, they awaken its soul, subordinating the assumptions of positivist historiography to the spirits, whose "power flows through texts and whose words are a force in action" (Goldman 2011:424–425). Texts containing shamanic power facilitate communication between the living and the dead and between the present, past, and future. As Dipesh Chakrabarty (2000:238–239) argued, a rational historical consciousness limits the lived relationship between the observing subject and other historical or ethnographic times. Machi, however, seek to maintain a living relationship with the past.

Francisca used her graphic literacy—the ability to understand and interpret visually represented data—to view alphabetic script as a technology inscribing meanings on a physical object. She believed that she and other shamans could manipulate these inscriptions for spiritual ends. Like Andean natives, Francisca focused on the phenomenology of the ritual object that bore the graphic inscription or, in the words of Joanne Rappaport and Tom Cummins, "how the inscription makes the absent present and therefore precedes and authorizes any decoding of the word" (2012:192). She saw my writing as representing both her oral narrations and historical events in

Millali; the words were designs with force that were partially disembodied from their written meanings. These designs could stand for the materiality of her body in the same way that the physicality of altars, relics, and scriptures bring forth the presence of the divine. Francisca believed that she could use her shamanic *newen* (power or force) to shape how and what I wrote; simultaneously, if I learned about her shamanic lore and allowed her to control my dreams, she could then imbue my writing with her shamanic power. By having me write her biography using alphabetic script, Francisca also believed, she could appropriate the non-Mapuche power, *wingka newen*, contained in the form of the written word. It is this interdependent relationship between alphabetic literacy, graphic literacy, and native oral and performative memory that has shaped the making of Francisca's bible as an intertextual object.

Alphabetic writing also has allowed the Mapuche to represent and share their culture in ways recognizable to Europeans. Writing became a source of legitimacy for indigenous people, giving them political and cultural power and allowing them to use official texts in unintended and adversarial ways (Bacigalupo 2014).[16] While writing may transform native forms of memory, written legal documents can also tie indigenous peoples irrevocably to their original rights, places, and events (Rappaport 1998). By the nineteenth century, Mapuche were writing mostly in Spanish but also in their own language, Mapudungun, to subvert the discourses embedded in official state texts and to create autonomous Mapuche archives. Literate Mapuche created their own stamps, letters, and newspapers to circulate the political correspondence of unconquered war leaders (Pavez 2008). They also produced family histories, ethnic national histories, and Mapuche prophetic bibles. Today 95 percent of Mapuche are literate, which has allowed them to expand the ideology of sorcery into the realm of legality.

THE POWER OF OFFICIAL DOCUMENTS IN COUNTERSORCERY AND REVIVING THE PAST

Our spoken histories are just like the law of wingka, just like the law of God, like the law of authority. . . . But we also learn wingka law to write documents to denounce them for their abuses and for taking our land. What the wingka and gringos did to us was sorcery. Now, we send their sorcery back to them.

—ALEJANDRO HUENCHUÑIR, JUNE 8, 2010

Throughout Latin America, the judicial sphere has become a domain for displaying shamanic power and producing countersorcery against the colonizers. Mapuche resist the power of settlers and the state by surreptitiously manipulating bureaucratic documents through ritual means so that they become "hidden transcripts" (Scott 1990) that work for Mapuche. The archive is at the root of modern indigenous identities because through it native peoples attempt to "appropriate the forms of European legal discourse and inscription in order to bind the colonizers in their own terms" (Platt 1992:144). In eighteenth-century Peru, shamans learned Hispanic law to extend the ideology of sorcery into colonial and national politics and to invert the colonists' penetration. Colonial magistrates confirmed shamans' powers as real and efficacious by trying them for demonological crimes rather than political crimes (Salomon 1983:424, 2004:414).[17] Similarly, Mapuche learned Chilean legal discourse to continue their confrontations with landowners on written, legal terms with practical and spiritual effects. *Longko* Domingo Katrikura noted, "We need our grandchildren to know the letters and control the papers so that we can protect our ancestral lands and lore and take the power of the *wingka*" (June 16, 2007).

For Mapuche in Millali, countersorcery and the production of legal documents of denunciation are useful modes of action against powerful non-Mapuche settlers who have usurped their lands. On October 15, 1928, Juan Millañir, *longko* of Millali, produced a sorcery-laden document to denounce Carlos Rosselot and Carlos Schleyer (Juan Schleyer's son) for illegally occupying half the Mapuche reservation and to demand its restoration to the community.[18] People in Millali believed that Juan Millañir effectively represented them in the court of law because he combined Mapuche notions of historic land possession with Chilean notions of legal property in order to justify his claim. He argued that Mapuche owned the land because their ancestors had lived there before the colonizers and because the state had recognized their possession of the land by granting them the 1909 title. The settlers, he argued, had to buy the land precisely because they were not the legitimate owners, and then they violated the law by moving their fences to usurp more Mapuche land. By using countersorcery, writing, and the law against the colonizers, he sought to participate equally in the powers of the state in order to wrest the land from Rosselot and Schleyer.

But Juan Millañir's claims were not effective because of the complicity between the settlers, the police, the judicial system, and the Chilean government, which people in Millali attributed to contracts with the devil. Millañir's great-nephew explained, "Nothing happened because even though the document was *cargado* [had sorcery], Rosselot was friends with the judge, the chief of police, and the devil, so everything was arranged

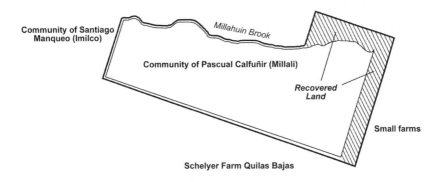

FIGURE 5.1

Map of the community of Pascual Calfuñir (Millali) with the fifty-one hectares of land recovered by the community in 2009 shaded (map commissioned by author).

between the compadres" (January 7, 2012). By February 1929 the government had modified the law to make the restoration of Mapuche land more difficult,[19] and officials ignored the subsequent complaints that people in Millali filed against Rosselot (who sold his lands to German settler Carlos Lüer in 1942) and Schleyer.[20] After further reductions by the Chilean government in 1947 and 1952, the people of Millali were left with 202 hectares, 51 hectares fewer than the community land title of 1909 granted to them. The failure of the Chilean judicial system to investigate Mapuche claims against powerful settlers or to resolve internal disputes attests to the marginalization of Mapuche within Chilean discourses of power and politics. Some people in Millali believe that in order to outdo the powerful settlers they need to create their own connections with the government and the devil, who are more powerful than local sorcerers.

Francisca, however, believed that she could manipulate the power that resides in the materiality of legal documents for the benefit of the community. Official documents do not just "leak the magic of the state into the hands of the people they dominate" (Taussig 1987:264), but some Mapuche believe they can appropriate the power of these documents and transform their meanings. In 1996 Francisca tried to revive Millali's 1909 land title map to bring into the present the realities under which the map was produced and thus recover the lands that had been usurped. She blew tobacco smoke over the map as she chanted, "Just as it is in the skies, so it is on the earth below [*Chumlei ta wenu mapu ka feli ta nang mapu*]" (February 2, 1996). In 2008 the community made a written land claim to the National Corporation of Indigenous Development (CONADI), denouncing non-Mapuche landowners for land usurpations and asking for the restitution of the fifty-one hectares it had lost since 1909. CONADI returned the fifty-one hectares, which now constitute 20 percent of Millali's land, in December 2009 (fig. 5.1).

The community's written claim was both a legal document of petition to the state and a form of countersorcery against the state—a strategy for changing history that harnessed the power of official texts for the community's benefit (Bacigalupo 2014). Francisca believed that her chanting and smoking over the document had the power to change history: by reviving the collective past in the present, she helped to recover the community's land and offered its members a better future long after she died.

FAMILY AND ETHNIC HISTORIES AS ALTERNATIVE MAPUCHE ARCHIVES

Scholars have vigorously debated the ways that shamanic and other kinds of indigenous histories are affected by Global North linear histories of events and nations. Anthropologists agree that differences exist between indigenous histories and histories *about* indigenous people, but they disagree about what counts as indigenous history and whether and how it should engage with histories of colonial and state rule over indigenous people.[21] Some scholars have explored how indigenous people construct their own histories to make sense of their encounters with complex, contradictory historical processes and the power dynamics of colonial and state societies.[22] Many Mapuche intellectuals take this approach to writing their own family, political, and ethnic histories, which follow clear genealogies.

Since at least the sixteenth century, Mapuche have traced their history through the lives and deeds of prominent individuals—chiefs, shamans, orators, politicians—rather than through the institutions or nations these individuals represent.[23] Consequently, Mapuche negotiations with, discourses around, and actions toward individuals and institutions are always conceived in terms of personalized, hierarchical relationships—relationships of power and subjugation—between individuals and their descendants, such as those between men and their patrilineal elders or between shamans and ordinary Mapuche. Thus Mapuche ideas about relationships and collectivity are also conveyed through the stories of prominent individuals, even though the importance of the actual individual may be secondary to generalized notions about leadership, shamanhood, or personhood.

Since the early twentieth century Mapuche intellectuals have been writing family and ethnic histories rooted in their own ways of understanding the past. They counter the dominant Chilean notions that Mapuche are ahistorical and irrational by focusing on the secular, political histories of prominent men and their patrilineages, preserving them and showing how they intersect with the national linear history (Guevara and Mañkelef 2002). However, Mapuche lineage histories based on aggregated lives are incompatible with the individually focused Chilean genealogical record, and the emphasis on the histories of conflicting Mapuche patrilineages has prevented the development of a broader ethnic history. Mapuche oral historian Antonio Painekura explained, "Our history is the history of the family and the social structures that we had in place, *rewe* and *aillarewe*. But if we create a history of the families, and I am Wenteche, then I do not identify with the Nangche families, and there is no history" (January 7, 2010).

Patrilineal kinship histories and men's political biographies are the parts of Mapuche history that are most appealing to non-Mapuche scholars who are interested in stories of subaltern resistance to state power, indigenous intellectual creativity, and the power of particular indigenous families.[24] Some have described Mapuche history according to the tenets of positivist historiography (Bengoa 1991; Pérez-Sales, Bacic Herzfeld, and Durán Pérez 1998); others have written about prominent Mapuche intellectuals and politicians as individuals rather than as representatives of larger collective histories.[25] A few have written about how women and gender-variant people create and reproduce knowledge and meanings in their encounters with the state (Richards 2004; Bacigalupo 2004b, 2007) and in their everyday lives (Montecino 1984; Bacigalupo 1996c); others have written biographies about prominent Mapuche women who are feminists (Reuque 2002) or machi (Bacigalupo 2007, 2013, 2014; Montecino 1999). However, there are few machi biographies. More particularly, little has been written about parallel shamanic lineages as traced through the mother's line in which the identities of prominent shamans (like Francisca) have been conflated with those of deceased machi (like Rosa Kurin) and primordial shamans in order to create multitemporal machi and place them ubiquitously in time (Bacigalupo 2010, 2013). Although local histories of patrilineages and shamanic lineages exist in dialogue with pan-Mapuche and Chilean national histories and official genealogies, Mapuche intellectuals have tended to justify their own secular historical practices by construing machi as ahistorical and apolitical, although they do acknowledge that machi are central to Mapuche tradition and identity.

SHAMANIZING DOCUMENTS *and* BIBLES

The most important Mapuche intellectuals of the first half of the twentieth century—Manuel Mañkelef and Venancio Coñuepan—sought to reinsert Mapuche into Chilean linear, textual history. They proposed that Mapuche become coauthors in the construction of Chilean history and mediate or fuse the political projects of Mapuche and members of the mainstream Chilean society, and they constructed Mapuche history by selectively engaging with *mestizaje* and some aspects of Christianity and Chilean culture without necessarily integrating Mapuche into a homogeneous Chilean national identity.[26] Mañkelef wrote *Comentarios del pueblo araucano* (Commentary on the Mapuche Nation; 1911), which had parallel columns of text in Spanish and Mapudungun, to present his vision of Mapuche's "double consciousness" in constructing Chilean history (see Mallon 2009; Menard 2006). He and other intellectuals created continuities between epic Mapuche heroes and individual Mapuche living during their time, and they defined Mapuche cultural difference in ways acceptable to the Chilean state (Menard and Pavez 2005:227). Coñuepan and Mañkelef shifted between their Chilean and Mapuche identities, combined them, or enacted both simultaneously (Crow 2010:148). They drew on the discourses of equality and individual rights to represent Mapuche as equal citizens and as key symbols of Chilean nationalism while at the same time calling for differential treatment because of their vulnerability as natives. Their writings had an impact on Chilean and Mapuche elites because these scholars offered a new way of expressing Mapuche historical consciousness and relating to the nation. But this ostensibly coauthored project did not enable the development of an independent, pan-Mapuche ethnic history.

In the twenty-first century a new generation of Mapuche intellectuals has created a larger Mapuche ethnic history, reconciling rural and urban experiences and decolonizing historical discourses (see Nahuelpan et al. 2012; Antileo Baeza 2012; Nahuelpan Moreno et al. 2012; Marimán et al. 2006, Cayuqueo 2012; Caniuqueo 2006; Marimán 2012). Like Hayden White (1973), these Mapuche scholars have argued that a historical narrative contains the ideological message of the writer, and they question Chilean historians' ability to write about the colonial past as it actually happened, arguing that many are still influenced by the colonialist agenda. These Mapuche scholars reinterpret the past and its official documents through their own epistemologies and systems of knowledge, and they establish points of convergence and antagonism with other forms of knowledge. They have created an autonomous Mapuche history independent from Chilean national history, and they have challenged Chileans' interpretation of their own national history.

Their Mapuche ethnic history emphasizes colonial power relations and state expansion, the history of Mapuche engagements with the state, and Mapuche local and national histories as an ideological discourse of decolonization. According to Pablo Marimán and colleagues (2006:260), "History should narrate what happened in the past, make us reflect on the present, and project us towards the situation we want in the future." But despite their oppositional and alternative strategies for challenging conventional assumptions about history, Mapuche intellectuals rely on rational, secular, academic, and linear protocols to counteract European depictions of indigenous people as irrational and lacking historical consciousness.[27] They have been reluctant to explore the crucial roles played by shamanic biography, spiritual inheritance, and spiritual rebirth in the recasting of local histories in an ethnic national context.

Francisca and her family were aware of this dynamic and thus wanted me to write a book on the experience, transmission, and remembrance of the past through a shamanic lens.[28] Shamanic historical consciousness can also contribute to the larger Mapuche project of historical decolonization and recovering historical knowledge because shamanic practices offer a productive entry point for thinking about indigenous people in terms other than their political asymmetry with the nation-state or as local native collectivities.[29] As Jonathan Hill (1999:394) writes, "Indigenous systems of representation still embodied today in the shamanic practices and the poetic evocations of a mythic and historical past constitute a parallel approach to the contradictions between nationalism and indigenous identities." Mapuche from Millali use the language of the spirits to challenge rational, secular discourses that posit development, modernization, law, and positivist historiography as the tenets of civilization. But instead of protesting against the colonists by organizing politically and retaking ancestral lands, they subject official documents and Bibles to the demands of deceased shamans and spirits and incorporate them into local spiritual epistemologies.

THE PRODUCTION OF MAPUCHE BIBLES

The creation of indigenous legal documents grants native peoples legitimacy in their own eyes and in the view of the state, and significantly reconfigures native memory (Rappaport and Cummins 2012; Salomon and Niño-Murcia 2011). Most texts produced by Mapuche serve the political purpose of asserting their collective claims to identity and greater legitimacy. But Mapuche bibles express a more deeply alternative historical consciousness, so neither they nor the processes of their production have been easily legible to non-Mapuche.

In nineteenth-century Chile, as in Africa, the Bible—a nonindigenous sacred text—became a metonym for colonial power and an instrument of Christian religious authority, but it was used in different ways. While the church in Zimbabwe was committed to an immaterial faith and adherents were not taught to read the Bible (Engelke 2003), the Pentecostal charismatic church in Zambia linked the materiality of the Bible with the Holy Spirit. Spirituality was seen as a prerequisite for healing, prophecy, and the divinely ordained literacy of the Bible (Kirsch 2008). Mapuche believed that the mysterious language of the Bible had potency and efficacy, which emerged from the book but was also separate from it (Menard 2013).[30] They appropriated Capuchin Catholic and Anglican Protestant Bibles but rejected German Lutheran Bibles because these denominations played radically different roles in the process of colonization. German Lutherans did not proselytize and did not try to engage with or incorporate Mapuche and their beliefs as did the Catholics and Anglicans. Lutheran Bibles were therefore linked to the usurpation and exploitation of Mapuche land by wealthy German settlers and to the German project of "civilizing" Mapuche by making them work as wage laborers. Mapuche still believe that the devil wrote the Lutheran Bible and imbued the sacred text with his powers so Germans could destroy Mapuche morality and sociality.

In contrast, Mapuche associated the Anglican and Capuchin Bibles with God's power, missionization, and literacy. These Bibles inspired the production of Mapuche bibles and were themselves put to shamanic use as ritual objects.[31] Mapuche in the Quepe area were heavily influenced by the Bible readings given by Italian Capuchin Catholic and North American Anglican Protestant missionaries during the nineteenth century. The Capuchins' goal was to evangelize the Mapuche and fully incorporate them into the Chilean state and the Catholic Church, so they created parallels between Catholic figures, beliefs, and practices and those of the Mapuche people. Capuchins gained followers by expelling devils, and in this effort machi and priests found parallels in their identities and ritual practices (Bacigalupo 1995, 2007, 2008). The Anglican missionaries were even more open to Mapuche culture than were the Capuchins and allowed polygamy and Mapuche *palin* games to persist. But the Anglican missionaries and teachers in Quepe also taught literacy, integration with the state, and the Christian Bible as early as 1895 (Menard and Pavez 2007).

Mapuche valued the Capuchin and Anglican Bibles, which gave them access to the healing powers of the Bible's authors, saints, and deity as well as to a new way of expressing prophetic power and recording historical memory. Many Mapuche leaders who were educated in the Quepe mission used the Bible in novel ways that made sense in terms of their identities but did not help them to integrate into a homogenous Chilean society (Menard and Pavez 2007). These leaders were conscious of the symbolic power of written production and appropriated it for themselves to enhance their status as "civilized."

In the early twentieth century Mapuche prophets (*profetas*) experienced revelatory dreams about the Mapuche's future. These leaders embarked on new forms of engagement with the church through the production of their own Mapuche bibles in Spanish, and they situated the European Christian symbolic system within a Mapuche sociopolitical and spiritual context. Through these bibles, the prophets created parallels between Mapuche spirituality, Judaism, and Christianity. Literate prophets manipulated orality and literacy according to multiple cultural criteria to negotiate between their views of the world and Chilean postcolonial society. They wrote down previously oral narratives of dreams and encounters with saints and spirits in ways that combined the "before time" and "today time." They wove these stories into bibles, incorporating the power of Jesus and the apostles into shamanic epistemologies and legitimating shamanic conceptions of history. But unlike machi, these prophets did not engage directly with spirits during altered states of consciousness to perform rituals and heal. Instead, Mapuche prophets subverted the discourse of the Catholic and Protestant missionaries by claiming that God speaks directly to Mapuche shamans and prophets, thus making priests and ministers unnecessary (Delrío 2005:108–109). Prophet Manuel Aburto Panguilef, for example, was "possessed by writing" and viewed his text as a potent object. He produced hundreds of pages describing his dreams and his reflections on political and spiritual practice. Aburto's son Germán compared his father to the prophet Samuel (Menard 2013:xciv). Although Panguilef was a prophet and not a shaman, he created parallels between the roles of Catholic priests, shamans, and prophets. He described himself as a prophet, as "the *machi* of all machi," and as the "king of Araucanía" (Menard 2003:7–8).

Panguilef argued that Mapuche should maintain a political and ethnic identity separate from the Chilean state by retaining their traditional social norms, dreams, and rituals. He argued for the maintenance of polygamy, *datun*, and *ngillatun* while also engaging with progressive intellectuals (Foerster 1983:115). He celebrated the "brilliant history" of Mapuche resistance to assimilation by the Chilean state, arguing that Mapuche ancestral lands were a space for traditional culture, spiritual practice, and historical memory (Crow 2010; Mallon 2005:90; Menard and Pavez 2005). He incorporated Christianity into his practice and asked for the God of all saints to bless the Mapuche, "the chosen people," by affirming their unique relationship with divinity and nature (Menard 2013). At the same time, he drew on

Jewish prophetism and the Christian concept of divine justice rather than on Mapuche shamanic historicity.

Severiano Alcaman, a Mapuche educated by the Capuchins in the second half of the twentieth century, who later became a priest and an anthropologist, wrote a bible in which he recorded shamanic power and Mapuche rituals. He sought to legitimate them as divine teachings akin to those of Jesus. He used his prestigious position to justify Mapuche beliefs and shamanic powers in the eyes of the Chilean majority.

For some Mapuche, reading and interpreting Christian Bibles competes with and undermines the agency of shamans and their direct experience of spirits through prayer and possession. *Longko* Jorge Sandoval argued that "machi who use texts and Bibles are not spiritual. Machi must follow their spirits and not have the Bible in front of them [to guide them]" (January 4, 2011). But some machi use Bibles as subjective ritual objects, and those texts become crucial instruments in shamanic practices and machi biographies.

Some male shamans in Quepe identified themselves as "Mapuche machi priests" or as "biblical machi" in order to gain power from Catholicism and its rituals and to revitalize Mapuche shamanic traditions. The Mapuche machi priests sought to establish their spiritual superiority over nonindigenous clerics and missionaries on the basis of their direct communication with the divine. They used their Christian title to criticize the ambiguous side of Mapuche shamanism—amorality, sorcery, gender shifting[32]—and to construct themselves as moral, celibate men who were legitimate both in local terms and in those of the Chilean majority (Bacigalupo 2005, 2008).[33] As a woman, Francisca could not claim the identity of a Mapuche machi priest or a biblical machi. And she did not perform rituals in the Catholic Church of Quepe, which some female machi did. But she identified herself as a Catholic machi and obtained powers from the Virgin Mary, the Bible, and Saint Francis.

"Celestial bibles" figure prominently in machi dream narratives and compete with those revered by evangelical Mapuche, who say that the names of the saved are written in golden letters in such a bible.[34] Machi, in contrast, link celestial bibles to their own life histories. In machi Marcelina's initiatory dream, for example, the Virgin Mary had a "paper like a will in her hand . . . and on top of her purse she had a huge Bible with [Marcelina's] name in it and a silver cross" (Bacigalupo 2004b:442). Machi José learned in his dream that my ethnographic writings about him would be mirrored in his celestial bible: "If you do your work well, Mariella, it will be written in the sky. . . . It will be like a 'bible' about me" (Bacigalupo 2007:142). Several machi told me that on the Christian Day of Judgment, time would end and the dead would be judged on the basis of what was written about them and their works in the book of life, which they interpreted as celestial bibles about their lives. Machi Francisca did not dream of a celestial bible, however. She wanted me to write a bible about her that would exist on this earth after she died, and she believed that through this bible her shamanic spirit would return.

Michael Taussig (1993) and Paul Stoller (1995) argued that less powerful people may copy their dominators in an attempt to appropriate the oppressors' extraordinary power. But as Fernando Santos-Granero (2009b:492–493) has pointed out, this creative strategy may also be an attempt by the less powerful to subdue the hegemonic other by using the cultural tools at their disposal. Panguilef, Alcaman, Francisca, and other machi sought to appropriate their dominators' powers through magically produced, indigenized versions of Anglican and Capuchin Bibles, and in doing so, they construed their personal and ethnic identities as well as their political autonomy in a new context. Mapuche men identified as Catholic machi, machi priests, or biblical machi (Bacigalupo 2005, 2008), but they did not want to permanently become like the Christian *wingka*. They used indigenized Christian concepts and symbols to "wrestle control of Christianity from whites while reshaping them to meet the needs of Indian people" (Brown 1991:401) and to produce bibles of their own. Francisca identified as a Catholic machi and referred to her biography as a bible because she wanted to contribute to the existing genre of prophetic bibles, which make sense of multiple and mutable identities, as others had done under the influence of Christian missionaries.

Francisca demanded that I write a bible about her because she wanted her words to have the weight and permanence of the authoritative text of the church *and* the power of a Mapuche prophetic bible. Francisca's bible is a sacred and powerful object that contains her machi spirit. It is not a commoditized fetish whose power is determined by abstract market values. She believed that my shamanic biography of her would absorb her shamanic power and validate her as a powerful prophet and Catholic shaman in much the same way that the Christian Bible had absorbed the powers of God, Jesus, and the apostles and validated them along with the power of the Christian *wingka*. Francisca also believed that her bible would store and circulate her shamanic power after her death.

This multiplicity of bibles—those used by different Christian denominations, those produced by Mapuche prophets, the celestial bibles of machi, and the bible I have written about Francisca—has implications for Mapuche's personal and collective memories, identity making, and perceptions of the sacred. Prophets wrote bibles to record their interpretations of Mapuche collective memory in textual form and to negotiate traditional spiritualities and new identities in relation to but separate from the Chilean nation-state and the church. Machi incorporate Bibles into their shamanic practices, and these texts become sacred objects that store and circulate the personal power of a machi's spirit. Bibles can also serve collective ends and be used for healing (Anglican Capuchin and Mapuche bibles) or to destroy the other (Lutheran Bibles). By appropriating the dominator's powers and using these powers for their own ends, machi challenge the processes of colonization and missionization and create new collective memories in which Mapuche become the spiritual victors of history.

SHAMANIC BIBLES, SPIRITUAL AGENCY, AND HISTORY

I have shown that while many indigenous people use texts as ritual objects independent from Global North ways of reading and understanding the alphabet, Mapuche also produce or commission sacred texts of their own to narrate indigenous histories and to circulate shamanic power. Francisca's bible offers a new understanding of the role of the written word in shamanic literacies and of shamanic biographies in the creation of indigenous historical consciousness and in the production of history. Machi expand notions of indigenous literacy and temporality by linking bibles to Mapuche individual and collective memories; to shamanic experiences of colonization, missionization, and *mestizaje*; and to disputed ideas about historical continuity, death, and rebirth. Mapuche shamanic biographical narratives are not only a mechanism through which individual histories become collective primordial histories and vice versa, they are also instrumental in shamanic rebirth.

Shamanic literacy expands ideas about how *grafismo* and writing operate as discourses of power because Mapuche shamans infuse Bibles with a new kind of intertextuality that emphasizes nonliterate oral narrations, shamanic perceptions of reality, and performative ways of storing and circulating power. The permanence of alphabetic script preserved in books has been brought into Mapuche notions of history and memory, and writing thus provides a new medium through which Mapuche can appropriate the power of outsiders and propagate shamanic power. In this shamanic literacy, alphabetic script not only channels the words and histories of shamans but also holds the power of shamanic spirits themselves. When smoked and chanted over, alphabetic script can produce history by enabling the rebirth of shamanic spirits in the bodies of new machi. Belief in this rebirth has provided Francisca's community with both structural continuity and the possibility of transformation—in other words, with local history—even in the new textualized form of Mapuche shamanic bibles. And this alternative history is able to explain new interethnic relations and other fundamental changes that occur in the dynamic context of modernity and colonialism.

Spirits can become effective historical agents if we allow for experiences, narratives, and worlds that are beyond the intentions of authors, exceed the limits of the archive, and acknowledge new forms of prophetic engagement between spirits and texts (Fausto and Heckenberger 2007:14; Salomon 1999). Mapuche spirits are unique in that they acquire historical agency as they animate texts, transforming them into ritual objects and linking them to the transformations of personhood and the processes of disremembering and remembering that take place after a shaman's death. Francisca's historical agency was evident when she used her spirit to manipulate the community's land title map, reviving the past reality under which the map was produced and changing history for the benefit of present and future Mapuche.

Francisca understood that Christian Bibles are sacred texts, but in her hands they also became ritual objects infused with power and had the ability to transform the world and the future. She and her family believed that her bible would store her disembodied powers within the quotations of her words printed on the page and would circulate them through time and space. The transformation of Francisca's shamanic power into text would not diminish the force of her words, which would continue to exert her agency even in her absence. But since the physicality of writing also affects that which it represents, I had to be precise and careful about what I wrote. Francisca's being is situated in the otherworld and in the past, while my text is of this world and the present, and this potent new textualized object has the potential to reinforce her authority by offering her a transcendental position from which to speak to an audience in the distant future.[35]

Bibles can transform the shape of Mapuche history and the sacred. Francisca's powers, individual life history, and dreams are now mediated by this bible and are stored permanently in alphabetic text. This bible also defies Mapuche shamanic perceptions of history-making because it challenges Francisca's changing personhood through the politics of remembering and forgetting in Mapuche communities—from historical figures during life, to ancestral ones at death, and then back as individuals cleansed of their antisocial qualities at the moment of rebirth. It was only after the community rewrote their own memories of Francisca that her family allowed me to write her bible. This bible will allow Francisca's individual identity to reemerge in a new context and presumably aid her spiritual rebirth in a new machi's body.

Shamanic literacy—and Francisca's bible as a ritual object—suggests a new medium that both documents and makes possible her reindividualization, rehistoricization, and perhaps rebirth in the future, perpetuating historical consciousness and making history. And as I show in the next chapters, Francisca's shamanic bible and histories also played a central role in the way people in Millali conceived of their relations with settlers and the state during the achronological "time of civilization" and "time of wilderness and warfare."

CHAPTER SIX

The TIME of WARRING THUNDER, the SAVAGE STATE, and CIVILIZED SHAMANS

Francisca's body tensed and quivered, her eyes dark with fury, as she pounded her small fist on the blue plastic tablecloth. She was shouting at Enrique Huenchuñir and Julio Huilcan, who sat sheepishly before her with downcast eyes. It was April 25, 1995, and they had cut down machi Rosa Kurin's colossal *boldo* tree in order to plant eucalyptus—an invasive tree brought by settlers that damages the soil, depletes the water table, and kills the spirit masters of the forests. Worse yet, Enrique was machi Rosa's great-grandson and should have known better. For Francisca, this native *boldo* tree was Rosa in person—in body and in thunder spirit. And Francisca shared personhood with Rosa, who had prayed beside this very *boldo* tree to save the world from destruction. It embodied the history of Rosa's kinship with past shamans, with Francisca, and with shamans yet to come. "Why did you cut me? My own family is cutting me?" Francisca wailed.

By axing the *boldo*, Enrique and Julio had destroyed the tree of life that tied the people of Millali to their land, its history, and the complex set of human and spirit relations in it. People in Millali called this *boldo* a *rewe*, which refers both to the relations of humans and nonhumans in a specific territory and to the tree of life that connects different times and spaces—the "before time" with "today time" and the human physical world with the spiritual worlds.[1] For machi, the tree of life complements the drum. Drums allow machi spirits to travel to many geographic and spiritual worlds and express their mobile histories; trees of life ground the different temporal and spatial worlds in local histories embedded in a specific landscape, to which machi spirits must return after their spiritual travels. Enrique and Julio had destroyed Millali's connection with other worlds and times. They had also marred Millali's history, including its interconnections with the wild spirits, the cycles of animals and plants, and the *newen* of the people who belonged to that place, as well as with Rosa's kin (whether through blood, adoption, or affinity)—including Enrique and Julio themselves, Julio's son Jorge (who had told them to cut the tree and had then fallen ill), Francisca, and many others in Millali. "Why did you hit that *boldo* if you knew it had the power of thunder and the knowledge of the forests and the past?" Francisca screamed, tears streaming down her face. "Go and bring your sister and your family to support you in the *datun*, because you won't be able to do this alone. And if Jorge dies, you can't blame me or say that I killed him."

That dark night Francisca performed a *datun* ritual, which brings forth the time of warfare. Francisca first invoked and appeased the wild thundering power of the *boldo* tree. Then, like a warrior, she confronted the neoliberal spirits of greed and individualism that had led Enrique and Julio to cut the tree down. Francisca lunged at these spirits with crossed knives. She shot her gun, which also carried the wild unmediated power of thunder (*tralkan*).[2] But when Huenchuñir family members were clashing sticks over Francisca's head to help her enter into trance, Jacinto Huenchuñir's stick broke—a bad omen. The spirits of thunder machi and the masters of the forest—amoral and concerned with their own well-being—would exact revenge against the perpetrators for their transgression. Francisca cursed and spat on the floor to counteract the fury of the thunder spirit in the *boldo* tree.

Francisca managed to heal Jorge, but a short time later, both Julio and Enrique died. Jorge's brother Pedro became lame in one leg and fled Millali. Francisca prayed at the stump of Rosa's *boldo* several times a day, asking for forgiveness and trying to restore the force of the tree, and the stump quickly sprouted new shoots, regenerating the historical continuity between times, generations, and worlds joined by Rosa's thundering spirit (fig. 6.1). Francisca and other community members believed that this new growth was proof that Rosa's powers remained in Millali, as did her shamanic temporalities—even if in a diminished form.

For Francisca and many Mapuche, wild unmediated power and violence take the shape of thunder, which acts in an achronological "time of wilderness and warfare" interpreted by Mapuche as the "time of spirit masters of the forest and warfare." In this time, machi use thunder to link the spirit masters of the native forests and stones with ancient warriors and military men. Thunder is used to exorcise evil spirits during healing rituals and to conduct spiritual warfare against enemies, such as representatives of the state-sponsored timber companies that cut down native species. Some Mapuche use these thundering powers to fight for the recovery of their ancestral lands. The Chilean state endorses the settlers' project—their claim to land rights, belonging, and history in southern Chile during the "time of

FIGURE 6.1
The stump and shoots of Rosa Kurin's massive boldo *tree (photo by author).*

civilization." But the unmediated power of native forest spirits and thunder legitimizes shamanism, the Mapuche people's rights to the land, and
the historical continuity between past, present, and future during the time
of spirit masters of the forest and warfare. This time also encompasses the
Mapuche's wars with various *wingka* forces, though these took place during various chronological periods.[3] For Mapuche, the time of spirit masters
of the forest and warfare did not precede the advent of the nation-state and
"civilization"; instead, it is a condition across time—a "social formation defined by its relationship with the state" (Scott 2009:208).

Mapuche in Millali consider acts like those of Enrique and Julio—who
damaged the *boldo* tree and betrayed the wild spirit masters—as belonging to the negative time of wilderness and warfare created by *wingka*. Pedro
Morales, *longko* of Imilco, explained: "Those who cut sacred trees and plant
eucalyptus trees think they are civilized entrepreneurs, but they really have
wesh wesh rakiduam [bad thoughts] and then become savages like Schleyer"
(December 17, 2012). Enrique and Julio disrupted the community's close
relationships with the beings of the forest and challenged the interests of
their own families and community. But they were not what Eduardo Kohn
(2013:117) called "soul blind"—unable to see beyond themselves and their
need for money to recognize the selfhood, or the soul stuff, of trees. Rather,
Enrique and Julio chose money over the powerful *boldo* tree and the com-

munity's well-being because they were willing to risk the tree's anger to make a better living for their children.

By celebrating their connection to the past through thunder, the spirits of native forests, and warriors, Francisca and other Mapuche inadvertently reinforce settlers' perceptions of shamans as wild people, living at the periphery of the state's sedentary social order of "governance and civilization" (Scott 2009:121). The settlers' mythology sees the "wild shamans" as existing in an unchanging past of prophetism, disorder, and difference, and as using magic to kill or to heal socially caused illnesses; the settlers simultaneously see the shamans as less than and more than human. The colonists sought healing from shamans while at the same time using the brutal technologies of civilization to kill them and other "savage" natives. Although settlers attempted to tame the wilderness, they needed the shamans to keep their wild force while serving as handmaidens to the civilized order (Taussig 1987:220, 240). Francisca explained, "My enemies are afraid of my healing powers. 'People killer,' they say. 'The people will all finish [die] if you are around'" (January 10, 1992). Although some Mapuche internalize these labels, others reverse the colonists' perspective by construing logging companies and the state as savage and the spirit masters of the ecosystem as truly civilized.

Scholars have worked with the rhetoric of savagery and civilization as forms of colonial discourse, but Mapuche have a unique way of shaping that ideological discourse to fit their struggles for alliance, resistance, and realpolitik. In this chapter I describe how the forces of the spirit masters and thunder disrupt current hegemonic political formations, allowing the emergence of a modern Mapuche politics combining spiritual, ecological, and social factors. These forces cannot be reduced to the realms of nature or symbolism. Instead, Mapuche need to be understood and recognized as political and historical agents with their own ways of engaging Chilean histories, the politics of land appropriation and exploitation, and the political ideologies of state leaders over time. To this end, I analyze the complex and diverse political usages of *civilization*, *wilderness*, and *savagery* by Francisca and her community, as well as the grounding of these responses in an alternative indigenous spiritual politics combined with realpolitik.

Shamanic power does not reside on the same plane as political ideology, although it can support political movements. The fluid and contradictory ways in which Francisca and other people in Millali have understood the time of spirit masters of the forest and warfare do not reflect the ideologies of political parties or Mapuche resistance movements. Instead, their notions derive from shamanic understandings of power, warfare, and time, through which people in Millali articulate conflicts within the community, wars with the Chilean state (1861–1883) and with Allende's socialist regime (1970–1973), and disputes with Pinochet's military regime (1973–1989) and with subsequent democratic and authoritarian governments (1990–present). In this chapter I consider the relationships among contrasting (and sometimes ambivalent) narratives about the time of spirit masters of the forest and warfare, the agents who produce and consume them, and the particular histories of state violence in which they are embedded. I also analyze the settlers' and the Mapuche's politics of confrontation, including local visions of how to defeat hostile forces and the efforts made to accomplish those goals. I describe how Mapuche conceive of deforestation and the timber industry, as well as the regimes of Allende, Pinochet, and those that followed, as one entity directing armies of foreign trees to kill the spirit masters of the ecosystem.

I also show how for Francisca and others, Pinochet's military power came to intersect with the military power of Mapuche warrior chiefs and with Mapuche sociopolitical and spiritual hierarchies and epistemologies. Not without political irony, Francisca invoked the "wild" military powers of Pinochet to perform spiritual warfare against evil spirits, "communist sorcerers," and collective Mapuche enemies, such as *wingka* civilization, the timber industry, *awingkamiento*, and the broader neoliberalism that thrived during the post-Pinochet democratic regimes.

Since Mapuche experience the savagery of the state as one persistent whole, female machi have developed a pragmatic politics that allows them to negotiate with a wide range of political authorities for the benefit of Mapuche, without committing to any one party. When settlers revived the ideologies of violence and domination from the War of Pacification, projecting them onto their relations with Mapuche during Pinochet's military regime and the violent democratic regimes that followed, they constructed Mapuche as savage "terrorists." People in Millali reacted by dreaming a new moral order in which civilized shamanism with a broad vision of the universe was separated from military power and led to the revival of parliaments among equals that could engage democratic presidents. As I discuss below, the terms *nature* and *culture*, like *civilized* and *savage*, came to have radically altered meanings among Mapuche, who experience their reality in such different ways.

SPIRIT MASTERS AND MAPUCHE POLITICS OF HOME

Domingo Katrikura and Pedro Morales, *longko* of the communities of Chihuimpilli and Imilco, respectively, huddled close to the wood-burning stove in Pedro's home, carefully avoiding the chili peppers, garlic, and dried meat hanging from the ceiling as they sipped yerba mate from a gourd they passed. Like most Mapuche in the Quepe area, they had challenged the German colonists' claims of civilization, morality, and belonging by asserting claims of priority, moral indigeneity, the presence of spirit masters, and sustainable land use. Although both men agreed that Mapuche practice a politics of multiple belonging rather than identifying solely with one place, they also embraced the notion of a specific homeland. Domingo denied that the German settlers were legitimate inhabitants of Araucanía: "The Germans are not from here. They are foreign immigrants who came to steal our land. We Mapuche are the original, native inhabitants of this region. We were born here and lived here way before the settlers arrived. The spirits of the ancestors are in this land." Pedro added, "Every little thing in nature has a spirit owner. In every part there are *ngenmawida* [spirit owners of forests], *ngenko* [spirit owners of water]. We just don't see them. On the top of the Millali hill, we have a powerful stone that is growing. . . . Next to it is a *palo trébol* that people use to make herbal remedies, and [they] leave money or some wool as an offering. . . . Nature is what moves us" (June 9, 2010; fig. 6.2).

Using a shamanic lens, Mapuche in the Quepe area construct relational histories that are inseparable from their territories and the beings that inhabit them: humans, animals, plants, ancestors, a variety of spirit masters of particular ecosystems (*ngen*), and other spirits. Reciprocity is key to these relationships, and humans make offerings of maize, wool, and coins to *ngen* in order to get their permission to extract herbal remedies, cut wood, and work the soil. In this ecosystem, spirits and deities are superior to shamans and chiefs, who in turn are superior to ordinary Mapuche in the hierarchy of knowledge and power (Bacigalupo 1996b, 1997). Spirits have agency and understand human language, actions, and thoughts. While ordinary Mapuche can only communicate and gain power or knowledge from spirits through dreams and visions, machi employ spiritual kinship, spiritual marriage, and their mastery over spirits and animals.

The Mapuche people's spiritual and environmentally sustainable approach to the land challenged the settlers' fantasies of wild emptiness. The arrowheads, ceramics, yokes, precious stones, planting and grinding stones, and vestiges of settlements found on the Millali hill indicate that the people combined cattle raising and rotational field cultivation so as not to deplete the land.[4] Many years prior to the arrival of the Chileans and Germans, the Mapuche had much land, and their way of cultivating made a minimal visual impact on the landscape (McFall 2002; Le Bonniec 2009). *Ngen* grant individuals or families permission to cut small clearings in the woods

FIGURE 6.2

The ngenko *or spirit owner of the waterfall at Millali hill (photo by author).*

to cultivate crops for subsistence purposes, but the spirit masters hex those who practice large-scale intensive farming or who cut down trees for the timber industry (Bacigalupo 1996b, 2007). Native forests were essential to Mapuche medicinal and spiritual practices. Mapuche left some native forests untouched and gave offerings to the *ngen*, who granted them permission to take herbal remedies for healing. Mapuche also performed rituals on the top of the Millali hill, a sacred landscape imbued with deep cultural significance, for hills are living kin that maintain relationships between the patrilineages, the living and the dead, and the past, present, and future. For Mapuche, hills serve as memorials for ancestors and family histories and are the loci for ceremonies, feasts, and political speeches (Dillehay 2007). The loss of land is therefore not just an economic issue for Mapuche, but a historical and ontological one. Without their sacred landscapes, the Mapuche's ways of being and local history are threatened.

The idea of a culturally and ethnically distinct Mapuche homeland inhabited by spirit masters has had even more salience since the imposition of the reservation system and the advent of an increasingly urban Mapuche culture. In response to such challenges, displaced people often cluster around remembered or imagined communities attached to imagined homelands (Gupta and Ferguson 1997:39), and being "from the motherland" has become a more important form of engagement with Mapuche identity than the reality of being fixed in a rural community (Bacigalupo 2004c, 2007:155). For example, Mapuche use the term *rewe* to refer simultaneously to a kin-based community tied to a particular landscape; to a machi's *axis mundi*, which both ties her spirit to a particular landscape and allows her to travel to other spiritual realms; and to the collective tree of life of a ritual community, which ties it to a particular land in the present. Although most Mapuche living in Chile and Argentina today are urban dwellers, their rural ancestral territories and the ancient forests remain central to their notions of identity, autonomy, and self-determination.

Because the United Nations views indigeneity as bound to culture and territory, this position is the one from which indigenous people have been able to argue most convincingly for their rights to land and self-determination (Bacigalupo 2004c; Muehlebach 2003:251, 253). As Rudi Colloredo-Mansfeld (2002) showed for the Ecuadorian Otavalo, indigenous self-determination is not bounded by indigenous territories; instead, the Otavalo engage in "relational" and "situational autonomy" linked to the geographical mobility of peasant labor. Similarly, urban Mapuche are not tied to their ancestral lands, but they do not have the political clout to negotiate the terms of their "relational self-determination" apart from cultural and territorial demands. As Andrea Muehlebach (2003:258) has written, "The rights to self-determination and territory are a starting point from which indigenous peoples could properly negotiate more equitable futures for themselves." To the Mapuche from Millali, land is central to their identity, autonomy, and self-determination, but their impoverished holdings cannot sustain the growing local population. Those who have stayed in their community do not have enough capital to buy seed, fertilizers, and machinery to farm the land, and many end up working as farmhands for settlers.

THE COSMOPOLITICS OF SPIRIT MASTERS AND THE SAVAGE ARMIES OF PINE AND EUCALYPTUS TREES

On January 7, 2012, Fernando Añiwal and Pedro Millañir (both *longko* of Millali after Segundo Millañir died in 2004) walked me around their dry plots of land. Fernando pointed at the rows of eucalyptus trees planted on the *fundo* just above Millali. Francisca had complained that these eucalyptus trees "dried up" her shamanic power, and Fernando described them as "savage armies of eucalyptus and pine trees that kill the *ngenmawida* [spirit masters of the forest], our community, and our history." Pedro and Fernando saw the history of Millali as located in the time of civilization because this history was constructed collectively through the knowledge of human and nonhuman beings. This broad, civilized history allowed these interrelated beings to live well in the present and to construct a better future. But Pedro and Fernando viewed thunder and spirit masters as existing in the time of spirit masters of the forest and warfare; they protected the community against foreign species and against *wingka* notions of nature as separate from history and politics. Pedro viewed the Chilean state and forestry companies as creating the *wingka* time of savagery and warfare, which included state violence, greed, timber harvesting, and plantations of eucalyptus and pine trees:

> The *wingka* are destroying our history, which is in the cycles of the plants and animals, and separating us from our people. . . . The settlers and timber companies live among us. They have cut down the native forests and plants, which is changing the generation, which is changing the soil, the cycles, which is changing our lives, our history. It is the same thing that they do with us Mapuche. They hope to eliminate us. The farms all have tree plantations, and they [the settlers] fumigate, and the birds eat those fumigated seeds and die. The *copiwe* flowers, the partridges, the hares are all gone. The *perimotu* [visions], the spirit owners

have left. . . . The *wingka* advances forward, but doesn't learn from nature and doesn't look at the past. . . . Our warriors defended our land and our *kimün* [wisdom], and all the Chilean presidents fought on the side of greed, with guns.[5]

Fernando described the spirit masters of the forests as angry beings that are producing accidents, earthquakes, and drought—all because the marriage between capitalists, the state, and timber companies introduced nonnative trees:

> *Wingka* brought armies of pine and eucalyptus and destroyed [the] spirit masters of native forests. Now, nature is asking for payback. It is claiming what belonged to it. The spirit masters of forests rejected Piñera, the multimillionaire president. When he was sworn in there was an earthquake, and we knew that a bad time was coming. There was the disaster with the miners, a plane fell, and there have been all these fires and drought. We did a *ngillatun*, and machi asked for rain. But it only rained for one day. We pray for all Chile in our *ngillatun* rituals, but some people don't behave well, and then nature punishes everyone. We poor Mapuche are paying for it. But all Chilean presidents say we are savages and terrorists, and they shoot us. We Mapuche, [the] plants, and [the] forests are at war with the timber companies and settlers. The time of spirit masters of the forest and warfare has returned. (January 7, 2012)

Like most Mapuche, Pedro and Fernando situate the spirit masters as simultaneously in the sacred world and in modernity; they are beings with demands, agency, and intentionality who relate to humans and play a central role in both Mapuche history and politics. Spirit masters practice what Marisol de la Cadena (2015) has called "cosmopolitics." They are crucial actors in local Mapuche and national politics, which are intertwined within the same socionatural world. Mapuche spirit masters, like Runa ones (Kohn 2013:133), make value assessments based on what is good or bad for their living components and their potential for growth. The wild thundering power of spirit masters protects Mapuche ways of life and confronts the savage devils and the armies of pine and eucalyptus along with the state, settlers, and timber companies driven by greed.

When Pedro and Fernando made demands to the state, NGOs, or environmental movements, however, they excluded the spirit masters from politics and represented them as "nature." Unlike Andeans (de la Cadena 2015), Mapuche do not frame the colonialist and Mapuche views of nature as political conflicts. Instead, they see the dominant modern order of life, in which nature belongs to science, in contrast with the human order, in which nature belongs to culture and politics (Latour 1993:27). While arguing that native forests must be protected from the damage wrought by logging, pesticides, and the acidic soil produced by pine and eucalyptus plantations, Pedro and Fernando constructed the Mapuche demands in terms of cultural rights, ethnic identity, and ecology, not as the demands of a sentient forest. In Elizabeth Povinelli's terms, Pedro and Fernando accepted the frame of indigeneity that liberalism requires (2002:329). Francisca, in contrast, refused to reduce her opposition to the timber industry to political economics, cultural politics, or challenges to state secularism. Rather, she expanded the concept of nature by using the shamanic notion of power, so that it included the agency of thunder and of the spirit masters of the forests in addition to the agency of politicians. Francisca's politics of power was a specific kind of Mapuche cosmopolitics. Beings like the *boldo* tree retained their political agency, although *wingka* were not able to see and understand them.

THE BATTLE OF SACRED LANDSCAPES AGAINST AGRARIAN REFORM AND THE TIMBER INDUSTRY

People in Millali speak of the time of savagery and warfare produced by the Chilean state as a historical continuum across different political regimes. Within this time, Mapuche temporal dislocation conflates several phenomena: the Chilean state's secularization of indigenous people's land; its support for the individualistic, capitalist perspective of *wingka* settlers; the egalitarian, class-based consciousness advanced by socialist president Allende; and the continued alliance between the military, settlers, and timber companies forged during the government of Pinochet and prevalent even during the subsequent democratic regimes. The battles Mapuche have waged to protect their sacred landscapes have been broadly consistent throughout this "time," but also different in form under each regime.

The secular, class-based ideas of socialism and egalitarianism advocated by Allende challenged Mapuche ideas about social order, spiritual agency, and ethnicity. Allende would not consider Mapuche-specific ethnic demands (Bengoa 1999:138; Mallon 2005:83, 88); instead, he challenged their hierarchical sociopolitical models and allowed no space for Mapuche spirituality and shamanic practices. Many Mapuche rejected the Communist Party's view that Mapuche are "peasants and workers with the same economic problems as other poor Chileans" and that those problems can only be "solved through social revolution" (Bengoa and Valenzuela 1984:203–

205). Francisca and others in Millali feared that one communist credo—
"the land belongs to those who work it"—would allow outsiders to take
their remaining lands and kill the spirit masters inhabiting them. Mapuche
argued that communist ideologies are incompatible with a Mapuche culture focused on relationships with animals and spirits (Ayllapan and Munizaga 1971).

Allende tried to solve the problems of low productivity and underutilization of land on the large farms in the province of Cautín (in the region of Araucanía), which had emerged between 1940 and 1970, by helping the settlers to modernize their estates and by implementing agrarian
reforms to break up large, unproductive farms into small plots for non-
Mapuche family farming.[6] In 1972 the agrarian reform law expropriated
and divided up some large farms in the Quepe area to create *asentamien-*
tos, which are collective, non-Mapuche peasant settlements.[7] Elizabeth
Schleyer—who owned some of those expropriated farms—experienced
Allende's agrarian reform as an illegal usurpation of her family's land and
a destruction of the economic, social, and political power of settlers in the
region:[8]

> The Allendistas gave Mapuche the idea that they could take over the
> lands of their *patrones*. . . . Mapuche here became divided. Most of them
> followed the Rapiman family of Imilco, who supported us because they
> know we are the ones who give them jobs. A few went with the Allendis-
> tas, who cut down all the trees of our groves except for one. There is no
> memory of our history left. . . . We worked those lands, and then Allende
> expropriated them and we had to buy them back. (June 28, 2007)

Mapuche's engagement with the agrarian reform varied by region. The
reform benefited Mapuche in some areas, like the coastal community of
Alio, which after much debate decided to adopt a socialist, class-based perspective and associate with the Movimiento Campesino Revolucionario
(Revolutionary Peasant Movement) so the socialist state would give them
some of the lands it expropriated from wealthy farmers (Mallon 2005). In
the Quepe area—where the authority of machi and *longko* tied to specific
landscapes predominated—*ngillatun* rituals helped maintain networks of
sociality and encouraged ethnic claims to Mapuche ancestral land in the
community. Most Mapuche in this area, including Francisca, opposed the
agrarian reform because Allende did not recover specific Mapuche ancestral lands that had been usurped by settlers. Mapuche in the Quepe area
saw the *asentamientos* as a government system designed to control their lives
even more than individual settlers had. One man from Millali recalled:

The workers started telling us we had to expropriate the farms without weapons. Even I went to a march in Temuco with a little stick on my shoulder like an idiot. They expropriated the lands of Puig family and gave them to Chilean peasants, who then sold them back to the settlers. They expropriated some land from Schleyer, which he then bought back, but they took nothing from the Lüer family here in Manzanar because the Mapuche workers protected their patron. The only Mapuche from around here that benefited a bit from the agrarian reform were the Lefian family [Francisca's maternal relatives], who gained some land from Ernst family in the Tumuntuco farm. We gained nothing. (June 15, 2007)

Francisca supported the Millali residents who asked Allende's government to expropriate the farms belonging to the Roth Schleyer family, which contained Mapuche sacred landscapes, and return them to the community. They specifically requested the farms Rucañanco and Campamento, home to RukaÑamku, the cosmic place of origin, the destination of ancestral souls, and a site of shamanic power. They also requested the farms Chucao and Europa, the home of Rüga Platawe, an old cemetery with buried treasures, where the owners of the ecosystem live. Francisca explained: "We asked for RukaÑamku and Rüga Platawe back because they have *newen* and belonged to our ancestors. The Millali mountain is angry that the gringos live there, and that's why we are suffering so much" (March 24, 1992).

During 1971 and 1972, when the Allende government denied the Mapuche's request because it did not advance agrarian reform—sacred landscapes, officials felt, only intensified the problem of underutilization of land in Cautín—Mapuche in the Quepe area occupied several large farms belonging to the Roth Schleyer, Ernst, and Lüer families.[9] Many Mapuche in the Cautín area did the same, recovering 300,000 hectares of land. But Allende's government deemed these occupations illegal and returned the land to the settlers. The Lüer and Ernst families tried to prevent further occupations by reporting some Mapuche in the Quepe area to the police.[10] People in Millali viewed these actions as proof that the agrarian reform subjugated Mapuche and favored settlers. They experienced Allende's denial of the validity of their occupying actions as symbolic violence and secular socialist sorcery because he recognized neither the agency of the mountain nor that of people in Millali, and he instead deemed Mapuche spiritual practices to be irrational and counterproductive.

General Augusto Pinochet, who took over in 1973, endorsed the power of the right-wing settlers, declaring both the agrarian reform and Mapuche and peasant occupations of farms to be illegal. Most of the lands that had been expropriated were returned to the German settlers. The land expropriations in the Quepe area were annulled, and the *wingka* recovered their farms (Reporte, Corporación Reforma Agraria, November 20, 1973). Under the radical free-market economic model instituted by Pinochet, harvesting timber and reforesting with eucalyptus and pine trees experienced a boom. Privatization, lowered environmental and labor standards, tax exemptions for foreign investors, and the promotion of forest exports all stimulated the modernization and expansion of the agricultural and timber industries. Deforestation worsened during the subsequent democratic regimes, which allowed national and transnational timber companies to invest in the region of Araucanía (Aylwin 2002; Klubock 2004, 2006). These profound ecological and social dislocations have greatly affected Millali.

Pinochet's land division law of 1979 prompted Francisca and other Mapuche to put their personal interests over those of the community. This law subdivided land titles held collectively by Mapuche into individual titles that were no longer considered indigenous land and thus were salable to outsiders.[11] The result was further assimilation, factional conflicts, and the loss of an additional 300,000 hectares of Mapuche land (Haughney 2007). The community of Millali was reduced to 202.26 hectares—a loss of 50.74 hectares from the original land title—and was divided into sixty-five individual plots. Francisca sold some of the land inherited from her father, Juancito Kolipi, to her maternal cousin Julia Lefian because she needed the money.[12] The Millañir family and other Mapuche who opposed Pinochet believed that by promoting individual interests, this law was directly responsible for the loss of Mapuche land to *wingka* and for an increase in sorcery. Francisca invoked Pinochet's power as a military *ülmen* (powerful Mapuche leader) to defend herself: "I had eight hectares, and we planted peas, maize, beans. But the people in the community let their animals into my field, and we had no harvest. I sold some of my land to my cousin Julia and bought wheat and potatoes so that we could survive for the year. . . . But the community came to pull my hair; they abhorred me because they said I had sold it to a rich *wingka*. I told them not to bother me, or General Pinochet would get them" (March 24, 1992).

Since 1990, the democratic governments have argued for a multicultural state and increased the number of cultural and development projects for Mapuche. But they have not recognized that the land division, the timber industry, racism (Richards 2013:2–3), and the dispossessed spirit masters of the land are at the root of their conflicts with indigenous people. The Chilean democratic presidents practice a form of neoliberal multiculturalism: they recognize indigenous peoples and grant them a limited measure of autonomy, but reject as counterproductive their demands for radical redistribution of resources, an autonomous territory, and self-determination (Hale 2002; Richards 2013:11).

Francisca and other Mapuche in the Quepe area believed that even the government's limited plan to return land was a trick because they did not recover the full rights to their ancestral lands. Although the democratic governments transferred more than 416,000 hectares to indigenous families between 1994 and 2004,[13] the law recognizes as "indigenous lands" only those deeded to Mapuche since the pacification, thus precluding Mapuche people's claims for the restoration of their ancestral territories. The state still owns the subsoil resources—such as water and minerals—near and within Mapuche communities and can sell the rights to exploit them (Haughney 2007).

People in Millali complain that the National Corporation of Indigenous Development (CONADI) violated their networks of emplacement—their relationships with specific lands and their spirits—when returning indigenous land. Pedro Morales (*longko* of Imilco and Francisca's brother-in-law) explained, "We asked CONADI to buy back our lands from Schleyer, but he charged too much, so CONADI offered us land for timber production in La Unión, near Osorno. But we are agriculturalists and don't want to live far away. We have to live here in our original lands. . . . This is where the spirits of the Millali hill are. Our *ngillatun* rituals have to be here" (December 17, 2012).

Mapuche in the Quepe area believe that Mapuche who recovered their lands from *wingka* have suffered because the land is now devoid of *ngenmawida*, the spirit masters of the native forest, and it contains some of the foreign settlers' life force, which is associated with the devil. Francisca said: "The gringos exploit the land with the help of the devil, who stays there even if the gringos leave. The land has to be plowed with salt to cleanse it" (March 24, 1992). *Longko* Jorge Sandoval suggested that Mapuche perform rituals to appease the violent gringo forces: "When the gringos make a farm, the *ngenmawida* leave and go to another place. But the *newen* of the gringo owner of the farm stays there. Mapuche who got some land back from a farm near Vilcún divided the land where the gringos used to be and put up fences without asking a machi to do a ritual first. Now they are all dead" (January 9, 2010).

PINOCHET AND MAPUCHE WARRIOR-SHAMANS

In the times of Pinochet, one could not speak. He was a powerful military man. He controlled everything. Those who left the house after

the 10 p.m. curfew were killed by the military police. . . . We didn't
perform ngillatun *rituals during Pinochet's time because we were afraid*
we would get shot. They shot people every night on the bridge at Pichi-
Quepe right next to the ngillatun *field. There were bullet holes and*
blood on the bridge. And screaming every night. . . . The police also
took advantage of the situation and killed those people they didn't like.
Jimenez, who was a policeman, would say, "You will be the next one.
I will chase you like cats in the plaza." He beat people like animals.
There was a sergeant, Juan Pinilla, who would come here, and he said,
"I killed Alejandro Ancao [Euladio Ancao's cousin]; we put him on
the bridge and shot him with our machine guns." Euladio went inside
himself. He didn't say anything, because his grandfather was in the
military, and he respects them. . . . The old [nineteenth-century] ülmen
like Mañkelef, Kolipi, Coñuepan were all authoritarian. People had to
obey them, or they would kill them, just like Pinochet. That's why here
in Araucanía, Mapuche always support the right [wing], the military.
They are afraid because if you talk badly about the military, they kill
you. And the rich settlers say, "If you don't support the right [wing],
the military, there will be no jobs."

—CONVERSATION WITH AMELIA AND
EULADIO ANCAO, JUNE 30, 2007

I was surprised to learn that Francisca, Euladio, and many Mapuche in the
Quepe area supported Pinochet. Since the 1970s most Latin American indigenous people had turned to the left, but this did not occur on a massive scale in the Quepe area until much later, in 2013. Having lived in Chile
through ten years of Pinochet's brutal dictatorship myself (1978–1988), I
could not fathom why so many Mapuche in the Quepe area during those
years embraced him. I knew it was not because they endorsed his right-
wing regime. I initially assumed that they supported Pinochet because they
had to if they wanted to save their lives and keep their jobs working for
right-wing settlers. But more was involved, which I came to understand by
examining the particular historical circumstances that led Mapuche in the
region of Araucanía to identify with military power. Central to their positioning was their understanding of local politics and shamanic practices,
along with the notions of parliaments and peace agreements. For people in
Millali, endorsement of Pinochet was an attempt to make sense, through
the lens of shamanic practice, of their complicated, contradictory history
and their vulnerability. By refusing to see the world through national politics, Francisca, Euladio, and others privileged shamanic ways of being and

seeing and shamanic practices of power in a kind of alternative machi politics that challenged *wingka* epistemologies, ideologies, and politics.

The alliance between settlers, the military, and the government was a central component of Mapuche people's experience of the time of spirit masters of the forest and warfare. Although many Mapuche supported the narratives of military regimes, they used these narratives for different ends. Euladio, Francisca, and other Mapuche in Quepe supported Pinochet because they read his military authority through Mapuche notions of power, hierarchy, and masculinity. Mapuche in the Quepe area hated police officers like Jimenez and Pinilla, but consented to the authoritarian military system that endorsed their crimes from 1973 to 1989. Comparable proportions of Mapuche and non-Mapuche were arrested, tortured, and killed during Pinochet's regime—not necessarily because they were militants in left-wing parties, but because the military believed they were a menace to development and could be manipulated by extremists. Nevertheless, most Mapuche in Araucanía, including Francisca and others in the Quepe area, supported Pinochet and voted for right-wing president Sebastián Piñera (2010–2014), and they continue to join the Chilean army in droves.[14] Like Euladio, many Mapuche are bitterly aware of their people's subordinate position and respond to it with fear and silence, and even by supporting the military and the right-wing parties to which settlers belong.

Francisca and other Mapuche in the Quepe area did not consider Allende to be a powerful *ülmen* like Kalfukura because he had no *newen*. Francisca argued: "His words had no force or justice. He was weak, stingy, and didn't respect machi" (February 2, 1992). Allende was an atheist with a class-based ideology who ignored Mapuche ethnic identity and spirituality. Although he was the president, Allende did not redistribute goods, impart justice, or otherwise provide for Mapuche, and they viewed his secular, egalitarian views as diminishing his authority and credibility. The Confederation of Araucanían Societies described Allende's government as "economic, social and moral chaos, . . . not interested in solving Mapuche problems, but in subjugating them through hunger and disorder, manipulating them through a regime of terror. . . . Instead of giving them land, seeds, machines and fertilizer, they gave them guns."[15] Mapuche did not see themselves as part of the national project, recognizing instead their own sovereignty. Mapuche who allied with the left did so for strategic reasons, not because they had developed a class or national consciousness (Foerster 1983:63; Caniuqueo 2006:195). Those who became political representatives of Allende and received benefits from the government were envied and criticized by other Mapuche—both for the challenge they posed to the Mapuche ethnic perspective and to local sociopolitical and spiritual hier-

---

archies (especially those of *longko* and machi) and for their failure to redistribute wealth to other community members (Caniuqueo 2006:198–199). In Millali, Allende supporters were accused of causing sorcery through *awingkamiento*. The only positive thing community members spoke of in terms of the Allende regime was that their textiles commanded higher prices.

In contrast, Mapuche in the Quepe area supported Pinochet's Catholic authoritarianism because they understood it in relation to the political power of nineteenth-century Mapuche *ülmen*, who developed their personal authority through a combination of charisma, persuasion, and force. *Ülmen* were lauded for their honorable behavior and for acting with respect toward their followers, to whom they granted wealth and benefits. Ordinary Mapuche sought to gain *newen* through personal interactions with *ülmen* and with non-Mapuche political, military, and spiritual authorities. In the nineteenth century, Mapuche traveled to Patagonia to gain prestige and to become men by associating with and warring against enemies, raiding for cattle and captives, and making money by selling cattle and salt. These Mapuche men also acquired spiritual powers from sacred stones. Alberto Calfuñir from Chihuimpilli characterized Kalfukura, the Mapuche who created the pan-Mapuche confederation in Salinas Grandes in 1835, as an *ülmen* with unlimited warrior-shaman powers: "He had more power than a president and controlled all the people. . . . When he wanted it to thunder, it thundered. . . . He did what he wanted, and he had his army that applauded him. . . . They searched his body and found that he had three hearts. . . . The spirits had given him three *newen*" (June 7, 2007).

Mapuche in the Quepe area also supported the right-wing settlers because the relationship of *patronazgo* endorsed by the settlers seemed to be compatible in many respects with Mapuche hierarchical social systems and the social value of mutual recognition. Some Mapuche viewed the settlers as generous, antisocialist, wealthy *ülmen* who gave them jobs, protected them, and understood that Mapuche were ethnically different. Even after Pinochet was deposed in 1990, most Mapuche continued to support their *patrones* and the right-wing ideologies that promised "order, progress, and jobs" for indigenous peoples (Caniuqueo 2006:198).[16] Euladio Ancao stated, "I vote for the party of the rich people, because they have money, they give us jobs, and they have power." Euladio boasted that Walter Lüer, lieutenant general of the Chilean air force in Colina under Pinochet, helped him to achieve material benefits and recognition: "I had a butcher shop, [and] he asked me to send four cows a week for the high military authorities in Colina. Lüer was a good *patrón*. 'Come in and drink chicha,' he would tell me. 'Bring this man a sack of potatoes,' he would tell one of the workers.

He trusted me to take his cattle to Freire for him and sell it. He paid me well" (June 15, 2007).

But despite all this resonance with Mapuche values, the *wingka* settlers' powerful position in the sociopolitical hierarchy of the nation-state conflicted with *longko* and machi authority in their own hierarchies. Francisca's sense of Mapuche ethnicity in the past and the present helped her reject hierarchical relations in which settlers were paramount. To this end, she sought to assert her authority as a machi by constructing her meeting with German settler Elizabeth Schleyer in 1971 as one of reciprocity and mutual recognition between equals: "I gave her flour, and she was grateful. She respected me. 'I work alone in my vegetable garden. I have garlic, cilantro, cumin, but no fruit,' she said. 'I am thirsty, Mamita,' I said, and she brought me chicha, and I swallowed it all. 'Are you a machi?' she asked me. 'Yes, and I stay home and do my work. I don't go with the Mapuche who take the patrons' land,' I said. 'Go ahead and look for remedies, and then when I am sick, you have to come and heal me. . . . I will go and see you,' she said. But she didn't come. . . . I sent her a basket of cherries" (February 2, 1992).

At other times Mapuche criticized *ülmen* for being despotic men who gained their authority and economic power by force and who used violence against those who opposed them. *Longko* Euladio Ancao remembered, "The old men Kolipi, Mañkelef, Coñuepan, Hueche had a lot of land and authority here. They were hard in their commands and punishments. They made their own justice and killed those they disliked like sheep. Manuel Antonio Katrikura married a Mañkelef girl, and the in-laws didn't like him. So they tied the girl to the wheel of the cart, and they killed him" (June 11, 2007).

Some Mapuche in the Quepe area viewed Pinochet as the most powerful *ülmen* in Chile, one who granted them benefits and protection in exchange for their loyalty. As a dictator, Pinochet had the power to subject citizens of the state to his will through torture and other forms of violence. He also protected those who were loyal to him, rewarding them with money and positions of power. Other Mapuche drew parallels between *admapu* (customary law), which is enforced by powerful *ülmen*, and "Pinochet's law" during the military dictatorship. Francisca said, "In ancient times, when a Mapuche was accused of sorcery, the *ülmen* like Kolipi [and] Mañkelef killed them. That was Mapuche law. With Pinochet, it was the same. If he thought someone was guilty, he would kill them. No defense" (March 24, 1992). But machi Juan from the Quepe area argued that Pinochet was not an *ülmen* because he did not respect Mapuche sociopolitical hierarchies:

"Pinochet had several machi and *longko* shot on Puente Quepe, and they were thrown into the river" (April 27, 1992).

The tensions in this complex Mapuche relationship to military power are not new. During the nineteenth century, Mapuche began to mimic the aesthetic of the Chilean army. Mapuche leaders often sent their eldest sons to study in Santiago or Buenos Aires (Foerster and Menard 2009), and some were buried in uniforms of the Chilean or Argentine militaries. In the nineteenth century Mapuche boys became men warriors by allying with others and participating in raiding parties for cattle and women in Patagonia. Once Mapuche were incorporated by the Chilean and Argentine states, they endorsed state military training of their boys to turn them into men. In effect, the nineteenth-century mounted warrior was replaced by the sergeant riding in a jeep with a gun. After the defeat of Mapuche by the Chilean army in 1881, Mapuche boys could no longer become men by warring against enemies and raiding for cattle in Patagonia; instead, they joined the ranks of the Chilean army to learn about weapons and military tactics, to enhance their strength and resistance, and to learn not to fear Chilean society (Pérez-Sales, Bacic Herzfeld, and Durán Pérez 1998:90–91).[17] They believed that joining the army would allow them to ascend socially and to become manly, brave, and disciplined.

Francisca had predicted that one of Euladio's descendants would join the military. In January 2012, eighteen-year-old Flavio Ancao returned from the military barracks wearing a camouflage uniform and a black beret. Flavio proudly showed me pictures of himself with other members of the army that had killed his great-uncle Alejandro. "I joined the army so that my heart and body would become strong and to develop character to become a man and not cry," he explained. "The Mapuche's blood is more warring and that's why we like the military, to become men." In contrast to this view of military service as an expression of Mapuche culture, the Chilean Ministry of War viewed military service as a way for Mapuche to gain the tools they needed to integrate into Chilean society: "to civilize Mapuche into becoming orderly, hard-working citizens, and to transform precapitalist peasant masses into a work force apt for industry" (Bengoa 1991:382).[18]

But the embrace of military forms and values cut both ways for Mapuche, as seen in the increasingly militarized character of the non-Mapuche elite. In the 1970s, settlers, the military, and the police created a right-wing alliance. Some settlers joined the right-wing paramilitary movement Patria y Libertad (Fatherland and Freedom), which was funded by the CIA between 1971 and 1973 to overthrow Allende's government. Enrique Pinochet Campos, a relative of Pinochet, became the mayor of the municipality of

Freire between 1973 and 1977, the most violent years of the military dictatorship. The German settler Walter Lüer served as lieutenant general of the Chilean air force in Colina under Pinochet, and Schleyer also had connections with the military and the government.

Violence became an uncontrollable force with a life of its own, like thunder, emblematic for Mapuche of the time of spirit masters of the forest and warfare. Mapuche in Millali believed that the *wingka* settlers used power granted to them by the devil to manipulate the government and the military, gain additional lands, intimidate workers into being loyal to them, legitimize their role in Chilean history, and have Mapuche resisters killed by the military. Pinochet's regime and the right-wing settlers who allied with him had stigmatized communists as fanatical, violent, immoral betrayers who destroyed family and society (Pérez-Sales, Bacic Herzfeld, and Durán Pérez 1998:215). Settlers collaborated with the police and military, identifying Mapuche who created problems as communists, which led to their arrest, torture, or even execution (Morales 1999; Pérez-Sales, Bacic Herzfeld, and Durán Pérez 1998:17). This, of course, created a climate of fear and vulnerability in the community. One Mapuche man from Millali told me, "Patrón Schleyer arrived in a military helicopter, and the Mapuche got scared and ran away. The police would ride in the trucks of the *patrones*, who would pay the police to eliminate Mapuche" (January 7, 2006). According to people in Millali, the settlers would then offer these lives to the devil in exchange for additional power and wealth. Francisca and many others supported right-wing settlers in order to avoid being labeled communists, but Francisca still reported seeing the devil wandering down from the Schleyer farm to the community center at night to claim the lives of Mapuche.

Since Mapuche from the Quepe area were estranged from the political ideologies of the state, they blamed themselves rather than the state for the suffering experienced during this time of violence. These Mapuche argued that neither left-wing nor right-wing political ideologies addressed Mapuche interests and that Mapuche who denounced Pinochet's land division law or participated in politics were *awingkados* operating to the detriment of their own people. Many turned their backs on fellow Mapuche who disappeared or were killed during the Pinochet regime, claiming that they were paying the price for participating in *wingka* politics.[19] Most Mapuche in Millali identified not as right wing but as Mapuchistas (ethnic Mapuche) and "*apolíticos*" (apoliticals) (Martínez and Caniuqueo 2011). These Mapuche claimed to be apolitical because they viewed "right wing" as the state's default category; they did not agree with right-wing political ideologies, but valued the opportunities they believed would follow from association with the right. Machi and *longko* in particular are said to lose their credibility and spiritual power if they become involved in politics. But Francisca and many other machi derived spiritual power from the *newen* held by *ülmen* such as Pinochet, using it to protect themselves from all kinds of sorcery, including that of so-called communist sorcerers.

FRANCISCA'S WARRING THUNDER
AGAINST COMMUNIST SORCERERS

Francisca's unmediated thunder power linked wilderness, warfare, sorcery, the Patagonian shamanic military complex, and Pinochet's military power. Just as the mounted Mapuche warriors traveled between Chile and Patagonia to kill enemies, take captives and cattle, and gain power and wealth, so Francisca mounted her spirit horse to travel between the human and spirit worlds to kill evil spirits, take spirits and prayers to the Mapuche sky, and gain knowledge of the universe. Francisca had a poster of Rambo in her living room to ward off evil spirits. She drew on Mapuche and Chilean military imagery and viewed gunshots and thunder as equivalent:

> I have four powerful ones, four warriors, four *likanche* [precious people], my four sergeants that protect me. I have my staff and salt and two knives. If I didn't have them, they would have killed me a long time ago. . . . In a dream they gave me a rifle, a revolver, my two *tralkan* [thunders] to kill the *añchimallen* and *witranalwe* [evil spirits]. I pull out my revolver and shoot *tralkan* from my gun . . . to get the filth out. . . . Pinochet was the great warrior. His rule, his word kills everything, even the *wekufü*. (December 18, 1993)

Francisca and many other machi understood Pinochet's military power as more spiritual than political.[20] For machi, nature beings, political figures, and spirits all have *newen*. They operate on the same ontological plane, performing as political actors and agents of history. Pinochet was not just a president, but a hypermasculine figure of great military power whom they could use for spiritual ends—to wage war against *awingkamiento*, communists, sorcerers, and evil spirits—and for individual protection against enemies. The violence of Pinochet and the violence of native spiritual warfare and sorcery worked through each other.

Historically, the Chilean state has viewed male and female machi through a gendered lens. Since the advent of democracy under a civilian government in 1990, male machi have increasingly defined themselves in terms of national political ideologies and engaged with political authorities through such ideologies, as other Mapuche men do (Bacigalupo 2007:200, 214). Female machi, by contrast, use their marginality to engage in creative resistance in their engagement with the dominant culture.²¹ Thus, female machi in the Quepe area have not consciously set out to transform political and ideological hegemonies. They have much more fluid and ambiguous understandings of ideology and military power that relate to their notions of *newen* and spiritual power, which exist apart from the ideologies of political parties or resistance movements. Machi Angela said: "Since [Ricardo] Lagos has been president [2000–2006], there has been a lot of disorder. People are insolent and don't respect the police. I have less power. In the time of Pinochet, people did not rebel because Pinochet would kill them. People need to respect me, like they need to respect Pinochet. He has *newen*, and I admire him. I need that kind of *newen* to chase the devil away" (December 15, 2003).

Francisca projected onto her interactions with political and military figures a Mapuche spiritual model of personalized, reciprocal relationships with deities and other spirit beings. This is an approach to politics concerned with interpersonal power, recognition, and identity. In their rituals, female machi greet the spirits and deities using the honorary titles "king," "queen," and "chief." They shower the spirits with offerings and prayers. In return, the spirits recognize machi as powerful and worthy of the knowledge that the spirits give them. In the same manner, female machi forge relationships with Mapuche and national political and military authorities, honoring them with rituals to bolster the shamans' own *newen* and to gain recognition. In 1986, Pinochet legitimated machi and *longko* from the city of Nueva Imperial, and they in turn legitimated him as "*ülmen, füta longko*"—a powerful political and military man and chief. They hoped Pinochet would return the land he had usurped and believed they could gain power through their encounters with him.

Machi Francisca believed that as president Pinochet had the positive qualities of an ideal *ülmen*: generosity, good judgment, oratorical skills, and respect for and commitment to his people. She believed that Mapuche should support Pinochet because he would distribute wealth and favors to those loyal to him. As she put it, "Many of us here are *momios* [right wing]. Pinochet took care of the Mapuche more than other people. He gave us things like a good *ülmen*" (March 24, 1992). Female machi view the state as a father and donor, replicating the nation's gendered kinship tropes and mirroring the relationship between the Mapuche deity Ngünechen and the ritual community. Just as Ngünechen grants good crops, remedies, and other blessings to machi who perform rituals, so associations with the state will bring them social and economic benefits (Bacigalupo 2007:244).

The TIME *of* WARRING THUNDER, *the* SAVAGE STATE, *and* CIVILIZED SHAMANS

There are deep historic roots for Mapuche's personalized relationship with the state authorities and their active resistance to them in some contexts. During resistance in the eighteenth century, Mapuche incorporated new social forms and developed new identities. Institutions of colonial power were transformed into local native political mechanisms, becoming part of Mapuche consciousness. The concentration of power in the hands of a few representatives and parliaments became the local way of practicing politics (Boccara 1998). Mapuche today want their autonomy, but they also seek associations with state and military officials who hold national political power and can grant them benefits (Marimán 1990:26–27). They resist the state's neoliberal policies and control of their territories, but Mapuche are also pragmatists who participate actively in the space made available to them by civil society (Foerster and Lavanchy 1999; Millaman 2001:12).

Mapuche continue to practice cosmopolitics. They invoke the power of wild warriors during protests and other confrontations with timber companies, settlers, and the Chilean state, while machi ritually invoke wild thunder warrior-shamans to kill evil spirits. Mapuche demands for autonomy—as well as attempts to retake their territories from settlers, loggers, state highway authorities, and hydroelectric plants—are conceptualized within the *tiempo de ngen mawida y weychan* (time of spirit masters of the forest and warfare).

Machi's ability to transform *newen* obtained from the spirits into powerful symbolic tools has allowed them to practice a kind of nonpartisan, situational politics and to negotiate with a wide range of powerful political and military authorities without committing to the ideologies of particular parties (Bacigalupo 2007:244). Francisca sought to enhance her power and prestige through her associations with Pinochet, but in 1993 she drummed at an event to celebrate the passing of an indigenous law under democratic president Aylwin that recognized the Mapuche as a people: "He greeted me and shook my hand. He knew I was an important machi," she said (March 24, 1992). Domingo Katrikura added, "She agreed to go because I told her that it was an event to do a little justice to the Mapuche, who were so marginalized and had lost their lands. . . . She said she would put all her *newen* into it" (January 6, 2006). Although they see the police and the military as representatives of the state, Mapuche have also used these forces to resolve local conflicts (Pérez-Sales, Bacic Herzfeld, and Durán Pérez 1998:99). Francisca identified parallels between Pinochet's persecution of communists and the community's punishment of alleged sorcerers, and she used the terms *communist* and *sorcerer* interchangeably to refer to evil or undesirable people. Francisca claimed that communists were sorcerers who transformed the minds of Mapuche, making them *awingkados*. She feared that the Millañir family and *longko* José Cayupi—the indigenous representative for Pinochet's government—would report her as a communist sorcerer and get her arrested and killed just because she had disputes with them. However, Francisca also boasted that Pinochet would protect her, because she was a "wild, warring thunder machi" and had treated his niece in a healing ritual.

Mapuche activist Ana Llao-Llao, by contrast, interpreted machi engagements with political and military figures as a form of political ideology. Ana argued that Mapuche women (including machi like Francisca) who posed in photographs with right-wing men like Pinochet were participating in what Pierre Bourdieu (2002:167, 1977:126) called invisible "symbolic violence"—unrecognized as such, and therefore "chosen as much as undergone"—that naturalizes unjust relations of power. Ana argued, "History repeats itself, but memory is not lost. It is always a rural Mapuche woman worshiping these right-wing guys. This is very bad. Do these Mapuche know about the Mapuche on hunger strikes, the Mapuche political prisoners?" (June 24, 2013). In Ana's view, Mapuche who supported Pinochet accepted his description of the state as a "fraternal community of mestizo unequals" based on class (Foerster 2001), which did not recognize the Mapuche's separate ethnic identity.

By 1995, Mapuche had begun to reconsider and reconceptualize state power in relation to the new democratic governments rather than Pinochet's authoritarian regime. Some people in Millali viewed the democratic regime as the time of civilization, which allowed Mapuche to think of themselves as a separate ethnic nation within the Chilean state and to demand sovereignty and the return of their lands. They believed that Mapuche would leave the Chilean army and become active in the ethnonational project (Foerster 2001). Other Mapuche viewed the democratic regime as the return of the time of spirit masters of the forest and warfare, a moment of open confrontation between the Mapuche ethnic perspective and capitalistic national and transnational interests. When I met Francisca for the first time in 1991, she was struggling with this new sociopolitical context and the demise of her authority and power, which had been closely associated with Pinochet. A new democratic regime led by President Patricio Aylwin (1990–1994) was in place, and Pinochet was openly discredited in the media. Francisca's self-image as a "wild, warring thunder machi" who transgressed gender norms but retained Pinochet's support had become suspect.

The TIME *of* WARRING THUNDER, *the* SAVAGE STATE, *and* CIVILIZED SHAMANS

"She's a bad-tempered sorcerer, and you'll never know if she's going to heal you or kill you," a woman of Millali warned me when I first began working with Francisca in 1991. "She is a crazy, promiscuous widow who has no morals. She is a *maricona* [butch], a *mujer de la calle* [street woman] who is always away from home and knows both Mapuche and *wingka* sorcery." I was puzzled at the gravity of these assertions. Francisca was unusual among Mapuche women in that she was independent, gruff, and demanding. But people from many communities came to her house for healing, and I had heard others in the community explain Francisca's behavior as the result of her unmediated power of thunder. "Why do you call Francisca a sorcerer?" I asked. The woman retorted, "She's like a military man, not a woman."

Francisca needed the unmediated powers of thunder and the military in order to conduct spiritual warfare against evil spirits and to gain recognition as a thunder shaman within the Calfuñir-Huenchuñir faction's hierarchical model. She needed to travel as a warrior-shaman, mounted on her horse, to other realms and heal patients in distant lands. But these shamanic practices challenged everyday Mapuche gender ideals grounded in nineteenth century practices: men should be highly mobile and forge alliances through multiple marriages and exchange, while women should remain close to their families and homes and be modest, and prudent. In many ways, female shamans do have more authority than ordinary Mapuche women and are not bound by the same gender norms: they take on public ritual roles, move between masculine and feminine identities during rituals, and travel away from home to heal patients. But the spirits see menstruation and birth as weakening their powers, and family life as a distraction from their professional spiritual roles. Marriage, children, and domestic chores all limit a machi's advancement, and machi must prioritize their spiritual marriage over their human one. Separation and widowhood thus allow machi to dedicate themselves to the spirits, but these transitions also stigmatize them and make them vulnerable to accusations of sorcery. Mapuche accept female machi's ritual gender transgressions for the maintenance of the collective good—so long as they remain representatives of tradition and continue to be respectable daughters, mothers, and wives, as determined by the dominant Catholic Chilean culture (Bacigalupo 2007:212–252).[22] A machi's transgressions are tolerated, but she must still uphold local traditions and Catholic ideals.

Francisca, however, engaged in behaviors outside her machi role that Mapuche defined as manly transgressions. She drank and swore in public, criticized *longko* for their lack of knowledge, had liaisons with men, refused to remarry, performed men's tasks, and generally made her own decisions and spent her own money. "I have to tell José Calfuñir [her brother-in-law] what to do, just like my husband. I can't send him to town to buy salt, grease, soap because he spends the money on drink. . . . I work alone in my house like a man for my money. I grab my hammer, my axe to cut wood. I yoke my ox. I dig the ditch, mend the fence, plow the land. Women also have strength" (March 20, 1992). Francisca's behavior challenged Mapuche gender hierarchies and roles, Mapuche notions of tradition and sociality, and Catholic moralities (Bacigalupo 2005). And her behavior was extreme even for female machi. Her friends teasingly called her "Francisca *loca*" (crazy), and some people in Millali came to regard her gender transgressions as signs of selfishness and sorcery, and thus as opposed to her machi practice.

Gendered expectations surrounding marriage and motherhood conflicted with Francisca's practice as a thunder machi married to her spirit. She struggled to raise her children and perform healing, while her husband rejected her machi practice. In March 1992 she told me: "My babies cried because I couldn't attend to them." Her mother-in-law cared for the children when Francisca was away, and her husband, José Pancho, was jealous of the time she spent healing. He said, "I don't like machi. They wander like beggars. Machi are not real wives. They are never at home. Machi are bossy, and the *chamall* stinks." Francisca gave precedence to her machi spirit over her husband and children, so José Pancho had sex with other women. Francisca's son and daughter-in-law also opposed her machi practice because they read her gender transgressions as sorcery:

My son Francisco told me, "Why are you playing your *kultrung* so much? I would split that *kultrung* and throw it away." His wife, Aureliana, accused me of putting *füñapuwe* [poison] into his soup. We hit each other. Then they had bad luck with harvests and animals. Three of their children died, and they blamed me, saying I killed them with sorcery. One day when I was looking for herbal remedies on the hill, Francisco clubbed me on the head. I was bleeding. They twisted my arm. Francisco told me never to go there again and said that he would kill me if I did. My arm was so bad I couldn't wash, cook, or lift anything for four months. Ngünechen told me, "Look, you don't even have confidence [from] your son. Your daughters are far away." I became very sad. I cried and cried because I am *guacha* [without family] and am all alone here working. (February 19, 1992)

The TIME *of* WARRING THUNDER, *the* SAVAGE STATE, *and* CIVILIZED SHAMANS

Francisca's brother-in-law José Calfuñir married Ignacia Millañir and lived with her in a house on the land where Francisca lived: "Ignacia said I was lazy and dirty and that I had a pact with the *witranalwe* to become wealthy and become friends with the *patrones*. She said I had other men and was trying to steal her husband with love magic." Francisca became angry and confronted Ignacia: "I told her to stop saying things about me, that I was always here at home with my kids. I slapped her and turned around to leave, and she picked up the axe and cut me on my arm, right here [pointing to her scar]. That woman was no good" (February 19, 1992). José and Ignacia eventually split up, and he went to work as a guard up north. Ignacia married a Chilean and left.

After Francisca's husband died in 1974, José Calfuñir returned to Millali and lived with Francisca. The Calfuñir family pressured Francisca to marry him to legitimate her position on their land, but Francisca refused because marriage conflicted with her machi practice: "Some husbands are jealous and bad-tempered. I prefer to be alone. Chau Díos is the one who bosses me around, not a husband. The machi spirit does not want me to remarry" (March 20, 1992). According to Francisca, José's ex-wife, Ignacia, then converted herself into a jaguar (*nawel*) and killed one of Francisca's sheep. Mapuche consider jaguars to be nonhuman persons with souls who have the powers of healing and sorcery. But since they live in the forest, they can also become soulless beings and nonpersons who are not capable of sharing or caring about others. Regardless of their position at a particular moment in time, however, jaguars and humans participate in and experience each other in the same world. Ignacia and Francisca were both human persons, but since they treated each other as sorcerers and predators, they also adopted amoral nonhuman forms who took revenge on each other.

As a were-jaguar, Ignacia was an ambiguous being who hunted and performed sorcery on her enemies—including members of the Calfuñir and Huenchuñir factions—but who also had emotional connections and obligations to her relatives in the Millañir faction. Francisca was afraid that the jaguar Ignacia would come back, kill more sheep, and then kill Francisca and José Calfuñir for revenge. But Francisca's wild, unmediated power of thunder was stronger than that of the jaguar, and she confronted it by playing her *kultrung* and by shooting her thunder (pistol) in its direction. The jaguar never reappeared. Some people in Millali claimed that Francisca had shot and killed the jaguar. Others argued that the jaguar transformed back into Ignacia when it heard the gunshots. Francisca explained, "My *tralkan* scared away the *kalku* jaguar" (November 21, 1991).

The Calfuñir, Lefian, and Huenchuñir families initially endorsed Francisca as a legitimate thunder machi who embraced Mapuche political and spiritual hierarchies. But when Francisca refused to abide by Mapuche gender norms, marry José Calfuñir, or share her wealth with her family, the Calfuñir family rejected Francisca and called her a sorcerer. They tried to expel Francisca from the lands of her deceased husband, but she considered them her own and refused to leave. She explained that her attachment to her *rewe* was the same as a man's ties to the land: "I was born in this community. I am like a man. I cannot get married and leave. My thunder spirit is here, in this *rewe*, in this land. When I go away, my *rewe* calls me back in dreams." José Calfuñir allowed her to stay, but Alberto Huenchuñir complained, "Francisca acted like a crazy woman. She liked to fight with the neighbors. She rode her horse with her skirt tucked up and defended herself with a stick. She was very nervous. When she would get mad at me, I was afraid that maybe she would poison my food" (June 19, 2007).

Despite pressure from the Calfuñir and Huenchuñir families to change her behavior, Francisca was unyielding: "They are frightened of me because I am a thunder machi and work like a man. They say I am a *maricona* because I am the boss in the house. They say I'm a *mujer de la calle* because I have men friends who help me to plow and harvest. But I am a machi, and I'm too old to care what they say about me" (March 20, 1992). To her, thunder machi and widows were freed from the demands of gender norms and patrilineages. She openly challenged these traditions and was impervious to the community's objections. In a society governed by men, Francisca was a powerful, independent woman who was feared as a sorcerer. The hostility Francisca experienced in her community is emblematic both of the Mapuche people's violent history of intra- and interethnic conflict and of the violence Mapuche experience at the hands of the Chilean state.

STATE AND SETTLER CONSTRUCTIONS OF MAPUCHE AS SAVAGE TERRORISTS

The government is united in its effort to combat the terrorism that affects the settlers in Araucanía. We will not hesitate to use any measure or action that the Constitution, the law and the state allows us. . . . We will apply the anti-terrorist law. We will promote police action that allows us to have more efficacy in the war against these terrorist groups.

—ANDRES CHADWICK, MINISTER OF
THE INTERIOR, JANUARY 6, 2013

On January 3, 2014, Chile's new minister of the interior, Cecilia Pérez, drew on the discourse of the nineteenth-century Chilean War of Pacification, during which "savage" rebel Mapuche were said to be foreigners challenging the "civilized Chilean nation." She visited police forces in Araucanía on the anniversary of the death of Mapuche activist Matias Catrileo and said: "We need more diligence to obtain the result that we are all looking for: the Pacification of Araucanía" (Pérez 2014).

Since the Mapuche lost their lands in the nineteenth and twentieth centuries, the Chilean state has tried to tame Mapuche "savages" using three contradictory approaches: celebrating Mapuche of the past as mythologized museum pieces and heroic warriors of the nation; criticizing contemporary Mapuche as having lost their culture and territories because they have lacked the capital or knowledge to work the land; and characterizing Mapuche who make land claims and demand sovereignty as not "real" integrationists but "insurrectionist Indians" (Hale 2006) and subversive terrorists manipulated by foreigners who threaten Chilean national sovereignty and impede development and progress (Pinto Rodríguez 2003; Bacigalupo 2004c). By arguing that Mapuche claim land rights only when manipulated by outsiders, the settlers and the state deny Mapuche agency as autonomous political actors who are capable of making their own economic and political alliances toward a variety of ends.[23] To combat them, the state revived the symbolism and history of the War of Pacification of Araucanía. As in other places in Latin America, the government of Chile and the colonizers have used narratives of culture, integration, and terrorism to undermine indigenous people's land claims and their demands for collective and cultural rights (Jackson and Warren 2005; Mallon 1996; Richards 2013).

In Chile, the Anti-Terrorism Law passed in 1984 proved an effective tool for Pinochet's suppression of Mapuche and other so-called counterrevolutionary groups opposing the dictatorship. It denied due process and tripled the punitive sentences against Mapuche. And the democratically elected presidents, starting with Ricardo Lagos in 2000, embraced this law as well. Since the end of Pinochet's dictatorship in 1990, at least twelve unarmed Mapuche activists have been killed by the military police, and the government has ignored Mapuche complaints about the violence and harassment perpetrated by military police in Mapuche communities (Vidal 2011; *The Guardian* 2013). During Michelle Bachelet's presidency (2006–2010), the police used Raul Castro Antipán as an agent provocateur to carry out incendiary attacks and other "terrorist" acts. Under the Anti-Terrorist Law they then used him as a protected witness to incriminate Mapuche leaders in court, perpetuating the image of Mapuche as terrorists (*The Clinic* 2014).

Claiming a native status as people born on these lands, some settlers argue that their ancestors did not participate in the War of Pacification. But they have revived the image of that state war against Mapuche by condemning activists as terrorists who threaten their livelihood and lands. One settler said:

> We practically live in a war zone. There is not one day when something doesn't happen. The Mapuche take over our lands, they steal our animals, they harvest our crops and take them, they cut our trees, they send their animals to graze on our land. This has been our home for more than twenty years. And we are in the same situation as thousands of other settlers who do not know what to do about the terror these Mapuche cause. We give work to people in the area, and we are victims of a minority group of violent Mapuche. (February 12, 2013)

Some settlers have also revived the symbolism and army practices that trace to the War of Pacification. In 2009 some colonists created the fascist paramilitary group Comandancia Trizano, named after Captain Hernán Trizano, who supported settlers in the nineteenth century and brutalized Mapuche. Members of Comandancia Trizano have threatened to blow up Mapuche activists with dynamite to "finish with the Mapuche problem."

The government and the police have not intervened to stop the Comandancia or to address abuses by European settlers. The Swiss Luchsingers arrived in Vilcún in 1906 and illegally usurped some 1,200 hectares of land granted to Mapuche and recognized in land titles. Jorge Luchsinger returned fifty-six hectares of the usurped lands in 1971, but other claims are still pending. The Swiss settler complained that some of his houses had been burned down and fences damaged. He dug a deep canal, into which animals regularly fell and died, to separate his property from that of his Mapuche neighbors. Luchsinger also employed a private police force on the farm to defend him from his Mapuche neighbors (Correa 2008). "It is not possible [to give Mapuche back their lands]," Luchsinger said in an interview with the newspaper *Que Pasa*. "It would be absolute misery because Mapuche don't work the land. Have you seen the land that the state has bought for them through the CONADI? Nothing is left. Not even one tree is standing. They produce nothing. The Mapuche is a predator. He lives from what nature gives him. He has no intellectual capacity, no will, no infrastructure. He has nothing."[24]

Just as in the War of Pacification, the Chilean state continues to protect the settlers' interests and support their self-serving historical narratives.

The state has become "the punishing arm of the settlers' war against Mapuche rather than being at the service of all its citizens" (Marimán 2013). In January 2013 two members of the Luchsinger family died in an arson attack. Minister of the Interior Andrés Chadwick and Minister of Agriculture Luis Mayol labeled the Mapuche and their allies as "dangerous, powerful, organized enemies" and as "terrorists." Andrés Molina, the governor of this region of Araucanía, exacerbated the conflict by calling the attackers "savages" and linking the deaths by arson to the deaths of timber company workers in 2012. President Sebastián Piñera said that the settlers were victims of violence and told them to defend themselves with weapons while ignoring the violence perpetrated upon Mapuche by the military police and Comandancia Trizano. Piñera declared a state of national emergency, again applying General Pinochet's antiterrorism law to the region. He sent military police to control Mapuche activists, to violently cleanse Mapuche communities of "terrorists," and to protect the settlers from the indigenous people (Vasquez 2013). Chileans also depict machi who engage in spiritual warfare against the spirits of neoliberalism as terrorists.

Mapuche see the Chilean government, the military police, and the settlers collaborating against the Mapuche people, regardless of the regime in power (Marimán 2012). *Longko* Juana Calfunao wrote a letter to President Piñera in which she said that she had been tortured and that her uncle had been killed in an arson attack on her home, but "there was no visit from the Chilean president or his ministers, and there was no state of siege declared; nor did the state apply the anti-terrorist law against the perpetrators. And yet the government continues to talk about 'equality before the law.' The life of a Mapuche does not have the same value and meaning as that of a *wingka*. All the Mapuche brothers who have been assassinated are a testimony to that" (January 5, 2013).[25]

MACHI SPIRITUAL WARFARE AGAINST THE EVIL SPIRITS OF NEOLIBERALISM

With all your teachings I will ride my horse. . . . Take me, you twelve
chueka *sticks of war, my twelve arrows of war, my twelve knives of*
war that will allow me to travel through the universe and give me my
knowledge. My twelve horse breaths, my twelve walking horses, my
twelve spirit horses, . . . they take me to the sky. I shall go to the sky.
I shall be doing war, . . . knowledge of war, teachings of struggle.[26]

—MACHI JAVIERA, PRAYER COLLECTED BY JUAN ÑANCULEF

Machi experience themselves as masters of time and alterity who—through their senses, rituals, ritual objects, and narratives—remember the Mapuche past in order to transform the present and the future both at the spiritual level and for the community of the living. Machi use spirits to protect Mapuche genealogies and histories, performing spiritual warfare against the state, logging companies, and the spirit of neoliberalism that drives them (Bacigalupo 2004c:519). They wage this war through personified, male mounted warriors (*machi weychafe pura kawellu*, often referred to as "guardians," "nobles," and "kings") who shelter machi during altered states of consciousness. Machi José viewed his spirit horse itself as a weapon against the timber companies: "I'll knock down evil with my horse and finish with it" (December 17, 2001).

Since the redemocratization of Chile in 1990, Mapuche communities have drawn on a revitalized sense of ethnic identity to challenge the authority of the transnational corporations that preside over monocultural timber production and to demand the return of their lands (Klubock 2004:338). Mapuche activists have politicized machi, casting them as representatives of Mapuche traditions, pan-Mapuche history, their ancestral rights to land, and the right to a Mapuche nation, which uses the machi drum as its symbol.[27]

Mapuche believe that machi suffer physical illness, spiritual harm, and loss of power if Mapuche ancestral territories are appropriated by others or affected by ecological disasters. For that reason, the logging of Mapuche land has become a key issue in both physical and symbolic confrontations between the Mapuche and the state. Heavy logging has produced severe soil erosion and crippled Mapuche communities' self-sufficiency and their relationship with the spirit masters. When Francisca's grandson Cesar Calfuñir began harvesting trees for the Roth Schleyer farm in January 1995, Francisca lamented, "My own blood is cutting pine trees and eucalyptus trees for the gringo. I am losing my strength, my power to heal. The thunder machi will defend the *ngenlawen* [spirit owners of herbal remedies]."

The timber companies and the government are aware of the symbolic relationship between machi and ancestral territories and recognize the central role that machi play in Mapuche resistance movements. Mapuche shamanic war metaphors and spiritual contests are often misconstrued by Chileans and used against Mapuche. After a confrontation between Mapuche protesters and police in Catrio Ñancul, agents of Forestal Mininco cut down the community's *ngillatuwe* (collective *axis mundi*) (Barrera 1999:186). By symbolically destroying machi powers and legitimacy, Mininco was attempting to prevent the shamans from performing rituals in which spiritual power, sacred landscapes, and the appeal of tradition could be used to mobilize the Mapuche against the logging industry. Although Francisca did not perform collective rituals to conduct spiritual warfare against timber companies, other machi have.

Some female machi have enthusiastically enacted the idea of the spiritual warrior in order to strengthen the notion of Mapuche nationhood based on landscape, the revival of tradition, and resistance to the state's neoliberal policies. The *ngillatun* has also acquired political implications. It expresses a sense of community and a spiritual relationship to the homeland, and it helps to maintain a boundary between Mapuche and outsiders. *Ngillatun* rituals are sometimes tailored to specific conflicts with timber companies and the government over particular landscapes. I participated in one in Lumaco on December 20–21, 1997, where machi Tegualda propitiated the ancestral spirits and spirit masters of the forests for help to battle Forestal Mininco. She and the *longko* exhorted the community to be brave warriors:

> Tegualda: Lift your *chuekas* [sticks] every time you scream "Marichiweu!" [We will win ten times over!] As if you were winning. You are brave men. You are Mapuche.
>
> *Longko*: You shall win. You are a warring woman, a warring machi. Give us your wisdom, your words, your advice. With your help, we shall have strength. We will unite to continue our struggle. Marichiweu, marichiweu!
>
> Tegualda: That's right. You should scream "Marichiweu" all the time! It is the cry of our ancestors, which you should not forget. We should recover what is ours—our territories, our ancient forests. We shall remember our ancestral laws.

Machi Tegualda resignified a collective ritual in political terms, invoking the support of ancient warriors to battle the spirit of the timber companies and regain local territory.

Mapuche resistance movements have fostered what Beth Conklin has described as an increasing "shamanization of indigenous identities" (2002:1058), which includes the politicization of shamanic roles. For example, Mapuche protest graffiti features the machi drum to highlight the role of *newen* and machi spiritual warfare in resistance, and it makes statements like "Leave, Usurper of Land" (in Spanish) and "Newen, Mapuche Brothers" (in Mapudungun; fig 6.3). Machi's spiritual performances to recover the Mapuche's ancestral lands, language, and traditions—along with their spiritual warfare against capitalism, timber companies, and *wingka* greed—are part of their fundamental role in the individual and collective

FIGURE 6.3

Mapuche protest graffiti in Metrenco featuring the machi's kultrung (drum) as a symbol of Mapuche identity and resistance. The expression "Fuera Usurpador de Tierra" (Leave, Land Usurper) is a protest against Chilean farmers, forestry companies, and the state highway system, which have usurped land from Mapuche communities. The expression "Newen Peñis" (Power or Strength, Mapuche Brothers) incites Mapuche to unite against the usurpers (photo by author).

healing of Mapuche and in the defense of Mapuche cultural and sociopolitical processes. However, the government views the politicization of machi as an internal threat to the state because the shamans fuse social, spiritual, and material aspects of Mapuche life with the concept of Mapuche territory. The Chilean government has wrongly assumed that machi who confront timber companies on legal and spiritual terms will also do so through physical violence.

Andrés Cuyul (2014) has referred to the persecution of machi since 2000 as a "witch hunt" in which Chilean tribunals have replaced those of the Inquisition, using the Anti-Terrorism Law of 1984 to coerce and control machi as spiritual authorities. In the process, they have caused moral, spiritual, and physical damage to machi. In 2002 the Ministry of Justice summoned machi Juan Huentemil to discuss the burning of timber company trucks, though he was neither the instigator nor the perpetrator of the attacks, because he had performed spiritual warfare against the company (Bacigalupo 2007:206–207). When two Swiss settlers died in an arson at-

tack in Vilcún in 2013, machi Francisca Linconao was harassed, humiliated, and charged with terrorism (Radio Bio-Bio 2013). The Chilean government assumed that she was involved in the attacks because in 2009 she
had won a legal battle against the transnational company Sociedad Palermo
that allowed her to collect herbal remedies from a sacred landscape belonging to the community (*La Opinion* 2013). In the end, machi Celestino Cor-
doba was held responsible for the deaths of the Luchsingers and sentenced
to eighteen years in prison (Soto Galindo 2014). Other machi, including
Millaray Huichalaf and Tito Cañulef, have been imprisoned for protesting
the construction of hydroelectric dams in sacred Mapuche landscapes (*Pais
Mapuche* 2013).

Even though Mapuche relationships with the military seem inconsis-
tent from a Global North political viewpoint, the shamanic frames of the
time of spirit masters of the forest and warfare and the time of civilization
remain consistent throughout, emerging in shamanic rituals and dreams.
Mapuche in the Quepe area have responded to the persecution of machi by
the state and military powers by radically changing their perceptions of the
relationship between shamanic power, narratives about the "before time,"
and military power. And this new perspective has emerged in their dreams.

MAPUCHE DREAMS AND REVISIONIST NARRATIVES
TO END SAVAGERY AND WARFARE

Mapuche in the Quepe area who began dreaming and narrating revisionist
stories that challenged their experiences of state-sponsored violence created
"moral projects" (Cole 2003), local visions of what constitutes a community of people and how they can attain a good life.[28] Their dreams challenged Francisca's perception of warring thunder machi, and they opposed
shamanic and military power. These dreams included fragments of Mapuche narratives about the "before time," in which military power appeared
to work against machi, decreasing shamanic power, and in which military men arbitrarily harmed people in the community rather than bene-
fiting them. In 2006, Domingo Katrikura, *longko* of Chihuimpilli, shared
with me one of his dreams about machi Francisca. Domingo had dreamed
about a military coup during Lagos's democratic regime and interpreted it
as an instance of *wingka* "wilderness and warfare" in which the triple alliance forged during Pinochet's regime between the military, the government, and settlers had remained intact. In this dream, which incorporated
a fragment of the narrative about the primordial serpents Trengtreng and

Kaykay, Francisca's shamanic powers were not enough to protect Domingo from harm:

> In the dream, I am visiting Millali when there is a coup d'état led by the military and the patrones. They shoot one group of people. They take another group to the top of the hill. And I was in that group. We were the ones saved by Trengtreng at the top of the hill. Machi Francisca was there protecting us, but she was weak. And I said, "I will be alive, but something bad is going to happen to me." And a few days later, a bus ran over my foot. (January 5, 2006)

Domingo's dream reflected all of the Mapuche people's wars with various *wingka* forces of wilderness over time, since that history is seen to form genealogies of and structural correspondences with the military-political realities of the present. Mapuche use cyclical narratives about the "before time" to fill in the holes in historical memories of state warfare against Mapuche. And like other native peoples (Rappaport 1998:18), they stress the repetitive structure of historical progress to link the past to the future, providing a template through which they understand where they came from and where they are going.

Katrikura's dream reflects indigenous history, Mapuche agency, and ethnic identity, and can be used for the "transformation of consciousness" (Burke 1999; Gramsci 1971 [1925–1935]:323; Strinati 1995:165) through "truth effects" (Artexaga 2000:52). It is a narrative that constitutes an immediate, affective, charged political reality. As Katrikura's dream was passed down to younger generations, it helped people in the Quepe area to maintain a sense of local history separate from the savage cycle of warfare and wilderness associated with governmental and military force.

For some Mapuche in Millali, this cycle of wilderness and warfare ended after 2013 when international pressure forced the Chilean government to change its strategies and when Mapuche stopped supporting right-wing regimes. The Inter-American Court of Human Rights condemned the Chilean state for violating human rights and due process, and the United Nations and Amnesty International criticized Chile for using the Anti-Terrorism Law against Mapuche (Long 2013). Socialist candidate Michelle Bachelet won the presidency, having promised in her campaign that she would not use the Anti-Terrorism Law against Mapuche (Cooperativa 2013). In that election, held in November 2013, 58.73 percent of the population of Araucanía voted for Bachelet over her right-wing opponent, Evelyn Matthei. This was a radical change in the voting pattern of the formerly right-wing Mapuche in the region, signaling a shift in their relationship with the military authorities and the conservative settlers who hold power over them. One Mapuche man in Millali said, "We got tired of the *weychan*, the abusive military men, the violence, the killing of *ngenmawida*. We voted for Piñera because we thought we would get jobs, and he brought war, disaster, and the transnational timber companies. Now we vote for Bachelet because she might let us talk in parliaments and let our forests speak. We are civilized Mapuche. We cannot understand each other with guns" (January 14, 2014). By divorcing shamanism from military power, people in Millali reinvented machi practice as a moral, civilized, spiritual order superior to the "civilization" of the settlers.

Mapuche in the Quepe area also have created revisionist narratives that "civilize" Chilean history through interethnic dialogue and parliaments. In order to legitimate their historical narratives of a civilized, moral, sovereign nation, Mapuche conflate their current realities with Mapuche historical practices, such as holding summits and making treaties, first with Spaniards and then with Chileans. Domingo Katrikura and Euladio Ancao argued that until 1881, the Mapuche were a sovereign nation that interacted as an equal with the colonizers in civilized parliaments. And it was the "savage colonizers" who breached this civilized dialogical practice by massacring Mapuche and taking their lands during the War of Pacification. Mapuche view treaties and parliaments between sovereign nations as civilized engagements that did much to guarantee peaceful relations between the Mapuche nation and the Chilean nation during that period (Pinto 2000; Pichinao Huenchuleo 2012). Mapuche believe that these need to be reinstated.

Although the Chilean state accuses contemporary Mapuche of being violent terrorists, most Mapuche organizations, leaders, and academics today publicly reject violence as a way of dealing with interethnic conflict and propose ongoing parliaments as a way to guarantee social peace through dialogue.[29] People in Millali and Imilco have used the civilized strategy of diplomacy rather than violence to try to recover their lands from the German settlers. Pedro Morales explained, "We are civilized Mapuche. We negotiate and don't like to fight with our neighbors, like they do in other communities. If we had, maybe we would have recovered land, but we would not be in peace because in a conflict, Mapuche always die" (January 5, 2012).

On January 16, 2013, Mapuche political and community leaders invited the government and civil society organizations to participate in a meeting on top of a hill called Cerro Ñielol to address the deaths of the two Swiss settlers from the Luchsinger family. Cerro Ñielol is a historical site of great symbolic significance: Mapuche used it in pre-Hispanic times, and the Mapuche nation and the Chilean state signed their last peace treaty there in 1881. In choosing this significant site, Mapuche sought to negotiate peace with Chile by reviving the tradition and rhetoric of historical meetings between nations. They also hoped to create the basis for a new civilized relationship with the Chilean state: conflicts would be resolved through dialogue rather than through violence, and the stigmatization of Mapuche as second-class citizens would be eliminated (CLACPI 2013). But despite these efforts, the relationship between Mapuche and the Chilean state remains tense.

CIVILIZED SHAMANS AND MORAL EXISTENTIALISM

Toward the end of her life, Francisca redefined her healing practices as those of a "civilized, moral machi" with broad knowledge who performed humanitarian healing for all. She had changed her previous perception that illness and healing were born from interethnic conflict mapped onto the dichotomy between the time of civilization and the time of spirit masters of the forest and warfare. Francisca challenged *wingka* discourses of otherness, arguing that her morality and her rhetorical and ritual practices were more civilized than those of *wingka* because her expansive knowledge of the universe accommodated different Mapuche and *wingka* systems of knowledge and belief, which she used to increase both individual and collective well-being. Pedro Morales, *longko* of Imilco, said, "Machi Francisca had her *kimün* [wisdom] and *newen* [power] in the ancestors, [in the] laurel trees on the top of the Millali hill, [in] the plants, and in the thunder, but she knew *wingka kimün*. That's why nobody could beat her" (January 5, 2012).

Francisca was concerned with fostering good and alleviating suffering for herself and other subjects—people living in pain or poverty, or under conditions of violence.[30] In her focus on suffering subjects, people's shared humanity, and the collective good, Francisca turned to larger questions about the value, morality, and well-being of individuals, and she challenged both Mapuche and Chileans who did not live up to her standards: "People are bad. I only like some Chileans, some Mapuche. I don't like some Mapuche because they are jealous, envious, deceitful. . . . They say false gossip. . . . They say I am [a] *wingka* sorcerer and maybe [they] can give me *füñapuwe* [poison] so I die. But Chileans are selfish, greedy, and deceitful too, and they also say I am a sorcerer. . . . I only heal those who have faith, regardless of their race" (September 6, 1996).

As a moral, civilized shaman Francisca understood illness and suffering in relation to Catholic beliefs of good and evil and in relation to older

Mapuche notions of the collective good, which conflict with the politics of revenge and sorcery. She pursued morality and well-being to create a livable world in the midst of *awingkamiento* and community factionalism. In this context, Francisca did not incorporate powers, symbols, technologies, or characters from folk medicine, Catholicism, biomedicine, or other literate traditions into her Mapuche shamanic ontology and epistemologies. Instead, she used *wingka* systems of knowledge and belief in parallel with Mapuche ones to construct herself as a machi with a broad, civilized vision of the world.

Machi and *longko* in the Quepe area have been creating a new, intimate, existential concept of the time of civilization that is focused on people's capacities and forms of being rather than on a person as a representative of larger geopolitical histories or forms of social organization, productivity, and interethnic relationships. Mapuche are using this existential notion of civilization to create a new pan-Mapuche historical and political project. Jorge Sandoval, *longko* of Huenchual, fused the moral, harmonious relationship with the land and its history experienced by sovereign Mapuche who lived 130 years ago with contemporary Mapuche experiences to create a civilized, moral Mapuche temporality. Jorge argued that civilized Mapuche do not act like angry *wingka* but have Mapuche *rakiduam* (wisdom) and behave seriously, calmly, respectfully, and responsibly. "We civilized Mapuche are *kümeche* [good people] and *kimche* [wise people]," he said (July 17, 2007). Jorge believed that by living lives of civilized morality today, Mapuche would transform their place in history and civilize the settlers' selfish, immoral "savagery."

Even though Francisca tried to move away from an ethnic reading of the time of spirit masters of the forest and warfare and the time of civilization, they remained in her shamanic repertoire as discourses capable of causing and relieving misfortune. The dynamics of power and resistance in her civilized practice were complex. Francisca gained power by showing that she used other systems of knowledge for the collective good and that she resisted the politics of revenge and sorcery. But by resisting the notion of illness as the result of interethnic conflict, she challenged her own legitimacy as a Mapuche thunder shaman. Mapuche in Millali suspected Francisca's "civilized" shamanic knowledge, which they associated with sorcery and *awingkamiento* because many Mapuche associate thunder machi with wildness. Many interpreted Francisca's appropriation as a loss of Mapuche culture to the dominant culture, a kind of complicity with the dark side of civilization, and ultimately as an act of betrayal. People in Millali wondered whether Francisca was truly embodying a broad shamanic civilized knowledge of the universe for the benefit of suffering subjects. Or was she collaborating with the civilization of the outsiders and becoming a *wingka* in the process for her own individualistic benefit? Should a thunder shaman ever let go of her wildness?

CIVILIZED AND WILD: WARRING TEMPORALITIES

The time of civilization and the time of spirit masters of the forest and warfare illustrate the complex web of relations between different narratives, the agents who tell them, their motivations, and the larger political and historical context of colonization and confrontation. The different ways in which settlers and Mapuche experience these times suggest that history is shaped by moral projects. The two different times situate Francisca's stories about the past and her life within wider political, ecological, and spiritual contexts. Mapuche sometimes situate these contexts in the realm of ethics and morality, and at other times see them as systems of value. What is included and what is silenced in these temporalities are therefore very important.

Settlers and Mapuche attribute radically different significance to the events of colonization and the relationship between Mapuche and the state. In their competing, continuous, intergenerational histories, the Mapuche and the colonizers each see themselves as participating in civilized time and see the other as inhabiting savage time. For each group, these historical constructions conflate particular moments of their respective histories. Both the Mapuche and the settlers justify their own physical or spiritual warfare during the time of wilderness and warfare, but they dismiss the other's warfare as "savage state violence" or Mapuche "terrorism."

German settlers construct Mapuche as savages and terrorists who exist permanently in a time of wilderness and warfare because Mapuche try to reclaim their ancestral lands, challenging the colonizers, the forestry companies, and the operators of hydroelectric dams that now hold the lands. *Wingka* view machi as savage because their wild, unmediated spiritual powers and nonideological practices are thought to be irrational. The settlers also link the spiritual warfare of machi against the spirits of neoliberalism with physical violence and terrorism.

The Mapuche, in contrast, see a savage state that has practiced indiscriminate violence against them continuously since the nineteenth century. The forestry companies' armies of eucalyptus and pine trees have destroyed Mapuche histories, which are linked to the cycles of the plants, animals, spirits, and humans that live in Millali. Mapuche have revived what they see as the positive side of the time of wilderness and warfare and transformed it into the time of spirit masters of the forest and warfare, calling

---

on the unmediated forces of thunder and the spirit masters of native forests, which shamans associate with autochthony and historical continuity. Francisca saw herself as forging relations between the past, present, and future of humans, forests, and spirits in order to wage war against settlers and the state, which are only interested in their well-being in the present. Spirit masters also use their wild powers to express their own histories through the dreams and visions they give to Mapuche and to encourage ordinary Mapuche and shamans to act to protect their common values.

During the time of civilization, Millali residents struggled to express a coherent moral Mapuche symbolic order that would oppose class-based, secular, socialist ideologies and bourgeois, liberal, capitalist ones. For Mapuche, being civilized means being calm, responsible, and serious. It also means embracing ideals of social egalitarianism and communal work, caring for the spirit masters, holding parliaments, valuing leisure and socializing, and having a broad knowledge of the universe. In this context, the moral behavior of Mapuche communities, factions, and individuals takes precedence over Mapuche blood ties. Moral Mapuche are those who focus on collective interests and interrelationships with nature and spirit beings. The *awingkados*, like Enrique and Julio, who cut down Rosa Kurin's *boldo* tree, have internalized the individualistic values of settler entrepreneurship: the ideologies and systems of power, politics, production, and consumption. During the time of spirit masters of the forest and warfare, people in Millali opposed the secularization of land; both right- and left-wing political ideologies; the alliance between settlers, the government, and the military; and the Chilean state's long-term politics of indiscriminate violence against indigenous people.

Although *wingka* and Mapuche claims to civilization and to wilderness and warfare are clearly opposed, the ways in which the two groups construct their temporalities are strikingly similar. Both conflate current experiences with moments in history so as to highlight their moral superiority and belonging or to justify their violence. Both compress memories. But the Chilean national imagination does not give equal weight to the competing intergenerational memories. The colonizers' version is recognized as history and as civilization by the Chilean state, which condemns the Mapuche as savage, nomadic pacifists or as terrorists. The Mapuche version, on the other hand, can emerge only as revisionist narratives about civilized Mapuche's transformed consciousness. Indigenous historical memory can be used to express new forms of healing for the collective good or to support political mobilization against settlers and the state. Mapuche argue for their legitimacy in narratives about civilized, moral Mapuche taming the savage state, the settlers' paramilitary groups and devils, and *wingka wekufü* spirits—deriving hope from these stories as they resist oppression and violence at the hands of the military and the colonizers.

Simultaneously, Mapuche conflate the machi warring power of thunder with the military power of Mapuche chiefs and the Chilean army and with the violence perpetrated by General Pinochet to confront inter- and intraethnic aggression during the Mapuche time of spirit masters of the forest and warfare. Francisca and other Mapuche used this machi power to combat state violence, the logging industry, factional conflicts, and *awingkamiento*, all of which can destroy Mapuche relationships with the spirit masters of the land. Although military imagery continues to mediate the historical narratives of machi, the shamans' relationship with the state is complex. By laying the responsibility for environmental destruction and violence on the state, machi ameliorated conflicts within the community and allowed enemies to continue to live together. Even so, when Francisca's practice as a thunder shaman with unmediated powers led her to transgress the community's gender roles, she suffered accusations of sorcery in Millali. These multiple, complex relationships illustrate what Michael Fischer (2003) calls "emergent forms of life," which challenge the dualisms of us/them and primitive/civilized and exist amid contingency, violence, and contradictory interests.

Twenty-first-century Mapuche dreams that separate shamanic power from military power have challenged the logic of the time of spirit masters of the forest and warfare to propose other, civilized forms of engagement with time—for example, a return to the practice of interethnic parliaments and caring for the spirit masters. Francisca argued that she was a "civilized machi" who accommodated different systems of knowledge and belief, and she challenged the perception that illness was due to interethnic conflict and attempted to alleviate suffering for all humans—Mapuche and non-Mapuche. But Francisca's death and contested rebirth would produce the greatest transformation of her shamanic history, changing her relationship to shamans of the past and the future.

CHAPTER SEVEN

TRANSFORMING MEMORY
through DEATH *and* REBIRTH

In August 1996, Francisca decided to die. She organized a *ngeikurewen* ritual to renew her powers, bought food and drink, and paid the helping machi and the musicians. Machi control their altered states of consciousness, and they know when they are near death. Also, Machi funerals are similar in format to renewal rituals, so some of her family believed that Francisca had prepared her own funeral and would will herself to die. She planned when and how she would be ritually finished as a person. And on September 11, 1996, shortly before the ritual was scheduled to begin, she died.

The Mapuche understand a living person on the basis of their social relationships, finding wholeness only in relation to others. Machi extend this network of relations who share personhood not only to kin and non-kin, but also to animal and spirit beings, including deceased machi from previous generations. The funeral rituals that finish a machi are therefore more elaborate than those of ordinary Mapuche, because they need to sever relationships with many different kinds of beings.

Francisca's funeral involved the staging of the *ngillatun* ritual, which included horses, *kultrung*, and flags. During the four-day wake preceding her funeral, patients, visitors, and people from Millali spoke about Francisca's life and lamented her departure. Those who had conflicts and unfinished business with Francisca spoke to her corpse, asking for forgiveness, making offerings, and resolving misunderstandings. After the wake, machi Angela came to perform the funeral, to finish Francisca as a person. In some Mapuche coastal communities, orators remember and condense the uniqueness of the deceased's life, objectifying the person to make her whole. In this way, the deceased is freed from reciprocal relations with the living and can move into the realm of the dead (Coña 1984 [1930]; Schindler 1996; Course 2011). But in Millali and the surrounding central Mapuche valleys, it is machi who ritually finish the dead (Bacigalupo 2010).

The machi's *amulpüllün*, a ritual of directed disremembering, was intended to make Francisca's *püllü* (spirit) leave, severing all of Francisca's shared personhoods with human, animal, and spirit beings. The ritual destruction of her possessions made her *püllü* distinct from those of the living and allowed it to merge with the collective ancestral *filew*.[1] Francisca's individual personality thus dissolved, and it would only be individualized again when a living person dreamed of her as an individual who would be reborn. People in Millali were particularly wary of Francisca's spirit because her life story reflected the uncomfortable realities of factionalism and accusations of witchcraft in the community. This made it important to conduct an especially meticulous *amulpüllün* to disremember her, placate her *püllü*, and send it on its way; otherwise, her *püllü* could return to avenge itself against the living through the *alwe*—the amoral force of the dead person. People in Millali explained the presence of evil *wekufü* spirits in the community as partly the result of *amulpüllün* rituals that were either improperly performed in that the *alwe* was allowed to lurk around the corpse, or incomplete because the living continued to remember the deceased after the funeral.

This unique Mapuche process—in which the deceased is disremembered immediately after the funeral and eventually re-remembered—transforms the personhood of machi from historical figures to ancestral ones, and then back. Individuals are cleansed of their antisocial qualities, to then be reborn and to create relational personhoods with a variety of others. But people in Millali were uncertain about the status of Francisca's personhood at death because of her multiple transgressive deaths and rebirths prior to her funeral in 1996.

In 1995, Francisca had slaughtered the horse with which she had shared bodily substances and personhood, so that its spirit would carry the spirit of her deceased son to the Mapuche sky. People in Millali viewed this as a form of social and spiritual suicide, since machi's horses are normally only killed when the machi dies. Because of her transgressive behavior, Francisca experienced three cataleptic "deaths" that year, and after each one, she revived in the same body. At her funeral, people in Millali were unclear about how they should finish and disremember Francisca. They wondered if during the previous cataleptic deaths she already had lost her lived and remembered relations to others. Was she already a whole, objectified person? Had she already become part of the collective *filew*, and had she simply forgotten the experience? Or was she already an evil spirit, hexing the living?

In this chapter I describe Francisca's nonconformist and personally dangerous act to ameliorate the soul state of her son. I also describe how her death was rescripted twice by her descendants—once as they moved in their own history and a second time through their collaboration with me.

———

TRANSFORMING MEMORY *through* DEATH *and* REBIRTH

Francisca's personhood was transformed and reshaped many times through contested processes of disremembering and remembering. The most recent transformation came after 2004, when people in Millali erased the negative aspects of Francisca's spirit and merged it with Rosa's spirit, anticipating the rebirth of a new machi spirit. I demonstrate how the process of mythologization was reversed as Francisca was rehistoricized in a new context, and I show that discourses of disremembering and the transformation of memory and personhood may both assert and deny social persistence and cohesion.

TRANSGRESSIVE DEATHS AND REBIRTHS

Francisca's son Francisco died on February 20, 1994, at the young age of forty-five. The medical cause of death was a myocardial infarction, due to an obstruction of the coronary artery by a thrombus. But some people of Millali believed he died from sorcery. Francisco was Francisca's blood descendant, her *küpalme*. According to Mapuche thought, they shared embodied traits, bodily substances, and character. When Francisco died, Francisca's family and community urged her to sever her social ties with him so his *püllü* could travel to another world and she could live a healthy life. If she continued to think about him, his spirit would remain trapped on this earth and become an evil spirit, or it could take her *püllü* to the afterworld with it.

But Francisca was unable to let go of her son, and she soon became physically ill. She felt pain in her chest, stomach, and head. She experienced fever, fainting, confusion, and amnesia. She interpreted these symptoms as soul loss: "My back hurts, my heart swells up, my liver swells, and that's why I can't move around. My bones don't work well; my blood doesn't move well. All my body itches. My knee [and] my heel hurt. I have sadness because my son died. I have weakness of the heart" (March 15, 1994). Bernardita, Francisca's granddaughter, explained the consequences of Francisca's inability to let go: "Francisca misbehaved, she cried too much for her son. He took her with him [to death] because she couldn't forget him" (January 4, 2006). Some people in the community claimed that Francisca had actually killed her son with sorcery in order to consume the blood of kin and thereby strengthen her own powers. But others said that Francisca could not have killed Francisco because she became weaker, not stronger, after his death.

Francisca sacrificed her spirit horse during her son's funeral, hoping that Francisco's *püllü* would ride on its back to the Wenu Mapu. Francisco's greediness and aggressive behavior had transgressed Mapuche moral codes, so Francisca worried that his *püllü* would not be able to get to the sky on its own: "The *püllü* of good people goes up to the sky; the people with bad tongues stay on the earth. Shit, my son wasn't so good. Where will his *püllü* be? Will he lurk around the cemetery and attack his family?" But Francisca and her horse had spiritual kinship ties (*küpalme püllü*) with each other, so killing the horse was a form of spiritual suicide that could also kill Francisca's body. Bernardita explained, "Francisca was already half-dead because she couldn't forget the death of her son. Then she killed her spirit horse to save [her son's] *püllü*. She lost her machi *püllü*. Her spirit horse got angry and killed her" (January 4, 2006). By severing her relationship with her spirit horse, Francisca finished herself as a person and defined herself as closed and bounded. This is ordinarily something that a machi does for a deceased person.

By slaughtering her spirit horse and remaining attached to her deceased son, Francisca transgressed social and spiritual relationships central to the constitution of machi personhood and the transformation of shamanic embodied history through death and rebirth. Francisca finished herself as a person, and yet her body remained alive. Without her spirit horse, Francisca could no longer be a mounted thunder shaman, a spiritual warrior, and a master of mobile histories—connecting different places, beings, and times to gain knowledge, facilitate healing, kill evil spirits, and forge a better future for Mapuche.

Francisca was hospitalized six times in 1995, and during that time she experienced her three cataleptic "deaths." She was treated for cardiomegaly (an enlarged and weakened heart), an auricular septal defect (a hole in her heart), and auricular fibrillation (heart arrhythmia) that caused thrombosis (blood clots in the circulatory system). Some blood clots lodged in a lung, causing a pulmonary embolism (blockage to one of the arteries of the lung), and at least one went to her brain, causing a stroke.[2] Francisca interpreted the medical diagnoses as symptoms of her spiritual suicide and the soul loss (*amun entuwi ñi püllü*) she experienced when she stabbed her spirit horse in the heart. Although Francisca had wanted to send off her son's spirit and sever her shared personhood with her spirit horse and the people in the society in which she lived, she realized this was impossible.

Francisca's cataleptic deaths were not part of a ritual to renew her shamanic powers; nor were they associated with rites of passage: initiation, renewal, and death rituals. Rather, they were associated with a series of social and spiritual transgressions. Her family attributed these deaths to *kastikukutran* (punishment illnesses) inflicted by various spirits. She described being revived and then individualized through the divine intervention of Ngünechen:

I was three times dead in the hospital in Temuco. Three times, they sent out messages saying that I was going to die, but the Celestial Mother, the Celestial Father protected me. That's why I was saved. One time, I was coming back from healing some people in Curarrehue [and] suddenly criminals stole the ox, and they brought my *kultrung* down from the cart. My head was dizzy. I jumped [from the cart], and I fell onto a stone in the road, and I broke my head. They took me to the hospital, and [I] was dead for about half an hour. I was almost buried. My daughter was crying. . . . Another time, my head was drunk. I felt like I was going to fall. I saw that all the people were around. I didn't know my family. I wondered, "Why are they crying?" Then they changed my clothes [for the funeral] and did prayers on me and asked God for favors. I felt things coming out of my head. Then a machi did a *datun* to me and I revived. . . . And then again I was in the hospital. The doctor, who is just like a machi, said I was dead. I felt nothing. I didn't know what they were doing to me. Then I looked up and saw the doctor, the nurse, but I didn't see who they were. "What happened to you, Panchi?" he asked. I couldn't speak. Thank God, Mamita, that God wanted me to revive. (November 13, 1995)

Francisca described her multiple deaths as the loss of her lived or remembered relations to self and others, which would be followed by the final death of her body and the rebirth of her spirit in the body of a new machi.[3] These preliminary deaths were very different from the altered states of consciousness she entered during spirit possession, when her spirit became temporarily fused with the *filew*. Although machi claim that they do not remember their possession experiences, in practice they are both aware and unaware, in what Carol Laderman (1992:192) calls "a balance between remembering and disremembering." Machi are aware of the spirit's presence and understand its advice and demands, but it is the spirit, not the machi, who speaks. Machi forget their own personas, but remember the ritual, the performance, and sometimes the actions and words of the possessing spirit. Machi Francisca described her personal soul as "sitting beside" her body and watching while the *filew* possessed her.

Like the Haitian Vodou practitioners whom Erika Bourguignon (1965) observed, machi perceive a continuity between the possessing spirit and the generic spirit of *filew* or Ngünechen, but they see a discontinuity between the possessing spirit and the human vehicle. The latter has no memory of or responsibility for the actions performed in that altered state of consciousness, while the machi's body is the residence of a more powerful spirit. Some cases of possession show an obvious continuity between the spirit and the conscious motivation of the possessed (Bourguignon 1965:47, 53, 57). However, in such cases the temporary replacement of the machi's self by a spirit does not challenge the integrity of the self, but rather provides it with an alternative set of roles. Francisca's cataleptic states, by contrast, produced not an altered consciousness, but a loss of consciousness. Francisca experienced a lack of personhood and bodily functions. She felt "brain dead" and was "feeling things coming out of [her] head," "feeling nothing," "losing [her] senses," and "looking at people and not seeing who they were."

The community debated what Francisca's multiple deaths meant, comparing them to the experience of other deceased machi and their eventual rebirth in the body of a new person. Ordinarily only the spirit, temperament, skills, and embodied performances of deceased machi are reborn in the body of a new machi. Francisca, however, was reborn in her own body and as her own social person, retaining her identity, emotions, thoughts, and relationships. Francisca experienced leaving her body and seeing herself from above, as a machi *püllü*: "I was looking from above. The doctor said I was dead. I felt nothing. I didn't know what they were doing to me" (November 13, 1995). Francisca sometimes claimed that her power and knowledge increased when she revived. At other times, she said she could not remember. Both of these statements make sense in the context of Mapuche thought, in which remembering and speaking require consciousness (*zuam*) and thought (*rakiduam*), which are physically located in the head of a living person in either a waking or altered state of consciousness. Francisca's cataleptic states involved neither. She could not remember these events because as the machi *püllü* or *filew* she had power, knowledge, and agency, but she had no consciousness or location in historical time.

Francisca's multiple deaths and rebirths back into her own body in historical time were ineffective because they did not purge her of her social transgressions. People in Millali considered them to be bad. They raised questions about her morality and even about the effectiveness of machi spirits as historical agents who actualize the "before time" and produce historical transformation.[4] By coming back into Francisca's body repeatedly and soon after death, her machi *püllü* prevented the community from disremembering her and did not allow her spirit to be stripped of the individual components of her social person and become part of the generic ancestral *filew*. Francisca's deaths and rebirths, therefore, did not strain out her negative qualities and transform her biography, which is what ordinarily occurs with deceased machi. Consequently, Francisca could not become mythologized like machi Rosa. One man from Millali argued that although Francisca might have temporarily become the ancestral *filew*, she could not transform the history of the community through divine action because she remembered nothing. Bernardita believed that since Francisca was dead for such a short time, the machi *püllü* just "sat beside her body and waited" (December 12, 2005). Another Mapuche man believed that Francisca was a sorcerer "who has all the knowledge because she never dies" (December 22, 2007). He believed that evil spirits, not the deity Ngünechen, brought her back to life each time. People in Millali wondered how Francisca—who was viewed with ambivalence—would use this ancestral shamanic knowledge.

Why was Francisca "killed" repeatedly by the spirits for her transgressions? And why did Ngünechen intercede each time, bringing her back to life and into historical time as the same social person? Francisca's multiple rebirths through divine intervention allowed her to correct her violations of social and spiritual relations by severing the inappropriate connections with her deceased son and reestablishing her shared personhood with a spirit horse. Francisca became whole again through her relational personhood with a new spirit horse.

When Francisca fell into a cataleptic state on January 28, 1995, machi Angela healed her. They belonged to the same machi cohort and therefore shared personhood, bodily substances, and spiritual essences. As I described in chapter 4, Angela performed *ülutun* and *datun* healing rituals for Francisca and strengthened her spirit through drumming, massage, and prayer. When Francisca regained consciousness, Angela explained that Ngünechen had killed Francisca because it had been five years since she performed a *ngillatun* ritual in the field beside her house. In addition, Francisca's spirit horse was angry because she had killed it and in doing so had killed herself in the same way—stabbed herself with a knife in the heart and lung. Machi Angela told Francisca not to think about her son and to buy another horse with which to exchange breath and saliva, thus making it her new spirit horse. Francisca elaborated, "I need the horse's panting, its *neyen*. I will put it [the *neyen*] on my head to be stronger and bless it. I will take out its heat with a little dish and put some water into it and drink it. That way, I will be strong again. And you, Mariella, will bring me a new goatskin for my *kultrung*, so that I will be strong." The *dungumachife* added, "Now people have interceded on her behalf, saying, 'She will have her saddled horse again. We already have it for her.'" By creating a relationship with a new spirit horse, Francisca was able to gallop once again to other realms.

Francisca also sought to increase the speed and range of her shamanic flight by merging her new spirit horse (which had both a corporeal and spirit form) with Rosa's pampean spirit horse and my airplane travel. She did so by renewing her spiritual kinship with Rosa and through her friendship and ritual partnership with me. Mapuche view *küpalme püllü* (the spirit of the social role one plays in the family and community) as central to the constitution of a shaman's spiritual essence, personhood, and powers (Bacigalupo 2007), while relations of friendship and partnership created through exchange (*wenüywen*) are one of the primary means through which one is constituted as a person (Course 2010). Francisca drew on the Wenteche-pampean shamanic horse complex and dreamed that she would get a spirit horse from the Argentine pampas that was imbued with the shamanic powers of ancient mounted warriors and machi Rosa: "In my dream, they gave me a Patagonian horse to ride. 'You shall ride this horse,' they told me. It had a white rose [*rosa*] on its face and mouth and a Chilean saddle. I rode my horse, that's why I am strong now" (May 24, 1995). White and blue are the colors of the Mapuche sky and the Virgin Mary, and the horse's "rose" implied that Francisca's spirit horse possessed Rosa's shamanic powers.

Through her persona as a machi mounted on a horse with her drum, Francisca was able to expand her relationships and mode of travel and engage in a productive connection with me—a partial outsider engaged with the world of academia—to produce her bible. Francisca conceived her bible as akin to her drum, in that it would carry her power and knowledge to different locations. But she imagined that I would travel with her bible on a jet plane rather than on a horse: "My bible will carry my force to many places. To all the places you travel to on the airplane and the people you know" (May 24, 1995). Francisca envisioned my experiences of jet travel as akin to her spiritual flight to other worlds through dreams and altered states of consciousness:

Francisca: You always go on the planes, and do you always dream that you fly?

Mariella: Yes.

Francisca: Do you travel okay? And when you look downward, do you see the houses, the earth, the hill?

Mariella: Yes. They look pretty. Everything is smaller.

Francisca: And then, when you want to come down, does your head get dizzy?

Mariella: Sometimes.

Francisca: Do you always have strength to move on?

Mariella: I try to be strong.

Francisca: When you are in another place, what remedies do you take to kill the fear?

Mariella: None, I just go. I'm afraid.

Francisca: You need to bring me the rain off the wings of your plane. I need to work it to protect you. I also see the houses, the fields, very small when I fly. I'm not afraid of death. I see everything. But Ngünechen doesn't like people who are not machi flying in the clouds. He throws the planes down with lightning. That's why when you fly, I pray a lot for you, my bud, my child. (May 25, 1995)

Francisca imagined that her new spirit horse would have the power and legitimacy of ancient mounted shamans from Patagonia and would fly with the force and speed of a jet plane.

Francisca reestablished herself as a machi by recovering her shared personhood with the spirit horse and therefore her power as a mounted thunder shaman. But this also highlighted her difference from other machi: Francisca had made herself ill by refusing to sever her relations with her son and finish him as a person, and her spiritual suicide in an effort to save his soul was unprecedented in machi practice. Ngünechen's intervention to revive Francisca allowed her to sever her social relationship with her deceased son and become a whole person again. Francisca then embraced the world of the living, strengthening her machi powers through her spiritual relationship with Rosa and her spirit animals, her friendship with me, and her participation in embodied shamanic cyclical and mobile histories. Now that Francisca was ritually remade as a whole person, she could orchestrate her own death, which would enable her community to finish her as a person.

PLANNED DEATH AND DISREMEMBERING

In August 1996 Francisca began preparations for her *ngeikurewen*, a ritual in which she would renew her powers and her relationships with her machi sheep, the spirit of Rosa, the thunder machi she embodied, and machi Angela, her "sister" in the same machi cohort. Francisca also hoped this ritual would serve as a collective *ngillatun* ritual for the Calfuñir-Huenchuñir faction of the community. Francisca planned her *ngeikurewen* for October 4, the day of Saint Francis (San Francisco)—the patron saint of animals, ecology, and agriculture—to ensure plentiful crops, animal fertility, and community well-being.

Machi renewal rituals closely resemble their funeral rituals, and both strengthen the machi's powers. But funerals do so with the purpose of finishing the living machi and sending her spirit off to the sky. Machi who know they are near death sometimes organize a *ngeikurewen*, buy food and drink, pay the helping machi and musicians, and then die shortly before the ritual. At the time, Francisca said:

> I had a dream that told me I had to do a machi *pürun* [dance of renewal, another name for *ngeikurewen*] here in the house. I dreamed that people were dancing *pürun* and *choyke* [the mating dance of the Patagonian ostrich]. "I have to do a machi *pürun*," I said. God said, "You have to go out and find people, get all the things you are going to need. You have to bring a good *trutrukatufe* [long horn player]. You have to have *choykes* for the *pürun*. There has to be meat. There has to be a powerful machi, a good machi." I dreamed that it was machi Angela who would come and help me make my spirit strong again. . . . I thought, "I will do my *pürun* the fourth of October, the day of Saint Francis. Maybe I will renew my powers, or maybe it will be my last machi *pürun*." (August 28, 1996)

Francisca asked me to take her to the social services office in Temuco a few days later to inquire about funeral subsidies. She was relieved to learn that the government would pay for a cheap pine coffin when she died. On September 10, 1996, the day before her bodily death, Francisca butchered a sheep and set aside a sack of potatoes for the participants in her machi *pürun*. She walked from house to house, inviting friends to her ritual, drinking large quantities of red wine, and paying in advance for the musicians and the machi who would officiate.

The next morning, José Calfuñir, her brother-in-law, could not wake her. He found blood on her mattress, and Francisca's granddaughter Bernardita realized that Francisca's heart was not beating. She and Francisca's daughter Alba wailed as they took off her jewelry. Each of them kept something. I was in Cambridge, Massachusetts, when Francisca died, so I was unable to attend her funeral in southern Chile. I have reconstructed the events here as they were narrated to me by Bernardita and machi Angela when I returned to Millali in December 1996.

After her death, the people of Millali willfully erased their memories of Francisca and finished her as a person. This allowed her spirit to merge with the generic spirit of all machi, the *filew*—an ancestral being beyond the exigencies of historical events. First, machi Angela prayed to Francisca's *püllü*: "You must leave now. You are now a different person. You are an outsider, a stranger. This is not your home. Go to your home in a different land. You no longer know anything about this world." Then the community performed a ritual of counterinscription—what Debbora Battaglia (1993:430) calls an "erasure of habitual practice"—in which they destroyed her belongings and refused to say her name in order to assist with the process of separation.[5] In a gesture common to all funerals in Millali, her brother-in-law broke off the heels of her shoes so her spirit would slip in the mud and not be able to clomp around the house, tormenting her family.

Francisca's family moved her house, changed the path to it, and planted new trees so her spirit would not recognize the landscape. Machi Angela pulled Francisca's old *rewe*, her shamanic tree of life, out of the ground and left it in a nearby stream to rot. The mourners killed and ate Francisca's spirit sheep, symbolically cannibalizing her body to release her spirit. Amazonian Wari often negate kinship relations, objectify their dead, and transform them into animals through ritual cannibalism to make them social outsiders (Conklin 2001; Vilaça 2000). But in Millali, where machi already share personhood with animals, deceased machi, and spirit animals, the spirits of recently deceased machi must become ontologically distinct from the living to erase their sociality. As Anne-Christine Taylor (1993:654–655) argued, people often transform their dead into paradigms of alterity or sociological foreignness in order to make them disappear as persons. The mourners finished Francisca as a person by constructing her as an outsider spirit who no longer had any relations with anyone or anything on earth. According to Mikhail Bakhtin (1986), it is only from the outside that one can see another person as a unique object and fix the person in time and space as closed and finished (Holquist 2002:22, 31). The Mapuche finished Francisca from the outside, but they also merged her with the non-unique *filew*, the generic ancestral shamanic spirit.

Francisca had commissioned me to write her bible in order to challenge the historical process of immediate disremembering and deindividualization after her death. But her family refused this challenge. They argued that Francisca's historical figure needed to be disremembered so that she could be transformed into the ancestral machi *filew*. This process of disremembering is an act of mental discipline, involving the control of emotions and a series of behavioral restrictions. The Mapuche and I could not speak Francisca's name or talk about her. We could not cry, and I could not write her bible. At the same time, her family knew that I could not fully disremember Francisca. They permitted me to write about some aspects of her life and practice, using the pseudonym of Pamela. Since Francisca's words were not linked to her name and individuality, they had no force, and they could not be used to practice shamanic literacy. And since the other books were not her bible, and therefore were not ritual objects containing her power, they could not bring back her spirit. Francisca's granddaughter was aware of the possibility of the re-remembering and rebirth of Francisca's spirit in Millali in the future. And it was because of this awareness that she

FIGURE 7.1
*Francisca Kolipi wearing her headdress of multicolored ribbons
and her ring (photo by George Munro).*

gave me Francisca's headdress and ring to take to the United States, to co-habit with my memories of Francisca—with the promise that I would return them if and when Francisca's spirit returned (fig. 7.1).

Francisca was buried after a blessing of the coffin by the local Catholic priest and dances by Mapuche mourners. Her brother-in-law slashed the skin of her drum and placed it on the casket together with the intestines of her spirit sheep and the blue and white flags that had been planted beside her *rewe.* Machi Angela and three of her helpers played *kultrung* while the men played trumpets and flutes to honor her as they would a military chief. The mourners painted her tombstone blue and placed an image of the Virgin Mary on it. Francisca had often called on the powers of Mary to help her heal, and Bernardita thought she would need the Virgin to accompany her on her voyage to the Wenu Mapu. The mourners buried the coffin with Francisca's feet facing east, so the next morning her *püllü* could walk up into the sky. There, it would merge with the *filew* and sit beside the deity Ngünechen, waiting for the right moment to become embodied as a new machi (Bacigalupo 2010). Battaglia (1992:14) has referred to this process, in which people create a new identity for the deceased in the afterlife, after they have been finished and disremembered, as the "willful transformation of memory."

For many peoples around the world, memories are constructed through a complex process of selective remembering and forgetting, and forgetting is seen as a fundamental component of the process of remembering (Battaglia 1993; Cole 2001; Fabian 2003; Ricoeur 2005; Augé 2004). These processes can extend well beyond an individual's life and death, and they are shaped by both the dynamic social realities of the living and the changing personhood of the deceased.[6] The multiple shamanic personhoods of machi are embodied in material and living entities and are transformed at different stages in the process of death and rebirth. These multiple personhoods are severed at death and replaced by new collective personhoods. The deceased machi can then be reindividualized and reborn in the body of a new machi, who reestablishes some of the deceased machi's shared personhoods and creates others anew. This cyclical process of the machi's spirit—death, severing, and disremembering leading to rebirth, relationality, and re-remembering—is central to the production of shamanic embodied histories.

In this cycle of disremembering and re-remembering, Mapuche spirits play a central role as agents of history. The goal of Mapuche death rituals is twofold: to undo the social and spiritual relationships that constitute a person so she can no longer be an agent in society, and to separate the different parts of the person—body, spirit, and life force—so the person as a whole is finished and the spirit can take a new form in a transcendent reality. Mapuche perceive the *kalül* (body) as separate from the *püllü* (living spirit, power), which carries the personality, abilities, and embodied experiences of the living, and the *am* (shadow of the deceased person). Mourners in Millali are particularly concerned with the *alwe*, the force of the dead person, which can be trapped on earth and lurk around the corpse. The *alwe* has no volition, personality, or morals. This means it can be easily manipulated by a sorcerer, who can transform it into an evil spirit, a *witranalwe* (visiting *alwe*) (Marileo 1995:106). If the death rituals are conducted properly, the *alwe* will disintegrate and the *püllü* will leave for another realm, losing its individuality as it merges with the *filew*. But if the mourners make mistakes or remember the deceased as an individual after the funeral, then the *alwe* will remain on earth, most likely as an evil spirit that harasses the living.[7]

All machi are expected to use their spiritual power to control their altered states of consciousness. By arranging the timing and conditions of her death, Francisca demonstrated her mastery, challenging Mapuche perceptions that death is often brought about by malevolent others. Francisca made sure that her death could not be blamed on her enemies and that she remained a machi who mediated between the worlds of the living and the dead and between the past, present, and future. By determining who would be at her funeral and what roles they would play in finishing her as a person, by hiring the necessary machi and musicians ahead of time, Francisca showed her ability to exist in transcendence while still remaining part of the social and shamanic world she was leaving behind. Machi control when, how, and by whom they will become whole during the rituals of the living—and sometimes the circumstances in which they will be finished in death, too—whereas ordinary persons do not.

People in Millali were particularly wary of Francisca's spirit because her life story reflected the factionalism and allegations of sorcery in the community. They feared that Francisca's spirit would return to avenge itself on the living, bringing scarcity, illness, and conflict to the community. When I returned to Millali in December 1996, Bernardita chided me for grieving for Francisca: "Don't cry. It is not good to remember her, because you will call her spirit back." "I want her back," I sobbed. "No," Bernardita countered, "you wouldn't know the spirit. The *alwe* would do sorcery on all of us." The recently dead remain alive in people's thoughts, and it is this "depersonified human deadness" (Taylor 1993:655) that is a menace to the living.[8]

The difference between Francisca's and Rosa's tombstones reflects their contrasting positions in the cycle of remembering and disremembering. Rosa's tomb has no birth or death dates and places her in the primordial "before time" by stating that she died at the age of 110. By making Rosa Kurin an ancestral but living presence in the community, the people of Millali ensured that she would not be disremembered and would serve as a model for future machi, who could embody her spirit and fuse their life history with hers. In contrast, Francisca's name and her birth and death dates were carved on the same plaque that held those of her husband, José Pancho Calfuñir Rañileo, who died in 1974, and her son, Francisco Calfuñir Kolipi, who died in 1994. This information fixed Francisca in linear time in her roles as wife and mother and as a machi who had died but would not return. Some people in the community wanted the memory of Francisca and the specifics of her life to die with her in what Slavoj Žižek and Mladen

Dolar (2001:135) call "the second death," which marks the death of memory and the process of mourning. This second death of Francisca's memory in the community was intertwined with the death of Francisca's memory of herself during her cataleptic states: a doubled second death.[9]

Community members often hold conflicting perceptions of the extent of disremembering (a willed act), which depend on their relationship to the deceased and their perceptions of their morality. When someone like Francisca dies—someone who is feared for being a sorcerer—many people will go to extreme measures to produce the second death, the death of memory, eradicating all reminders of the deceased so the spirit will never return and nobody will dream about them or remember them. But family members of exceptional figures, such as powerful shamans and chiefs, will often hold on to the idea that they will eventually return. So they will disremember the deceased, but they will not eradicate their memory completely through a second death. This can be dangerous. People in the community claimed that Francisca's granddaughter Bernardita died suddenly in 2007 because she dreamed of Francisca's spirit. In 2006 Bernardita had said: "Sometimes I am afraid I am going to die, because in my dream she smiles at me and shows me the path to follow her to the world of the dead."

People in the Quepe area consider machi to be wholly embodied persons as well as partial outsiders due to their relationships with spirits. Therefore it is machi who objectify ordinary deceased persons and transform them into spirits that stand outside the realm of sociality in a simple ritual called *tranatun*, in which they tell the person's disremembered spirit to go up to the sky. Machi also transform the spiritual kinship relations of deceased machi through complex *amulpüllün* rituals that release the dead machi from their matrilineal relations with spirits.[10] Machi Angela's transformation of Francisca's ontological self through ritual allowed Francisca's spirit to travel to the Wenu Mapu, unify with the ancestral *filew*, and become permanently whole until rebirth.

Generic *filew* spirits reestablish social and spiritual relationships with the living through prayer and ritual, grant knowledge to living machi during healing and divination rituals, and can intervene to help them. In Millali, the public memorialization of the *filew* takes place during *ngillatun*, which are held in the community's ritual field once every four years. But community members do not pray to the *filew* on *kuel*—collective sacred mounds where the bodies of prominent machi and chiefs are buried—as is the case among Mapuche in the Purén-Lumaco area (Dillehay 2007). In Millali, the generic *filew* eventually reindividuates when it is reborn in a new machi, and some people in the Quepe area believe that the preservation of the machi's body is central to the health of the machi's spirit and its return. *Longko* Jorge Sandoval wrapped his deceased machi mother's body in a thick nylon sheet "so that her spirit doesn't suffer, and since I have good dreams about her, I know that she is at peace" (December 19, 2005).

Most Mapuche disremember the dead, and eventual rebirth is a reward granted only to those shamans and chiefs who are ethical and powerful—and whose communities want them back.[11] People in Millali went to extreme lengths to ensure that Francisca's spirit would not come back because they feared she was a sorcerer. Special circumstances, however, made the people in Millali dramatically change their opinion of Francisca, opening up a path for her return. As Anne Becker (1995:2, 6) argued, the intrinsic moral binding of self to community lays the groundwork for both the embodiment of social processes within the personal body and the disembodiment of the person's agency and identity. Francisca's death rituals illustrate how personal, embodied experiences and knowledge can be relocated in the sociocosmic corpus and how social processes may in turn be reconstituted in individual bodies. The longevity of particular statements is always determined by a set of relations and conditions at a specific time, wrote Foucault (2002), and the historical archive is the general set of rules concerning the longevity of statements. The changing discourses about Francisca's character, personhood, and power reflected the new social and political conditions that would allow her spirit to emerge, to be transformed multiple times, and to possibly be reborn.

MYTHOLOGIZING, REMEMBERING, AND HISTORICIZING

Francisca's deaths map what might be thought of as the social life of memory and disremembering in a community at once imagined and material. Eventually some of the factional conflicts that had roiled Millali during Francisca's lifetime subsided, and the community reshaped her memory in a way that promoted historical continuity between the past and the present, the living and the dead. People relieved Francisca of her contentious and ambiguous qualities by reinventing her as a shaman who had granted blessings to the community and by conflating her identity with those of other deceased machi and the generic ancestral *filew*. There is no real process of forgetting in Millali; rather, people reshape the past to create the future. The community deliberately transformed her memory for future generations as it awaited the rebirth of her shamanic spirit. In this way, the dialectic between the individual and society shaped the remembering and forgetting (Cole 2004; Bloch 1996).

By 2004 one of Francisca's grandsons, Cesar Mellado Calfuñir, had married Irma Millañir, the granddaughter of Francisca's enemy *longko* Segundo Millañir, and Osvaldo Calfuñir had married Maria Teresa Millañir. Previously feuding factions were thus united. *Longko* Eduardo Añiwal drew on a larger sense of Mapuche ethnic identity to dissipate factionalism and sought to reunite the community in one *ngillatun* ritual: "The argument between [the] Millañir and the Calfuñir was between the old folks and has nothing to with the young people or with us because we are all Mapuche." Cesar became one of the *choyke* dancers in the *ngillatun* rituals organized by the Millañir and Añiwal families and dreamed that he would eventually become a *longko*: "In the dream, they gave me a white *longko* flag from the sky and all types of herbal remedies" (January 7, 2012). Other members of the Calfuñir family also joined in the rituals.

The community flourished: harvests were plentiful, Millali was legally reconstituted as an indigenous community, and governmental development programs were implemented.[12] During the democratic presidencies of Lagos and Bachelet, Millali finally got electric power and good dirt roads. People obtained government health care, education, and social security benefits. Bachelet supported cultural programs such as Origenes, which promoted the performance of collective *ngillatun* rituals by giving the community musical instruments and ritual attire.

With these changes, Millali entered into a new cycle of remembering. Prosperity, cooperation, and well-being allowed the people to envision a positive future for themselves as a community and to reconstruct their past within that framework. They now needed a new mounted machi warrior to forge relations with other beings and places, including the worlds of Chilean history and the state. This warrior would tie machi powers to the place of Millali through her *rewe*, perform healing as a civilized shaman, and protect the community from outsiders by drawing on the forces of Millali's primordial bull. Some people in the community began to willfully reverse the process of disremembering Francisca. They transformed their memory of her, erasing her allegedly malevolent qualities and reinventing her in a positive light. Eduardo Añiwal explained, "People didn't take Francisca seriously because she became a machi when she was older and didn't show her powers, but she was a good machi" (December 22, 2005). If community members had not successfully disremembered Francisca initially, and if positive circumstances had not pointed to the need for a new machi, Francisca's spirit would not have been able to return.

In order to erase any traces of Francisca's ambiguity, community members merged her personhood with that of Rosa, referring to the combined spirit as "the thunder machi" (*tralkan machi*) rather than as "Rosa" or "Francisca." By 2010 Francisca's name and birth and death dates had weathered from her tombstone, freeing her from her location in linear time; she was no longer a machi from the past who would not return. Some people now conceived of Francisca within the space of the "before time," where her identity merged with the *filew* and machi Rosa. Francisca was no longer disremembered, and like Rosa she became an ancestral presence in the community who would eventually be reborn in the body of a new machi. Filomena Katrikura conflated Francisca's identity with that of Rosa, her shamanic predecessor: "The machi here was powerful. The lightning struck around her head. At the beginning, they said she was a sorcerer. But then she saved the community. When the earth shook, the machi prayed, and it stopped. She lived for hundreds of years and was very, very old" (January 4, 2010).

Like the stories of past shamans, chiefs, and the multitemporal Schleyer, this new thunder shaman narrative compressed the memories of different people and different events. Once reborn in a new body, the thunder shaman would become a historical character again, rather than being relegated to the cyclical "before time." This type of condensed image affects Mapuche's experiences of particular relations through recursivity and spiritual agency, which function to emphasize cultural difference and group identity. Mapuche narrative fuses and mythologizes personal lives and historical events in order to distinguish Mapuche shamanic history from Chilean history, while also connecting the Mapuche collective memory to the experiences of the living. By mythologizing Rosa/Francisca as the restorer of cosmic order, Mapuche in Millali re-created their community's place in a new historical context. The oral historian Alessandro Portelli (1988) argues that such narratives need to be taken just as seriously as "real" events because they, too, are part of the historical process.

The compression and remaking of Francisca's story is similar to what is done by the Amazonian Piro (Gow 2001) and Kayabi (Oakdale 2005) in that the community referred to few specific dates or historical events. Instead, they condensed and dramatized long-term historical processes in what Raymond Fogelson (1985:84, 1989:143) would label an "epitomizing event." Some lowland biographical traditions encourage the use of memorized accounts of past human and mythic personages (Graham 1995; Oakdale 2005; Urban 1989), while other biographical narratives take on new meanings in new contexts with new narrators who are just as concerned with bringing the future into being as they are with documenting the past (Basso 1995). The Mapuche combine both modes when they deliberately conflate the identities of prominent shamans with those of primordial and deceased shamans and with spirits. In this process of narrating the past, they also transform it. Mapuche intellectual Juan Ñanculef elaborated,

"Mapuche invocation of ancestors is always in imprecise time. We don't say they are from a certain generation, but we link the ancestors to events that happened. Spirits are latent in all the times of the world. They are here. They will be in the future, and they will be in the past. So there is a memory of the cosmic presence of the spirits, a memory of the human past. But since we believe in a circular world, phenomena continue to repeat themselves cyclically. Then this becomes the memory of the cultural group" (January 4, 2011). By obliterating time in the Mapuche world and adapting the ancient people's stories, the new narrative allows them to take on new forms with meaningful connections to the experienced and the lived.

As their community flourished, Francisca's family believed that the machi spirit was ready to be reborn, and they engaged in another reversal. After people in the community transformed their memories of Francisca to allow her to reemerge, I was asked to write her bible after all. Although the machi spirit that would return would be differentiated from the *filew*, it was neither the individuated self of Rosa or Francisca; nor was it abstracted from its social role. Rather, it was the spirit of a thunder shaman with a social and spiritual role. It shared some qualities and biographical elements with those humans it had inhabited and with whom it had established spiritual kinship relations, but it was not determined by them. Francisca's bible would be a new medium, expressing the process of Francisca's re-individualization, rehistoricization, and perhaps her rebirth in the future, and would serve to perpetuate historical consciousness and make history.

By 2007 some people in Millali had begun speaking of the rebirth of the newly cleansed spirit of Rosa/Francisca in Bernardita's grandchildren or great-grandchildren because they are descendants of both machi Rosa (Bernardita's husband's maternal grandmother) and machi Francisca (Bernardita's maternal grandmother). Bernardita explained, "I thought the machi spirit would come back and make me a machi, but I am too old. Maybe it will initiate one of Francisca's great-granddaughters" (January 2, 2006). Amelia Ancao argued that Francisca's grandchildren would not inherit her spirit through dreams because she was a thunder machi, but that it could return during a massive earthquake or lightning storm and possess someone. *Longko* Domingo Katrikura believed that the machi spirit had already returned but had been ignored: "Sofia Huenchuñir and Melina Huenchuñir both have the spirit of a machi, but won't take on the machi role, which is why they are different, distant" (June 7, 2007). In 2008 a member of the Huenchuñir family saw four machi dancing at the *boldo* tree just outside Alejo Huenchuñir's property. Some people in the community interpreted this vision as a sign that Francisca's machi spirit wanted to return. Bernardita believed that the newly reborn machi *püllü* would retain Francisca's and Rosa's personalities and embodied performances, while taking on the thoughts, emotions, and individual relationships of the new machi. Specifically, Bernardita believed that if the spirit returned, it would retain Rosa's and Francisca's fiery tempers.

Francisca's return seemed imminent in 2009, when the *külon* tree that had been planted on her grave doubled in size. And in December of that year, the National Corporation of Indigenous Development (CONADI) returned the fifty-one hectares of land to Millali. Some people in the Quepe area said that there were signs that the spirit of the thunder machi was present, and an earthquake—8.8 on the Richter scale—and tsunami hit southern Chile on February 27, 2010. Then, the Puyehue volcano erupted in June 2011—the first eruption since Francisca's initiation in 1960. Francisca's presence and agency also became evident through her shamanic objects that remained with me.

THE REBURIAL OF FRANCISCA'S HEADDRESS AND RING

Bernardita had decided in December 1996 that I should keep Francisca's ring and her headdress of multicolored ribbons for the next machi, in the event that her spirit was reborn. Shamans in societies around the world defy physical death by infusing their power into objects like rings, shells, breastplates, headdresses, amulets, trees, and stones. Before their deaths, they or their families often give these power objects to trusted associates so the power link between shamans and their successors may be maintained (see Stoller 2008, 2014). Bernardita was aware that people in Millali might remember Francisca's spirit in positive terms in the future, which might precipitate the rebirth of that machi spirit. Bernardita believed that if she gave me some of the objects that embodied Francisca's shamanic power for safekeeping, Francisca's return would be more viable. As a Peruvian academic living in the United States, where the seasons are the opposite of those in Chile, I was an outsider and therefore closer to the world of the dead. Therefore Bernardita reasoned that I could keep these ritual objects for the future without running the risk of calling back Francisca's spirit prematurely. But as Francisca's *champuria* ritual assistant, I was also an insider who knew how to care for her shamanic objects and would know when it was time to return them.

Francisca's drum and *axis mundi* were destroyed because they were "subjective objects" (Santos-Granero 2009c:9) with their own agency and were vehicles of communication between the individual machi and her spirit and other worlds. Her clothes were also destroyed, because they contained her bodily substances and character. But many Mapuche associate head-dresses, breastplates, sleigh bells, and rings with the positive attributes of the machi's spiritual essence; they are associated with generic power and knowledge but not linked to mediation between worlds. Some argue that they too should be destroyed because they may take the holder to the land of the dead or bring other misfortune.[13] Others argue that they should be kept for future machi because these shamanic objects can grant the living power and knowledge through dreams, and they can help bring about the rebirth of the machi spirit in a new generation. *Longko* Jorge Sandoval from Huenchual and *longko* Luis Cayuman from Chihuimpilli both kept the sleigh bells and headdresses of their deceased machi mothers. Both dreamed that these machi returned to grant them the power of oratory, enabling them to become the main *longko* in their communities and to pray in collective *ngillatun* rituals.

Jorge Sandoval distinguished between subjective shamanic objects and art objects, claiming that machi objects have brought misfortune when their meaning was transformed and they were treated as "beautiful things to look at" rather than as "machi objects with power." Scholars have also made this distinction between commoditized, fetishized objects, which are imbued with exceptional material properties and abstract values and desires, and ritual objects, which are animated by a god, a spirit, or a soul that resides in and "enlivens" them (Pels 1998:94–95). Religious practitioners around the world sometimes complicate this distinction by trying to partially strip and "purify" ritual objects of their sacredness in order to transform them into neutralized art objects and sell them. However, this "purification" is seldom complete, and these objects remain dangerous.[14] Gods and spirits have agency in these decisions when they decide to enter or leave shamanic objects (Kendall and Yang 2014:15).

Machi do not believe that ritual objects can ever be stripped of their power and sacredness. The only objects machi consider acceptable to sell to museums or tourists as commodified art objects are those that are created specifically for that purpose and never imbued with shamanic power. Mapuche argue that when relatives sell objects that belonged to a deceased machi on the market to rid themselves of the ambiguity of the machi's spiritual essence, they are knowingly transferring misfortune to the buyers who treat them as art objects. I treated Francisca's ritual objects as she did during her life, but they still contained the essence of a thunder shaman whose anger and impatience could cause me misfortune.

In January 2011 I dreamed repeatedly that Francisca asked me to take her headdress and ring back to Millali. In my prayers, I told her I would return her objects in December, when I was finished with classes. But the spirit became increasingly impatient in my dreams, and in that same month I was involved in a car accident that resulted in severe vertigo and three herniated disks in my neck. In December 2011 I traveled to Millali to return Francisca's objects and to relay my dreams to her family. Francisca's daughter Aurora explained: "You dreamed, crashed, and became ill because you were close to Francisca and have her powerful things. The machi spirit is impatient. It wants them back." My dreams had become a way for the spirit of the deceased Francisca to intervene in the present.

I also told my dream to machi Maria, who shared spiritual kinship with Francisca. Francisca had initiated Maria's grandmother Juana as a machi, and thus machi Juana was Francisca's spiritual daughter. When Juana died, her spirit was reborn in the body of Maria, who was therefore also Francisca's spiritual daughter. Machi Maria explained that in order for Francisca's awakened spirit to regain its full potential, it needed to possess its shamanic objects and sever their relationship with me, a living human who would not become a machi:

> Even though you loved and remember Francisca, she is no longer the same person; she wanders in a different land. Francisca's *püllü* was in your house for many years. Now it has awakened and wants her objects back. You need to bury them at her tomb. Talk to Francisca's *püllü*. Her tomb is connected to the Wenu Mapu, and she will hear what you say. Tell her, "Thanks for letting me keep your things. Don't make me ill, and don't come back in my dreams because I have brought your objects back. I have fulfilled your request." (December 30, 2011)

The sun beat down as Aurora, Francisca's two great-grandsons, and I buried Francisca's headdress and ring in a shallow pit at her headstone and prayed. Next to the headstone, we placed hydrangeas from Aurora's garden and roses I brought from Temuco in a cut-down plastic bottle filled with water (fig. 7.2). Clouds soon covered the sky, and it began to rain. Aurora breathed a sigh of relief: "She accepted her things and our prayers. Now we can go" (January 3, 2012).

I returned to visit machi Maria. "Now you buried Francisca's things, you are free," she said, "but you still have *konün*—[where] the thoughts of the deceased are transposed onto a living person. You carried her things with her *newen* for many years, and that's why your thoughts are entrapped by her." Maria told me to drink an herbal medicine made from four *triwe* leaves, four *külon* leaves, and four *boldo* leaves to help me release Francisca before my cleansing ritual the following morning.

On January 9, 2012, Maria tied her blue headscarf tightly around her

FIGURE 7.2
Burial of Francisca Kolipi's headdress and ring next to her weathered tombstone,
where a gigantic külon *tree grows (photo by author).*

head. She fastened her black and blue woolen machi shawl with a heavy silver *trapelakucha* breastplate and flicked the ends over her back. I sat on a low stool in the doorway of her *ruka*, with the morning sun streaming in. I faced her thick *rewe*, which was flanked by branches of *triwe, foye,* and *külon.* Machi Maria pulled out a heavy silver cross and laid it on a small wooden table to her right, next to a bottle of *aguardiente.* Maria lit a cigarette and stood behind me, puffing clouds of smoke over my head. Her right hand rubbed *aguardiente* into my hair as she prayed in a booming voice. Maria invoked Ngünechen and the assemblies of ancient *longko* and machi who perform *kamarikun* (*ngillatun* rituals to prepare for war) to battle the bad smells of the dead, illness, and bad luck. Maria asked her spirit to refresh my bones and my heart, to reestablish my balance, and to heal me. She then explained my situation to Francisca's spirit: "A long time ago, she got the evil of the *püllomeñ* [literally, 'blue fly,' the spirit of the recent dead] because she was told to keep your objects. You were happy to live with this creature, but you cannot leave your bad breath of death on her. She has returned your things to the earth. You became earth a long time ago. Let the evil, the bad luck stay in the earth. Release this creature, let her go, untie her. You will not return in her dreams."

Since then, I have not dreamed about Francisca as a demanding spirit, but only as the ancestral *filew*, offering healing and advice. I have invoked her five times. When my partner, Steven Rubenstein, died suddenly on March 8, 2012, I asked Francisca to show me the path to the land of the dead. But instead, Francisca returned in my dreams singing and showering me with herbal remedies until I was ready to accept his death and let go. When my aunt Amelia Ancao died during a hernia operation on June 19, 2013, I begged Francisca—who was Amelia's midwife and close friend—to care for her spirit. I dreamed that Francisca and Amelia walked arm in arm along the path of death. When my friend Pedro Morales, *longko* of Imilco and Francisca's son-in-law, died on December 22, 2013, I asked Francisca if his spirit was well. In a dream, Francisca showed me his gigantic laurel tree reaching up to the sky to join the ancestors. When my uncle, *longko* Euladio Ancao, died from cancer on April 26, 2014, I asked Francisca what we needed to do. She appeared in my dreams to say that his children needed to take *alwe lawen* and *triwe* herbal remedies and perform a smoke exorcism to release Euladio's spirit, which was still attached to his house and family. And when I was editing this bible in January 2015, I asked Francisca if she liked the book. In a dream, she showed me her bible wrapped in royal blue headscarves—a positive color associated with machi mediation and the Mapuche sky, and a sign of acceptance. But her spirit also had a suggestion. Francisca showed me the narrative about her initiation by earthquake, the alphabetic characters dancing in organized lines to the ritual beat of the machi *purrun*, placed at the very beginning of the book, rather than in chapter 3, where I had originally put it. I have followed her direction, and her initiation narrative now opens the book.

When I visited Millali again in December 2012, nobody else in the family had dreamed of Francisca. They said that she had her power back and needed to have her bible finished, although they were uncertain whether the machi spirit would return in a new machi or not.

Spirits move through objects. The headdress and ring I was given for safekeeping and then returned, the objects that drew the dead Francisca into my dreams, are implicated in facilitating the presence of a new machi. Shamanic objects are powerful tools. They are also the means through which spirits can act as agents in their own history and produce their future.

CONTINUITY AND TRANSFORMATION THROUGH REMEMBERING AND DISREMEMBERING

Machi spirits not only carry history, they *are* history. Machi spirits become historical agents as they carry knowledge and shamanic power from past shamans into the bodies of new ones, who in turn will also act as historical agents. But spirits are also historical agents because they are transformed, cleansed, and reinvented in narratives about the primordium and historical events in response to the changing social and political needs of the community over time. Throughout this book, I have shown that machi's biographical narratives and personal experiences, including Francisca's, are central to Mapuche engagements with temporality and to the construction of historical consciousness in multiple ways. Mapuche experience and construct complex cycles of remembering and disremembering, and the personhood of spirits changes over time, both as historical individuals and as collective mythologized figures. My focus on Francisca's story has revealed norms, practices, and notions of Mapuche personhood—including its relationship to spirits and to history—that might not otherwise be evident.

There is an unresolved contradiction in Millali. On the one hand, the community creates historical continuity with the past through remembering and through machi's rebirth. On the other hand, the community disremembers deceased machi to ensure that their spirits travel to the Mapuche sky and transform into the collective ancestral spirit of all machi. If machi are not disremembered at death and do not properly sever their ties with the living, their life force (*alwe*) can be manipulated by a sorcerer and become an evil spirit that will harass the community. This *alwe* can also travel between the Miñche Mapu, the subterranean world associated with evil and sorcery, and the *mapu*, the Mapuche earth. But if machi are never re-remembered, all the wisdom from the past is lost, and a machi's *püllü* cannot be reborn in a new machi. Because only machi are fully reborn in the bodies of their spiritual descendants, they are crucial to the construction of Mapuche historical consciousness. Spirits act as historical agents, so the failure to be reborn in another shaman implies a loss of historical consciousness: the past can no longer be crafted into the present nor the present into the past.

The cycles of remembering and forgetting in Francisca's shamanic history exemplify the Mapuche perception of spiraling histories. Shamanic history offers a new understanding of the relationship between myth and history, which narrators creatively manipulate for various purposes at different moments. The cyclical, synchronic narratives about the primordium interweave with the linear, diachronic shamanic history in Millali to form a spiral along which people and events both repeat themselves and move through time. Narratives about Francisca's death and rebirth show that through Mapuche shamanic biographical narratives, history becomes myth and myth becomes history, and both are instrumental in shamanic rebirth. Shamanic spirits are transformed as they are recycled into the bodies of new machi and as the social realities in the community shift at significant historical-political moments in linear time. The recursive nature of the spiral of shamanic history is a product of the cycles of the primordial "before time" and shamanic rebirth, while the singleness of its path represents the individual and the specific historical event. The three-dimensionality of the spiral demonstrates that the cycle turns and returns, mapping onto persons and events, and that individuals and events in turn mark the beginnings and ends of cycles.

After the death and disremembering of individual machi and their histories, shamanic spirits are transformed as they merge with the *filew*, are collectively re-remembered as ancestral machi, and are then recycled in the bodies of new machi. Once the community's collective memory about the "before time" history and the "today time" history were restored, and after positive changes assured them that they were protected from sorcery, people in Millali resingularized and rehistoricized the spirit of Rosa/Francisca, distinguishing it from the generic *filew*, with which it had joined after her death.

Marc Augé (2004) and Paul Ricoeur (2004) have argued that oblivion is a necessary precondition for comprehending and remembering the past, for living fully in the present, and for finding the future by forgetting the past. Forgetting allows some people to interrupt temporal continuity or escape traumatic events and thus reimagine human experiences (Nietzsche 1983). But for Mapuche, the past is not forgotten; instead, it is controlled, put aside, and reshaped before it reemerges to become embodied in the present and future. Mapuche temporarily disremember recently deceased machi at particular moments in time in order to transform history and create a better future.

Like the autobiography of Sinek, the Karo "memory artist," Francisca's story is at once "collective history and singular testimony, literal chronicle of events and fabulated personal narrative" (Steedly 2000:814). The tension between individual identity and memory (Francisca's objects and biography, her desires, and this bible) and collective identity and memory (the *filew* spirit, the mythologized version of Rosa/Francisca, and community history) is evident throughout the process of disremembering and re-remembering. By deconstructing Francisca, unmaking her individual identity, undoing their social relations with her, and asking me not to write her biography, Mapuche in Millali erased and forgot her controversial individual history in favor of the communal memory of all shamans and the identity of the group. This process is common to most deceased machi. The individuality of Francisca's life and its traces—her powerful ritual objects and clothes—had to be destroyed, and her biographical text had to be subjected to local historical narratives of disremembering so that at a particular historical and political moment the collective identity could prevail. As Jennifer Cole (1998:627) has pointed out for the Betsimisaraka in Madagascar, all memories are not equally salient all the time, and the process of remembering and disremembering is tied to the flow of social life and people's attempts to control it.

The community's collective disremembering of Francisca also had emotional, social, and moral implications. The purposeful disremembering of her at death helped mourners to handle their grief, shielded them from sorcery, and protected the living from the dead. To remember her controversial persona at that moment would have projected the conflicted past into the present, which would have been damaging to the living. But not all traces of Francisca's life were destroyed. Her granddaughter Bernardita gave me some of her ritual objects to keep for future remembering because she hoped that, at some moment to come, Francisca would merge with Rosa's spirit and be remembered and reborn once again. The scattered selfhood of the spirit of Rosa/Francisca can be read through Foucault's (2004) notion of the discursive constitution of identity. The discourse and actions of this spirit are not the manifestations of a thinking, knowing subject; instead, they are a totality in which the dispersion of Francisca's and Rosa's identities and their discontinuity with their previous selves may be determined.

The relationship between a machi's individual and collective identities becomes ambiguous and contradictory as memory is reshaped and rehabilitated to suit new conditions. When a machi joins the collective *filew*, her individual animating personality is supposed to dissolve. It is only individualized again if a living person dreams of the machi as an individual who will then be reborn. But Francisca's spirit was not individualized again, and if it returns her spirit will be conflated with Rosa's spirit. The collective memory has been reshaped and condensed so that evocations of the dead appear true to the community's expectations of a particular role—what a Mapuche thunder shaman would say and do—rather than to the specifics of Francisca's or Rosa's life, which could reincite quarrels between factions.

This new, condensed machi thunder spirit is now remembered in a new form, devoid of Francisca's ambiguous qualities and rehabilitated in a new historical and political moment. Francisca's family wants to be reconciled with an appropriately cleansed machi spirit that could play a necessary role in her family's and the *longko's* political project—which aims to create a pan-community identity under a collective *rewe*. And it is this moment that calls for the appearance of a civilized thunder shaman. In its rituals of remembrance, the community has redefined its position in the world around ideals of reciprocity, traditional Mapuche shamanic practices, and Catholic moral values.

The transformation of memory is a complicated process. The community's memory was transformed when its members perceived that Francisca's spirit had forgotten—and therefore erased—her bad relationships with people in the community and was thinking and acting like a benevolent ancestral *filew* spirit, rather than as a selfish sorcerer. The community then flourished, crops were plentiful, and Francisca's grandson dreamed that she told him to marry the granddaughter of her enemy to unite Millali's factions. This new peaceful social and political context made members of the community want to transform their memories of Francisca—and in doing so, reshape their histories, hopes, and futures. These desires triggered narratives that collapsed Francisca's and Rosa's stories into each other, creating an image of a benevolent, mythologized shaman who was once a historical figure in their community. This image obliterated the past of conflict and factionalism in the community, creating a new past for the current generations, who are no longer bound by past sorcery. Francisca was rehabilitated to match the new moment, a successful process of disremembering and then re-remembering the spirit in its cleansed form, purified of sorcery.

All machi spirits go through this cycle of disremembering and losing personal qualities to become a collective *filew* spirit, and the most prestigious machi go through the process of re-remembering and reindividualizing where the particular qualities of their machi spirit are reborn in a new machi. These processes always occur at significant historical and political moments in linear time. But Francisca's story is unique, both in the extent to which her spirit was so decisively cleansed of sorcery and in the explicit way her spirit was merged with Rosa's to become a generic thunder shaman, allowing for the possibility of its rebirth in a new body.

CHAPTER EIGHT

RECONCILING DIVERSE
PASTS *and* FUTURES

Dancing, dancing
We have arrived here
We are happy, we are happy
I am Panchita [Francisca]
We have arrived . . .
It is valuable, it is valuable
To come this way
My poor orphaned heart, my poor heart
is now inside me
Old God, Chachai God
How happy I am,
My heart is happy
Where there are sick people
My solitary heart shall help
If I am here, I shall be singing when I arrive
I have arrived dear old ones
I have returned

———

—FRANCISCA'S *ÜL*, JANUARY 15, 1995

Francisca sang her experience as a lonely *champuria* machi traveling between places, times, and identities to reshape the past and the future and
to return. She experienced herself in the present ("I am Panchita," "My
heart is happy") and in the future ("Where there are sick people / My solitary heart shall help"). Francisca also saw where she had been and what she
had done in the past ("it is valuable / To come this way"), where she was
in the present ("I have arrived," "I have returned"), and where she would
be and what she would do in the future ("If I am here, I shall be singing
when I arrive"). Francisca's song shows the ever-changing past existing in

the present and also shows how the future is produced through social practices, altered states of consciousness, and rituals. She has arrived dancing—a highly social form of engagement with others—her machi spirit cleansed of prior ambiguities and of the tensions between the hierarchical histories of mounted machi as spiritual warriors and the conflicted histories of machi brides possessed by spirits in order to serve others. Such shamanic narratives challenge historical narratives of the Global North and give voice to an indigenous understanding of history. For machi, history is not given but enacted through the agency of spirits and ritual objects, including bibles.

I have discussed in this text how Francisca asked me to write her bible. The book you have just read is that bible—a collaborative personal, spiritual, and academic project. This bible is about Francisca's life and powers and how they became intertwined with mine as we healed together and talked about how she shaped Mapuche history. It is also a scholarly study of Mapuche shamanism and Mapuche perceptions of history. My close relationship with Francisca, my pact of solidarity with her, and what we experienced together allowed me to write about her in her terms. And my training as an anthropologist has enabled me to comment on her life and experiences and interpret and contextualize them. This bible is at once an academic book in my voice that can be read by others, and Francisca's bible, which can circulate her power and bring about her rebirth.

Perhaps history can be told in a way that does not exclude or override the historical consciousness of others (Chakrabarty 2000:41). To that end, I have presented what Alcida Ramos (2012:490) calls a "trans-epistemic" anthropology—one that approaches indigenous histories and systems of knowledge on their own intellectual terms. Mapuche consider shamanic history to be true history because it obliterates their traumatic experiences of subordination to powerful outsiders and their own past moral transgressions in the process of creating revisionist narratives that offer Mapuche a better present and future. In order to create these narratives, machi sacrifice themselves, use temporal dislocation to condense experiences from the Mapuche's sovereign past, and create a moral cosmic order. Mapuche inter- and intraethnic histories redefine outsiders' notions of the savage and the civilized in ways that prioritize broad knowledge, a moral Mapuche cosmic order, and the agency of Mapuche spirits in a spiraling history that cycles and recycles but is never exactly the same. Throughout this book I have also brought these perspectives into broader dialogue with many other forms of historical consciousness and explored their significance for Mapuche and for people around the world.

Like all histories, Mapuche histories define a moral community in the present. Mapuche histories differ from Chilean national history in their "standards of plausibility with regard to which 'pasts' might convincingly underwrite what presents" (Palmié 2010:374). Francisca embodied the past in order to divine the present and the future. She ritually manipulated the power that emerges from Catholic Bibles and official documents to revive some aspects of the past, change history, and construct a better future for her community. Memory is an elaborate process. For Mapuche, cycles of memory are conditioned by local political circumstances, cosmic events, shamanic transformations, and anthropological texts. I have shown that machi expand notions of indigenous literacy and temporalities by linking bibles to Mapuche individual and collective memory; to shamanic experiences of colonization, missionization, and ethnic intermixing; and to disputed historical continuity, death, and rebirth. Machi biographical narratives are the medium through which individual history becomes collective myth and vice versa. They also are instrumental in shamanic rebirth, a process that provides Francisca's community with structural continuity and transformation—that is, with local history.

The biographies of shamans link personal testimonies about historical processes—change and continuity, conflict and harmony, sorcery and healing, disremembering and remembering, death and rebirth—with transformations of personhood. Scholars differentiate between societies that remember in order to create permanence and transcendence for their people and those that obliterate time, have shallow genealogical memories, and disremember in order to create impermanence and transformation in every domain (see Chaumeil 2007). For Mapuche, remembering and disremembering coexist and play equal roles in the development of a shamanic historical consciousness. Although consigning events to oblivion is often a long historical process for some indigenous peoples (Fausto 2007; Santos-Granero 2007), the Mapuche rewrite history immediately after a major event, which is closely related to the way they recycle the spirits of their prominent dead, but different from forgetting in the name of nation-building and state formation.

Mapuche shamanic histories challenge long-standing conceptual dichotomies between individual and collective memory. Some classic scholarly works argue that social memory is constituted in contrast with personal memory, though it is still modeled on the individual thought process (Halbwachs 1992; Nora 1989; Kenny 1999; White 2008), while others contend that "communal memory" (Connerton 1989:71–72) is fundamentally different from personal memory and the same for all participants. But machi practice certain "memory techniques" (Cole 2001:1) that allow them to shape social memories and through which social and individual memories act upon the world. Mapuche create shamanic histories by aggregating the personal experiences of individual shamans, recognizing the periodic reembodiment of the spirits of past shamans in new machi, and identifying shamanic spirits alternately as collective and as individual identities.

Francisca's shamanic literacy, intertextual bibles, and transformation in memory indicate that she and people in Millali actively controlled their economy of alterity—the way that relations with kin are understood to be fashioned out of relationships with ancestors or outsiders (Viveiros de Castro 1996:190; Oakdale 2007:16). Shamanic power has not decreased with ethnic intermixing; nor do Mapuche experience an "absence of agency" or the "collapse of the controlled engagement with difference" (Course 2013:775). Francisca, for example, strategically manipulated alphabetic script for shamanic purposes and to legitimate her own mutable identities and the Mapuche moral order within a new context of literacy.

Mapuche constantly revise their identities—both the terms and their meanings—in order to make sense of themselves over time. Francisca participated in an economy of alterity that included a certain kind of "openness to the white Other," but on her own terms, which did not include a broad process of "symbolic exchange that cross[ed] sociopolitical, cosmological, and ontological boundaries" (Viveiros de Castro 1996:189–190). Mapuche shamanic histories reverse the political economy of spiritual power to perpetuate a moral cosmic order in the Mapuche community. Mapuche reject outside beings and forces, including evil spirits, devils, and sorcerers, that challenge this order as immoral others. But at the same time Mapuche appropriate and transform outside beings who support machi's production of shamanic power and indigenous history as heroes and shamans. Francisca tamed the savagery of the colonialist state by transforming its powers into part of the broad knowledge of the universe that she held as a civilized shaman.

Although the Global North often exoticizes shamans as exemplars of a radical ontological alterity because of their visions of other worlds, the machi and narratives about the "before time" are historically and politically grounded mediators between different cultures, worlds, and forms of being. This shifting positionality of shamanic alterity and identity is what allowed Francisca to create a better future for herself, her patients, and her community. Her politics of difference was not an assertion of "the possible, the could be" (Holbraad, Pedersen, and Viveiros de Castro 2014) within a modern project, nor was it a second-order effect of political economies. Francisca's utopian visions were based on contextual transformations of experience in rituals beneficial to herself and to other contemporary Mapuche.

RECONCILING DIVERSE PASTS *and* FUTURES

Through her multiple modes of historical consciousness, Francisca illustrated how and when difference matters, what kinds of difference are relevant to Mapuche lives, and how immanence and constraint are in constant tension. In shamanic practices, Mapuche claims to sovereignty emerge in opposition to *awingkamiento* and sorcery through processes of incorporation, resistance, and transformation. Francisca both challenged and reinforced representational politics; she fractured and multiplied difference. Her example shows that an ontological status of radical alterity is not a precondition for political or shamanic engagements with temporality, which exist in multiple worlds and express fluid ways of knowing and being. As Lucas Bessire and David Bond (2014:445) have argued, indigenous worlds are "unstable and rotational temporalities, of epistemic and material ruptures, of categories and things unraveling and being reassembled. [They are] world[s] composed of potentialities, of contingencies, of becoming, but also violence, wherein immanence is never innocent of itself."

Her *champuria* identity was at the heart of Francisca's form of shamanic literacy and her ability to effectively transform a non-Mapuche sacred text, the Catholic Bible, into an animated shamanic object. The lack of temporal anchors and the multiple vectors of deployment of that Bible, her own bible (this book), and the many variations of bibles that incorporate the textual traditions of the Global North into Mapuche culture offer a different perspective on indigeneity and colonialism. It was Francisca's identity as *champuria* that allowed her to foster this wider and strikingly less Global North form of temporality and historical consciousness. Francisca countered accusations of *awingkamiento* and sorcery by constructing her shamanization of the Bible and literacy as a form of mediation between different realities for the well-being of the collective. She indigenized Bibles and alphabetic script through her own identity as a machi.

Francisca was literate in such a way that her words always had double meanings. She perceived writing as a colonialist tool even though her bible remains partially embedded within the dominant discourse of literacy. Since the permanence of alphabetic script was already part of Mapuche history and memory, Francisca used it as a medium through which she and other Mapuche could appropriate *wingka* power and propagate their oral histories and shamanic power in a new context. By imbuing alphabetic script with her shamanic powers, Francisca gained control over the form, its meaning, and its use, creating not only graphic designs that represented her life and stored her shamanic force but also an animated object that would circulate her power after her death. Moreover, Francisca trained me (the *champuria* writer) in shamanic practice so the words I wrote would also have double meanings. I have therefore produced an academic text that is also an animated object that carries her *champuria* identity and her shamanic force rather than the force of positivist historiography.

Francisca's bible both reinterprets larger historical processes from a shamanic perspective and transforms regional history. By narrating and compressing shamanic biographies, rural Mapuche create regional histories that are presented as overcoming conventional Chilean history. In textualizing Francisca's story and merging her narrative with Rosa's, Francisca's bible becomes a kind of official regional history that holds and merges the power of both shamans. This purified shamanic spirit, which has had both individual and collective identities at different moments in time, has been shaped by the multiple historical, political, and social changes that have taken place in the community, yet it claims the continuity and legitimacy of an ancestral shamanic tradition. The history and power inherent in Francisca's bible compete with those of official documents about the community. But while official documents can be revived and animated only through the actions of shamans, Francisca's bible is an animated object in its own right. Perhaps people in Millali can also be the spiritual victors of historical texts now.

My own multiple identities and experiences also shaped the making of Francisca's bible and therefore the production of Mapuche shamanic history. Whose history is my history? How does my voice as a *champuria* granddaughter, ritual helper, and Peruvian-Chilean-American anthropologist emerge in the text? Anthropologists often experience the culture shock of the field first, and then the upheaval of going back home. But I experienced culture shock when I came to the United States to earn my Ph.D. in anthropology. Although returning to Chile was going back home to the place where most of my immediate family lived, I had changed, and they had not. The gulf between me and my family grew as my worldview and my writing continued to be shaped by American anthropology, feminism, and activism, all of which challenged the social norms by which they lived. My siblings had childhood memories of Mapuche on our grandparents' farm in Argentina, but I had close relationships with Mapuche in Millali. The deeply spiritual and moral Mapuche world became very much a part of my world, and my world became part of theirs. This gave me a sense of belonging and not-belonging: I was part of Millali's history and at the same time separate from it. As Vincent Crapanzano (1980:134, 140) and Steven Rubenstein (2002:218, 223) have argued, life histories demand both involvement and detachment, and those about whom we write become our teachers, friends, and families. I am grateful that departure is never an ending. I have returned periodically to Millali and also struggled across the miles to remain a loyal relative and friend. My life remains deeply entwined with that community. I wrote this book both because of its anthropological value and because I hope that in fulfilling my commitment to Francisca and writing her bible, her spirit will indeed return.

I also hope that Francisca's bible will expand Mapuche notions of history, the sacred, and bibles themselves. It was important to Francisca that I would write about her conflicted life in the community at a particular moment. But her narrative, as she told it, challenged the larger community's history and ideas about historical continuity as told in the present. My academic writing about Francisca would make evident the discrepancy between the history of Millali at different times—a discontinuous series of presents that are now all past—and the current ethnography of Millali in which the community creates a seamless, mythologized narrative about the past from the present. What would people in Millali do when they were confronted with the constructed nature of these different modes of pastness? Would older narratives about Francisca's alleged sorcery and about community conflicts challenge her new mythologized version and interfere with her shamanic rebirth?

Alejo Huenchuñir, Francisca's brother-in-law, laughed at my questions: "That is what people said then. But we are not the same people now. We think differently. You put it all in your book. Francisca will seize what she wants. And people can read the story. Fulfill your commitment to Francisca. Only then will you be free" (January 8, 2012). Alejo created a narrative of historical discontinuity between the present and the conflicted past of the community, while at the same time he maintained continuity with the positive aspects of the past—the melding of Francisca's and Rosa's shamanic identities and powers and my long-term commitment to Francisca. Writing an ethnography of Francisca's life history and practices, as told by her between 1991 and 1996, was my personal commitment to her, which I needed to fulfill so Francisca's individual spirit would fully disengage from me and become an autonomous machi spirit. And it was the collective recognition of that spirit as the melding of Rosa's and Francisca's powers and their positive impact on the community that would become part of the community's history and enable that spirit to be reborn in the body of a new machi.

People in Millali were not concerned with the "objectivity," "accuracy," or "factuality" of events and dates, but with the larger moral truths expressed through their ontology and history and the agency of spirit beings in the universe. Francisca's power was dependent on her ability to state the truth, which allowed her to make new worlds and had a practical effect on people's everyday lives. My interactions with the community as an anthropologist and ritual helper transformed community members' ways of telling their history and reshaped Mapuche perceptions of shamanism and writing. My presentation of Francisca's story is not just the revival of a mythologized past; it is the history of that past, the story of the present, and a projection into the future. Putting a mythologized shamanic oral narrative, along with the history of its production and the specifics of Francisca's biography, into a text means that people in Millali now have to simultaneously engage multiple narratives of the past, each with its own agenda.

Machi's mutability of self allows them to create new modes of understanding that transform their embodied memories of the past and open up the possibility of a better future. Machi temporal frameworks—based on the fluid relationship between past, present, and future—challenge contemporary memory studies that equate time primarily with pastness. Scholars have defined the anthropology of history as "how the past is known, understood, and represented in world societies" (Palmié and Stewart 2013), how history is put into social circulation (Hirsch and Stewart 2005:268), and how it is construed as a "truthful" representation of the "actual past" (Palmié 2010:375). Saklava mediums carry and embody the past through their possession by spirits who comment on the present (Lambek 2003), while machi face the past because they are the past and are interested mainly in the future behind them, which is illuminated by the past and present. Francisca ritually manipulated the power that emerges from Bibles and official documents to see and revive the past to change history and construct a better future for her community. Like dreamers in Naxos, Greece (Stewart 2012:217), Francisca was interested in mediating change to move into a future in which life will be different.

Machi also buck a contemporary trend in anthropology wherein "futures are replacing the past as a cultural reservoir" (Piot 2010:16) by continually establishing new relationships with time. Machi temporalities draw on the dynamic techniques of remembering and forgetting and on stories of lives, deaths, and rebirths, and project these onto sacred texts. Mapuche thus see the future as partly known, anticipated, and manipulated by machi. Francisca selected moments of the past and creatively drew on the Bible as a textual object to create "what would happen" and to bring about her shamanic rebirth. The future takes the form of the past as transformed by new mediums of expression and by the utopias dreamed in the present. The actual achievement of a utopian future is, however, uncertain and often contested (cf. Biersack 1991), and the failure to achieve a better future is a moral failure. If Francisca's spirit does not return, the withering of this utopian future will be attributed to moral failure—both hers and the community's. If her spirit does come back, some Mapuche will use her sacred text to reshape and revive the past through the realities and hopes of the present and to project themselves and their spirits into the future.

Francisca never meant for her bible to be a static, authoritative product: she expected the narratives in this book to be read and debated by many people over time. Mapuche narratives are always open and subject to contestation, reinterpretation, and adjustment. The Mapuche historian Sergio Caniuqueo said, "Writing is just another narrative. It is not a finished product. But then there is also the hegemony of documents and the role they played in colonialism. And we have to be careful not to allow our writings to become that. When I write, I include all version[s] of stories in the community so I don't create one narrative" (January 7, 2012). I have written a book that reflects the Mapuche dynamic notions of writing, personhood, and time. Francisca's bible includes her voice and mine, as well as those of her spirits, her community, and her many other Mapuche and non-Mapuche interlocutors. I hope readers will honor Francisca's intentions and see this text as a history in the making, one that will allow her spirit to return but in which nobody has the final word and Mapuche history never ends.

NOTES

CHAPTER 1: MAKING HISTORY IN FRANCISCA KOLIPI'S BIBLE

1. This multiple temporality, expressed in local imagery, offers credible solutions to social problems (De Martino 2012; Stewart 2012:7, 214).

2. In Christian perception, the right hand is the hand of God and is associated with blessings and greetings.

3. Throughout this book, *Bible* (capitalized) refers to the Christian text, and *bible* (lowercased) denotes various indigenous texts and local referents.

4. When Francisca died in 1996, 90 percent of indigenous people in Chile were literate in the Spanish language. Today, this figure has increased to 95 percent (Gobierno de Chile 2011).

5. See Molina 1901 [1787]:86–87; Barros Arana 1888:104–105; Rosales 1989 [1882]:29; Gay 1846:487; Olivares 1864:7:493–495; Luis de la Cruz 1953:42, 47–49; Intendencia de Cautin, vol. 12, oficio 1331 (n.d.):13–14, Temuco. Articles in *El Araucano* dated August 1, 1926 (9:6–8); January 1, 1928 ("La Juventud Araucana," 1:2–3); January 4, 1928; and April 1, 1928 ("Los Machis," 15:3–4). Villalobos 2000a; 2000b.

6. As Michel-Rolph Trouillot (1995) argues for the Haitian slave revolution of 1790, purposeful forgetting imposed by the state is integral to its domination and oppression of people.

7. Machi hold a kind of "empirical rationality" (Sahlins 1995:10) based on their experience of the world as a whole, on the properties of things, and on relationships between things—the everyday world, narratives about the primordium, historical events, personages, and nature.

8. See Linda Tuhawi Smith 2005 on decolonizing methodologies.

9. See, for example, Nahuelpan et al. 2012; Antileo Baeza 2012; Marimán et al. 2006; Cayuqueo 2012; Caniuqueo 2006; Marimán 2012. Ethnographers of Latin America have studied indigenous memories primarily through urban narratives of resistance or the ideologies of political parties (Warren 1998; Mallon 2005; Rappaport 2005) and through *testimonios*—first-person witness narratives that represent the experiences of marginalized peoples (Gugelberger and Kearney 1991; Beverly 1996). Less attention has been given to the role of shamans in the construction of indigenous history.

10. Peter Gow (1994) argues that there is a particular association of shamanism and mestizos in western Amazonia. Just as mestizos travel between cities and forests, shamans are the masters of the paths between multiple worlds and realities.

11. The oscillation between collective and singular personhoods is present among many Latin American indigenous people and is best understood through Mikhail Bakhtin's (1986) spatial metaphors: centripetal processes of incorporation of aspects of others and centripetal processes of condensation of those aspects into a singular person (Oakdale and Course 2014; Gow 2014).

12. See Urban 1989; Graham 1995; Oakdale 2005; Bacigalupo 2007; Fausto 2012; Rubenstein 2002; Rappaport 2007; Wright 2013; Kopenawa and Albert 2013.

13. These perceptions of Mapuche longevity created by the collapsing and rebirth of Mapuche lives remain current in Mapuche pop culture and jokes. On December 20, 2013, Mapuche poet Leonel Lienlaf tweeted: "According to an analysis of my twitter account, I have a mental age of 50,000 years which shows that we Mapuche are very old."

14. Supernatural forces are central to historical processes such as resistance to colonialism (Comaroff 1985; Steedly 1993; Lan 1985) and to the spread of capitalism (Kendall 2009; Ong 1987; Nash 1993). Spiritual practitioners around the world mimic, parody, and oppose colonialism (Taussig 1997; Stoller 1995) and remake the past for their own ends by narrating their stories in relation to socialism, neoliberalism, and despotism (Bacigalupo 2007; Shaw 2002; Buyandelger 2013; Kendall 2009).

15. Thomas Abercrombie (1998) has studied the way in which oral discourse is recast into documentation through "pathways of memory and power" and can be written on paper and upon the land.

16. Diverse biblical spiritual literacy practices have emerged in Africa. Some African healers infuse the Bible with their powers and then use it to reveal patients' afflictions but do not read in the sense of deciphering letters. In contrast, African preachers in the Spirit Apostolic Church utter the words in the Bible to free them from their materiality and instill them with the power of the Holy Spirit (Kirsch 2008:110–114, 153).

17. Webb Keane (2007:15) argues that textualized objects can "reinforce the authority of practitioners by offering them a transcendental position from which to speak."

18. Like Meme, the Yolmo Buddhist lama (Desjarlais 2000:271, 272), Francisca thought that the writing of her biography would allow some trace of her life to remain after she died, as though her body had become a text.

19. Amazonian shamanic biographies also express ideological shifts and complex relations with others (see Basso 1989; Oakdale 2005).

20. The original sixty-one people of Millali included the families of Pascual Calfuñir, Bartolo Calfuñir, José Añiwal, Federico Huenchuñan, Juan Millañir, Ignacio Huenchuñir, and Juan Kolipi (Corporación Nacional del Desarrollo Indígena [CONADI] Archivo General de Asuntos Indígenas, Temuco, volume 4, folio 1600:393).

21. For the laws that permitted the usurping of Mapuche land between 1883 and 1989, see "Tierras Mapuches: Despojo Por Ley," *Revista Análisis*, November 30, 1987.

22. Instituto Nacional de Estadistica Censo, Santiago, 2012.

23. Ministerio de Planeamiento (MIDEPLAN), Encuesta de Caracterización Socioeconómica Nacional (CASEN), Santiago, 2006.

24. Rodolfo Stavenhagen, the human rights commissioner for the United Nations who visited Chile in July 2003, criticized the Chilean government for violations of human rights and for the corrupt judiciary system used against Mapuche. He recommended that the indigenous law prevail over other national laws for exploiting resources, that CONADI be granted more money to buy indigenous land, and that Mapuche be consulted about development projects that take place in Mapuche territory.

He also stated that Mapuche's legitimate protests and social demands should not be criminalized and that the government should grant amnesty to Mapuche political prisoners (Marimán 2000).

25. Bruce Albert describes his relationship with Yanomami shaman Davi Kopenawa in similar terms (Kopenawa and Albert 2013:430–433).

26. See Rappaport and Pacheco 2005 on the coproduction of knowledge.

27. For examples of dialogical anthropology see Bakhtin 1981; Tedlock and Mannheim 1995; Tsing 1993; and Behar 1993, 1996.

CHAPTER 2: MOBILE NARRATIVES THAT OBLITERATE THE DEVIL'S "CIVILIZED HISTORY"

1. The most important sacred stone portals used by Mapuche travelers on the path between Araucanía and Patagonia include Pewinkantue (place to see destiny), Gupalkura (enchanted stone), Retrikura (stone containing a spirit), Curamalal (stone that makes Mapuche warriors invincible), and Pillankura (volcanic stone associated with shamanic power and warfare) (Lenz 1895:368; Bengoa 1991:102–103; Bello 2011:215–218).

2. This distinction has been criticized by Hill (1988), Turner (1988), Whitehead (2003), and Whitten (2011).

3. Maurice Bloch (1998) offers another example of multiple indigenous notions of time.

4. Several authors have argued that agency is a culturally defined quality; its definition varies according to native ontological premises and relational practices (Viveiros de Castro 2001; Fausto and Heckenberger 2007:12; Gow 1991; Strathern 1988; Taylor 2000; Wagner 1991).

5. Spanish military pressure and socioeconomic changes led Mapuche to expand into the Argentine Pampas, attracted by both the trade in salt from the natural salt flats there and the opportunity to raid farmers and rival indigenous groups and to become prestigious, wealthy men in the process (Alvarado, de Ramón, and Peñaloza 1991:84, 87, 89; Briones and Lanata 2002; Del Rio 2005:4–5; Mandrini 1992, 2010; Bello 2011:272, 275; Bengoa 1991:101–103; Mariman et al. 2006:56, 57).

6. See also Villalobos 2000a; Casanueva 1998:70–76; Hunter 1992:44.

7. See Silva 1993; Blakemore 1993; Collier and Sater 1997.

8. Nevertheless, prominent Chilean historians such as Diego Barros Arana (1888:32–33) and Benjamin Vicuña Mackenna (1939) wrote about settlers of European origin as the main protagonists of Chilean history, ignoring Mapuche as historical actors. These settlers acquired great socioeconomic and political power in the region, shaped public opinion, and created the material markers of local history.

9. See Bengoa 2004; Caniuqueo 2009; Congreso Nacional 1912; Klubock 2006:540; Pinto 2007a, 2007b.

10. See also El Mercurio de Valparaiso, "Comunicado de Arauco," January 30, 1856.

11. See also El Mercurio de Valparaiso, editorial page, June 25, 1859.

12. See Pinto 2003:143, 153–156; El Mercurio de Valparaiso, editorial page, June 7, 1959, and June 25, 1959.

13. Germans came to Patagonia and southern Chile in several waves: to Valdivia before the Pacification Campaign (1846–1860); to Patagonia and the central Mapuche valleys, where Millali is located (1868–1885), during the Pacification Campaign; to Pat-

agonia (1870–1914) after the Pacification Campaign; and to Chile and Argentina after World War I, during World War II, and after the war, when Nazi exiles and sympathizers found refuge. The term *German* was used to refer to any European immigrant who spoke the German language, which became the basis for the creation of new, independent settler communities that did not integrate into mainstream Chilean or Argentine society (Bjerg 2003; Lütge et al. 1981).

14. *El Mercurio de Valparaiso,* "Comunicado de Arauco," January 30, 1856; Barros Arana 1888:32–33; Vicuña Mackenna 1939; Lewis 1994; Foerster and Montecino 1988; Caniuqueo 2005.

15. In contrast, *ngenpin* (masters of the word) perform priestly roles during *ngillatun* rituals on the Mapuche coast, along the cordillera, and in the southern valleys (Bacigalupo 1995; Course 2012; Dillehay 2007; Foerster 1985).

16. Like Rosa, prophet-shamans Juan Santos Atahualpa (a Quechua Indian educated by priests) and Kamiko (a Baniwa educated by a black preacher) were mediators between the worlds of Indians and foreigners, the living and the dead, and they bridged sociopolitical, ethnic, or spiritual divides for the benefit of their communities. They had spiritual knowledge which allowed them to foretell the future and oppose the world of whites. Baniwa and Mapuche conceived colonization by whites through the idiom of sorcery. And like Rosa, according to oral traditions, Kamiko and his successor, Uetsu, demonstrated that they had greater power than the whites; at the same time, they attempted to eliminate sorcery in the villages and encourage harmony. Both preached autonomy from the whites, who were seen as corrupt and violent (Wright 2013). In the eighteenth and nineteenth centuries, Atahualpa led the Amazonian Ashaninka, Arawakan, and Panoan peoples in a revolt to throw off the yoke of Spanish rule and expel Franciscan missionaries. He transformed Christianity and argued that Spanish priests should be replaced by native clerics (Brown 1991:393; Santos-Granero 1993:143; Cepek 2009). Kamiko and Uetsu both took on a priestly role and assumed the title of Christo (Christ), arguing that Arawakans could perform their own rituals and had no use for missionaries (Wright and Hill 1986:37; Wright 2013). Rosa is unique among South American indigenous shamanic leaders in that she did not incorporate and reshape aspects of Christianity to meet the spiritual needs of her community; nor did she propose a reversal of the dominant order of foreign settlers in favor of a Mapuche one.

17. Suzanne Oakdale (2007:70) observed a similar process occurring in the case of a Kayabi shaman named Prepori.

18. In November 1885 the Ministry of War moved the fort to a strategic location by the Toltén River, where the town of Pitrufquén was built (Archivo del Ministerio de Guerra, vol. 1368, sin folio. 1884. Santiago: Archivo Nacional. Santiago).

19. People in Millali, as in Amazonian societies, perceive long cycles of political and interethnic consolidation as punctuated by critical periods of rapid change, including episodes of millenarian enthusiasm that promise a new world order in which all things would be changed (Brown 1991:390; Hill 1988:7).

20. *Renü* originally referred to an epistemological principle concerning the transmission of knowledge. Mapuche believe that people must be able to perceive and interpret knowledge from ancestors and the environment so as to integrate it into their subjectivity (Cañumil and Ramos 2011).

21. In contrast, in highland Ecuador a white witch saint kills people listed in his book of names (Wogan 2003).

22. *Mingka* is voluntary communal work among Mapuche men who have relationships of *compadrazgo* (the bond between the parents and godparents of a child), who are allies, or who are either real or fictive kin and perform various forms of agricultural work, building projects, or repairs on community roads. This communal work is called *minga* or *mink'a* in the Andes (Alberti and Mayer 1974).

23. See Londoño (2012) on inhuman beings, morality, and perspectivism in the Amazon.

24. The Toba in the Argentine Chaco also believe that the *patrón* feeds the devil with workers (Gordillo 2004:133). In the European tradition, people offer their soul to the devil in exchange for knowledge, wealth, and power. In the Mapuche version (where Christian-Platonic notions of soul have little value) the payment is made in life-years. Either those who engage in contracts with the devil or their families die young.

25. As Fernando Santos-Granero (2007:51) argues, "There is no remembrance of the past that is not linked to a hope for immortality, and there can be no salvation without remembrance of the past."

CHAPTER 3: MULTITEMPORAL VISIONS AND BAD BLOOD

1. To many anthropologists the distinction between possession and ecstasy is a matter of control or lack of control over altered states of consciousness. But in practice, if the altered state is sought, "then the question of 'control' or 'possession' is a matter of ideology, theatrics, or audience perception" (Tedlock 2005).

2. See Tedlock 1981 for theories of dream interpretation.

3. The term *kastikukutran* is a neologism derived from the Spanish word *castigo* (punishment) and the Mapuche word *kutran* (illness).

4. The Amazonian Jivaro also see nurture rather than the transfer of bodily substance as making the parental relationship (Taylor 2000:19).

5. E. E. Evans-Pritchard (1937:387) distinguished between witchcraft as the innate, sometimes unconscious, inherited psychic ability to cause misfortune or death, and sorcery as the deliberate ritual act of manipulation, the uttering of spells, and the manipulation of organic substances such as herbs with the conscious intent of causing harm. *Kalku* possess both the innate psychic power to perform evil and the ability to manipulate medicines and perform rituals as spells and therefore do not fit this classification.

6. Lorenzo Marileo Kolipi and Juan Marileo Kolipi were executed in Chile, and Luis Marileo Kolipi and other surviving Kolipi who fled to Patagonia were executed there (Vicuña Mackenna 1939; Bengoa 1991:74–75, 295, 298, 301).

7. During the war of independence in 1810, the Kolipi gave Chilean patriot Bernardo O'Higgins three thousand Mapuche soldiers to fight the royalists (Nanculef interview, January 6, 2010). While nineteenth-century Wenteche gained military training under Kalfukura's Wenteche-Patagonian confederation, Nangche men joined the Chilean army. Wenteche men remembered Lorenzo Kolipi, the powerful Nangche *longko* from Purén, as a huge, despotic man who upheld military discipline (Coliman in Bengoa 1991:72). Lorenzo Kolipi's son, Felipe, became captain of the Chilean army to fight the Peruvian-Bolivian Confederacy (1836–1839). Another son of Lorenzo's, Juan Marileo Kolipi, was raised by Chilean general Cornelio Saavedra. Some Kolipi spied for the Chilean army, received government salaries, adopted Chilean customs, and abused the

rebel Mapuche in the area by pillaging their land and animals (Navarro 1909:214; Bengoa 1991:73, 143, 267). Ambrosio Pinolevi (Painevilu) Kolipi was a spy for Colonel Saavedra. He behaved and dressed like a Chilean and was assassinated in 1868 by the Wenteche *longko* Kilapan (son of Mangin) for being a traitor (Bengoa 1991:71–75, 201–203, 301). Pinolevi's nephew explained his uncle's actions as an attempt to help Mapuche by integrating them into Chilean society: "He didn't know the thoughts of the Chilean government and thought that the Mapuche could not dominate all of those *wingka* and that many young Mapuche would die."

8. For examples of the interplay between subject, experience, and the narratives in the context of individual spiritual practitioners' storytelling, see Steedly (1993:18–21) and Buyandelger (2013:134).

9. Julio converted to evangelical Christianity because the previous *ngillatun* had not granted him plentiful harvests and he hoped that Jesus would. Evangelicals are popular in some Mapuche communities because, like machi, they directly experience the divine, heal with spirits, and propitiate ancestors (Foerster 1993:156–157). Mapuche Pentecostal evangelicals prohibit shamanic practice, *admapu* (Mapuche customs), the drinking of alcohol, and the performance of collective *ngillatun* rituals. Julio also converted in order to condemn the heavy drinking of his enemy, *longko* Segundo Millañir. Francisca claimed that evangelicals brought chaos and conflict to the community.

10. A *ngillatun* can be any type of prayer or petition to the spirits, whether individual or collective, but Mapuche most commonly apply the term to collective rituals involving several communities that come together before and after the harvest.

11. How they deploy identity depends, for example, on how long others have lived and eaten with them and if they behave according to Mapuche moral norms in particular contexts (Bacigalupo 2001, 2003, 2005; Course 2011).

12. As is the case for other indigenous peoples; see Comaroff and Comaroff 1991:17; de la Cadena 2000:222–223.

13. This illustrates how natives alter sociohistorical processes and the course of historical events through political actions (Rappaport 1998:22; Trouillot 1995:22–29) and how they reinterpret historical processes through narrative and shamanic stories and rituals.

CHAPTER 4: EMBODIED HISTORY

1. See Stoller 1995; Steedly 1993; Lambek 2003; Nielssen 2011; Kendall 1999; Shaw 2002; Buyandelger 2013.

2. See Bourdieu 1984 and Comaroff 1985 for linkages between colonial memories, embodiment, and historical imagination.

3. Jennifer Cole (2001:281) finds a similar phenomenon among the Betsimisaraka of Madagascar.

4. This contrasts with Betsimisaraka mediums in Madagascar (Nielssen 2011) who appropriated the outside power of *tromba* spirits to enable local autonomy despite their peripheral position in relationship to Malagasy state politics.

5. Modern subjects attempt to objectify the past because they desire to be free of it and to create a modern present (Chakrabarty 2000:248).

6. For example, kinship, property, and work (De Martinao 2012).

7. Michael Lambek (2003:17) argues that "historical consciousness entails the con-

tinuous, creative bringing into being and crafting of the past in the present and the present in respect to the past (poesis), and judicious interventions in the present that are thickly informed dispositions cultivated in, and with respect to the past, including understandings of temporal passage and human agency (phronesis)."

8. See Kristensen 2010 and Pandolfi 2007 for additional perspectives on illness as history.

9. Joanna Overing (1990) noted a similar process in Piaroa healing chants.

10. Carlo Severi (2000) finds a similar process among the Panamanian Cuna.

11. See for example the work of Abercrombie (1998), Gaston Gordillo (2004), Charles Hale (2002), Michael Taussig (1987), and many others.

12. West Africans also view sorcery as an amoral form of power (Rouch 1960; Stoller 2005).

13. Likewise, Anne-Christine Taylor (2007) notes that Shuar do not imitate whites but compete with them.

14. Gordillo finds similar processes among shamans in the Argentinean Chaco (2003:111, 113).

15. Similarly, the Amazonian Baniwa who are hexed temporarily lose their humanity and go the forest to become like tree animals for a few days (Wright 2013:124).

16. Some of the typical cultural logics of spirit possession played out: the "paradox of agency," whereby mediums gain a voice by giving their own voice up to the spirits (Jackson and Karp 1990); the embodied political metaphor of a spirit "mounting" a subordinate human (Matory 1994); and the machi as a bride of the spirit and also a masculine mounted warrior, which also reflects gendered and colonial hierarchical relations (Bacigalupo 2007).

17. Both the individual sacrifice of machi in healing rituals and the collective sacrifices of *ngillatun* rituals are expected to ensure a better future, but they have different focuses. In healing rituals, machi sacrifice their present lives, the knowledge and power of the spirits who possess them, and their bodies in order to create a better future for their patients. Mapuche sacrifice their animals and work during collective *ngillatun* rituals for the benefit of the entire community; the goal is to integrate the ritual community and to maintain a reciprocal relationship with other people, spirits, and the deity Ngünechen in the present. Mapuche pray to give thanks for abundance and well-being and to request the same on behalf of the entire ritual congregation (Bacigalupo 1995, 2001). Their interactions with friends, relatives, spirits, and deities always involve a greeting (*chalintun*), asking about the health of relatives (*pentukun*), and the sacrifice (*langümün*) of an animal that represents the human and is collectively consumed. Gifts of wine can also replace animal meat (Foerster 1993:112; Course 2011). The assumption is that these collective sacrificial acts will be reciprocated by Ngünechen.

18. Life is the primary metavalue in sacrifice (Lambek 2003).

19. See Freud (1976 [1900]:399) and Stewart (2012:212–213) for other examples of how those who access a multitemporal plane become different people.

20. Some *ngenpin* (ritual orators) and *werken* (messengers) believe that ancestral knowledge comes from outside of them—from spirits and ancestors—and that they acquire authority by virtue of being able to channel this knowledge of the past although they do not possess authorship over it. They argue that the knowledge that they wield is true because it is not a personal product but is collective ancestral knowledge that emerges from the anonymous force of the machi and *longko* who sustain it. Similarly, the *werken* transmit Mapuche political messages as independent from those of

Chilean political parties. The authority of the *werken* resides in their capacity to transmit the teachings of an anonymous and invisible mass (Menard 2003:22).

21. *Nervios* is an illness with physical, emotional, and often spiritual components that is common to Mapuche and many other people in Latin America and may be caused by the breakdown of family or spiritual networks, loss of loved ones, and concern for the well-being of friends and family members. As Setha Low (1994:141–142) describes it, "Nerves is constructed by local discourses and institutions, then expressed and acted upon as a *metaphor* of social, psychological, political or economic distress. The relationship between nerves and embodied distress, therefore, is culturally mediated, both in terms of what forms of distress cause suffering and in terms of its metaphorical expression" (emphasis in original). Francisca experienced disorientation, dizziness, and fainting, fits of crying or anger, insomnia and headaches, sensations of hot and cold, and body aches.

22. Taussig (1993:2, 19) argued that the image affects the thing it represents, that the representation shares in or takes power from the represented, and that the ability to mime is the capacity to make "other."

23. The anthropologist Mischa Titiev (1968:303) argues that "there is often an element of bisexualism in a machi's dealings with the other world," and Alfred Métraux (1942:333) states that when machi are healing, "they may address various supernatural beings, one of whom is likely to be a female-male personage." What these authors fail to notice is that the machi actually becomes these different gendered beings in healing and that these ritual gendered performances do not necessarily translate into bisexualism in the machi's everyday life.

24. Peruvian *curanderos* use similar categories for illness and healing (Glass-Coffin 1998; Joralemon and Sharon 1993).

25. Likewise, the goal of West African Dogon Sigui rituals and those of Songhay healers is to pass on the knowledge to the next generation (Stoller 1980).

CHAPTER 5: SHAMANIZING DOCUMENTS AND BIBLES

1. Scholars have explored this question by analyzing myth and ethnohistories (Hill 1988, 2009; Turner 1988), narrative (Basso 1995; Fausto 2002; Oakdale 2005), ritual (Graham 1995; Wright 1998; Conklin 1995; Taylor 1993), landscape (Santos-Granero 1998; Vidal 2000), kinship (Gow 2001), and historicity (Whitehead 2003; Taylor 2007; Fausto and Heckenberger 2007).

2. For other examples of native publications of sacred narratives, see Hugh-Jones (2010).

3. Janet McIntosh (2009) discusses how Giriama diviners of Kenya create a mystical literacy where possessing spirits "read" and "write" the Qur'an in Arabic, a language that their hosts do not understand.

4. Likewise, Trouillot (1995:73, 82) argues that the successful slave insurrection leading to the creation of an independent state in Haiti was unthinkable within the ontologies and epistemologies of colonial Western thought.

5. See Pietas in Gay 1846:487; Olivares 1864:7:493–495; Cruz 1953:42, 47–49; Barros Arana 1888:104–105.

6. See *El Araucano*, September 1, 1927; Foerster and Montecino 1988:59–60; Guevara and Mañkelef 2002; Pangul, "Los machis y su obra destructora," *Diario Austral de*

Temuco, December 6, 1927; *Diario Austral*, "Viejas supersticiones aun subsisten," January 3, 1935, p. 37; Mario Rubello, "De los machis is las brujas santiaguinas," *Diario Austral*, February 26, 1941, p. 3; Marcelino Ñanculeo, "Machitunes," *Diario Austral*, November 17, 1942, p. 3; *Diario Austral*, "Enfermeras quitaron enferma grave a una machi en Huanacura," March 9, 1956; *El Mercurio*, "Los Araucanos," April 11, 1930.

7. See Intendencia de Cautin, vol. 12, oficio 1331 (n.d.):13–14, Temuco; articles in *El Araucano* dated August 1, 1926 (9:6–8); January 1, 1928 ("La Juventud Araucana," 1:2–3); January 4, 1928; and April 1, 1928 ("Los Machis," 15:3–4).

8. See also *La Nación*, December 26, 1924.

9. See Gordillo 2006 and Allard 2012 for other examples of indigenous fetishism of ID cards.

10. For other native examples of invisibility, see Fogelson 1989:142.

11. See Alarcón 2008:66; Valdivia 1887 [1606]:52–53; Latcham 1924:595–596; González de Nájera 1889 [1614]:96.

12. For an example of political name exchanges, see Menard 2013.

13. Dennis Tedlock (2010) shows that Mayan iconic inscriptions of animal spirits is a reinforcement of phonetic inscriptions in a complex rendering of ideas.

14. Unlike Sangama, the Piro shaman studied by Peter Gow (1990:92), Francisca did not experience a text as a person with lips that could speak; nor did she see the paper as possessing a body.

15. For action and nonaction modes of communication, see Gill 1985:226, 228, 233.

16. Johannes Fabian noted that by the mid 1990s anthropologists could no longer maintain the illusion of a clear distinction between literate and illiterate societies, as "natives" use literacy for their own projects of survival (1993:84).

17. Natives often see similarities between the materiality of colonizers' books, guns, and shamanic ritual objects (Hugh-Jones 2010; Hill 1993:6). Signatures on documents are consubstantial with the person, as they can be used as a mechanism to obtain gifts (Allard 2012). Shamans often name pathogenic entities such as poisonous darts or sorcerers in order to control and destroy them in the same way that bureaucrats control people by writing down their names and ID numbers (Allard 2012; Gordillo 2006). They also take revenge on their enemies by denouncing them in documents (Walker 2012). Indigenous people include alphabetic literacy metaphors in shamanic speech and traditions, and shamanic séances are full of metaphors drawn from native experiences of the colonial archive (Salomon and Urioste 1991; Platt 1992:139).

18. Tribunal de Leyes Comunitarias Indígenas, Exped. 1305:32[2], Temuco.

19. See Bengoa 1991:372; Foerster and Montecino 1988:73–74, 79, 81; Mallon 2001:147.

20. Archivo de la Oficina Fiscal de Colonización 1933:10–12, Ministerio de Relaciones Exteriores, Tierras y Colonización, Santiago.

21. See Sahlins 1995; Wolf 1982:19, 385; Turner 1988:238; Gow 2001:303.

22. See Hill 1988; Santos-Granero 1998; Wright 2013; Oakdale 2005; Whitehead 2003; Taylor 2007; Graham 1995; Fausto and Heckenberger 2007; Rappaport and Cummins 2012; Salomon and Niño-Murcia 2011.

23. In contrast, native societies worldwide often downplay individualism in favor of collective histories and values, while celebrating the individual feats of prestigious native leaders and cultural heroes (Fogelson 1989:140).

24. See Pérez-Sales, Bacic Herzfeld, and Durán Pérez 1998; Pavez 2003; Pinto Rodríguez 2003; Bengoa 2004.

25. See Foerster and Montecino 1988; Pávez 2003; Menard 2006; Menard and Pavez 2005; Crow 2010.

26. See Pavez 2003; Menard 2006; Mallon 2009.

27. For another example, see Rappaport 1998.

28. Scholars have argued for two forms of social memory: lived experience, or how people remember, forget, and reinterpret the past; and cultural persistence, or the remembrance of past events and experiences, and a past transmitted and stored (Battaglia 1992:14; Berliner 2005:201). Mapuche historical consciousness incorporates both within its construction of the collective memory of the group.

29. The relationship between Mapuche shamanic historical consciousness and the production of Chilean national history recalls Constantine Fasolt's (2004) comparison between the Eucharist as the major ritual of Catholicism and contemporary historians' ritual of producing evidence. As Stephan Palmié (2010) has pointed out, in both cases (the body of Christ and the historical past), we are arguably dealing with a "reality" that ultimately cannot be substantiated but that must be represented and rendered socially binding through ritualized procedures. As Fasolt (2004) argues, the sacredness (in Durkheim's sense) of evidence, central as it is to such rituals, arises out of and in turn stabilizes liberal visions of personal freedom and accountability—two key components of a credo at the very core of modern historiographical praxis.

30. Bibles are partly temporal because they are material texts consisting of words that represent Christian notions of time as unique, non-repeatable events, and partly eternal because they represent God's speech and aim to take the reader out of time and into encounter with the eternal (Engelke 2004:156, 169).

31. Amazonian people see books and tape recordings as ritual objects. For the Tukano, books are ritual objects; for the Kayapo, tapes are. Both are what they also record so that the medium is a part of the message. A VCR records in a primarily visual register, with verbal content secondary. The book is a primarily verbal register but also acts as a substitute for past oral and visual displays. Books and video cameras fit in with the practices and ideas of people who use them and also relate to an ongoing process of cultural transformation (Hugh-Jones 2010).

32. Priests mediate between the natural and supernatural worlds on behalf of humans and hold moral authority, but they also wear skirts and practice a sexuality that is distinct from that of ordinary family men (Bacigalupo 2008).

33. Indigenous Amazonian millenarian movements such as Orden Cruzada (Cocama and Tikuna peoples in Peru and Brazil) and Hallelujah (Carib-speaking peoples of Guyana, Venezuela, and Brazil) rejected aspects of native society they considered negative, such as sorcery and drunkenness (Regan 1988:136; Brown 1988, 1991:401).

34. In contrast, in the Ecuadorian highlands God's book contains people's birth and death dates (Wogan 2003).

35. See Keane 2011 on the relationship between absence, the past, and otherworldliness.

CHAPTER 6: THE TIME OF WARRING THUNDER, THE SAVAGE STATE, AND CIVILIZED SHAMANS

1. For many Amazonians, the cosmic tree transcends time and serves as a vehicle for transformation back into the past (Wright 2013:171).

2. In Sierra Leone, people use the strategy of concealment—"closure of their homes and bodies" (Shaw 2002). Amazonian people use both concealment and confrontation (Wright 1998).

3. *Weychan* (war) refers to many wars, including those with the Inca state (1483–1485), the Spaniards (1536–1818), the Chilean army (1861–1883), Allende's socialist regime (1970–1973), and Pinochet's military regime (1973–1989), and to the post-Pinochet clashes between Mapuche and the police over disputes with settlers and timber companies (1990–present).

4. See Archivo Ministerio de Tierras y Colonización, vol. 60, 1909, Ministerio de Relaciones Exteriores, Tierras, y Colonización, Santiago; Bengoa 1991:349; Aldea 1902; Domeyko 1871.

5. The Kogi of Columbia and the Yanomami of Venezuela and Brazil (Kopenawa and Albert 2013) have noticed a similar phenomenon.

6. See Mallon 2001:156–158 and Klubock 2006:567 on the modernization of settlers' estates during Allende's time. For example, the German elite settler family Lüer, who owned the Manzanar farm in Quepe, obtained incentives from the Inter-American Institute to reforest, cultivate pastures, build irrigation canals, install irrigation equipment, and purchase fertilizer.

7. Reporte, Corporación Reforma Agraria, Archivos de Titularidad Publica, Archivo Central, Santiago, November 20, 1973. The government expropriated the hacienda of Tumuntuco to create the collective peasant settlement named Cooperativa "El Esfuerzo" (Cooperative "The Effort"). Several farms belonging to the Roth Schleyer family—Alameda, Araucaria, Hacienda Freire, and Los Perales—were converted into a peasant settlement named Alameda (Informe de Comisaría de Carabineros de Temuco Tenencia Freire, March 19, March 23, and March 26, 1971; Correa, Molina, and Yañez 2005:annex).

8. Reporte, Corporación Reforma Agraria, Archivos de Titularidad Publica, Archivo Central, Santiago, November 20, 1973.

9. This included the farms Gloria y Suerte, Predio Mapuche, Huilquilco, Arancanía, Santa Ana, and San Luis (Roth Schleyer); Huichahue Chico and Manzanar (Lüer); and Tumuntuco (Ernst) (Correa, Molina, and Yañez 2005:annex; Informe Comisaría de Carabineros de Temuco Tenencia Freire, March 19, 1971, March 23, 1971, March 26, 1971, May 11, 1971 [#1085], and June 17, 1971 [#1441]; Segundo Juzgado de Letras Temuco, August 1, 1973 [#10-7-13], October 9, 1971, and February 25, 1972 [#202]).

10. See Informe Comisaría de Carabineros de Quepe, January 8, 1972 (#24), January 11, 1972 (#70), January 12, 1972, March 6, 1972, March 10, 1972 (#76); Informe Comisaría de Carabineros de Padre de las Casas, January 14, 1972 (#35), February 25, 1972 (#202), March 10, 1972 (#76); Informe Comisaría de Carabineros de Temuco, March 8, 1972 (#296), March 13, 1972 (#147), February 24, 1972 (#642), February 29, 1972 (#247), March 6, 8, 10, and 13, 1972 (#5–6), March 17, 1972 (#31), March 23, 1972 (#149).

11. See *Diario Oficial* 30:326, March 28, 1979; Comisión Asesora en Temas de Desarrollo Indígena 1999; Aylwin 1999.

12. Ministerio de Agricultura, Instituto de Desarrollo Indígena, Departamento Jurídico, 1979, #C-13-6, Temuco.

13. Ministerio de Planeamiento (MIDEPLAN), Encuesta de Caracterización Socioeconómica Nacional (CASEN), Santiago, 2006.

14. See Marimán 1990; Foerster and Lavanchy 1999.

15. Intendencia de Cautín, Archivo Regional de la Araucanía oficio 505, Temuco, September 14, 1973.

16. See also *El Mercurio*, December 30, 2001.

17. *Diario Austral*, "De los 900 voluntarios inscritos para el servicio militar cerca de 800 son indígenas," February 26, 1929.

18. See also Memorias del Ministerio de Guerra, 1910, Archivo Nacional, Santiago; *Diaro Austral de Temuco*, April 6, 1920.

19. For example, Carlos Aillañir Huenchual and Pedro Millalen Huenchuñir were militants in the Communist Party and relatives of people in the Quepe area (Correa, Molina, and Yañez 2005:278, 280).

20. In the Euroamerican context, politics is often understood as a secular ideology that is ontologically separate from spirituality and nature. This distinction between nature and culture, science (the knowledge of nature) and politics (the organization of human beings), is basic to modern Western institutions (Latour 1993). These categories and notions of secular politics have permeated academic discourses and those of nation-states so that indigenous politics make sense only in modern terms (Chakrabarty 2000:4; de la Cadena 2015). The emergence of political ideology is closely tied to the concept of power and refers to "shared ideas or beliefs which serve to justify the interests of dominant groups" (Giddens 1997:583).

21. See Tsing 1993:254 for examples of this strategy in Indonesia.

22. Women become shamans not because they are suppressed by patriarchal state authorities (Basilov 1997; Humphrey and Onon 1996; Kendall 1985; Tedlock 2005) but because of specific historical conditions (Balzer 1996; Kendall 1999:894) that allow them to create "new forms of speech and new local and global histories" (Tsing 1993:254), to temporarily shift their identities (Steedly 1993), and to create new identities to work alongside male shamans (Tedlock 2005; Bacigalupo 2007). Among Mapuche, female and male shamans coexist, with one or the other predominating according to specific economic, social, and political circumstances and the gendering of social and spiritual space (Bacigalupo 2007:98).

23. The Mapuche intellectuals Rosamel Millaman and José Quidel argue that traditional political alliances between Mapuche lineages should be revitalized and made permanent in order to create large, independent Mapuche political organizations.

24. *Que Pasa*, June 18, 2005.

25. Some academics think of Mapuche in ways that recall what Giorgio Agamben (1998) calls a "bare life" as subjects living close to nature and excluded by the state, stripped of their land and human rights, and abandoned to sovereign violence and left to die. But most Mapuche define themselves as active agents in indigenous politics, histories, and ways of life.

26. Mapuche norms dictate that ritual objects, ritual actions, and deities be referred to in sets of twos and fours, but the Catholic notion of the twelve apostles has also been incorporated into Mapuche sacred numerology.

27. Religious faith has provided a basis for revitalizing rebellion among Latin American indigenous people in the twenty-first century (Nash 2012).

28. Lydia Degarrod (1990) and Roberto Morales (1999) have analyzed dreams as a medium to express and resignify political trauma, but not as a medium to create revisionist histories.

29. See Aylwin 2013; Marimán 2013; Calfunao 2013; Conuepan 2013; Cayuqueo 2012.

30. Francisca's efforts speak to a recent ethnographic turn toward an "anthropology of the good" (Robbins 2013:457–459).

CHAPTER 7: TRANSFORMING MEMORY THROUGH DEATH AND REBIRTH

1. The Japanese dead also go through a process of generalization in which they are given posthumous Buddha names and then ritually absorbed into a more generalized body of protective household tutelary being—the *kami* (Smith 1974).

2. Medical Records for Francisca Kolipi, Servicio de Salud de la Araucanía, Temuco, Chile.

3. Machi, like shamans around the world, experience symbolic death and rebirth during rituals to initiate or renew their powers (Eliade 1967:82–84, 102; 1974 [1964]:45, 53, 56). The symbolic death of machi initiates during these rituals often involves catalepsy and includes loss of consciousness, lack of response to external stimuli, decreased sensitivity to pain, rigidity of muscles, inability to move, lethargic sleep, and a partial suspension of vital functions (Métraux 1942:315–316). This experience is then followed by a "rebirth" with new or renewed shamanic powers, and a return to an ordinary state of consciousness and the historical time in which they live with their clients and communities.

4. Like the Kwakiutl from the Pacific Northwest coast (Mauzé 1994:188), Mapuche believe that the reincarnation of a soul (the substance of being that makes the individual) in a new being cannot be considered the reincarnation of a social person with all of his or her attributes, rights, and obligations. Shamans who maintain their social person and acquire increasing power through successive deaths and rebirths are often feared and viewed ambivalently in their communities (Radin 1994:57, 65).

5. The Tehuelche of Argentina, who were heavily influenced by Mapuche, are like mourners in Millali in that they bar mention of the names of the deceased until they are forgotten. Later they often name their grandchildren after their deceased grandparents. The Tehuelche also bury the deceased's personal objects with the body and kill and eat the deceased's favorite animals (Priegue 2002:51, 52, 55).

6. See, for example, Weller 1985; Kwon 2008; Kim 1989; and Buyandelger 2013.

7. Deceased Mapuche are like deceased native Amazonians in that they are not considered human because they are separated from their bodies, and therefore radically different from the world of the living. Deceased spirits can therefore transform into animals and other forms of bodily alterity such as enemies and evil spirits (Viveiros de Castro 1998:482).

8. Forgetting spirits can have opposite effects in different cultures: While the uncontrolled spirits of deceased Buryat become bad and cause misfortune when forgotten (Buyandelger 2013), Mapuche spirits become bad and cause sorcery if remembered immediately after mortuary rituals, as this prevents them from leaving.

9. Like Francisca, Alzheimer's survivors in India experience the death of their own memories as a critical metaphor for death itself. But their senility is also a metaphor for a bad Indian family, the death of good, caring social relations (Cohen 1998:126). Francisca's death of memory, by contrast, was attributed to punishment by spirits due to her inappropriate social and spiritual relations and her inability to detach affect from the deceased.

10. Amelia Ancao explained, "We only do *amulpüllün* for those who perform im-

portant roles in *ngillatun* rituals: *longko*, machi, and sometimes *choyke*. We do not have orators who say how the person was in their life, as they do in other places. People are afraid that the words of one orator will contradict those of another and that then there will be fights. In the *amulpüllün* the machi says that the family will do well, that the children will grow without any problems. She tells the spirit not to bother the family and to go. Then they forget the person and don't say the name anymore."

11. As in some North American Indian cultures (Mills and Slobodin 1994; Matlock 1994), Mapuche shamans have a series of souls or spirits, some of which can be reborn in the bodies of their descendants or community members. Mapuche are also like Buddhists (Bernstein 2012) in that they see reincarnation as journeys and relationships between bodies across multiple lifetimes. But the meaning of Mapuche rebirth is different from that concept in Hindu and Buddhist traditions, in which humans seek to escape the cycle of rebirth (*samsara*) through ethical behavior in order to reach salvation and transcendence.

12. Corporación Nacional del Desarrollo Indígena (CONADI) Archivo General de Asuntos Indígenas, Temuco, folio 908:8.

13. Korean shamanic objects passed from one shaman to her successor are ambiguous and may cause misfortune and death if they are not given sufficient care and respect as ritual objects (Walraven 2009:64). Korean shamans can bury their shamanic paintings, imbued with sacred power, if they lack disciples or have ruptured relationships with them, or they can purify and sell them (Kendall and Yang 2014).

14. See Kendall and Yang 2014:5; Wiener 2003:140; Hill 2007; Keane 2006; Pels 1998.

BIBLIOGRAPHY

Abercrombie, Thomas. 1998. *Pathways of Memory and Power: Ethnography and History among an Andean People*. Madison: University of Wisconsin Press.

Abu-Lughod, Lila. 1991. "Writing against Culture." In *Recapturing Anthropology: Working in the Present*, ed. G. Fox Richard, 137–162. Santa Fe, N.M.: School of American Research Press.

Agamben, Giorgio. 1998. *Homo Sacer: Sovereign Power and Bare Life*. Redwood City, C.A.: Stanford University Press.

Alarcón, Ana María. 2008. *Estructura y significado de los apellidos mapuche*. Santiago: Impresos Maigret.

Alberti, Giorgio, and Enrique Mayer. 1974. *Reciprocidad e intercambio en los Andes peruanos*. Lima: Instituto de Estudios Peruanos.

Aldea, Pedro Ruiz. 1902. *Los araucanos y sus costumbres*. Santiago: Guillermo Miranda Ediciones.

Allard, Olivier. 2012. "Bureaucratic Anxiety: Asymmetrical Interactions and the Role of Documents in the Orinoco Delta, Venezuela." *HAU: Journal of Ethnographic Theory* 2(2): 234–256.

Alvarado, Margarita, Ema de Ramón, and Cecilia Peñaloza. 1991. *Weichan, la guerra de Arauco: Una mirada desde la estética 1536–1656*. Unpublished Manuscript. Instituto de Estética, Universidad Católica de Chile. Santiago, Chile.

Antileo Baeza, Enrique. 2012. "Migración mapuche y continuidad colonial." In *Ta iñ fijke xipa rakizuameluwün: Historia, colonialismo y resistencia desde el país mapuche*, ed. Héctor Nahuelpan Moreno et al. Temuco, Chile: Comunidad de Historia Mapuche.

Appadurai, Arjun. 2006. *Fear of Small Numbers: An Essay on the Geography of Anger*. Durham, N.C.: Duke University Press.

Argyrou, Vassos. 1999. "Sameness and the Ethnological Will to Meaning." *Current Anthropology* 40(S1): S29–S41.

Artexaga, Begoña. 2000. "Playing Terrorist: Ghastly Plots and the Ghostly State." *Journal of Spanish Cultural Studies* 1: 43–58.

Ashforth, Adam. 2000. *Madumo: A Man Bewitched*. Chicago: University of Chicago Press.

Atkinson, Jane Monning. 1989. *The Art and Politics of Wanna Shamanship*. Berkeley: University of California Press.

Attwood, Bain. 2005. *Telling the Truth about Aboriginal History*. Sydney, Australia: Allen and Unwin.

Augé, Marc. 2004. *Oblivion*. Minneapolis: University of Minnesota Press.

Ayllapan, Lorenzo, and Carlos Munizaga. 1971. *Vida de un araucano*, 2nd ed. Santiago: Departamento de Ciencias Antropológicas y Arqueología de la Universidad de Chile.

Aylwin, José. 1999. "Indigenous Peoples' Rights in Chile: Progress and Contradiction in a Context of Economic Globalisation." *Indigenous Law Bulletin* 72. www.austlii .edu.au/au/journals/ILB/1999/72.

———. 2002. "Políticas pública y pueblos indígenas: El caso de la política de tierras del estado chileno y el pueblo mapuche." Working paper. University of Texas, Austin. Center for Latin American Social Policy.

———. 2013. "Hacia un Parlamento en la Araucanía," January 15. Temuco, Chile: Observatorio Ciudadano. www.observatorio.cl/node/8234.

Bacigalupo, Ana Mariella. 1995. "El rol sacerdotal de la machi en los valles centrales de la Araucanía." In *Modernización o sabiduría en tierra mapuche?*, ed. Ricardo Salas, Ramón Curivil, Cristián Parker, Ana Mariella Bacigalupo, Alejandro Saavedra, and Armando Marileo, 51–98. Santiago, Chile: Ediciones San Pablo.

———. 1996a. "Adaptación de los métodos de curación tradicionales mapuche: La práctica de la machi contemporánea en Chile." Santiago, Chile: PAESMI Monographs.

———. 1996b. "Identidad, espacio y dualidad en los perimontun (visiones) de machi mapuche." *Scripta Ethnológica* 18:37–63.

———. 1996c. "Mapuche Women's Empowerment as Shaman/Healers." *Annual Review of Women in World Religions* 4:57–129.

———. 1997. "Las múltiples máscaras de Ngünechen: Las batallas ontológicas y semánticas del ser supremo Mapuche en Chile." *Journal of Latin American Lore* 20(1): 173–204.

———. 1998. "The Exorcising Sounds of Warfare: Shamanic Healing and the Struggle to Remain Mapuche." *Anthropology of Consciousness* 9(5): 1–16.

———. 2001. *La voz del kultrun en la modernidad: Tradición y cambio en la terapeútica de siete machi*. Santiago: Editorial Universidad Católica.

———. 2003. "Rethinking Identity and Feminism: Contributions of Mapuche Women and Machi from Southern Chile." *Hypatia* 18(2): 32–57.

———. 2004a. "Ritual Gendered Relationships: Kinship, Marriage, Mastery, and Machi Modes of Personhood." *Journal of Anthropological Research* 60(2): 203–229.

———. 2004b. "The Mapuche Man Who Became a Woman Shaman: Selfhood, Gender Transgression, and Competing Cultural Norms." *American Ethnologist* 31(3): 440–457.

———. 2004c. "Shamans' Pragmatic Gendered Negotiations with Mapuche Resistance Movements and Chilean Political Authorities." *Identities: Global Studies in Culture and Power* 11(4): 501–541.

———. 2005. "The Creation of a Mapuche Sorcerer: Sexual Ambivalence, the Commodification of Knowledge, and the Coveting of Wealth." *Journal of Anthropological Research* 61(3): 317–336.

———. 2007. *Shamans of the Foye Tree: Gender, Power, and Healing among Chilean Mapuche*. Austin: University of Texas Press.

———. 2008. "The Re-Invention of Mapuche Male Shamans as Catholic Priests: Legitimizing Indigenous Co-Gender Identities in Modern Chile." In *Native Chris-

tians: Modes and Effects of Christianity among Indigenous Peoples of the Americas, ed. Robin Wright and Aparecida Vilaça, 89–108. Aldershot, U.K.: Ashgate.

———. 2010. "The Life, Death, and Rebirth of a Mapuche Shaman: Remembering, Forgetting and the Willful Transformation of Memory." *Journal of Anthropological Research* 66(1): 97–119.

———. 2013. "Mapuche Struggles to Obliterate Dominant History: Mythohistory, Spiritual Agency, and Shamanic Historical Consciousness in Southern Chile." *Identities: Global Studies in Culture and Power* 20(1): 77–95.

———. 2014. "The Potency of Indigenous Bibles and Biography: Mapuche Shamanic Literacy and Historical Consciousness." *American Ethnologist* 41(4): 648–663.

Bakhtin, Mikhail. 1981. *The Dialogical Imagination*, trans. Caryl Emerson and Michael Holquist. Austin: University of Texas Press.

———. 1986. *Speech Genres and Other Late Essays*, ed. Caryl Emerson and Michael Holquist, trans. Vern W. McGee. Austin: University of Texas Press.

Balzer, Marjorie Mandelstam, ed. 1990. *Shamanism: Soviet Studies of Traditional Religion in Siberia and Central Asia*. London: M. E. Sharp.

———. 1996. "Sacred Genders in Siberia: Shamans, Bear Festivals, and Androgyny." In *Gender Reversals and Gender Cultures*, ed. Sabrina Ramet, 164–182. London: Routledge.

Barrera, Aníbal. 1999. *El grito mapuche (una historia inconclusa)*. Santiago: Editorial Grijalbo.

Barros Arana, Diego. 1888. *Historia General de Chile*, vol 9. Santiago: Librería Central de Mariano Servat.

Basilov, Vladimir. 1997. "Chosen by the Spirits." In *Shamanic Worlds: Rituals and Lore of Siberia and Central Asia*, ed. Marjorie Mandelstam Balzer, 3–48. Armonk, N.Y.: M. E. Sharpe.

Basso, Ellen. 1989. "Kalapalo Biography: Psychology and Language in a South American Oral History." *American Anthropologist* 91(3): 551–569.

———. 1995. *The Last Cannibals: A South American Oral History*. Austin: University of Texas Press.

———. 2003. "Translating 'Self-Cultivation.'" In *Translation and Ethnography: The Anthropological Challenge of Intercultural Understanding*, ed. Tulio Maranaho and Bernhard Streck, 85–101. Tucson: University of Arizona Press.

Bataille, Georges. 1992 [1973]. *Theory of Religion*, trans. Robert Hurley. New York: Zone Books.

Battaglia, Debbora. 1992. "The Body in the Gift: Memory and Forgetting in Sabari Mortuary Exchange." *American Ethnologist* 19(1): 3–18.

———. 1993. "At Play in the Fields (and Borders) of the Imaginary: Melanesian Transformations of Forgetting." *Cultural Anthropology* 8(4): 430–442.

Bauman, Richard. 2004. *A World of Others' Words: Cross-Cultural Perspectives on Intertextuality*. Malden, M.A.: Blackwell.

Bechis, Martha. 1994. "Matrimonio y Política en la Génesis de Dos Parcialidades Mapuche Durante el Siglo XIX." *Memoria Americana: Cuadernos de Etnohistoria* 3: 41–62.

Becker, Anne. 1995. *Body, Self, and Society: The View from Fiji*. Philadelphia: University of Pennsylvania Press.

Behar, Ruth. 1993. *Translated Woman: Crossing the Border with Esperanza's Story*. Boston: Beacon.

———. 1996. *The Vulnerable Observer: Anthropology that Breaks Your Heart*. Boston: Beacon.

Bello, Álvaro. 2011. *Nampülkafe: El Viaje Mapuche a las Pampas Argentinas o Puelmapu* (siglos XIX y XX). Ediciones Universidad Católica de Temuco. Temuco: Chile.

Bem, Sandra. 1993. *The Lenses Of Gender: Transforming the Debate on Sexual Inequality*. New Haven, C.T.: Yale University Press.

Bengoa, José. 1991. *Historia del pueblo Mapuche, siglo XIX y XX*. Santiago: Ediciones Sur.

———. 1992. "Mujer, tradición y shamanismo: Relato de una machi mapuche." *Proposiciones* 21:135–155.

———. 1999. *Historia de un conflicto: El estado y los Mapuches en el siglo XX*. Santiago: Editorial Planeta.

———. 2000. "Políticas públicas y comunidades mapuches: Del indigenismo a la autogestión." *Revista Perspectivas* 3(2): 331–365.

———. 2004. *La memoria olvidada: Historia de los pueblos indígenas de Chile*. Santiago: Presidencia de la República, Comisión Bicentenario.

Bengoa, José, and Eduardo Valenzuela. 1984. *Economía mapuche: Pobreza y subsistencia en la sociedad mapuche contemporánea*. Santiago: Pas Ediciones.

Benjamin, Walter. 1969. "Theses on the Philosophy of History." In *Illuminations*, ed. Hannah Arendt. New York: Schocken.

———. 1999. *The Arcades Project*. Cambridge, M.A.: Harvard University Press.

Berliner, David C. 2005. "The Abuses of Memory: Reflections on the Memory Boom in Anthropology." *Anthropological Quarterly* 78(1): 197–211.

Bernstein, Anya. 2012. "On Body-Crossing: Interbody Movement in Eurasian Buddhism." *Ab Imperio* 2:168–195.

Bessire, Lucas, and David Bond. 2014. "Ontological Anthropology and the Deferral of Critique." *American Ethnologist* 41(3): 440–456.

Beverly, John. 1996. "The Margin at the Center." In *The Real Thing: Testimonial Discourse and Latin America*, ed. Georg Gugelberger, 23–41. Durham, N.C.: Duke University Press.

Biersack, Aletta. 1991. "Prisoners of Time: Millenarian Praxis in a Melanesian Valley." In *Clio in Oceania: Toward a Historical Anthropology*, ed. Aletta Biersack, 231–296. Washington, D.C.: Smithsonian Institution Press.

Bjerg, Samuel. 2003. "The Danes in the Argentine Pampa: The Role of Ethnic Leaders in the Creation of an Ethnic Community, 1848–1930." In *Mass Migration to Modern Latin America*, ed. Samuel Bailey and Eduardo José Miguez, 147–166. Wilmington, D.E.: Scholarly Resources.

Blakemore, Harold. 1993. "From the War of the Pacific to 1930." In *Chile since Independence*, ed. Leslie Bethell. Cambridge, U.K.: Cambridge University Press.

Bloch, Maurice. 1996. "Internal and External Memory." In *Tense Past: Cultural Essays in Trauma and Memory*, ed. Paul Antze and Michael Lambek, 215–231. New York: Routledge.

———. 1998. "Time, Narratives, and the Multiplicity of Representations of the Past." In *How We Think They Think*, by Maurice Bloch, 100–113. Boulder, C.O.: Westview.

Boccara, Guillaume. 1998. *Guerre et ethnogenese mapuche dans le Chili colonial: L'invention du soi*. Paris: L'Harmattan.

Bourdieu, Pierre. 1977. *Outline of a Theory of Practice*, trans. Richard Nice. Cambridge, U.K.: Cambridge University Press.

———. 1984. *Distinction*. New York: Routledge.

———. 2002. *Interventions, 1961–2001: Science Sociale et Action Politique*, ed. Franck Poupeau and Thierry Discepolo. Marseille: Agone.

Bourdieu, Pierre, and Loïc Wacquant. 1992. *An Invitation to Reflexive Sociology*. Chicago: University of Chicago Press.

Bourguignon, Erika. 1965. "The Self, the Behavioural Environment, and the Theory of Spirit Possession." In *Context and Meaning in Cultural Anthropology*, ed. Spiro Melford, 39–60. London: Macmillan.

Briones, Claudia. 1993. "'Qué importa quién gane si nosotros perdemos siempre': Los partidos políticos desde la minoría mapuche." *Cuadernos de Antropología Social* 7:79–119.

———. 1998. *La alteridad del "Cuarto Mundo": Una deconstrucción antropológica de la diferencia*. Buenos Aires: Ediciones del Sol.

———. 2007. "Our Struggle Has Just Begun: Experiences of Belonging and Mapuche Formations of Self." In *Indigenous Experience Today*, ed. Marisol de la Cadena and Orin Starn, 99–121. Oxford: Berg.

Briones, Claudia, and José Luis Lanata, eds. 2002. *Archaeological and Anthropological Perspectives on the Native Peoples of Pampa, Patagonia, and Tierra del Fuego to the Nineteenth Century*. London: Bergin and Garvey.

Brooks, James. 2008. "Seductions and Betrayals: La Frontera Gauchesque, Argentine Nationalism, and the Predicament of Hybridity." In *Small Worlds: Method, Meaning and Narrative in Microhistory*. Santa Fe, N.M.: School of Advanced Research Advanced Seminar Series.

Brown, Michael Forbes. 1984. *Una paz incierta: Historia y cultura de las comunidades agarunas frente al impacto de la Carretera Marginal*. Lima: Centro Amazónico de Antropología y Aplicación Práctica.

———. 1988. "Shamanism and Its Discontents." *Medical Anthropology Quarterly* 2:102–120.

———. 1991. "Beyond Resistance: A Comparative Study of Utopian Renewal in Amazonia." *Ethnohistory* 38(4): 388–413.

———. 1996. "On Resisting Resistance." *American Anthropologist* 98(4): 729–749.

Burke, Barry. 1999. "Antonio Gramsci and Informal Education." In *The Encyclopedia of Informal Education*. http://infed.org/mobi/antonio-gramsci-schooling-and-education.

Buyandelger, Manduhai. 2013. *Tragic Spirits: Shamanism, Memory and Gender in Contemporary Mongolia*. Chicago: University of Chicago Press.

Calfunao, Juana. 2013. Carta Abierta de Longko Juana Calfunao al Presidente Chileno Sebastian Piñera. January 6. www.rebelion.org/noticia.php?id=162186.

Caniuqueo, Sergio. 2005. "Antagonismo en las percepciones territoriales: Un marco de interpretación." *Revista Historia y Geografía* 19:9–48.

———. 2006. "Siglo XX en Gulumapu: De la fragmentación del Wallmapu a la unidad nacional Mapuche 1880 a 1978." In *¡Escucha, winka!: Cuatro ensayos de historia nacional Mapuche y un epílogo sobre el futuro*, ed. Pablo Marimán, Sergio Caniuqueo, José Millalén, and Rodrigo Levil, 129–217. Santiago: LOM.

———. 2009. "Particularidades en la instauración del colonialismo chileno en Gulumapu, 1884–1950: Subordinación, alianzas y complicidades." In *Las disputas por la etnicidad en América Latina: Movilizaciones indígenas en Chiapas y Araucanía*, ed. Christian Martínez and Marco Estrada, 191–212. Santiago de Chile: Catalonia.

Cañumil, Pablo, and Ana Ramos. 2011. "Knowledge Transmission through the Renu." *Collaborative Anthropologies* 4:67–89.

Cárcamo-Huechante, Luis. 2011. "The Long History of Indigenous Textual Cultures: A Response." *Textual Cultures: Texts, Contexts, Interpretation* 6(2): 142–146.

Casanueva, Fernando. 1998. "Indios malos en tierras buenas: Visión y concepción del mapuche según las elites chilenas del siglo XIX". In *Modernización, inmigración y mundo indígena: Chile y la Araucanía en el siglo XIX,* ed. Jorge Pinto, 55–132. Temuco, Chile: Ediciones Universidad de la Frontera.

Cayuqueo, Pedro. 2012. *Solo por ser indio y otras crónicas Mapuches.* Santiago: Editorial Catalonia.

Cepek, Michael L. 2009. "The Myth of the Gringo Chief: Amazonian Messiahs and the Power of Immediacy." *Identities: Global Studies on Culture and Power* 16: 227–248.

Chakrabarty, Dipesh. 2000. *Provincializing Europe: Postcolonial Thought and Historical Difference.* Princeton, N.J.: Princeton University Press.

Chaumeil, Jean-Pierre. 2007. "Bones, Flutes and the Dead: Memory and Funerary Treatments in Amazonia." In *Time and Memory in Indigenous Amazonia: Anthropological Perspectives,* ed. Carlos Fausto and Michael Heckenberger, 243–283. Gainesville: University Press of Florida.

Chureo, Francisco. 2001. "Nuestras familias no tienen tierras y eso enferma al pueblo Mapuche," Entrevista de Manuel Holzapfel al director del Hospital Intercultural Makewe Pelales. In Centro de Documentación Mapuche Ñuke Mapu. http://linux .soc.uu.se/mapuche/mapu/redChilenaIndo10829.html.

CLACPI (Coordinadora Latinoamericana de Cine y Comunicación de los Pueblos Indígenas). 2013. "Chile: La irresponsabilidad del gobierno y la prensa con el pueblo Mapuche." Santiago de Chile, January 4. www.yepan.cl/chile-la -irresponsabilidad-del-gobierno-y-la-prensa-con-el-pueblo-mapuche.

Clinic, The. 2014. "Testigo protegido de Fiscalía confiesa que se infiltró en comunidades mapuches para realizar atentados incendiarios por orden de Carabineros," February 12. www.theclinic.cl/2014/02/12/testigo-protegido-de-fiscalia-confiesa -que-se-infiltro-en-comunidades-mapuches-para-realizar-atentados-incendiarios -por-orden-de-carabineros/.

Cohen, Lawrence. 1998. *No Aging in India: Alzheimer's, the Bad Family, and Other Modern Things.* Berkeley: University of California Press.

Cohn, Bernard. 1981. "Anthropology and History in the 1980s: Toward a Rapprochement." *Journal of Interdisciplinary History* 12(2): 227–252.

Cole, Jennifer. 1998. "The Work of Memory in Madagascar." *American Ethnologist* 25(4): 610–633.

———. 2001. *Forget Colonialism? Sacrifice and the Art of Memory in Madagascar.* Berkeley: University of California Press.

———. 2003. "Narratives and Moral Projects: Generational Memories of the Malagasy 1947 Rebellion." *Ethos* 31(1): 95–126.

———. 2004. "Memory and Modernity: Overcoming the Social/Individual Divide in Memory Studies." In *A Companion to Psychological Anthropology,* ed. Conerly Casey and Robert B. Edgerton, 103–120. London: Blackwell.

Collier, Simon, and William F. Sater. 1997. *A History of Chile, 1808–1994.* New York: Cambridge University Press.

Colloredo-Mansfeld, Rudi. 2002. "Autonomy and Interdependence in Native Movements: Towards a Pragmatic Politics in the Ecuadorian Andes." *Identities: Global Studies in Culture and Power* 9:173–195.

Comaroff, Jean. 1985. *Body of Power, Spirit of Resistance*. Chicago: University of Chicago Press.

Comaroff, Jean, and John Comaroff. 1991. *Of Revelation and Revolution*, vol. 1: *Christianity, Colonialism, and Consciousness in South Africa*. Chicago: University of Chicago Press.

———. 1992. *Ethnography and the Historical Imagination*. Boulder, C.O.: Westview.

———. ed. 2001. *Millennial Capitalism and the Culture of Neoliberalism*. Durham, N.C.: Duke University Press.

Comisión Asesora en Temas de Desarrollo Indígena. 1999. *Informe*. Santiago: Ministerio de Planificación (MIDEPLAN).

Comisión de Verdad Histórica y Nuevo Trato con los Pueblos Indígenas. 2008. *Informe de la Comisión de Verdad Histórica y Nuevo Trato con los Pueblos Indígenas*. Santiago: Comisionado Presidencial para Asuntos Indígenas. www.memoriachilena.cl/602/articles-122901_recurso_2.pdf.

Coña, Pascual. 1984 [1930]. *Testimonio de un cacique mapuche*. Santiago: Pehuen.

———. 1995 [1927]. *Lonco Pascual Coña ñi tuculpazugun: Testimonio de un caique mapuche dictado por Wilhelm de Moesbach, Ernesto, 1882–1963*. Santiago: Pehuén Editores.

Congreso Nacional. 2012. *Comisión Parlamentaria de Colonización: Informe, proyectos de ley, actas de las sesiones y otros antecedentes*. Santiago de Chile: Imprenta y Litografía Universo.

Conklin, Beth. 1995. "'Thus Are Our Bodies, Thus Was Our Custom': Mortuary Cannibalism in an Amazonian Society." *American Ethnologist* 22(1): 75–101.

———. 2001. *Consuming Grief: Compassionate Cannibalism in an Amazonian Society*. Austin: University of Texas Press.

———. 2002. "Shamans versus Pirates in the Amazonian Treasure Chest." *American Anthropologist* 104(4): 1050–1061.

Connerton, Paul. 1989. *How Societies Remember*. Cambridge, U.K.: Cambridge University Press.

Conuepan, Venancio. 2013. "Arson Deaths in Chile Spark Anti-Terror Measures: President Announces New Anti-Terrorist Measures after Attack on Couple Who Owned Land Wanted by Indigenous People." *The Guardian*, January 4. www.theguardian.com/world/2013/jan/04/arson-chile-land-dispute.

Cooperativa. 2013. "Michelle Bachelet: En ningún caso volvería a aplicar la Ley Antiterrorista," April 11. www.cooperativa.cl/noticias/pais/politica/michelle-bachelet/michelle-bachelet-en-ningun-caso-volveria-a-aplicar-la-ley-antiterrorista/2013-04-11/063613.html.

Correa, Martín. 2008. "El Fundo Santa Margarita: Origen, historia y relación con las comunidades mapuche vecinas y colindantes." Documento de Trabajo, Observatorio Ciudadano, Temuco, Chile.

Correa, Martín, Raul Molina, and Nancy Yañez. 2005. *La reforma agraria y las tierras mapuches, Chile, 1962–1975*. Santiago: LOM.

Course, Magnus. 2010. "Making Friends, Making Oneself: Friendship and the Mapuche Person." In *The Ways of Friendship: Anthropological Perspectives*, ed. A. Desai and E. Killick. New York: Berghahn.

———. 2011. *Becoming Mapuche: Person and Ritual in Indigenous Chile*. Champaign: University of Illinois Press.

———. 2012. "The Birth of the Word: Language, Force and Mapuche Ritual Authority." *HAU: Journal of Ethnographic Theory* 2(1): 1–26.

BIBLIOGRAPHY

———. 2013. "The Clown Within: Becoming White and Mapuche Ritual Clowns." *Comparative Studies in Society and History* 55(4): 771–799.

———. n.d. "The General and the Boy: The Efficacy of Sacrifice in Chile." Unpublished paper.

Covarrubias Orozco, Sebastián de. 1995 [1611]. *Tesoro de la Lengua Castellana o Española*, ed. Felipe C. R. Maldonado. Madrid: Editorial Castalia.

Crapanzano, Vincent. 1980. *Tuhami: Portrait of a Moroccan*. Chicago: University of Chicago Press.

Crow, Joanne. 2010. "Negotiating Inclusion in the Nation: Mapuche Intellectuals and the Chilean State." *Latin American and Caribbean Ethnic Studies* 5(2): 131–152.

Cruz, Luis de la. 1953. "Tratado importante para el conocimiento de los indios pehuenches según el orden de su vida." *Revista Universitaria* 38(1): 29–59.

Curivil, Ramón Francisco, ed. 2002. *Lenguaje mapuche para la educación intercultural: Aproximaciones al mapucezugun*. Santiago de Chile: Centro de Documentación, Instituto Nacional de Derechos Humanos.

Cuyul, Andrés. 2014. "Machi terrorista o machi esterilizada: Persecución politica y criminalización de autoridades tradicionales mapuche en Chile." *Mapuexpress*, January 31.

de Augusta, Felix José. 1996 [1835]. *Diccionario Araucano. Mapuche–Español/Español–Mapuche*. Santiago: Ediciones Cerro Manquehue.

de Boeck, Filip. 1999. "Domesticating Diamonds and Dollars: Identity, Expenditure and Sharing in Southwestern Zaire (1984–1997)." In *Globalization and Identity: Dialectics of Flow and Culture*, ed. B. Meyer and Paul Geschiere, 177–209. Oxford: Blackwell.

Degarrod, Lydia. 1990. "Punkurre y Punfuta, los cónyuges nocturnos: Pesadillas y terrores nocturnos entre los Mapuche de Chile." In *Antropología y experiencias del sueño. Colección 500 años, #21*, ed. M. Perrin, 179–194. Quito: Ediciones Abya Yala.

———. 1998. "Landscapes of Terror, Dreams, and Loneliness: Explorations in Art, Ethnography, and Friendship." *New Literary History* 29(4): 699–726.

de la Cadena, Marisol. 2000. *Indigenous Mestizos: The Politics of Race and Culture in Cuzco, Peru, 1919–1991*. Durham, N.C.: Duke University Press.

———. 2015. *Ethnographic Cosmopolitics: Beings across Andean Worlds*. Durham, N.C.: Duke University Press.

Delrío, Walter. 2005. *Memorias de expropriación: Sometimiento e incorporación indígena en la Patagonia, 1872–1943*. Buenos Aires: Universidad Nacional de Quilmes.

de Martinao, Ernesto. 2012. "Crisis of Presence and Religious Integration," trans. Tobia Farnetti and Charles Stewart. *HAU: Journal of Ethnographic Theory* 12(2): 431–450.

Derrida, Jacques. 2007. *Psyche: Inventions of the Other*, vol. 1. Redwood City, C.A.: Stanford University Press.

Desjarlais, Robert. 2000. "Echoes of a Yolmo Buddhist's Life." *Cultural Anthropology* 15(2): 260–293.

Diario Austral. 2009. "Aparece vocero de 'Comando Trizano' y amenaza con 'hacer volar' a dirigentes y lonkos indígenas," July 30. www.australtemuco.cl/prontus4 _noticias/site/artic/20090730/pags/20090730003325.html.

Dillehay, Tom. 1985. "La influencia política de los chamanes mapuches." *CUHSO* 2(2): 141–157.

———. 1990. *Araucanía, presente y pasado*. Santiago: Editorial Andrés Bello.

————. 2007. *Monuments, Empires, and Resistance: The Araucanian Polity and Ritual Narratives.* New York: Cambridge University Press.

Domeyko, Ignacio. 1871. *Araucanía y sus habitantes.* Buenos Aires: Editorial Francisco de Aguirre.

Donoso, Ricardo, and Fanor Velasco. 1928. *Historia de la Constitución de la Propiedad Austral.* Santiago: Imprenta Cervantes.

Durkheim, Émile. 2001 [1912]. *Elementary Forms of Religious Life.* Oxford: Oxford University Press.

Edelman, M. 1994. "Landlords and the Devil: Class, Ethnic, and Gender Dimensions of Central American Peasant Narratives." *Cultural Anthropology* 9(1): 58–93.

Eliade, Mircea. 1967. *Myths, Dreams and Mysteries,* trans. Mairet Philip. New York: Harper & Row.

————. 1974 [1964]. *Shamanism: Archaic Techniques of Ecstasy.* Princeton, N.J.: Princeton University Press.

Engelke, Matthew. 2003. "The Book, the Church, and the 'Incomprehensible Paradox': Christianity in African History." *Journal of Southern African Studies* 29(1): 297–306.

————. 2004. "Text and Performance in an African Church: The Book, 'Live and Direct.'" *American Ethnologist* 31(1): 76–91.

Erikson, Philippe. 2004. "Chamanisme, écriture et ethnopolitique." *L'Homme* 171–172: 525–528.

Erize, Esteban. 1960. *Diccionario comentado mapuche–español: Araucano, pehuenche, pampa, picunche, rancülche, huilliche.* Bahía Blanca, Argentina: Instituto de Humanidades, Universidad Nacional del Sur.

Evans-Pritchard, E. E. 1937. *Witchcraft, Oracles and Magic among the Azande.* Oxford: Clarendon.

————. 1956. *Nuer Religion.* Oxford: Clarendon.

Fabian, Johannes. 1983. *Time and the Other: How Anthropology Makes Its Object.* New York: Columbia University Press.

————. 1993. "Keep Listening: Ethnography and Reading." In *The Ethnography of Reading,* ed. J. Boyarin, 8–97. Berkeley: University of California Press.

————. 2003. "Forgetful Remembering: A Colonial Life in the Congo." *Africa: Journal of the International African Institute* 73(4): 489–504.

Faron, Louis. 1964. *Hawks of the Sun: Mapuche Morality and Its Ritual Attributes.* Pittsburgh: University of Pittsburgh Press.

Farriss, Nancy M. 1987. "Remembering the Future, Anticipating the Past: History, Time, and Cosmology among the Maya of Yucatan." *Comparative Studies in Society and History* 29(3): 566–593.

Fasolt, Constantine. 2004. *The Limits of History.* Chicago: University of Chicago Press.

Fausto, Carlos. 2002. "Faire le mythe: Histoire, récit et transformation en Amazonie." *Journal de la Société des Américanistes* 88:69–90.

————. 2007. "If God Were a Jaguar: Cannibalism and Christianity among the Guarani (16th–20th Centuries)." In *Time and Memory in Indigenous Amazonia: Anthropological Perspectives,* ed. Carlos Fausto and Michael Heckenberger, 74–105. Gainesville: University of Florida Press.

————. 2012. *Warfare and Shamanism in Amazonia.* Cambridge, U.K.: Cambridge University Press.

Fausto, Carlos, and Michael Heckenberger. 2007. "Indigenous History and the History of Indians." In *Time and Memory in Indigenous Amazonia: Anthropological Perspectives*, ed. Carlos Fausto and Michael Heckenberger, 1–43. Gainesville: University Press of Florida.

Febres, Andrés. 1882 [1765]. *Diccionario araucano–español*. Buenos Aires: Juan A. Alsina.

Feierman, Steven. 1995. "Healing as Social Criticism in the Time of Colonial Conquest." *African Studies* 54(1): 73–88.

Finley, M. 1965. "Myth, Memory, and History." *History and Theory* 4(3): 281–302.

Fischer, Michael. 2003. *Emergent Forms of Life and the Anthropological Voice*. Durham, N.C.: Duke University Press.

Foerster, Rolf. 1983. *Martín Painemal: Vida de un dirigente mapuche*. Santiago: Grupo de Investigaciones Agrarias.

———. 1985. *Vida religiosa de los huilliches de San Juan de la Costa*, vol. 1. Santiago: Ediciones Rehue.

———. 1993. *Introducción a la religiosidad mapuche*. Santiago: Editorial Universitaria.

———. 2001. "Sociedad mapuche y sociedad chilena: La deuda histórica." *Polis: Revista Académica de la Universidad Bolivariana* 3(2).

Foerster, Rolf, and Javier Lavanchy. 1999. "La problemática mapuche." In *Análisis del año 1999: Sociedad-política-economía*, ed. Departamento de Sociología, Universidad de Chile, 65–102. Santiago: Universidad de Chile.

Foerster, Rolf, and André Menard. 2009. "Futatrokikelu: Don y autoridad en la relación mapuche-wingka." *Atenea* 499:33–59.

Foerster, Rolf, and Sonia Montecino. 1988. *Organizaciones, líderes y contiendas mapuches: 1900–1970*. Santiago: Centro de Estudios de la Mujer.

Fogelson, Raymond. 1985. "Interpretations of the American Indian Psyche: Some Historical Notes." In *Social Contexts of American Ethnology, 1840–1984*, ed. June Helm, 4–27. Washington, D.C.: American Anthropological Association.

———. 1989. "The Ethnohistory of Events and Nonevents." *Ethnohistory* 36(2): 133–147.

Foucault, Michel. 1979. *Discipline and Punish: The Birth of the Prison*. New York: Vintage.

———. 1986 [1954]. "Dream, Imagination and Existence." In *Dream and Existence*, ed. Keith Hoeller, 30–78. Atlantic Highlands, N.J.: Humanities Press.

———. 2002. *Archaeology of Knowledge*. New York: Routledge.

———. 2004. *Abnormal: Lectures at the Collège de France, 1974–1975*. Paris: Edicion de Seul/Gallimard.

———. 2006. *History of Madness*, ed. Jean Khalfa. New York: Routledge.

Freud, Sigmund. 1976 [1900]. *The Interpretation of Dreams*, vol. 4. London: Penguin.

Gay, Claudio. 1846. *Historia física y política de Chile*, vol. 1. Paris: Imprenta de Maulde y Renos.

Gerbhart-Sayer, Angelika. 1985. *The Cosmos Encoiled: Indian Art of the Peruvian Amazon*. New York: Center for Inter-American Relations.

Geschiere, Peter. 2009. *Perils of Belonging: Autochthony, Citizenship, and Exclusion in Africa and Europe*. Chicago: University of Chicago Press.

Giddens, Anthony. 1997. *Sociology*, 3rd ed. Cambridge, U.K.: Polity Press.

Gill, Sam. 1985. "Nonliterate Traditions and Holy Books: Toward a New Model." In *The Holy Book in Comparative Perspective*, ed. Frederick M. Denny and Rodney L. Taylor, 224–239. Columbia: University of South Carolina Press.

Glass-Coffin, Bonnie. 1998. *The Gift of Life: Female Spirituality and Healing in Northern Peru*. Albuquerque: University of New Mexico Press.

Gobierno de Chile. 2011. *Pueblos originarios CASEN*. Santiago: Gobierno de Chile. http://observatorio.ministeriodesarrollosocial.gob.cl/layout/doc/casen/Pueblos _Indigenas_Casen_2011.pdf.

Goldman, Marcio. 2011. "Cavalo dos deuses: Roger Bastide e as transformações das religiões de matriz africana no Brasil." *Revista de Antropologia* 54(1): 407–432.

González de Nájera, Alonso. 1889 [1614]. *Desengaño y reparo de la guerra del reino de Chile*. Colección de Historiadores de Chile, vol. 16. Santiago: Imprenta del Ferrocarril.

Goodall, Heather. 2002. "Too Early Yet or Not Soon Enough? Reflections on Sharing Histories as Process." *Australian Historical Studies* 33(118): 7–24.

Goody, Jack. 1977. *The Domestication of the Savage Mind*. Cambridge, U.K.: Cambridge University Press.

Gordillo, Gastón. 2003. "Shamanic Forms of Resistance in the Argentine Chaco: A Political Economy." *Journal of Latin American Anthropology* 8(3): 104–126.

———. 2004. *Landscapes of Devils: Tensions of Place and Memory in the Argentinean Chaco*. Durham, N.C.: Duke University Press.

———. 2006. "The Crucible of Citizenship: ID-Paper Fetishism in the Argentinean Chaco." *American Ethnologist* 33(2): 162–176.

Gould, Jeffrey L. 1990. *To Lead as Equals: Rural Protest and Political Consciousness in Chinandega, Nicaragua, 1912–1979*. Chapel Hill: University of North Carolina Press.

Gow, Peter. 1990. "Could Sangama Read?: The Origin of Writing among the Piro of Eastern Peru." *History and Anthropology* 5:87–103.

———. 1991. *Of Mixed Blood: Kinship and History in Peruvian Amazonia*. Oxford: Clarendon.

———. 1994. "River People: Shamanism and History in Western Amazonia." In *Shamanism, History, and the State*, ed. N. Thomas and C. Humphrey, 90–113. Ann Arbor: University of Michigan Press.

———. 2001. *An Amazonian Myth and Its History*. Oxford: Oxford University Press.

———. 2007. "La ropa como aculturación." *Amazonía Peruana* 15(30): 283–304.

———. 2014. "'This Happened to Me': Exemplary Personal Experience Narratives Among the Piro (Yine) People of Peruvian Amazonia." In *Fluent Selves: Autobiography, Person, and History in Lowland South America*, ed. Suzanne Oakdale and Magnus Course, 69–92. Lincoln: University of Nebraska Press.

Graham, Laura. 1995. *Performing Dreams: Discourses of Immortality among the Xavante of Central Brazil*. Austin: University of Texas Press.

Gramsci, Antonio. 1971 [1925–1935]. *Further Selections from the Prison Notebooks*. New York: International.

Graw, Knut. 2009. "Beyond Expertise: Reflections on Specialist Agency and the Autonomy of the Divinatory Ritual Process." *Africa* 79(1): 92–109.

Grebe, Maria Ester. 1973. "El kultrún mapuche: Un microcosmo simbólico." *Revista Musical Chilena* 123–124:3–42.

Grebe, María Ester, Sergio Pacheco, and Jorge Segura. 1972. "Cosmovisión mapuche." *Cuadernos de la Realidad Nacional* 14:46–73.

Guardian, The. 2013. "Arson Deaths in Chile Spark Anti-terror Measures." Associated Press in Santiago, January 4. www.theguardian.com/world/2013/jan/04/arson -chile-land-dispute.

Guevara, Tomás. 1913. *Las últimas familias y costumbres araucanas*. Santiago: Imprenta Cervantes.

Guevara, Tomás, and Manuel Mañkelef. 2002. *Kiñe mufu trokiñche ñi piel: Historias de familias, siglo XIX*. Santiago de Chile: CoLibris Ediciones.

Gugelberger, Georg, and Michael Kearney. 1991. "Voices for the Voiceless: Testimonial Literature in Latin America." *Latin American Perspectives* 70(18): 3–14.

Gupta, Akhil, and James Ferguson. 1997. *Culture, Power, Place: Explorations in Critical Anthropology*. Durham, N.C.: Duke University Press.

Guzman-Gallegos, María. 2009. "Identity Cards, Abducted Footprints and the Book of San Gonzalo: The Power of Textual Objects in Runa Worldview." In *The Occult Life of Things: Native Amazonian Theories of Materiality and Personhood*, ed. Fernando Santos-Granero, 214–234. Tucson: University of Arizona Press.

Halbwachs, Maurice. 1992. *On Collective Memory*. Chicago: University of Chicago Press.

Hale, Charles. 2002. "Does Multiculturalism Menace?: Governance, Cultural Rights, and the Politics of Identity in Guatemala." *Journal of Latin American Studies* 34: 485–524.

———. 2006. *Mas Que un Indio: Racial Ambivalence and Neoliberal Multiculturalism in Guatemala*. Santa Fe, N.M.: School of American Research Press.

Harris, Grace. 1989. "Concepts of Individual, Self and Person in Description and Analysis." *American Anthropologist* 91(3): 599–612.

Haughney, Diane. 2007. "Neoliberal Policies, Logging Companies, and Mapuche Struggle for Autonomy in Chile." *Latin American and Caribbean Ethnic Studies* 2(2): 141–160.

Hill, Jonathan. 1988. *Rethinking History and Myth: Indigenous South American Perspectives on the Past*. Urbana: University of Illinois Press.

———. 1993. *Keepers of the Sacred Chants: The Poetics of Ritual Power in an Amazonian Society*. Albuquerque: University of Arizona Press.

———. 1999. "Nationalisme, chamanisme et histories indigenes au Venezuela." In *Ethnologie Française* 29:387–396.

———. 2007. *Sacred Landscapes as Environmental Histories in Lowland South America*. Paper presented at the American Anthropological Association meetings, Washington, D.C., November 30.

———. 2009. "History, Power, and Identity: Amazonian Perspectives." Theme issue: "Identity Politics: Histories, Regions, and Borderlands," *Acta Historica Universitatis Klaipedensis* 29, *Studia Anthropologica* 3:25–47.

Hirsch, Eric, and Charles Stewart. 2005. "Introduction: Ethnographies of Historicity." *History and Anthropology* 16:261–274.

Holbraad, Martin. 2012. *Truth in Motion: The Recursive Anthropology of Cuban Divination*. Chicago: University of Chicago Press.

Holbraad, Martin, Morten Axel Pedersen, and Eduardo Viveiros de Castro. 2014. "The Politics of Ontology: Anthropological Positions." Fieldsights—Theorizing the Contemporary, *Cultural Anthropology Online*, January 13, http://culanth.org/fieldsights/462-the-politics-of-ontology-anthropological-positions.

Holquist, M. 2002. *Dialogism: Bakhtin and His World*. New York: Routledge.

Hubert, Henri, and Marcel Mauss. 1968 [1898]. *Sacrifice: Its Nature and Functions*. Chicago: The University of Chicago Press.

Huenchulaf, Ernesto, Prosperino Cárdenas, and Gladys Ancalaf. 2004. *Nociones de Tiempo y Espacio en la Cultura Mapuche*. Temuco: Corporación Nacional de Desarrollo Indígena (CONADI).

Hugh-Jones, Stephen. 1988. "The Gun and the Bow: Myths of White Men and Indians." *L'homme* 28(2–3): 106–107, 138–155.

———. 2010. "Entre l'image et l'ecrit: La politique tukano de patrimonialisation en Amazonie." *Cahiers des Amériques Latines* 63–64:195–227.

Humphrey, Caroline, and Urgunge Onon. 1996. *Shamans and Elders: Experience, Knowledge and Power among the Daur Mongols.* Oxford: Oxford University Press.

Hunter, Eduardo. 1992. *Historia de Freire Ediciones Sicom.* Freire, Chile: Ediciones Sicom.

Irvine, Judith T. 1979. "Formality and Informality in Communicative Events." *American Anthropologist* 81(4): 773–790.

Jackson, Jean, and Kay Warren. 2005. "Indigenous Movements in Latin America, 1992–2004: Controversies, Ironies, New Directions." *Annual Review of Anthropology* 34:549–573.

Jackson, Michael. 1995. *At Home in the World.* Durham, N.C.: Duke University Press.

———. 2007. *Excursions.* Durham, N.C.: Duke University Press.

Jackson, Michael, and Ivan Karp. 1990. *Personhood and Agency: The Experience of Self and Other in African Cultures.* Washington, D.C.: Smithsonian Institution Press.

Joralemon, Don, and Douglas Sharon. 1993. *Sorcery and Shamanism: Curanderos and Clients in Northern Peru.* Salt Lake City: University of Utah Press.

Kapferer, Bruce. 1997. *The Feast of the Sorcerer.* Chicago: University of Chicago Press.

Keane, Webb. 2006. "Subjects and Objects." In *Handbook of Material Culture,* ed. Chris Tilley, Webb Keane, Susanne Küchler, Mike Rowlands, and Patricia Spyer, 197–202. London: Sage.

———. 2007. *Christian Moderns: Freedom and Fetish in the Mission Encounter.* Berkeley: University of California Press.

———. 2011. "What Eludes Speech: A Dialogue with Webb Keane by Rosemary A. Joyce." *Journal of Social Archaeology* 11(2): 158–170.

Keenan, Dennis King. 2005. *The Question of Sacrifice.* Bloomington: Indiana University Press.

Kendall, Laurel. 1985. *Shamans, Housewives, and Other Restless Spirits: Women in Korean Ritual Life.* Honolulu: University of Hawaii Press.

———. 1999. "Shamans." In *Encyclopedia of Women and World Religions,* ed. Serenity Young, 892–895. New York: Macmillan.

———. 2009. *Shamans, Nostalgias, and the IMF: South Korean Popular Religion in Motion.* Honolulu: University of Hawaii Press.

Kendall, Laurel, and Jongsung Yang. 2014. "Goddess with a Picasso Face: Art Markets, Collectors and Sacred Things in the Circulation of Korean Shaman Paintings." *Journal of Material Culture* 1:1–23.

Kenny, Michael G. 1999. "A Place for Memory: The Interface between Individual and Collective History." *Comparative Studies in Society and History* 41(3): 420–437.

Khalfa, Jean. 2006. "Introduction." In *History of Madness,* by Michel Foucault, ed. Jean Khalfa. New York: Routledge.

Kim, Seong-nae. 1989. "Lamentations of the Dead: The Historical Imagery of Violence on Cheju Island, South Korea." *Journal of Ritual Studies* 3(2): 252–286.

Kirsch, Thomas. 2008. *Spirits and Letters: Reading, Writing, and Charisma in African Christianity.* New York: Berghahn.

Kleinman, Arthur. 1988. *The Illness Narratives: Suffering, Healing and the Human Condition.* New York: Basic Books.

———

Klubock, Thomas Miller. 2004. "Labor, Land, and Environmental Change in the Forestry Sector in Chile, 1973–1998." In *Victims of the Chilean Miracle: Workers and Neoliberalism in the Pinochet Era, 1973–2002*, ed. Peter Winn, 337–387. Durham, N.C.: Duke University Press.

———. 2006. "The Politics of Forests and Forestry on Chile's Southern Frontier, 1880s–1940s." *Hispanic American Historical Review* 86(3): 535–570.

Kohn, Eduardo. 2013. *How Forests Think: Toward an Anthropology beyond the Human*. Berkeley: University of California Press.

Kopenawa, Davi, and Bruce Albert. 2013. *The Falling Sky: Words of a Yanomami Shaman*. Cambridge, M.A.: Harvard University Press.

Kracke, Waud. 1987. "Myths in Dreams, Thought in Images: An Amazonian Contribution to the Psychoanalytic Theory of Primary Process." In *Dreaming: Anthropological and Psychological Interpretations*, ed. Barbara Tedlock, 31–54. Cambridge, U.K.: Cambridge University Press.

Kristensen, Dorthe. 2010. "Uncanny Memories, Violence and Indigenous Medicine in Southern Chile." In *Remembering Violence: Anthropological Perspectives on Intergenerational Transmission*, ed. Nicolas Argenti and Katharina Schramm, 63–80. New York: Berghahn.

Kuhn, Thomas. 1962. *The Structure of Scientific Revolutions*. Chicago: University of Chicago Press.

Kuramochi, Yosuke. 1990. "Contribuciones etnográficas al estudio del machitun." Paper presented at the Cuartas Jornadas de Lengua y Literatura Mapuche. Temuco, Chile.

Kwon, Heonik. 2008. *Ghosts of War in Vietnam*. Cambridge, U.K.: Cambridge University Press.

Laderman, Carol. 1992. "Malay Medicine, Malay Person." In *Anthropological Approaches to the Study of Ethnomedicine*, ed. M. Nichter, 191–206. New York: Routledge.

———. 1994. "The Embodiment of Symbols and the Acculturation of the Anthropologist." In *Embodiment and Experience: The Existential Ground of Culture and Self*, ed. Thomas Csordas, 183–197. Cambridge, U.K.: Cambridge University Press.

Lambek, Michael. 1996. "The Past Imperfect: Remembering as Moral Practice." In *In Tense Past: Cultural Essays in Trauma and Memory*, ed. Paul Antze and Michael Lambek, 235–254. New York: Routledge.

———. 1998. "The Saklava Poiesis of History: Realizing the Past through Spirit Possession in Madagascar." *American Ethnologist* 25(2): 106–127.

———. 2003. *The Weight of the Past: Living with History in Mahajanga, Madagascar*. Basingstoke, U.K.: Palgrave Macmillan.

Lan, David. 1985. *Guns and Rain: Guerillas and Spirit Mediums in Zimbabwe*. Berkeley: University of California Press.

Latcham, Ricardo. 1924. *La organización social y las creencias religiosas de los antiguos araucanos*. Santiago: Publicaciones del Museo de Etnología y Antropología de Chile.

Latour, Bruno. 1993. *We Have Never Been Modern*. Cambridge: Harvard University Press.

Lazzari, Axel, and Diana Lenton. 2002. "Araucanization, Nation: A Century Inscribing Indians in the Pampas." In *Contemporary Perspectives on the Native Peoples of Pampa*, ed. C. Briones and J. L. Lanata, 33–46. Westport, C.T.: Greenwood.

Le Bonniec, Fabien. 2009. "Del territorio independiente araucano al walmapu: Transformaciones sociales y ambientales del paisaje de la frontera entre los siglos XIX y XXI." In *Paisaje, espacio y territorio: Reelaboraciones simbolicas y reconstrucciones identitarias en América Latina*, ed. Nicolas Elison and Mónica Martínez, 47–67. Quito: Abya Yala.

Lenz, Rodolfo. 1895. *Estudios Araucanos: Viaje al país de la manzaneros, Contado en Dialecto Huilliche por el Indio Domingo Quintuprai de Osorno*. In *Anales de la Universidad de Chile* 90:359–385.

León, Leonardo. 1991. *Maloqueros y Conchavadores en Araucanía y las Pampas 1700–1800*. Temuco: Universidad de la Frontera.

———. 1995. "Mapu, Toquis y Weichafes Durante la Primera Guerra de Arauco: 1546–1554." *Revista de Ciencias Sociales* 40:277–344.

Lévi-Strauss, Claude. 1955. *Tristes tropiques*. Paris: Plon.

———. 1981. *The Naked Man*. London: Jonathan Cape.

———. 1987. *Anthropology and Myth: Lectures 1951–1982*. Oxford: Basil Blackwell.

———. 1991. *Histoire de Lynx*. Paris: Plon.

Lewis, Stephen. 1994. "Myth and History of Chile's Araucanians." *Radical History Review* 58:112–141.

Londoño, Carlos. 2012. *People of Substance: An Ethnography of Morality in the Colombian Amazon*. Toronto: University of Toronto Press.

Long, Gideon. 2013. "UN Criticises Chile for Using Terror Law on Mapuche." *BBC News*, Santiago, July 31. www.bbc.com/news/world-latin-america-23512784.

Low, Setha M. 1994. "Embodied Metaphors: Nerves as Lived Experience." In *Embodiment and Experience: The Existential Ground of Culture and Self*, ed. Thomas Csordas. Cambridge, U.K.: Cambridge University Press.

Lütge, Wilhelm, Werner Hoffmann, Karl Wilhelm Körner, and Karl Klingenfuss. 1981. *Deutsche in Argentinien: 1520–1980*. Buenos Aires: Verlag Alemann.

Mallon, Florencia. 1995. *Peasant and Nation: The Making of Postcolonial Mexico and Peru*. Berkeley: University of California Press.

———. 1996. "Constructing Mestizaje in Latin America: Authenticity, Marginality, and Gender in the Claiming of Ethnic Identities." *Journal of Latin American Anthropology* 2(1): 170–181.

———. 2001. "Land, Morality and Exploitation in Southern Chile: Rural Conflict and Discourses of Agrarian Reform in Cautín, 1928–1974." *Political Power and Social Theory* 14:141–193.

———. 2005. *Courage Tastes of Blood: The Mapuche Community of Nicolás Ailío and the Chilean State, 1906–2001*. Durham, N.C.: Duke University Press.

———. 2008. "El Cambiante mundo politico Mapuche: Magiñ Wenu y los Arribanos." Lecture. Department of History, Universidad Diego Portales. Santiago, Chile.

———. 2009. "El siglo XX Mapuche: Esferas públicas, sueños de autodeterminación y articulaciones internacionales Catalonia." In *Movilizaciones Indígenas en Chiapas y Araucanía*, ed. C. Martinez Neira and M. E. Saavedra, 155–190. Santiago: Catalonia.

———. 2010. "La doble columna y la doble conciencia en la obra de Manuel Manquilef." *Revista de Antropología* 21:59–80.

Mandrini, Raul Jose. 1992. "Pedir con vuelta: Reciprocidad difeida o mecanismo de poder?" *Antropoligas* 1:59–69.

Marileo, Armando. 1995. "Mundo mapuche." In *Medicinas y culturas en la Araucanía*, ed. Citarella Luca, 91–108. Santiago: Editorial Sudamericana.

Marimán, José. 1990. *Pueblo Mapuche: Estado y Autonomía Regional*. Santiago: Centro Estudios y Documentación Mapuche Liwen y Fundación para el Progreso Humano.

———. 2000. "El Nacionalismo Asimilacionista Chileno y su Percepción de la Nación Mapuche y sus Luchas." Centro de Documentacion Mapuche Nuke Mapu, Department of Sociology, Uppsala University, Uppsala, Sweden. www.mapuche.info /mapuint/marimanooioii.html.

———. 2012. "Manu militari con los Mapuche." *El Desconcierto* 2.

———. 2013. "A propósito de la cumbre mapuche." *El Quinto Poder*, January 13. www .elquintopoder.cl/politica/a-proposito-de-la-cumbre-mapuche/.

Marimán, Pablo, Sergio Caniuqueo, José Millalén, and Levil Rodrigo. 2006. *¡Escucha winka!: Cuatro ensayos de historia nacional mapuche y un epílogo xobre el futuro*. Santiago: Lom Ediciones.

Martínez, Christian. 2009. "Comunidades y redes de participación mapuche en el siglo XX: Nuevos actores étnicos, doble contingencia y esfera pública." In *Movilizaciones Indígenas en Chiapas y Araucanía*, ed. C. Martinez Neira and M. E. Saavedra, 135–153. Santiago: Catalonia.

Martínez, Christian, and Sergio Caniuqueo. 2011. "Las políticas hacia las comunidades mapuche del gobierno militar y la fundación del Consejo Regional Mapuche, 1973–1983." *Veriversitas* 1(1): 146–186.

Matlock, James. 1994. "Alternate Generation Equivalence and the Recycling of Souls: Amerindian Rebirth in Global Perspective." In *American Rebirth: Reincarnation Belief among North American Indians and Inuit*, ed. Antonia Mills and Richard Slobodin, 263–283. Toronto: University of Toronto Press.

Matory, Lorand. 1994. "Rival Empires: Islam and the Religions of Spirit Possession among the Ọyọ-Yoruba." *American Ethnologist* 21(3): 495–515.

Mauzé, Marie. 1994. "The Concept of the Person and Reincarnation among the Tlingit Indians of Southeastern Alaska." In *American Rebirth: Reincarnation Belief among North American Indians and Inuit*, ed. Antonia Mills and Richard Slobodin, 177–191. Toronto: University of Toronto Press.

Mayblin, Maya, and Magnus Course. 2014. "The Other Side of Sacrifice: Introduction." *Ethnos* 79(3): 307–319.

McFall, Sara. 2002. "Paisajes visuales, opticas distíntas: Cambios" In *El Medio Ambiente y la Territorialidad Mapuche y Expansión Forestal*, ed. Sara McFall, 43–56. Temuco, Chile: Instituto de Estudios Indígenas (Universidad de la Frontera).

McIntosh, Janet. 2009. *The Edge of Islam: Power, Personhood, and Ethnoreligious Boundaries on the Kenya Coast*. Durham, N.C.: Duke University Press.

Mege, Pedro. 1997. *La imaginación araucana*. Santiago: Lom Ediciones.

Memorias del Ministerio de Guerra. 1910. Imprenta de la Época. Santiago.

Menard, André. 2003. "Manuel Aburto Panguilef: De la República Indigena al sionismo mapuche." Nuke Mapu Working Papers. http://repositorio.uchile.cl/handle /2250/121816.

———. 2006. "Emergencia de la tercera columna en el texto: 'La faz social' fragmento de los Comentarios del pueblo araucano de Manuel Manquilef. Presentación y comentario." *Anales de Desclasificación* 1(2): 927–938.

———. 2013. "Manuel Aburto Panguilef y los archivos de la Federación Araucana (estudio preliminar)." In *Diario del Presidente de la Federación Araucana, Manuel Aburto Panguilef,* ed. André Menard, xciii–cxx. Santiago: CoLibris.

Menard, André, and Jorge Pavez. 2005. "El Congreso Araucano: Ley, raza y escritura en la política mapuche." *Política* 44:211–232.

———. 2007. *Mapuche y Anglicanos.* Santiago: Ocho Libors.

Métraux, Alfred. 1942. "Le shamanisme araucan." *Revista del Instituto de Antropología de la Universidad Nacional de Tucumán* 20(10): 309–362.

Millaman, Rosamel. 2001. "Mapuches Press for Autonomy." *NACLA Report of the Americas* 35(2): 10–12.

Mills, Antonia, and Richard Slobodin, eds. 1994. *Amerindian Rebirth: Reincarnation Belief among North American Indians and Inuit.* Toronto: University of Toronto Press.

Molina, Juan Ignacio. 1901 [1787]. *Compendio de la historia civil del reino de Chile.* Colección de Historiadores de Chile, vol. 24. Santiago: Imprenta del Ferrocarril.

Montecino, Sonia. 1984. *Mujeres de la tierra.* Santiago: CEM-PEMCI.

———. 1999. *Sueño con menguante: Biografía de una machi.* Santiago: Editorial Sudamericana.

Morales, Roberto. 1999. "Cultura Mapuche y Represión en Dictadura." *Revista Austral de Ciencias Sociales* 3:81–108. Universidad Austral, Valdivia, Chile.

Morphy, Howard, and Frances Morphy. 1985. "The Myths of Ngalakan History: Ideology and Images of the Past in Northern Australia." *Man* 19:459–478.

Muehlebach, Andrea. 2003. "What Self in Self-Determination? Notes from the Frontiers of Transnational Indigenous Activism." *Identities: Global Studies in Culture and Power* 10:241–268.

Municipalidad de Freire. 1983. "Los Alemanes en Chile: La aventura, la confianza, el trabajo y la naturaleza. Homenaje en los 125 años a los Alemanes colonos en Chile." Unpublished manuscript. Freire, Chile.

Nahuelpan Moreno, Héctor, et al. 2012. *Ta iñ fijke xipa rakizuameluwün: Historia, colonialismo y resistencia desde el país mapuche.* Temuco, Chile: Comunidad de Historia Mapuche.

Ñanculef, Juan, and Juan Carlos Gumucio. 1991. "El trabajo de la machi: Contenido y expresividad." *Nütram* 25:2–12.

Nash, June. 1993. *We Eat the Mines and the Mines Eat Us: Dependency and Exploitation in Bolivian Tin Mines.* New York: Columbia University Press.

———. 2012. "Faith, Hope, and Rebellion: Indigenous Movements in the Twenty-First Century." Paper presented at the Religion and Rebellion conference, Trondheim, Norway.

———. Forthcoming. *Llevando el cargo del tiempo.* San Cristóbal and Merida: Universidad Nacional de Chiapas/Universidad Nacional de Yucatan.

Navarro, Leandro. 1909. *Crónica militar de la conquista y pacificación de la Araucanía.* Santiago: Lourdes.

Nielssen, Hilde. 2011. *Ritual Imagination: A Study of Tromba Possession among the Betsimisaraka in Eastern Madagascar.* Leiden: Brill.

Nietzsche, Friedrich. 1983. *Untimely Meditations.* Cambridge, U.K.: Cambridge University Press.

Nora, Pierre. 1989. "Between Memory and History: Les Lieux de Mémoire." *Representations* 26:7–24.

Núñez de Pineda y Bascuñán, Francisco. 1996 [1673]. *Cautiverio felíz y razón de las guerras dilatadas de Chile.* Santiago, Chile: Editorial Universitaria.

Oakdale, Suzanne. 2002. "Creating a Continuity between Self and Other: First-Person Narration in an Amazonian Ritual Context." *Ethos* 30(1–2): 158–175.

———. 2005. *I Foresee My Life: The Ritual Performance of Autobiography in an Amazonian Community.* Lincoln: University of Nebraska Press.

———. 2007. "Anchoring 'The Symbolic Economy of Alterity' with Autobiography." *Tipiti Journal of the Society for the Anthropology of Lowland South America* 5(1): 58–78.

Oakdale, Suzanne, and Magnus Course. 2014. *Fluent Selves: Autobiography, Person, and History in Lowland South America.* Lincoln: University of Nebraska Press.

Olivares, Miguel de. 1864. *Historia militar, civil y sagrada de Chile.* Colección de Historiadores de Chile, vol. 4. Santiago: Imprenta del Ferrocariles.

Ong, Ahiwa. 1987. *Spirits of Resistance and the Capitalistic Discipline: Factory Women in Malaysia.* Albany: State University of New York Press.

Opinion, La. 2013. "Francisca Linconao, machi de la comunidad Pedro Linconao, detenida y luego en la calle. Sigue el hostigamiento tras el ataque a la mansión de Luchsinger," January 10. https://publicacionrefractario.wordpress.com/2013/01/10/temuco-francisca-linconao-machi-de-la-comunidad-pedro-linconao-detenida-y-luego-en-la-calle-sigue-el-hostigamiento-tras-el-ataque-a-la-mansion-de-luchsinger/.

Overing, Joanna. 1990. "The Shaman as a Maker of Worlds: Nelson Goodman in the Amazon." *Man* 25:601–619.

Pais Mapuche. 2013. "Seis meses de prisión preventiva para machis y comuneros por defender el Ngen Mapu Kintuante." January 31. http://paismapuche.org/?p=6454.

Palmié, Stephan. 2010. "Slavery, Historicism and the Poverty of Memorialization." In *Memory: Histories, Theories, Debates,* ed. Susannah Radstone and Bill Schwarz, 363–375. Bronx, N.Y.: Fordham University Press.

Palmié, Stephan, and Charles Stewart. 2013. "For an Anthropology of History." Paper presented at the 112th Annual Meeting of the American Anthropological Association, Chicago, November 20.

Pandolfi, Mariella. 2007. "Memory within the Body: Women's Narrative and Identity in a Southern Italian Village." In *Beyond the Body Proper: Reading the Anthropology of Material Life,* ed. M. Lock and J. Faquhar, 451–458. Durham, N.C.: Duke University Press.

Pavez, Jorge. 2003. "Mapuche ñi nütram chilkatun. Escribir la historia mapuche: studio posliminar de Trokinche müfu ñi piel: Historia de las familias siglo XIX." *Revista de Historia Indígena* 7:7–51.

———. 2008. *Cartas mapuche: Siglo XIX.* Santiago: Ocho Libros.

Pels, Peter. 1998. "The Spirit of Matter: On Fetish, Rarity, Fact, and Fancy." In *Border Fetishisms: Material Objects in Unstable Spaces,* ed. Patricia Spyer, 91–121. New York: Routledge.

Pérez, Cecilia. 2014. "Queremos lo que todos buscan, la Pacificación de la Araucanía." *El Mostrador,* January 3.

Pérez-Sales, Pau, Roberta Bacic Herzfeld, and Teresa Durán Pérez. 1998. *Muerte y desaparición forzada en la Araucanía: Una aproximación étnica.* Santiago: Ediciones LOM Ltda.

Perrin, Michel. 1986. "Savage Points of View on Writing." In *Myth and the Imaginary in the New World*, ed. Edmundo Magaña and Peter Mason, 211–231. Dordrecht, Netherlands: Foris.

Pichinao Huenchuleo, Jimena. 2012. "Los parlamentos hispano-mapuche como escenario de negociación simbólico-político durante la colonia." In *Ta iñ fijke xipa rakizuameluwün: Historia, colonialismo y resistencia desde el país mapuche*, ed. Héctor Nahuelpan Moreno et al. Temuco, Chile: Comunidad de Historia Mapuche.

Pinto Rodríguez, Jorge. 2000. *De la inclusión a la exclusión: La formación del estado, la nación y el pueblo Mapuche*. Santiago: Instituto de Estudios Avanzados, Universidad de Santiago.

———. 2003. *La formación del estado y la nación y el pueblo Mapuche: De la inclusión a la exclusión*. Santiago: Ediciones de la Dirección de Bibliotecas, Archivos y Museos.

———. 2007a. "Del antiindigenismo al proindigenismo en Chile en el siglo XIX." In *La Reindianización de América, siglo XIX*, ed. Leticia Reina. Mexico City: Editorial Siglo XXI.

———. 2007b. "Expansión económica y conflicto mapuche: La Araucanía, 1900–1940." *Revista de Historia Social y de las Mentalidades* 1(11): 9–34.

Piot, Charles. 2010. *Nostalgia for the Future: West Africa after the Cold War*. Chicago: University of Chicago Press.

Platt, Tristan. 1992. *Writing, Shamanism and Identity, or Voices from Abya-Yala*. Oxford: Oxford University Press.

Portelli, Alessandro. 1988. "Uchronic Dreams: Working Class Memory and Possible Worlds." *Oral History* 16(2): 46–56.

Povinelli, Elizabeth. 2002. *The Cunning of Recognition: Indigenous Alterities and the Making of Australian Multiculturalism*. Durham, N.C.: Duke University Press.

Priegue, Celia. 2002. "Mortuary Rituals among the Southern Tehuelche." In *Contemporary Perspectives on the Native Peoples of Pampa, Patagonia and Tierra del Fuego: Living on the Edge*, ed. Claudia Briones and José Luis Lanata, 47–56. London: Bergin and Garvey.

Radin, Paul. 1994. "The Reincarnations of Thunder Cloud, a Winnebago Indian." In *Amerindian Rebirth: Reincarnation Belief among North American Indians and Inuit*, ed. Antonia Mills and Richard Slobodin. Toronto: University of Toronto Press.

Radio Bio-Bio. 2013. "Machi acusada de guardar armas en su casa recupera su libertad en Temuco," January 5. http://www.biobiochile.cl/2013/01/05/machi-francisca-linconao-recupera-su-libertad-en-temuco.shtml.

Ramos, Alcida Rita. 2012. "The Politics of Perspectivism." *Annual Review of Anthropology* 41:481–494.

Raoni and Jean-Pierre Dutilleux. 2010. *Memoirs of an Indian Chief*. Paris: Rocher.

Rappaport, Joanne. 1998. *The Politics of Memory: Native Historical Interpretation in the Colombian Andes*. Durham, N.C.: Duke University Press.

———. 2005. *Intercultural Utopias: Public Intellectuals, Cultural Experimentation, and Ethnic Pluralism in Colombia*. Durham, N.C.: Duke University Press.

———. 2007. "Anthropological Collaborations in Colombia." In *Anthropology Put to Work*, ed. Les W. Field and Richard G. Fox, 1–43. Oxford: Berg.

Rappaport, Joanne, and Tom Cummins. 2012. *Beyond the Lettered City: Indigenous Literacies in the Andes*. Durham, N.C.: Duke University Press.

Rappaport, Joanne, and Abelardo Ramos Pacheco. 2005. "Una historia colaborativa: Retos para el diálogo indígena-académico." *Historia Crítica* 29:39–62.

Rausch, G. B. 1999. *Conflict in the Southern Cone: The Argentine Military and the Boundary Dispute with Chile, 1870–1902*. New York: Praeger.

Reed-Danahay, Deborah. 1997. *Auto/ethnography: Rewriting the Self and the Social*. Oxford, U.K.: Berg.

Regan, Jaime. 1988. "Mesianismo Cocama: Un movimiento de resistencia en la Amazonia Peruana." *América Indígena* 48(1): 127–138.

Reuque, Rosa Isolde Paillalef. 2002. *When a Flower Is Reborn: The Life and Times of a Mapuche Feminist*, ed. and trans. Florencia Mallon. Durham, N.C.: Duke University Press.

Richards, Patricia. 2004. *Pobladoras, Indígenas, and the State: Conflict Over Women's Rights in Chile*. Piscataway, N.J.: Rutgers University Press.

———. 2013. *Race and the Chilean Miracle: Neoliberalism, Democracy, and Indigenous Rights*. Pittsburgh: University of Pittsburgh Press.

Ricoeur, Paul. 2004. *Memory, History, Forgetting*. Chicago: University of Chicago Press.

———. 2005. *The Course of Recognition*, trans. D. Pellauer. Cambridge, M.A.: Harvard University Press.

Rio, Knut. 2014. "A Shared Intentional Space of Witch-Hunt and Sacrifice." *Ethnos* 79(3): 320–341.

Robbins, Joel. 2013. "Beyond the Suffering Subject: Toward an Anthropology of the Good." *Journal of the Royal Anthropological Institute* 19:447–462.

Rodriguez, Carlos Ruiz. 2001. "Antecedentes históricos y ambientales de Lumako y la identidad Nagche." *Revista de Historia Indígena* 5:83–118.

Rosales, Diego. 1989 [1882]. *Historia general del reyno de Chile*. Santiago: Editorial Andrés Bello.

Rose, Michael. 1985. *Reworking the Work Ethic: Economic Vales and Socio-Cultural Politics*. London: Schocken.

Rouch, Paul. 1960. *La religion et las magie songhay*. Paris: PUF.

Rubenstein, Steven. 2002. *Alejandro Tsakimp: A Shuar Healer in the Margins of History*. Lincoln: University of Nebraska Press.

———. 2007. "Circulation, Accumulation, and the Power of Shuar Shrunken Heads." *Cultural Anthropology* 22(3): 357–399.

Sahlins, Marshall. 1995. *How 'Natives' Think about Captain Cook, for Example*. Chicago: University of Chicago Press.

———. 2011. "What Kinship Is (Part One)." *Journal of the Royal Anthropological Institute* 17:2–19.

Salomon, Frank. 1983. "Shamanism and Politics in Late Colonial Ecuador." *American Ethnologist* 10(3): 413–428.

———. 1999. *Testimonies: The Making and Reading of Native South American Historical Sources*. Cambridge, U.K.: Cambridge University Press.

———. 2004. *The Cord Keepers: Khipus and Cultural Life in a Peruvian Village*. Durham, N.C.: Duke University Press.

Salomon, Frank, and Mercedes Niño-Murcia. 2011. *The Lettered Mountain: A Peruvian Village's Way with Writing*. Durham, N.C.: Duke University Press.

Salomon, Frank, and George L. Urioste, eds. and trans. 1991. *The Huarochiri Manuscript: A Testament of Ancient and Colonial Andean Religion*. Austin: University of Texas Press.

Santos-Granero, Fernando. 1993. "Anticolonialismo, mesianismo y utopía en la sublevación de Juan Santos Atahuallpa, siglo XVIII." *Revista del Instituto de Estudios Andinos y Amazónicos* 4:133–152.

———. 1998. "Writing History into the Landscape: Space, Myth, and Ritual in Contemporary Amazonia." *American Ethnologist* 25(2): 128–148.

———. 2007. "Time Is Disease, Suffering, and Oblivion: Yanesha Historicity and the Struggle against Temporality." In *Time and Memory in Indigenous Amazonia: Anthropological Perspectives*, ed. Carlos Fausto and Michael Heckenberger, 47–73. Gainesville: University Press of Florida.

———. 2009a. "From Baby Slings to Feather Bibles and from Star Utensils to Jaguar Stones: The Multiple Ways of Being a Thing in the Yanesha Lived World." In *The Occult Life of Things: Native Amazonian Theories of Materiality and Personhood*, ed. Fernando Santos-Granero, 105–127. Tucson: University of Arizona Press.

———. 2009b. "Hybrid Bodyscapes: A Visual History of Yanesha Patterns of Cultural Change." *Current Anthropology* 50(4): 477–493.

———. 2009c. "Introduction: Amerindian Constructional Views of the World." In *The Occult Life of Things: Native Amazonian Theories of Materiality and Personhood*, ed. Fernando Santos-Granero, 1–23. Tucson: University of Arizona Press.

———. 2009d. *Vital Enemies: Slavery, Predation, and the Amerindian Political Economy of Life*. Austin: University of Texas Press.

Santos-Granero, Fernando, and Frederica Barclay. 2011. "Bundles, Stampers, and Flying Gringos: Native Perceptions of Capitalist Violence in Peruvian Amazonia." *The Journal of Latin American and Caribbean Anthropology* 16(1): 143–167.

Sartre, Jean Paul. 2004 [1940]. *The Imaginary: A Phenomenological Psychology of the Imagination*, trans. J. Webber. London: Routledge.

Saunders, George. 1995. "The Crisis of Presence in Italian Pentecostal Conversion." *American Ethnologist* 22:324–340.

Schindler, Helmut. 1988. "'Con Reverencia Nombreys al Pillan y Huecuvoe' (Sermón IV, Luis de Valdivia, 1621)." *Revista Indigena Latinoamericana* 1:15–27.

———. 1996. "Amulpüllün: Un rito funerario de los Mapuches chilenos." *Lengua y Literatura Mapuche* 7:165–180.

Schindler, Helmut, and Minerva Schindler-Yáñez. 2006. "La Piedra Santa del río Lumaco." In *Acerca de la espiritualidad Mapuche*, ed. Helmut Schindler, 1–68. München: Martin Meidenbauer Verlagsbuchhandlung.

Scott, James. 1990. *Domination and the Arts of Resistance: Hidden Transcripts*. New Haven, C.T.: Yale University Press.

———. 2009. *The Art of Not Being Governed: An Anarchist History of Upland Southeast Asia*. New Haven, C.T.: Yale University Press.

Seixas, Peter. 2004. "Introduction." In *Theorizing Historical Consciousness*, ed. Peter Seixas, 3–120. Toronto: University of Toronto Press.

Severi, Carlo. 2000. "Cosmologia crise e paradoxo: De imagem de homens e mulheres brancos na tradicao Xamanica Kuna." *Mana* 6(1): 121–155.

Shaw, Rosalind. 2002. *Memories of the Slave Trade: Ritual and the Historical Imagination in Sierra Leone*. Chicago: University of Chicago Press.

Sider, Gerald. 1998. *Lumbee Indian Histories*. Cambridge, U.K.: Cambridge University Press.

Sierra, Malu. 1992. *Gente de la tierra*. Santiago: Editorial Persona.

Silva, Eduardo. 1993. "Capitalist Conditions, the State, and Neoliberal Economic Restructuring: Chile 1973–1988." *World Politics* 45(4): 526–559.

Silverstein, Michael, and Greg Urban. 1996. *Natural Histories of Discourse*. Chicago: University of Chicago Press.

Smith, Edmund Reul. 1855. *The Araucanians, or Notes of a Tour among the Indian Tribes of Southern Chili*. New York: Harper and Brothers.

Smith, Linda Tuhiwai. 2005. "On Tricky Ground: Researching the Native in the Age of Uncertainty." In *The SAGE Handbook of Qualitative Research*, ed. N. K. Denzin and Y. S. Lincoln, 85–107. Thousand Oaks, C.A.: Sage.

Smith, Robert J. 1974. *Ancestor Worship in Contemporary Japan*. Redwood City, C.A.: Stanford University Press.

Socolow, Susan. 1987. "Los Cautivos Españoles en las Sociedades Indígenas: El Contacto Cultural Através de las Fronteras Argentinas." *Annuario IEHS* 2:70–156.

Soto Galindo, Karen. 2014. "Celestino Córdova es condenado a 18 años de cárcel por la muerte del matrimonio Luchsinger-Mackay." *La Tercera*, February 28. www.latercera.com/noticia/nacional/2014/02/680-567408-9-celestino-cordova-es-condenado-a-18-anos-de-carcel-por-la-muerte-del-matrimonio.shtml.

Steedly, Mary. 1993. *Hanging without a Rope: Narrative Experience in Colonial and Postcolonial Karoland*. Princeton, N.J.: Princeton University Press.

———. 2000. "Modernity and the Memory Artist: The Work of Imagination in Highland Sumatra, 1947–1995." *Comparative Studies in Society and History* 42(4): 811–846.

Stern, Steven. 2001. "Between Tragedy and Promise: The Politics of Writing Latin American History in the Late Twentieth Century." In *Reclaiming the Political in Latin American History*, ed. Gilbert M. Joseph, 32–77. Durham, N.C.: Duke University Press.

Stewart, Charles. 2012. *Dreaming and Historical Consciousness in Island Greece*. Cambridge, U.K.: Harvard University Press.

Stoller, Paul. 1980. "The Epistemology of Sorkotarey: Language, Metaphor and Healing among the Songhay." *Ethos* 8(2): 117–131.

———. 1995. *Embodying Colonial Memories: Spirit Possession, Power, and the Hauka in West Africa*. New York: Routledge.

———. 2008. *The Power of the Between: An Anthropological Odyssey*. Chicago: University of Chicago Press.

———. 2014. *Yaya's Story: The Quest for Well-Being in the World*. Chicago: University of Chicago Press.

Strathern, Marilyn. 1988. *The Gender of the Gift*. Berkley: University of California Press.

———. 1992. "Parts and Wholes: Refiguring Relationships in a Post-Plural World." In *Conceptualizing Society*, ed. Adam Kuper. London: Routledge.

Strinati, Dominic. 1994. *An Introduction to Theories of Popular Culture*. London: Routledge.

Stuchlik, Milan. 1976. *Life on a Half Share*: London: C. Hurst.

Taussig, Michael. 1980. *The Devil and Commodity Fetishism in South America*. Chapel Hill: University of North Carolina Press.

———. 1984. "History as Sorcery." *Representations* 7:87–109.

———. 1987. *Shamanism, Colonialism, and the Wild Man: A Study in Terror and Healing*. Chicago: University of Chicago Press.

———. 1993. *Mimesis and Alterity: A Particular History of the Senses*. New York: Routledge.

———. 1997. *The Magic of the State*. London: Routledge.

Taylor, Anne-Christine. 1993. "Remembering to Forget: Identity, Mourning and Memory among the Jivaro." *Man* 28(4): 653–678.

———. 2000. "Le sexe de la proie: Représentations jivaro du lien de parenté." *L'Homme* 154–155:309–334.

———. 2007. "Sick of History: Contrasting Regimes of Historicity in the Upper Amazon." In *Time and Memory in Indigenous Amazonia: Anthropological Perspectives*, ed. Carlos Fausto and Michael Heckenberger, 133–168. Gainesville: University of Florida Press.

Tedlock, Barbara, ed. 1981. *Dreaming: Anthropological and Psychological Interpretations*. Cambridge, U.K.: Cambridge University Press.

———. 2005. *The Woman in the Shaman's Body: Reclaiming the Feminine in Religion and Medicine*. New York: Bantam.

Tedlock, Dennis. 2010. *2000 Years of Mayan Literature*. Berkeley: University of California Press.

Tedlock, Dennis, and Bruce Mannheim. 1995. *Dialogic Emergence Culture*. Champaign: University of Illinois Press.

Titiev, Mischa. 1968. "Araucanian Shamanism." *Boletín del Museo Nacional de Historia Natural* 30:299–312.

Trouillot, Michel-Rolph. 1995. *Silencing the Past: Power and the Production of History*. Boston: Beacon.

———. 2003. *Global Transformations: Anthropology and the Modern World*. New York: Palgrave Macmillan.

Tsing, Anna Lowenhaupt. 1993. *In the Realm of the Diamond Queen*. Princeton, N.J.: Princeton University Press.

Turner, James W. 1986. "The Water of Life: Kava Ritual and the Logic of Sacrifice." *Ethnology* 25(3): 203–214.

Turner, Terence. 1988. "Ethno-Ethnohistory: Myth and History in Native South American Representations of Contact with Western Society." In *Rethinking History and Myth: Indigenous South American Perspectives on the Past*, ed. Jonathan D. Hill. Urbana: University of Illinois Press.

Urban, Gregory. 1989. "The 'I' of Discourse." In *Semiotics, Self and Society*, ed. Ben Lee and Greg Urban, 27–51. Berlin: Mouton de Gruyter.

Urrutia, Gregorio. 1882. *Correspondence with the Chilean Ministry of War, December 8, 1882*. Santiago: National Archives of the Ministry of War.

Valdivia, Luis de. 1887 [1606]. *Arte, vocabulario y confesionario de la lengua de Chile*. Leipzig: Teubner.

Varese, Stéfano. 1973. *La sal de los cerros: Una aproximación al mundo campa*. Lima: Retablo de Papel Ediciones.

Vasquez, Carla. 2013. "Gobierno evalúa decretar estado de excepción en zona afectada por el conflicto mapuche." *La Tercera*, January 6. http://diario.latercera.com /2013/01/06/01/contenido/pais/31-127047-9-gobierno-evalua-decretar-estado-de -excepcion-en-zona-afectada-por-el-conflicto.shtml.

Vicuña Mackenna, Benjamín. 1939. *Discursos Parlamentarios*. Santiago: Ediciones de la Universidad de Chile.

Vidal, Aldo. 2011. "Lista de mapuche muertos post dictadura en relación al llamado conflicto mapuche." *Enlace Mapuche Internacional*, April 27.

Vidal, Silvia. 2000. "Kuwé Duwákalumi: The Arawak Sacred Routes of Migration, Trade, and Resistance." *Ethnohistory* 47(3–4): 635–667.

Vilaça, Aparecida. 2000. "O que significa tornar-se outro? Xamanismo e contato inter-étnico na Amazônia." *Revista Brasileira de Ciências Sociais* 15(44): 56–72.

———. 2002. "Making Kin Out of Others in Amazonia." *Journal of the Royal Anthropological Institute* 8(2): 347–365.

———. 2005. "Chronically Unstable Bodies: Reflections on Amazonian Corporalities." *Journal of the Royal Anthropological Institute* 11(3): 445–464.

Villalobos, Sergio. 2000a. "Araucanía: Errores Ancestrales." *El Mercurio*, May 14, A2.

———. 2000b. "Caminos Ancestrales." *El Mercurio*, September 3.

Viveiros de Castro, Eduardo. 1992. *From the Enemy's Point of View: Humanity and Divinity in Amazonian Society*, trans. C. V. Howard. Chicago: University of Chicago Press.

———. 1996. "Images of Nature and Society in Amazonian Ethnology." *Annual Review of Anthropology* 25:179–200.

———. 1998. "Cosmological Deixis and Amerindian Perspectivism." *Journal of the Royal Anthropological Institute* 4(3): 469–488.

———. 2001. "GUT Feelings about Amazonia: Potential Affinity and the Construction of Sociality." In *Beyond the Visible and the Material: The Amerindianization of Society in the Work of Peter Riviére*, ed. Laura Rival and Neil Whitehead, 19–44. Oxford: Oxford University Press.

———. 2003. "And." After-dinner speech given at Anthropology and Science, the 5th decennial conference of the Association of Social Anthropologists of the U.K. and Commonwealth. Manchester, U.K.: University of Manchester Department of Social Anthropology.

Wagner, Roy. 1991. "The Fractal Person." In *Big Men and Great Men: Personifications of Power in Melanesia*, ed. Maurice Godelier and Marilyn Strathern, 159–173. Cambridge, U.K.: Cambridge University Press.

Walker, Harry. 2012. "The Pen and the Dart: Dark Arts of Amazonian Lawfare." Paper presented at the 54th International Congress of Americanists, Vienna. July 15–20.

Walraven, Boudewijn. 2009. "National Pantheon, Regional Deities, Personal Spirits? Musindo, Sŏngsu, and the Nature of Korean Shamanism." *Asian Ethnology* 68(1): 55–80.

Walther, Juan Carlos. 1973. *La conquista del desierto*. Buenos Aires: Eudeba.

Warren, Kay B. 1998. *Indigenous Movements and Their Critics: Pan-Maya Activism in Guatemala*. Princeton, N.J.: Princeton University Press.

Watson, Lawrence C., and Maria-Barbara Watson-Franke. 1985. *Interpreting Life Histories: An Anthropological Inquiry*. New Brunswick: Rutgers University Press.

Weller, Robert P. 1985. "Bandits, Beggars, and Ghosts: The Failure of State Control over Religious Interpretation in Taiwan." *American Ethnologist* 12(1): 46–51.

Werbner, Richard. 2015. *Divination's Grasp: African Encounters with the Almost Said*. Bloomington: Indiana University Press.

White, Geoffrey. 2008. "Histories and Subjectivities." *Ethos* 28(4): 493–510.

White, Hayden. 1973. *Metahistory: The Historical Imagination in Nineteenth-Century Europe*. Baltimore: Johns Hopkins University Press.

———. 1978. *Trophies of Discourse: Essays in Cultural Criticism*. Baltimore: John Hopkins University Press.

Whitehead, Neil. 2003. "Histories and Historicities in Amazonia." In *Histories and Historicities in Amazonia*, ed. Neil Whitehead, 59–80. Lincoln: University of Nebraska Press.

Whitten, Norman. 2011. "Ethnogenesis and Interculturality in the 'Forest of Canelos': The Wild and the Tame Revisited." In *Ethnicity in Ancient Amazonia: Reconstructing Past Identities through Archaeology, Linguistics, and Ethnohistory*, ed. Alf Hornborg and Jonathan D. Hill, 321–334. Boulder: University Press of Colorado.

Wiener, M. 2003. "Hidden Forces: Colonialism and the Politics of Magic in the Netherlands Indies." In *Magic and Modernity: Interfaces of Revelation and Concealment*, ed. B. Meyer and P. Pels, 129–158. Redwood City, C.A.: Stanford University Press.

Wogan, Peter. 2003. *Magical Writing in Salasaca: Literacy and Power in Highland Ecuador*. Boulder, C.O.: Westview.

Wolf, Eric. 1982. *Europe and the People without History*. Berkeley: University of California Press.

Wright, Robin M. 1998. *Cosmos, Self, and History in Baniwa Religion: For Those Unborn*. Austin: University of Texas Press.

———. 2013. *Mysteries of the Jaguar Shamans of the Northwest Amazon*. Lincoln: University of Nebraska Press.

Wright, Robin, and Jonathan Hill. 1986. "History, Ritual, and Myth: Nineteenth Century Millenarian Movements in the Northwest Amazon." *Ethnohistory* 33:31–54.

Yankelovich, D. 1981. *New Rules: Searching for Self-Fulfillment in a World Turned Upside Down*. New York: Random House.

Zeballos, Estanislao. 1981. *Callvucurá y la dinastía de piedra*. Buenos Aires: Centro Editor de América Latina.

Žižek, Slavoj, and Malden Dolar. 2001. *Opera's Second Death*. New York: Routledge.

INDEX

Note: Italic page numbers refer to illustrations.

authoritarian ideologies, 88, 89, 159, 169–176, 179

Aylwin, Patricio, 19, 178, 179

Bachelet, Michelle, 184, 191–192, 214

Bakhtin, Mikhail, 208, 236n11

Battaglia, Debbora, 207, 210

Bibles: Anglican Protestant Bibles, 14, 148–149, 151, 152; Capuchin Catholic Bibles, 14, 148–149, 151, 152; Catholic Bible of Francisca Kolipi, 6–7, 13–14, 151; contrasting meanings for Mapuche and Chilean state, 131; Francisca Kolipi's bible compared to, 7, 14, 140; Francisca Kolipi's use as object of power, 14, 30, 107, 130, 132, 140, 153, 228, 230, 233; Lutheran Bibles, 14, 140, 148, 152; Mapuche leaders' use of, 14, 148–150, 152; Mapuche production of, 132, 141, 147–152, 153, 230, 232; temporality of, 244n30

biomedicine, 17, 108, 135, 194

boldo tree: Huenchuñir family's vision at, 216; and Francisca Kolipi's rituals, 112, 156; on Millali hill, 17, 32, 55, 62, 155–158, *157*, 196; political agency of, 165

Bourdieu, Pierre, 48, 179

Buryat culture, 38, 98–99, 129–130, 247n8

Calfuñir, Aurora (daughter), 68, 69, *113*, 124, 219

Calfuñir, Bernardita (granddaughter): death of, 212; drawing picture with Francisca Kolipi of initiation, *26*, 94; on grieving, 211; and Francisca Kolipi's burial, 209–210; on Francisca Kolipi's cataleptic deaths, 204; and Francisca Kolipi's death, 207; and Francisca Kolipi's headdress and ring, 208–209, 217, 224; and Francisca Kolipi's healing, 126; on Francisca Kolipi's reaction to son's death, 200, 201; as Francisca Kolipi's ritual assistant, 93; marriage of, 78; and rebirth of Francisca Kolipi, 216–217

Calfuñir, José (brother-in-law), 137, 181–183, 207–209

Calfuñir, Osvaldo, 82–83, 214

Calfuñir, Pascual, 16, 137, 236n20; map of community of, *143*

Calfuñir family: administrative roles on Mapuche reservation, 50; hierarchical ideology of, 79, 86, 180; and Francisca Kolipi, 78, 79–83, 86–87, 182–183, 206; and Millali factions, 54, 88; and Millañir family, 87, 214; and Wenteche-Patagonian military-shamanic power, 55, 78, 79

Calfuñir Kolipi, Francisco (son), 6, 78, 123, 181, 200–201, 204, 206

Calfuñir Rañileo, José (Pancho) (husband), 6, 78, 79, 87–88, 181

capitalism: Chilean state's support of, 165; of German settlers, 60–61, 65; in Rosa Kurin's shamanic history, 57, 59, 66; and machi, 36, 86–89, 236n14; Mapuche's spiritual warfare against, 188, 196; and tree plantations, 164

Catholic Church: and female machi, 180, 181; Francisca Kolipi as Catholic machi, 1, 4, 5, 75, 79–80, 89, 150, 193–194, 209; Francisca Kolipi's dreams with Catholic significance, 3–4, 5, 89; Francisca Kolipi's resignification of, 108–109; and male machi, 150; and Mapuche sacred numerology, 246n26; and Millañir family, 55; and Pinochet, 172; rituals of, 244n29. *See also* Christianity

Chadwick, Andres, 183, 186

champuria identity: author as ritual assistant, 21–22, 24, 25, 27, 28, 29, 93–95, 217, 230, 231; as distrusted in Millali, 50; and kinship, 73; Francisca Kolipi's identity as, 13–14, 21, 30, 74, 78, 81, 82, 84, 226, 230–231

Chihuimpilli, Chile, 17–18, 23, 159, 218

Chile: construction of Mapuche as savage terrorists, 183–186, 189–190, 192, 195, 196; democratic regimes of, 19–20, 135, 159, 165, 168–169, 176–179, 184, 186–187, 214; earthquake of February 27, 2010, 217; independence of, 42, 239–240n7; Francisca Kolipi's bible as

INDEX

forest industry: and civilized/savage dichotomy, 45, 195–196; Francisca Kolipi's moral critique of, 26; and Mapuche community, 30, 82, 96; and Mapuche cosmopolitics, 163, 164, 178; and Mapuche resistance movements, 187–189, 192; *ngen* spirits' hexing of, 162; and tree plantations, 155, 163–165, 168, 187, 195

Fort Freire, 44, 47, *47*, 54, 238n18

Foucault, Michel, 10, 128, 133, 213, 224

Freire, Chile, 46–47, 60, 174–175

gender norms, 5, 74, 135, 150, 176–177, 179–183, 197, 244n32

German settlers: and agrarian reform, 167–168, 245n6; and civilized/savage dichotomy, 29, 44–49, 59, 65, 160, 195; contrasting temporalities with Mapuche, 36–37; intermarriage with Mapuche, 51–52; and land appropriation, 48–49, 148, 192, 195; Mapuche associating with devil, 58–61; Mapuche taking captives from settlements of, 32, 42, 50; Mapuche as wage laborers for, 60, 81, 148; and Millali hill, 56–57, 59, 64; waves of settlement, 237–238n13

Global North: chronology of, 18; documentation practices of, 131, 138; historical consciousness of, 7, 10, 11, 30, 34, 45, 99–101, 134, 144, 227, 230; idioms of historicism, 100, 133, 240n5; and literacy, 152; machi exoticized by, 229; and Mapuche relationship with military, 190; personhood and individuality in, 12, 137

Global South, as premodern, 133

grafismo, 132–133, 138–141, 152

Haitian slave revolution of 1790, 235n6, 242n4

hierarchical ideologies, 15, 20, 58, 79, 84, 86–89, 171–175, 180

historical consciousness: and civilized/savage dichotomy, 45, 195; of Global North, 7, 10, 11, 30, 34, 45, 99–101, 134, 144, 227, 230; Michael Lambek on, 240–241n7; linear temporal rela-

tionship of positivist historiography, 7, 8, 10, 34, 101, 131–134, 144, 145, 231; of Mapuche, 146–147, 152, 187, 195, 227–228, 244n28; and myth, 34–37; shamanic historical consciousness of Francisca Kolipi, 22, 23, 26, 197, 229; shamanic historical consciousness in Francisca Kolipi's bible, 5–8, 10–13, 26, 28–30, 216, 222, 230, 231; shamanic historical consciousness of Mapuche, 28, 29, 61, 64–67, 116, 138, 144, 147, 222, 227–229, 244n29

historical continuity: and descendants of German settlers, 46; and kinship, 1, 65; of Francisca Kolipi's bible, 15, 232; machi's creation of, 83, 99, 152, 156–157, 196, 213, 222, 228; and Mapuche achronological cyclical narrative, 64

Huenchuñir, Alberto, 1, 17, 31, 52, 55, 62, 82, 183

Huenchuñir, Alejandro, 55, 80, 141

Huenchuñir, Alejo, 1, 78, 216, 232

Huenchuñir, Enrique, 155–158, 196

Huenchuñir, Ignacio, 52, 138, 236n20

Huenchuñir family: administrative roles on Mapuche reservation, 50; hierarchical ideology of, 79, 86, 180; and Francisca Kolipi, 79–83, 87, 156, 182–183, 206; and Millali factions, 54; vision at *boldo* tree, 216; and Wenteche faction, 78; and Wenteche-Patagonian military-shamanic power, 55

Huilcan, Julio, 155–158, 196

Imilco, Chile, 17, 18, 19, 53, 159, 192

Incas, 18, 21, 36, 38

indigenous people: and Chilean democratic governments, 168–169; definition of indigenous history, 144, 227; *grafismo* of, 139–141; historical agency of shamanic narratives, 64–65; historical processes interpreted through narrative and shamanic stories, 240n13; literacy of, 131, 132, 141, 235n4, 242n3; marginalization in documentation practices, 131, 133; and politics, 246n20; religious faith as basis for revitalizing rebellion, 246n27; role of

Kolipi, Francisca (*continued*)
temporal dreams of, 29, 89–93; mythologizing of, 200, 213–217, 225, 233; narrating attachment to sacred landscapes of Millali, 13; and *ngillatun* rituals, 80, 82–83, 86, 87, 92, 198, 204, 206; perception of warring thunder machi, 190; and Pinochet's land division law of 1979, 168; Pinochet supported by, 170, 171, 177, 179; powers in right arm, 3–5, 88, 109–111, 113, 128; preparing herbal remedies, 105, *106*, 112, *113*; reburial of headdress and ring of, 217–221, *220*; ritual modes of historicization, 29, 102, 109–129; ritual practices of, 5, 11, 13, 24, 25, 29, 68–69, 96, 98, 102, 105, 130, 156, 193, 197; sacrifice of spirit horse as form of spiritual suicide, 123, 200–201, 204, 206; and Elizabeth Schleyer, 173; sexual liaisons of, 78, 180, 181, 182; shamanic historical consciousness of, 22, 23, 26, 197, 229; and shamanic literacy, 139, 140–141, 239; shamanic rebirth of, 12–14, 27, 29–30, 227, 232–233; sheep as spirit animal of, 78, 127, 128, 206, 208, 209; song of, 226–227; spiritual matrilineage from Rosa Kurin, 5, 74, 79–80, 81, 138, 145, 206; tombstone of, 108, 211–212, 214–215; trances of, 96, 113–115, 127–128; utopian visions of, 229, 233–234
Kolipi, Francisca, bible of: author's writing of, 5–7, 11–13, 15–16, 22, 25–28, 30, 93, 109, 132, 140–141, 147, 151, 153, 205, 208, 216, 221, 227, 231–232; collaboration in making of, 25–28, 205, 227; family's position on writing of, 208–209, 216, 223, 224; historic power of, 13–16, 231, 234; immortalizing Francisca Kolipi's powers, 14–15, 25, 93, 130, 132, 140, 151, 153, 205–206, 234, 236n18; as intertextual object, 14, 25, 141, 151, 229, 236n17; literacy of, 14, 25, 132, 229; and Millali relations with European settlers, 154; performative function of, 7, 14, 153; rituals recorded in, 25, 123, 128; role of written word in

shamanic literacies, 152, 231; shamanic historical consciousness in, 5–8, 10–13, 26, 28–30, 216, 222, 230, 231
Kolipi, Juan, 76, 138, 236n20
Kolipi, Juancito (father), 76–77, 78, 80, 138, 168
Kolipi family, 76, 77–78, 239n6, 239–240n7
Kurin, Rosa: balance of identities, 52, 58, 65–66; birthplace of, 21, 25; *boldo* tree on Millali hill, 17, 62, 155–158, *157*, 196; and Christianity, 238n16; death of, 55; initiation of, 17, 32, 51, 54, 74, 80; Francisca Kolipi embodied by spirit of, 1, 3, 12, 15, 16, 64, 65, 67, 79, 96, 99; Francisca Kolipi's connecting through trance, vision, and dream, 71, 111; Francisca Kolipi's spiritual matrilineage from, 5, 74, 79–80, 81, 138, 145, 206; Francisca Kolipi's thunder-based kinship with, 5, 67, 79, 84, 215, 224, 225, 232; marriage of, 78; as mestiza, 21, 31, 50, 51–52, 67, 81; mobile histories surrounding, 37–38, 41; and multiple personhoods, 73, 214, 224; as multitemporal machi, 29, 63, 64; mythologizing of, 55–56, 63–64, 65, 79, 203, 215, 225; narratives of, 15, 16, 31–33, 36; and *ngillatun* rituals, 54, 57, 62, 86; Pampean spirit horse of, 204, 205; rituals of, 54, 58, 59, 62, 66, 67; and sacred landscapes of Millali, 13; sexual liaisons of, 52, 53, 78; shamanic history of, 31, 36, 57, 58, 62, 64–67, 211, 231; socioeconomic status of, 32, 52, 53, 54, 81; and split in Wenteche faction, 54–55; subversion of state archive, 137, 138; as thunder machi, 4, 32, 38, 67, 214, 216–217; thunder stone of, 91; tombstone of, 211; Trengtreng associated with, 36, 62, 63, 80; and Gregorio Urrutia, 36, 45, 53–54, 56, 62, 65, 78

Lagos, Ricardo, 20, 177, 184, 190, 214
land appropriation: and agrarian reform, 166–167; and Chilean democratic governments, 168–169, 187; and

machi (shamans) (continued)

machi (shamans) using headscarves, 97, 113, 125; preservation of body, 212–213; regalia of, 6, 23; reinvention of machi practice, 192; relations with Chilean state, 197; ritual objects of, 218, 221, 223; rituals of, 23, 35, 41, 50, 72, 75, 85, 105, 187, 212, 219–220; role in construction of indigenous history, 34–35, 235n9; role of drums, 155; sacrifices of, 115–121, 123, 227, 241n17; shamanic bibles, 132, 152–154, 227; songs of, 127; sorcery distinguished from, 83–86, 116, 121; spirit animals of, 38–41, 39; spirit possession, 113, 124, 202–203, 242n22; spiritual warfare of, 186–190, 195; symbolic death and rebirth during rituals, 203, 247n3, 247n4; and visions of bulls, 32; women as, 9, 23, 72, 135, 150, 159, 176–177, 179, 180–183, 188, 246n22. See also thunder machi; and specific machi

Mapuche: achronological narratives of, 11, 16, 30, 35, 64; archival narratives, 41–44; bibles produced by, 132, 141, 147–152, 153, 230, 232; Chilean state's construction of Mapuche as savage terrorists, 183–186, 189–190, 192, 195, 196; civilized, moral temporality, 194, 196–197; collective memory of, 151–152, 215, 223–224, 228; communal ideals of egalitarianism, 60, 86–89, 96; communal work ideals, 60, 196, 239n22, 241n17; cosmopolitics of, 30, 163–165, 178; cycle of subjugation to Chilean and Argentine states, 36, 63, 65, 167, 171; cyclical narrative of, 64, 65, 191, 216, 227, 228; decolonization of knowledge production, 26; dreams and revisionist narratives to end savagery and warfare, 190–191, 192; ethnic identity of, 19, 50–51, 66, 88–89, 165, 171–172, 175, 179, 187, 191, 214, 229; evangelical Christians, 7, 82, 240n9; exclusion from positivist history, 134, 145; family and ethnic histories, 144–147; funeral rituals of, 209, 210–211, 247n7, 247n8; gra-

fismo of, 139–141; guerrilla warfare of, 18, 20; hierarchical ideologies of, 15, 20, 79, 84, 86–89, 171–175, 180; historical consciousness of, 146–147, 152, 187, 195, 227–228, 244n28; identity categories in flux, 84, 88–89; identity in relation to Chilean state, 11, 19–20, 27, 49, 51, 99, 103, 146; identity tied to sacred landscape, 162, 163; illness and conceptualization of history, 29, 102–109, 123, 242n21; interethnic alliances, 38, 41, 42, 50, 228; interethnic conflict, 102–103, 183, 192, 193, 197; and intergenerational memory, 29, 37, 195, 196; intermarriage of, 52–53, 81; intraethnic conflict, 102–104, 183, 197; Francisca Kolipi's bible perpetuating historical continuity, 15, 232; Francisca Kolipi's social critiques of, 27; longevity created by, 12, 236n13; longko as local political authority, 5, 20, 42, 49, 50, 79, 166, 172, 173, 175–177, 194, 224; military culture, 174, 176, 190–193, 197; mobile histories of, 38–41; moral cosmic order of, 229; multiple belonging practiced by, 37–38, 52–53, 160; multiple modes of historicity, 30, 35–36; mythologizing of, 184, 222–223; Nangche faction, 39, 42, 43, 51, 75, 76, 81, 145, 239n7; narratives as open and unfinished, 31, 234; ngillatun rituals, 41, 41, 46, 49–50, 54–56, 58, 62, 74, 80, 82, 86–87, 92, 99, 149, 164, 166, 169–170, 188, 198, 204, 212, 214, 218, 238n15, 240n9, 240n10, 241n17; official documents produced by, 132, 135, 139, 141, 144–147; oral histories of, 135, 141, 145; origin stories of, 11, 34, 35–36; pan-Mapuche historical and political project, 172, 194; patrilineage of, 8, 42, 49, 71, 73, 76, 78, 134, 136–137, 144, 145, 162, 183, 246n23; and patronage, 172–173, 175; perception of body in time, 110; perception of spiraling histories, 37, 65, 222–223, 227; Pinochet supported by, 170, 179; as political agents, 158; population of, 18, 20, 43, 49, 162;

primordium narratives, 29, 35–36, 37, 46, 55, 61, 62–63, 102, 145, 214, 222–223; protest graffiti, 188, *189*; raids of, 32, 39, 174, 176, 237n5; regional histories of, 231; and reincarnation of a soul, 247n4, 248n11; reinterpretation of time of civilization and time of wilderness, 30, 36–37, 45, 154, 157–158, 190–193, 196, 227; relations with Chilean state, 19, 20, 36, 37, 38, 42, 43, 44, 49, 51, 54, 96, 129, 131, 133–134, 135, 142–143, 149–150, 178, 192, 192–193, 195, 196, 236–237n24, 239–240n7; reliability of narratives, 33–34, 45; resistance movements, 38, 45, 66, 136–138, 142, 145, 149, 152, 158, 159, 178, 187–188, 229; role of biography, 11, 12, 215–216; sacred numerology of, 186, 246n26; and sacrifice, 120; shamanic historical consciousness of, 28, 29, 61, 64–67, 116, 138, 144, 147, 222, 227–229, 244n29; sovereign territories of, 42–43, 46–49, 64, 105, 142–143, 160, 162–163, 166, 168–169, 179, 184, 187, 189, 194, 195; as spiritual victors of history, 29, 231; subversion of state archive, 132, 136–138; and temporal dislocation, 29, 165; truth tied to world of values, 10; *ülmen*'s personal authority, 172–173; virilocal norms, 73, 78; and visions of bulls, 32, 80; wars among rival groups, 32, 38, 41, 42; wars with colonial Spanish military, 40, 41, 42, 237n5; Wenteche faction, 38, 42, 43, 51, 52, 54–55, 75, 76, 78, 81, 138, 145, 239–240n7

Mapuche reservation: and Chilean naming system, 137; and Chile's land policies, 19, 43–44, 48–49, 54; defined land base and communal identity of, 5, 19, 43, 49–51, 96; imposition of, 18–19, 162; and legal documents, 142; yields of, 20

Mapuche spirit masters of forest and warfare: and battle of sacred landscapes, 165–169, 188, 190; and Chilean democratic regimes, 179; cosmopolitics of, 30, 163–165, 178; and Mapuche resistance of forest industry, 187–188, 189, 195; and moral existentialism, 194–195; and Pinochet, 169–176; and politics of home, 159–163, 188; and thunder machi, 30, 156–159, 164; and warring temporalities, 195–197

Mapudungun language: Francisca Kolipi's use of, 6, 69, 81, 104–105, 107, 123; lack of term for history or myth, 10, 35; Mapuche writing in, 141, 146; *wingka* captives learning, 73

María (machi), 97–98, 99, 219–220

Mellado Calfuñir, Cesar (grandson), *6*, 68, 124, 127, 187, 213–214, 225

memory: collective memory of Francisca Kolipi, 28, 199; collective memory of Mapuche, 151–152, 215, 223–224, 228; as complex heterogeneous process, 16, 228; continuity and transformation through remembering and disremembering, 221–225, 228; death of memory of Francisca Kolipi, 212, 247n9; discourses of disremembering, 198–199, 200, 206–213; embodied cultural memories, 100, 101; and immortality, 67, 239n25; intergenerational memory, 29, 37, 195, 196; as lived experience, 10; and machi's multitemporality, 233; performative memory, 141; personal memory, 228–229; Rosalind Shaw on, 110; social memory, 228–229, 244n28; and temporality experienced by spiritual practitioners, 72

men: and kinship, 73, 74; as machi, 8, *9*, 23, 72, 150, 151, 176–177, 246n22

mestizos: Chilean state's rejection of *mestizaje*, 51; German settlers' subjugation of, 48; Francisca Kolipi as, 5, 12, 15, 21–22, 67, 81, 82; Rosa Kurin as, 21, 31, 50, 51–52, 67, 81; machi associated with, 51–52, 235n10; Mapuche view of *mestizaje*, 50, 81, 146

Millali, Chile: and Allende, 166–167, 172; alterity and identity in, 65, 229; author's relationship with, 231–232; and Christian values, 78; collective memory of Francisca Kolipi, 28, 199; cycle of wilderness and warfare ending in,